THE COST OF CHILD MALTREATMENT: WHO PAYS?

We All Do

Kris Franey, M.A., Robert Geffner, Ph.D.,

and Robert Falconer, M.A.

Editors

A Project Funded By The Family Violence and Sexual Assault Institute
and
The Institute For Trauma Oriented Psychotherapy

2001

3rd Printing; Printed in the United States of America

Library of Congress Cataloging in Publication Data

Main entry under title: Costs of Child Maltreatment: Who Pays? We All Do.

This book provides articles from highly regarded international authors concerning the long-term effects and costs of child maltreatment.

Edited by: Kris Franey, Robert Geffner, and Robert Falconer
Artwork by: Brian Franey
Includes bibliographical references

ISBN 1882948-12-2

1. Physical effects of child maltreatment (including long-term medical effects and neurological disorders), 2. Mental health impacts (including hospitalization rates, suicide attempts and rates of psychological disorders), 3. Societal impacts (including homelessness, and incarceration), 4. Economic impacts (including projected annual costs of child maltreatment).

TABLE OF CONTENTS

PREFACE

Child maltreatment has tremendous, largely unrecognized costs for all of us. The most obvious result of child abuse is the long-term effects on the mental health and healthcare of the children as they grow up. But even here we are only beginning to appreciate the extent to which childhood trauma impacts future development. Depression, suicidality, eating disorders, substance abuse, urgent psychiatric hospitalizations, personality disorders, and many other serious mental health problems are associated with a history of child abuse, as has been documented in many of the articles in this book. People abused as children are 25% more likely to experience Post Traumatic Stress Disorder (PTSD) both following the abuse and into their lifetime (Spat Widom, 1999). As adolescents, abused children are three times more likely to endure depressive disorders and eight times more likely to attempt suicide (Friedman, 1999). These children experience educational difficulties, exhibit adverse behaviors and are more likely to be removed from their home (Frothingham, 2000). These themes are emphasized in the second section of this book.

Less recognized but equally debilitating are the many somatic manifestations that often occur after child maltreatment. People with histories of child maltreatment tend to over-utilize physicians much more than the non-abused population, as was noted by Felitti, et al in their article reprinted in this book. Gastro-intestinal distress, adult onset diabetes, chronic fatigue syndrome, fibromyalgia, and other physical conditions are correlated strongly with child abuse and trauma histories. Research has shown an increase in smoking (Etheridge, 1999), Breast Cancer, arthritis and Thyroid disease (Stein, 2000) among adult survivors of childhood maltreatment. Adults who were abused as children are more apt to have gastrointestinal pain, require surgery more often, and have slower recovery times than their nonabused peers (Leserman, 1996). Research has now shown that trauma permanently alters the structure of a child's brain, resulting in higher levels of depression and negative emotions (see Perry in this issue). Yet it appears to remain more convenient for society to focus on the individual hardships while ignoring the impact abuse has on all of us.

However, the cost in human misery, both psychological and physical, for those who were maltreated is only a small part of the problem. There is an intergenerational transmission of human violence, shame, and dysfunctional behavior that is "passed on" to children largely through child maltreatment. This is harder to document than the psychological and somatic sequelae, but studies show that a very high percentage of violent offenders and people on death row were abused as children, many of the female prison inmates had been abused, and domestic violence is correlated with histories of child abuse (e.g., Hart & Geffner, 1999, Rosenbaum & Geffner, 1997).

Child maltreatment, be it physical, sexual, emotional or neglect has far reaching consequences. It is easy for society to assume that abuse "hurts" in the moment, but those who were abused as children need to move on. Yet research shown in this book supports what adult survivors of childhood maltreatment have been stating all along: you can't just forget about abuse because it does not go away on its own most of the time. The research findings cited above and in this book help explain why an abuse survivor can not just "get over it."

Dr. James Gilligan (1996), long time prison psychiatrist, has noted that violence is fundamentally connected to shame rather than to anger, which appears to be counterintuitive. Gilligan's insights provide a theoretical pathway for understanding the connection between child abuse and a violent society. The connection is shame. Abusing a child, then preventing the child from talking about it and not allowing healing, creates shame-based adults. Thus, as long as child maltreatment continues at high levels, we are likely to have violence. This was the theme in a series of articles in the *Journal of Psychohistory* published by deMause. He explored the connection between child rearing practices and the cultures and political systems that result. His detailed historical studies show that in societies where children are abused and shamed, violence and reactive, repressive measures are highly correlated. Gilligan and deMause are but a few authors who are writing about the long-term societal impacts of childhood maltreatment. Their writings and the findings reported in this book indicate the importance of child maltreatment in the global arena. It is not just a "family matter" or a community problem. It is a significant social concern that must be treated as such.

Prevention May Be Better Than the Cure

Just as stopping smoking is the most cost effective and humane way to deal with lung cancer, stopping child maltreatment is the most cost effective and humane way to create a more healthy, peaceful and productive culture. Dealing with childhood trauma (i.e., preventing it or at least ameliorating its effects as soon as possible) is a powerful leverage point for the transformation of society. Using this fulcrum, grassroots change can be created in the mores of a culture and the behaviors prevalent in a society.

It can be said that there are three levels at which to address this problem: 1) preventing the abuse; 2) help for those who were abused; and 3) containing the effects of abuse. Currently the vast majority of society's efforts emphasize the third category: prisons for the offender, and treatment for medical ailments and addictions for adult survivors of childhood maltreatment. Some funding and efforts are starting to flow into therapy focused on the child abuse traumas themselves. However, relatively little funding is directed at prevention or research. We need to reverse these priorities.

There are many ways to reverse these priorities. The intergenerational transmission of violence and shame can be stopped. The focus must be on the prevention of child maltreatment. Two specific projects are examples of the type of work suggested by this understanding of child maltreatment. First, major universities can establish a department of trauma studies or programs to focus on this area. Currently this knowledge and training tends to be spread throughout departments, such as psychology, sociology, history, medicine, criminal justice, and biology, among others. Consolidating the information and energies will vastly increase the rate of growth of our knowledge, research, and programs in this area.

Secondly, we need to focus major efforts on the treatment of adolescent as well as adult offenders. Early intervention can prevent numerous others from being victimized. Sending offenders to jails or other detention facilities tends to "harden" rather than rehabilitating them. Prisons protect society and other victims for the time the offenders are incarcerated, but it does not help the long-term prognosis once the offender is released. Therefore, a treatment-based model for these young offenders is recommended, one in which society can be protected while helping the offenders change their attitudes, beliefs, and behaviors. The amount of funding and effort needed are substantial, but compared to what is now being spent on dealing with the after-effects of abuse, they are very small.

The Need for This Book

It is our hope that this book will help others recognize and understand the long-term impacts of childhood maltreatment. By enlarging the focus from the individual impact, that is physical and emotional impacts, to the wider society, we hope to focus the attention of a wider audience. It was difficult for us to choose among the outstanding research that exists. We attempted to choose those articles that kept the wider impact of abuse at its focus.

The book begins by looking at the medical impact of child maltreatment. The chapters range from an overview of medical difficulties to specifics about brain damage and diabetes. We then move into the impact on mental health. Here the authors address issues such as lifetime revictimization, suicidality and hospitalization. In keeping with our desired goal, the text then focuses on the societal and economic impacts of child maltreatment. Societal issues, such as homelessness and incarceration, are discussed in this section. Likewise, experts in the field of childhood trauma attempt to break down the actual economic impact of child abuse in the final section of the book. The numbers they have hypothesized are astronomical.

Our goal is that this book will move the scope of child maltreatment from an individual victim mindset to a long-term societal calamity. The abuser does not merely impact the child who often suffers alone in silence, but rather a culture and world full of anger, shame and hatred. The social cost of child maltreatment is significant. We have enough resources and we are beginning to have enough knowledge to deal with this at its root. It is time for society as a whole to take a stand against child maltreatment, and to put the necessary funding and priorities into research, intervention, and prevention efforts.

We would like to thank the authors of the chapters for their hard work and dedication to the field of childhood trauma. We would also like to extend our gratitude to those authors whose work we were not able to use in this text due to our narrowed focus. We hope this work serves as a wake-up call to those who believe child maltreatment only affects the people who are abused. When a child is abused we all pay.

Kris Franey, MA
Family Violence and
Sexual Assault Institute

Robert Geffner, Ph.D., ABPN
Family Violence and
Sexual Assault Institute

Robert Falconer, M.A.
The Institute for
Trauma Oriented
Psychotherapy

References

Etheridge, P. (1999). Study links childhood trauma and smoking: Children faced with a terrible burden of stressors. www.Cnn.com/Health/9911/02/smoking.kids. Washington, D.C.

Friedman, R. P. D. (1999). Sexual abuse a major risk factor for depression, suicide: Teens most at danger, study shows. WEBMD Medical News. Santa Cruz, CA.

Frothingham, T., Hobbs, C.J., Wynne, J.M., Yee, L., Goyal, A., & Wadworth, D.J. (2000). Follow up study eight years after diagnosis of sexual abuse. *Archives of Diseases of Childhood, 83,* 132-134.

Gilligan J. (1996). *Violence: Our deadly epidemic and its causes.* New York: Grosset/Putnam.

Hart, B. L., & Geffner, R. (1999, March). Development and analysis of a neuropsychological data base with comparison to a behavioral history of violence. Paper presented to the annual meeting of the Academy of Criminal Justice Sciences, Orlando, FL.

Leserman, J. D., Douglas, L. Z., Toomey T., Nachman G., & Glougau, L. (1996). Sexual and physical abuse history in gastroenterology practice: How types of abuse impact health status. *Psychosomatic Medicine, 58,* 4-15.

Rosenbaum, A., Geffner, R., & Benjamin, S. (1997). A biopsychosocial model for understanding relationship aggression. *Journal of Aggression, Maltreatment, & Trauma, 1,* 57-79.

Spat Widom, C. P. D. (1999). Posttraumatic stress disorder in abused and neglected children grown up. *American Journal of Psychiatry 156,* 1223-1229.

Stein, M. B. M., & Elizabeth, M. D. (2000). As cited in the "Center for Advancement of Health." *Psychosomatic Medicine* (November/December).

ABOUT THE EDITORS

Kris Franey, M.A. received her BA in psychology from the University of Washington and her Master of Arts degree in Psychology from the California School of Professional Psychology (CSPP) in San Diego, CA. She is completing her doctorate in clinical psychology at CSPP, Alliant University in San Diego, with specialized training in child and adolescent psychology. Her dissertation is focusing on the experiences of adolescent sexual offenders who have re-entered society following their treatment. Ms. Franey has worked with the Family Violence and Sexual Assault Institute since 1998.

Robert Geffner, Ph.D., ABPN is the Founder and President of the Family Violence and Sexual Assault Institute (and Executive Editor of the *Family Violence & Sexual Assault Bulletin)* located in San Diego, CA and Fort Worth, TX. Dr. Geffner is a Clinical Research Professor of Psychology at the California School of Professional Psychology, Alliant University in San Diego. He is a Licensed Psychologist and a Licensed Marriage & Family Therapist in Texas and in California, and was the clinical director of a large private practice mental health clinic in East Texas for over 15 years. He is Editor-in-Chief of Haworth's Maltreatment and Trauma Press, which also includes being the Editor of the: *Journal of Child Sexual Abuse; Journal of Aggression, Maltreatment, & Trauma* and co-editor of *Journal of Emotional Abuse,* all internationally disseminated. He also is Senior Editor of the Maltreatment, Trauma, and Interpersonal Aggression book program for Haworth Press. He has a Diplomate in Clinical Neuropsychology from the American Board of Professional Neuropsychology. He has served as an adjunct faculty member for the National Judicial College since 1990, and was a former Professor of Psychology at the University of Texas at Tyler for 16 years. He has been a researcher and consultant for several grants, as well as a grant reviewer for federal and state agencies and foundations during the past 20 years. Dr. Geffner has been invited as a keynote speaker or workshop presenter for over 450 international, national or regional conferences. He has served on several state and national committees relating to family violence, child maltreatment, forensic issues, and interpersonal violence.

Robert Falconer, M.A. received his B.A. in anthropology from the University of Chicago and his M.A. in psychology from Norwich University. He is currently the executive director of the Institute for Trauma Oriented Psychotherapy. He previously co-edited a book entitled, *Trauma, Amnesia & the Denial of Abuse,* which is also available from Family Violence Sexual Assault Institute. This book was published in 1995. Mr. Falconer has a strong interest in the long-term effects of child maltreatment, with a special focus on the ways foundations and other funding agencies can help prevent such abuse from occurring in the first place.

ABOUT THE AUTHORS

Evvie Becker, Ph.D., is a Senior Policy Analyst with the Office of the Assistant Secretary for Planning and Evaluation, U.S. Department of Health and Human Services. Dr. Becker was a 1992-93 Congressional Fellow, sponsored by the American Association for the Advancement of Science and the American Psychological Association (AAAS/APA). Dr. Becker was also a Fellow at Harvard University and Boston Children's Hospital (funded by an NIMH National Research Service Award), and a Psychology Fellow in Pediatrics at Harbor-UCLA Medical Center. Prior to returning to Washington, she was an Assistant Professor of Clinical Psychology at the University of Connecticut, where her research focused on high-risk populations, including incarcerated young men, pregnant teens, and high-school dropouts. Dr. Becker has served on various APA Committee dealing with legal issues and violence.

John Briere, Ph.D., is Associate Professor of Psychiatry and Psychology at the Keck School of Medicine, University of Southern California, and Director of the Psychological Trauma Clinic at LAC-USC Medical Center. Dr. Briere is a Fellow of the American Psychological Association, and President-elect of the International Society for Traumatic Stress Studies (ISTSS). He is author of a number of books, articles, chapters, and psychological tests in the areas of child abuse, psychological trauma, and interpersonal violence. He is a recent recipient of the Laufer Memorial Award for Outstanding Scientific Achievement from the ISTSS, and the Outstanding Professional Award from the American Professional Society on the Abuse of Children.

Claire Burke Draucker, RN, PhD, CS, is an Associate Professor in the College of Nursing at Kent State University, Kent, OH. She is a licensed psychologist and a clinical specialist in psychiatric-mental health nursing. Her research interests include the healing of adult survivors of childhood sexual abuse, the victimization of women throughout the lifespan, and sexual violence by intimate others. She is the author of *Counseling Survivors of Child Sexual Abuse* published by Sage.

Martha L. Coulter, Ph.D., received her doctorate in Maternal and Child Health Welfare at the University of North Carolina, School of Public Health. She received her M. S. W. from Tulane University. Dr. Coulter is an Associate Professor at the University of South Florida, College of Public Health and serves as Director of the James and Jennifer Harrell Center for the Study of Domestic Violence. She has numerous publications in the fields of family violence and child health.

Mark E. Courtney is the Director of the Chapin Hall Center for Children and an Associate Professor in the School of Social Service Administration at the University of Chicago. Dr. Courtney previously served on the faculty of the University of Wisconsin-Madison. Before moving into academia, he worked for several years in various capacities providing group home care to abused and neglected adolescents. He has served as a consultant to the federal government, departments of social services in several states and to local public and private child welfare agencies around the country. Dr. Courtney's research has focused on outcomes of out-of-home care placement including family reunification, reentry to out-of-home care, adoption, and the post-discharge well-being of youth who aged out of foster care. He has also written extensively about the relationship between public assistance and child welfare programs. He has authored numerous articles in professional journals and is co-author of Unfaithful Angels: How Social Work Has Abandoned Its Mission (New York: The Free Press, 1994) and From Child Abuse to Permanency Planning: Child Welfare Services, Pathways, and Placements (New York: Aldine de Gruyter, 1994).

Vincent J. Felitti, M.D., is Chairman, Department of Preventative Medicine, Kaiser Permanente, in San Diego, CA. He is also an Associate Clinical Professor of Medicine at the University of California, San Diego, and a Fellow of the American College of Physicians. He received his degree from Johns Hopkins School of Medicine.

Elizabeth Frenkel, M.A., is a doctoral student in clinical psychology at Miami University in Oxford, Ohio. She earned her Master's degree at Miami University and completed her predoctoral internship at the University of Medicine and Dentistry of New Jersey, Robert Wood Johnson Medical School. Ms. Frenkel is conducting her dissertation research in the area of revictimization of childhood sexual abuse survivors.

Dan Hoyt is at the Department of Sociology and Anthropology at the University of Central Florida in Orlando.

Kathleen Kendall-Tackett, Ph.D., received her doctorate from Brandeis University in social/ developmental psychology. She is currently a Research Associate at the Family Research Laboratory, University of New Hampshire. She has a long-standing interest in health, working in the fields of child sexual abuse, maternal depression and breastfeeding. Her current research is on the health effects of victimization. Dr. Kendall-Tackett is on the editorial boards of *Child Abuse & Neglect* and *Journal of Child Sexual Abuse* She is a member of several organizations dealing with behavioral medicine, health, and abuse.

Kathryn Kuehnle, Ph.D., is a Florida Licensed Psychologist who received her doctorate from the University of Minnesota. Dr. Kuehnle maintains a private practice where she specializes in evaluating and treating victims of abuse and neglect. She also holds the position of Assistant Research Professor at the University of South Florida in both the Department of Mental Health Law & Policy and in the College of Public Health, Department of Community and Family Health. She lectures extensively and is the author of a book, book chapters, and journal articles on evaluating and treating child abuse victims.

Eugene Maguin is an assistant research professor for the Center for Research on Urban Social Work Practice at the University of Buffalo in Buffalo, New York.

Lynette Menezes is a doctoral student in the Department of Community and Family Health at the College of Public Health, University of South Florida. She is currently a research assistant at the James and Jennifer Harrell Center for the Study of Domestic Violence.

Brenda Miller is the Director at the Center for Research on Urban Social Work Practice at the University of Buffalo in Buffalo, New York.

Brenda Morissette Joly is a doctoral candidate in the Department of Community and Family Health at the College of Public Health, University of South Florida. She is currently a research assistant at the James and Jennifer Harrell Center for the Study of Domestic Violence.

Sachiko Nobuyasu, M.B.A., M.P.A., was born and raised in Rome, Italy where she attended the University La Sapienza receiving a BS/MBA in Economics and Commerce in 1993. Ms. Nobuyasu attended Cornell University earning a Master in Public Administration with a concentration in social policy for children & youth in 1997. Ms. Nobuyasu has consulted in project management, strategic planning, and policy analysis for NGOs and international organizations in the U.S. and abroad. Ms. Nobuyasu recently relocated in Boston to pursue studies in not-for-profit management.

Bruce D. Perry, M.D., Ph.D., is Chief of Psychiatry at Texas Children's Hospital in Houston, Texas. Within Baylor College of Medicine, he serves as the Thomas S. Trammell Research Professor of Child Psychiatry in the Department of Psychiatry and Behavioral Sciences. Dr. Perry has secondary appointments in Pediatrics, Pharmacology and Neuroscience. Dr. Perry's neuroscience research has examined the effects of prenatal drug exposure on brain development, the neurobiology of human neuropsychiatric disorders, and the neurophysiology of traumatic life events. His clinical research and practice has focused on traumatized children, examining long-term cognitive, behavioral, emotional, social, and physiological effects of neglect and trauma in children, adolescents and adults.

Frank W. Putnam, M.D., is a child and adolescent psychiatrist specializing in the effects of child abuse, neglect and trauma on the psychological, social, and biological development of children. He was Director of the Developmental Traumatology Program at the National Institute of Mental Health Intramural Research Program for several years. He currently is at Children's Hospital in Cincinnati, OH, where he is Professor of Pediatrics, Director of the Mayerson Center for Safe and Healthy Children, and Scientific Director of Every Child Succeeds. Dr. Putnam has published over 100 articles and chapters, and authored two books.

Lillian Range, Ph.D., is a Professor of Psychology at the University of Southern Mississippi in Hattiesburg, where her research interests are suicide among adolescents and adults, and professional training issues.

John Read, Ph.D., is a Senior Lecturer and Co-Director of the Clinical Psychology Doctoral Training Programme, Psychology Department, The University of Auckland, in Auckland, New Zealand; he specializes in abuse and trauma and its long-term effects.

Kimberly A. Tyler, Ph.D., is an Assistant Professor in Sociology at the University of Central Florida in Orlando. Her research interests include sexual risk-taking behaviors, childhood sexual abuse and sexual victimization among homeless and runaway adolescents.

Bessel A. van der Kolk, M.D., is a Professor of Psychiatry at Boston University School of Medicine, and Medical Director of The Trauma Center. He is a Past President of the International Society of Traumatic Stress Studies. He is the author of over 100 scientific articles on the effects of trauma on children and adults, and of two books: *Psychological Trauma* and *Traumatic Stress: The effects of overwhelming experience on mind, body and society*

Les B. Whitbeck is at the Institute for Social and Behavioral Research in the Department of Sociology at Iowa State University.

Margaret O'Dougherty Wright, Ph.D. is an Associate Professor of Psychology at Miami University in Oxford, Ohio. She received her doctorate degree in Clinical Psychology from the University of Minnesota and completed an internship in Clinical Psychology at the Neuropsychiatric Institute at the University of California, Los Angeles. She has published a book on coping with chronic illnesses in childhood and her empirical research focuses on vulnerability and resilience following traumatic life events. She is particularly interested in developmental and cultural factors that mediate successful recovery from trauma and has written about adaptation following experiences of child abuse, massive war trauma, and chronic health conditions.

The Hidden Effects of Childhood Maltreatment on Adult Health
By Stephanie J. Dallam, RN, MS, FNP

Introduction

Over the past several decades, research has increasingly shown that child maltreatment, defined as neglect, physical abuse, sexual abuse, or emotional maltreatment, is a major social and public health problem that affects children from all cultural backgrounds, and socioeconomic levels. The Third National Incidence Study of Child Abuse and Neglect (a study involving 5,600 community professionals who come into contact with children) estimated that 42 children per 1,000 in the population were harmed or endangered by abuse or neglect in 1993 (U.S. Department of Health and Human Services, 1996). This translates into millions of cases of child maltreatment, much of which occurs at the hands of the child's primary caregiver and is thus never reported. Between 1986 and 1993, government figures show that the number of children seriously injured by abuse and neglect quadrupled, leading the U.S. Advisory Board on Child Abuse and Neglect to declare a child protection emergency. Evidence suggests that this represents an actual increase in child maltreatment, not just an artifact of improved reporting (Sedlak & Broadhurst, 1996).

Despite the millions of children impacted by abuse or neglect and the well-documented associations between childhood maltreatment and a host of neuropsychiatric conditions (e.g., post-traumatic stress disorder, dissociative disorders, mood disorders, conduct disorders), until recently there has been a relative lack of systematic research on the physiological after-effects of childhood maltreatment. As a result, few people are aware that childhood maltreatment is a powerful risk factor for health problems in adulthood. The present chapter will (1) summarize the effects of maltreatment on the neuroendocrine system; (2) provide an overview of the association between childhood maltreatment and adult health; and (3) examine the potential economic impact of childhood maltreatment on health care utilization.

Physiological Effects of Maltreatment
The Neuroendocrine System

The nervous and endocrine system engage in a back and forth dance through which they control the body's physiology by continuously increasing or decreasing the activity of various neurotransmitters and hormones. The brain orchestrates this dance with the goal of maintaining a state of homeostasis or equilibrium. Stressful events disrupt the dance, upsetting its delicate balance. The brain responds by activating the sympathetic nervous system and the hypothalamic-pituitary-adrenal (HPA) axis, and releasing endogenous opioids. Stimulation of the sympathetic nervous system results in the release of catecholamines into the blood, while the HPA axis induces the release of glucocorticoids (primarily cortisol). Both catecholamines and cortisol have been found to be chronically elevated in abused children (De Bellis, Baum, et al., 1999; Putnam & Trickett, 1997).

Catecholamines. Stressful events cause increased catecholamine (primarily epinephrine and norepinephrine) levels resulting in hyperarousal along with increased heart rate, respiration, blood pressure, and muscle tone. Simultaneous changes in the central nervous system cause a state of hypervigilance in which the child tunes out all non-critical information. This is called the "fight or flight" response, as the body prepares itself to fight with, or run away from, the potential threat. Over activation of the "fight or flight" response can lead to chronically elevated levels of catecholamines resulting in abnormalities in cardiovascular regulation, along with an increased startle response, profound sleep disturbances, affect regulation problems and generalized anxiety (Perry, 1994, 2000; Perry, Pollard, Blakely, Baker, & Vigilante, 1995).

Opioids. When fighting or physically fleeing is not feasible, the child may use a "freeze" or surrender response (dissociation) in which the child detaches from the events and withdraws inwardly (Perry, 2000). Evidence suggests that alterations of the endogenous opiate system and dopaminergic systems are involved in the dissociative response (Perry et al., 1995; Bohus et al. 1999). Most children experience a combination of hyperarousal and dissociation during stressful events. When confronted with a traumatic event, the child will feel threatened and the arousal systems will activate. With increased threat, the child moves along the arousal continuum. At some point along this continuum, the body releases endogenous opioids and the dissociative response is activated. This results in a marked decrease in arousal, decreased awareness of pain, and a decreased heart rate and blood pressure despite increases in circulating epinephrine (see Perry et al., 1995). Overall, females and younger children are more likely to dissociate and while older children and males are more likely to display a classic "fight or flight" response.

Cortisol. During acute stress situations cortisol enhances survival by depressing the body's reaction to injury. With regards to emotional behavior, experimental increases in cortisol have been shown to initially increase alertness, activity levels, and feelings of well-being; while prolonged elevations stimulate withdrawal, dysphoria, and feelings of "tiredness" (Plihal, Krug, Pietrowsky, Fehm, & Born, 1996). Chronic secretion of cortisol can also depress the immune system. One of the primary organs of the immune system, the thymus gland, has been found to be significantly smaller in abused and/or neglected children when compared to those of nonabused children. The size of maltreated children's thymus glands is correlated with the severity and length of maltreatment (Fukunaga et al., 1992).

Use Dependent Changes

When the trauma has ended, feedback mechanisms are activated to counteract the stress hormones and return the heart rate, blood pressure and other physiological adaptations to normal. However, if the stress is severe and chronic, compensatory mechanisms can become over-activated and incapable of restoring the previous state of equilibrium. The physiological system is then forced to re-organize its basal patterns of equilibrium. Research by Dr. Bruce Perry, Professor of Child Psychiatry at the Baylor College of Medicine in Houston, Texas, has shown that chronically traumatized children will often, at baseline, be in a state of low-level fear which is reflected in their body's physiology (e.g., increase heart rate, muscle tone, rate of respiration). According to Perry, the longer the activation of the stress-response systems (i.e., the more intense and prolonged the traumatic event), the more likely there will be a "use-dependent" change in these neural systems (for a review see Perry et al., 1995). The predominant adaptive style of the child in the acute traumatic situation will determine which post-traumatic symptoms will develop -- hyperarousal or dissociative (Perry, 2000).

Repeated exposure to threatening stimuli also causes sensitization of the nervous system. Sensitization results from a pattern of repetitive neural activation or experience. The nervous system comes to anticipate the trauma, and soon the same neural activation can be elicited by decreasingly intense stimuli. The result is that full-blown hyperarousal or dissociation can be elicited by apparently minor stressors (Perry et al., 1995). The developing brain organizes around this internalization of the fear response resulting in behavior that may be symptomatic of a number of psychiatric conditions. For instance, chronically traumatized children may display signs of post-traumatic stress disorder (PTSD), attention deficit hyperactivity disorder (ADHD), major depression, various dissociative disorders, oppositional-defiant disorder, conduct disorder, separation anxiety or specific phobia (see Perry & Azad, 1999).

Disorders Associated with Dysregulation of the HPA axis.

PTSD. Symptoms of post-traumatic stress are frequently found in traumatized children. One study of abused children reported that 34% of children experiencing sexual or physical abuse and 58% of children experiencing both physical and sexual abuse met criteria for PTSD (Ackerman, Newton, McPherson, Jones, & Dykman, 1998). PTSD is associated with a wide variety of symptoms such as impulsivity, distractibility and attention problems (due to hypervigilance), emotional numbing, social avoidance, dissociation, sleep problems, aggressive play, school failure, and regressed or delayed development. PTSD from childhood maltreatment can persist for many years after the original traumatic event and may never fully remit (Zlotnick et al., 1999).

Research suggests that dysregulation of the HPA axis and functional alterations in specific cortical and subcortical areas of the brain underlie many of the symptoms of patients with PTSD (Bremner, Narayan, et al., 1999; Bremner, Staib, et al., 1999). Individuals with PTSD show evidence of increased autonomic reactivity (Metzger et al., 1999), and in what appears to be the result of a sensitized feedback mechanism, adults with histories of childhood maltreatment often have lower baseline cortisol levels (Heim, Ehlert, & Hellhammer, 2000) and a blunted cortisol respond to subsequent stressors. These physiological changes appear to render adult victims of childhood victimization more vulnerable to stress-related disorders and more reactive when confronted with stressors during adulthood.

For instance, women with a history of prior physical or sexual assault have been found to have a significantly attenuated cortisol response to the acute stress of rape compared to women without such a history. Blood samples were drawn from 37 adult female rape victims within 51 hours after they had been raped. Approximately three months later they tested the women for PTSD. Women with a history of previous assault had a lower mean acute cortisol level after the rape and a higher probability of subsequently developing PTSD (Resnick, Yehuda, Pitman, & Foy, 1995). Stressful and traumatic events during childhood have also been found to predispose male and female solders to develop combat related PTSD symptomatology (Bremner, Southwick, Johnson, Yehuda, & Charney, 1993; Engel et al., 1993; Zaidi & Foy, 1994).

Dissociative Disorders. Dissociative disorders are associated with a severe, prolonged physical and/or sexual abuse in childhood (Coons, 1986). Unable to physically escape, small children tend to employ dissociation to mentally escape traumatic events. Dissociation tends to create a distorted sense of time, a detached feeling that what is happening is not real, and a diminished sensation of pain. Children who frequently dissociate are often quiet, compliant, and avoidant (Perry et al., 1995; Perry, 2000). During a traumatic event they appear to "tune out" and later may not remember what happened.

Depression. Childhood maltreatment is also a risk factor for developing depression, a condition associated with dysregulation of the HPA axis. For example, researchers who prospectively followed a randomly selected cohort of 776 children found that adolescents and young adults with a history of childhood maltreatment were 3 times more likely to become depressed or suicidal compared with individuals without such a history (Brown, Cohen, Johnson, & Smailes, 1999). Two community surveys found the incidence of depression to be 100% in women who suffered sexual abuse involving penetration during childhood (Bifulco, Brown & Alder, 1991; Cheasty, Clare, & Collins, 1998).

Stress-related disorders. Because cortisol helps regulate the immune system, the lower cortisol responses found in many trauma survivors may cause their immune systems to become overly reactive. For instance, adults with chronic PTSD have been found to have elevated leukocyte and total T-cell counts consistent with chronic immune activation (Boscarino & Chang, 1999). The chronic activation of the immune system along with the persistent lack of cortisol availability in traumatized or chronically stressed individuals may promote an increased vulnerability for the development of stress-related disorders. Disorders associated with hypocortisolism include chronic fatigue syndrome, fibromyalgia, rheumatoid arthritis, and asthma (Heim, Ehlert, et al., 2000).

Effect of Chronic Maltreatment on Brain Growth and Function

Neural systems respond to prolonged, repetitive stress by altering their structural organization and functioning. Brain scans using magnetic resonance imaging (MRI) have demonstrated that maltreated children and adolescents with PTSD have significantly smaller intracranial and cerebral volumes than matched controls with no history of maltreatment. Lower brain volume correlated with age of onset and duration of the abusive experiences and severity of dissociative and PTSD symptoms in the children studied (De Bellis, Keshavan, et al., 1999). Children with histories of severe physical or sexual abuse have also been found to have signs of subtle structural brain abnormalities on EEGs. Researchers have found that the left hemispheres of abused children have fewer nerve-cell connections between different areas (Ito, Teicher, Glod, & Ackerman, 1998). In addition, abused children show evidence of tiny seizures, similar to those of epileptics, through various sectors of their brains. These brain changes appear to have a deleterious effect on cognitive function as children with PTSD have been found to have poorer overall memory performance when compared with controls (Moradi, Doost, Taghavi, Yule, & Dalgleish, 1999).

Recent studies of adults indicate that extreme stress during childhood can lead to measurable physical changes in the hippocampus and medial prefrontal cortex, two areas of the brain involved in memory and emotional responses. For example, women reporting childhood abuse have been found to have significantly lower left-sided hippocampal volumes (a region of the brain involved in learning and verbal memory) when compared with matched controls without abuse histories. The degree of decreased hippocampal volume correlates with the severity of dissociative symptoms and PTSD found in the abused women (Stein, Koverola, Hanna, Torchia, & McClarty, 1997). These changes can also lead to ongoing problems with learning and remembering new information. When compared with healthy matched controls, adult survivors of severe childhood physical and sexual abuse have been found to demonstrate significant deficits in verbal short-term recall, which correlates with the severity of the abuse experienced (Bremner et al., 1995).

Health Consequences of Childhood Maltreatment

Dr. Vincent Felitti, at the Department of Preventive Medicine, Southern California Permanente Medical Group, was one of the first physicians to systematically study the relationship between childhood maltreatment and adult health. Dr. Felitti became interested in this area after finding that an inordinate number of patients failing a weight control program gave histories of child sexual abuse. To find out if there was a connection, Dr. Felitti (1991) studied 131 sequential adult patients who acknowledged a history of childhood sexual abuse. He found that severe sexual trauma during childhood was associated with marked reductions in physical, emotional, and vocational functioning in his predominantly female sample. For instance, compared with age- and sex-matched controls, sexually abused patients had significantly higher rates of chronic depression, morbid obesity, and certain psychosomatic symptoms such as chronic gastrointestinal distress and recurrent headaches. The abused subjects also had significantly higher rates of health care utilization; seeking medical care at a rate of more than three times that of the control group.

Subsequent studies have supported Felitti's findings and demonstrate a strong, linear relationship between childhood maltreatment and indices of adult health. In other words, the greater the severity of maltreatment during childhood, the more health problems reported during adulthood.

Physical Symptoms and Functional Disorders

Researchers have found that overall women who report a history of childhood abuse report problems in twice as many body systems as nonabused women (Lechner, Vogel, Garcia-Shelton, Leichter, & Steibel, 1993). In many cases no organic cause for the symptoms can be found (Boisset-Pioro, Esdaile, & Fitzcharles, 1995). For instance, a study of 239 women referred to a gastroenterology clinic found that when compared to nonabused patients women with abuse history, particularly those with severe abuse, were much more likely to report somatic symptoms related to panic (e.g. palpitations, numbness, shortness of breath), depression (e.g. difficulty sleeping, loss of appetite), musculoskeletal disorders (e.g. headaches, muscle aches), genito-urinary disorders (e.g. vaginal discharge, pelvic pain, painful intercourse), skin disturbance (e.g. rash) and respiratory illness (e.g. stuffy nose) (Leserman, Li, Drossman & Hu, 1998). When no source can be found to explain the patient's symptoms, the symptoms are considered "functional." In extreme cases, patients with unexplained medical symptoms may be diagnosed with somatization — a disorder characterized by somatic complaints that after appropriate medical assessment cannot be explained in terms of a conventionally defined medical condition. Somatization is frequently found in conjunction with depression, anxiety disorders and history of maltreatment. The association between somatization and maltreatment is perhaps best demonstrated by a study which found that out of 100 women with somatization disorder, over 90% reported some type of abuse, with 80% reporting sexual assault either as a child or an adult (Pribor, Yutzy, Dean, & Wetzel, 1993).

Although functional disorders are often blamed on psychological illnesses, research indicates that the relationship between the two may actually be mediated by HPA axis dysfunction. For instance, people with somatization have been found to HPA axis dysfunction similar to that found in patients with PTSD (Heim, Ehlert, Hanker, & Hellhammer, 1998). A study of 252 female primary care patients with unexplained symptoms found a strong linear relationship between the severity of sexual abuse and impairment in health-related quality of life, both before and after controlling for the effects of a current psychiatric diagnosis (Dickinson, deGruy, Dickinson, & Candib, 1999).

Health Perceptions and Quality of Life

A survey of 1,225 women randomly selected from the membership of a large health maintenance organization (HMO) found that a history of childhood maltreatment was significantly associated with perceived poorer overall health, increased numbers of distressing physical symptoms, and greater physical and emotional functional disability. Women reporting multiple types of maltreatment demonstrated the greatest health decrements for both self-reported symptoms and physician-coded diagnoses (Walker, Gelfand, et al., 1999). A similar survey of 668 middle class females in a gynecological practice revealed that women with histories of childhood abuse reported a greater number of physical and psychological problems, and lower ratings of their overall health. A linear relationship was found between the amount of abuse experienced and subsequent health problems; moreover, the number of abuses experienced during childhood was the only variable that contributed significantly to the prediction of adult well-being (Moeller & Bachmann, 1993).

Golding, Cooper and George (1997) examined health perceptions in victims of sexual assault either in childhood or adulthood by combining data on over 10,000 men and women from 7 population surveys. A meta-analysis of the data revealed that a history of sexual assault was associated with poorer subjective health, and this result was consistent regardless of gender, ethnicity, or sample. Controlling depression did not markedly change this result, indicating that depression did not account for or mediate the association. Individuals with histories of multiple assaults reported the worst health.

Chronic Pain

A history of physical and/or sexual abuse is also frequently reported among chronic pain populations and is associated with poorer adjustment to pain (Boisset-Pioro et al., 1995). For instance, a study of female patients with gastrointestinal disorders found that sexually and/or physically abused women reported more than twice the musculoskeletal pain (e.g., headaches, backaches, chest pain), four times the pelvic pain and three times more fatigue than women without abuse histories (Drossman et al., 1990). A study of outpatients diagnosed with fibromyalgia or myofascial pain found that over 60% had a history of abuse (Goldberg, Pachas, & Keith, 1999). An increased prevalence of childhood physical and/or sexual abuse has also been found in women with chronic pelvic pain (Heim et al., 1998; Harrop-Griffiths et al., 1988; Reiter, Shakerin, Gambone, & Milburn, 1991; Springs & Friedrich, 1992; Walker et al., 1992), irritable bowel syndrome (Drossman et al., 1990), and chronic headaches (Domino & Haber, 1987; Felitti, 1991).

Health Care Utilization

In addition to lower ratings of their overall health, adults with histories of childhood abuse tend to make significantly more visits to their doctor (Leserman et al., 1998). They also tend to be admitted to the hospital more frequently and undergo more surgical procedures than their nonabused peers (Moeller & Bachmann, 1993; Salmon & Calderbank, 1996).

Serious Illnesses

In addition to poorer subjective health, childhood maltreatment has also been associated with serious health problems. For example, the Adverse Childhood Experiences (ACE) study, lead by Dr. Felitti, surveyed over 9,000 adults on adverse childhood experiences soon after they had a standardized medical evaluation at a large HMO. The participants were questioned about abuse and family dysfunction including psychological, physical, or sexual abuse; violence against the mother; or living with household members who were substance abusers, mentally ill or suicidal, or ever imprisoned. The researchers found a strong graded relationship between the number of adverse experiences and the presence of serious adult diseases including ischemic heart disease, cancer, liver disease, chronic lung disease, skeletal fractures, and liver disease. These findings suggest that childhood maltreatment and household dysfunction may be related to the development of chronic diseases that are among the most common causes of death and disability in the United States (Felitti, et al., 1998).

The researchers also reported a strong graded relationship between the number of categories of childhood exposure and every adult health risk behavior they studied. For instance, a strong relationship was found between the number of adverse childhood experiences and self-reports of cigarette smoking, obesity, physical inactivity, alcoholism, drug abuse, depression, suicide attempts, sexual promiscuity, and sexually transmitted diseases. These findings suggest that the poorer health found in many survivors of childhood maltreatment may be related in large part to participation in high risk behaviors.

Associations have also been found between early sexual abuse and several health conditions in the elderly. Murray B. Stein, MD, of the University of California, San Diego's Anxiety and Traumatic Stress Disorders Program, and co-author Elizabeth Barrett-Connor (2000), analyzed health data on more than 1,300 elderly white, middle class men and women from a Southern California community. In women, early sexual assault appeared to increase the risk of arthritis and breast cancer, with multiple abuse episodes increasing disease risk by two- to three-fold compared with a single episode. In men, early sexual assault appeared to increase the risk of thyroid disease ("Sexual Abuse May," 2000).

High-Risk Behaviors

As noted previously, children raised in an environment of persistent threat have an altered baseline such that a state of internal calm is rarely obtained. As they grow up, many of these children find that they can artificially induce a more relaxed state by self-medicating with substances such as cigarettes, alcohol and drugs. They may also seek to escape chronic feelings of anxiety and depression through overeating or compulsive sexual behavior. Although, for the purposes of this section each high-risk behavior will be examined separately, it should be remembered that many of high risk or unhealthy behaviors are interrelated. In other words, these behaviors rarely occur in isolation and participating in one significantly increases the likelihood of participating in others (Zakarian, Hovell, Conway, Hofstetter, & Slymen, 2000).

For example, consider the results of the Commonwealth Fund Adolescent Health Survey, which was based on a nationally representative cross-section sample of 3,015 girls in grades 5 through 12. After controlling for demographic characteristics (grade level, ethnicity, family structure, and socioeconomic status) the researchers found that when compared to their nonabused peers, girls who reported experiencing both physical and sexual abuse were over five times more likely to experience depressive symptoms and over three times more likely to report moderate to high life stress. The abused girls were also many times more likely to report that they engaged in regular smoking, regular drinking, illicit drug use, or to give a history of bingeing and purging behavior.

In addition, they were almost twice as likely to rate their health status as fair to poor (Diaz, Simatov, & Rickert, 2000).

Cigarette Smoking. Research suggests that the risk of smoking following victimization is doubled even when controlling for the effects of race, education and past psychopathology (Resnick, Acierno, & Kilpatrick, 1997). The ACE study assessed the relationship between adverse childhood experiences and smoking in 9,215 mostly middle-aged adults. After adjusting for age, sex, race, and education, each type of adversity experienced during childhood significantly increased the risk for each type of smoking behavior assessed. For example, compared with those reporting no adverse childhood experiences, persons reporting 5 or more categories were over 5 times more likely to have started smoking before age 15, and over twice as likely to still be smoking (Anda et al., 1999). Similar results have been found in surveys of adolescents. For instance, Riggs, Alario and McHorney (1990) found that high school students with a history of physical abuse were three times more likely to smoke as nonabused students. The Commonwealth Fund Adolescent Health Survey found that adolescent girls who had been both sexually and physically abused were almost 6 times more likely to smoke than their nonabused peers (Diaz et al., 2000).

Alcohol and Illicit Drug Use. Numerous surveys have found that adolescents and adults who were abused during childhood are significantly more likely to drink alcohol and/or use illicit drugs than their peers. For instance, one study found that high school students with a history of physical abuse were 3 times more likely to drink alcohol and almost twice as likely to use illicit drugs (Riggs et al., 1990). The Commonwealth Fund Adolescent Health Survey found that adolescent girls who had been both sexually and physically abused were over 3.5 times more likely to engage in regular drinking or to have recently used illicit drugs when compared with their nonabused peers (Diaz et al., 2000). Similar results have been found with adults. For instance, longitudinal data from the National Women's Study demonstrated that both distant past and recent assault were associated with 2 to 3 times the risk of alcohol abuse in women, even when controlling for baseline alcohol use, age, race and education (Resnick et al., 1997). This relationship is even stronger in clinical populations. Briere and Runtz (1987) reported that female crisis center clients with a history of sexual abuse had 10 times the likelihood of a drug addiction history and over two times the likelihood of alcoholism relative to nonabused female clients.

Risky Sexual Behaviors. Victims of childhood maltreatment, especially those who have been sexual abused, have been consistently found to be more likely to engage in high-risk sexual behaviors then their peers. Researchers examined the relationship of sexual abuse history to sexual risk behaviors in representative sample of 9th through 12th graders (N = 4,014). After controlling for related demographics and risk behaviors, sexually abused female students were over twice as likely than those without such a history to have had earlier first coitus, to have had three or more sex partners, and were almost twice as likely to have been pregnant. Sexually abused male students were over three times more likely than those without such a history to have ever had multiple partners, and to have engaged in sex resulting in pregnancy (Raj, Silverman, & Amaro, 2000).

Other surveys have reported similar findings. For instance, a survey of 3,128 high school girls found that adolescents with a history of sexual abuse were more likely to report having had intercourse by age 15, to have not used birth control at last intercourse, and to have had more than one sexual partner compared to their nonabused peers (Stock, Bell, Boyer, & Connell, 1997). Another study followed 510 girls from birth to adulthood. At age 18, women who reported child sexual abuse, especially those reporting severe abuse involving intercourse, had significantly higher rates of early onset consensual sexual activity, multiple sexual partners, unprotected intercourse, sexually transmitted disease, and sexual assault after the age of 16. A multifactoral causal relationship was noted in which various factors such as family instability, impaired parent child relationships, and childhood sexual abuse resulted in the early onset sexual activity which, in turn, led to heightened risks of other adverse outcomes in adolescence (Fergusson, Horwood, & Lynskey, 1997).

For instance, abused women are more likely than their peers to be treated for venereal disease, pelvic inflammatory disease, and surgical evaluation of pelvic pain (Lechner et al., 1993). Women with a history of childhood sexual abuse also tend to report less efficacy concerning prevention of HIV (Johnsen & Harlow, 1996) – one of the most rapidly increasing causes of death in the United States (McGinnis & Foege, 1993). This potential connection is strengthened by the findings of a study of HIV-seropositive adolescents. Over 50% of the adolescents had a documented history of sexual abuse and 82% had a history of substance use (Pao et al., 2000).

Childhood maltreatment is also an important risk factor of adolescent pregnancy (Adams & East, 1999; Fergusson et al., 1997; Kellogg, Hoffman, & Taylor, 1999). Pregnancy during adolescence is accompanied with its own set of health risks in the form of complications such as preterm delivery, low birth weight, and neonatal mortality (Olausson, Cnattingius, & Haglund, 1999). In addition, infants born to teenage mothers are themselves at increased risk for being abused and/or neglected, thus perpetuating the cycle of maltreatment into the next generation (de Paul & Domenech, 2000).

Self Harm and Suicide

Research has shown that individuals who have suffered interpersonal abuse at or before age 14 often develop significant problems with modulating anger and self-destructive and suicidal behaviors (van der Kolk et al., 1996). For instance, a study of over 400 college students found that a history of child sexual abuse predicted depression, chronic self-destructiveness, self-harm ideation, acts of self-harm, suicide ideation, and suicide attempts for both men and women. The more frequent and severe the sexual abuse and the longer its duration, the more depression and self-destructiveness reported in adulthood (Boudewyn & Liem, 1995).

According to Dr. Judith Herman (1992), a psychiatrist specializing in treating victims of interpersonal violence, normal regulation of emotional states is disrupted by traumatic experiences that repeatedly evoke terror, rage, and grief. These emotions create a dysphoric state that may subsequently be evoked in response to perceived threats of abandonment and cannot be terminated by ordinary means of self-soothing. Abused children discover at some point that intolerable feelings can be most effectively terminated by a major jolt to the body. The most dramatic method of achieving this result is through the deliberate infliction of injury. In some instances the magnitude of these intolerable feelings can drive the victim to attempt suicide. One study found that high school students with a history of sexual abuse were three times more likely, and those who had been physically abused were five times more likely, to attempt suicide than their peers (Riggs et al., 1990). Another study found that sexually abused boys were 10 times more likely than their peers to report having attempted suicide (Garnefski & Arends, 1998).

The Cost of Childhood Maltreatment

Because childhood maltreatment is a hidden problem in our society, its true cost is concealed within the many medical and psychological disorders that appear to be caused or worsened by childhood maltreatment. Costs attributable to child maltreatment are imposed on society in a variety of ways. These include medical and psychological care; government services such as criminal justice and child protection agencies; and lost earnings and productivity related to impaired functioning in the labor market.

Increasing rates of childhood maltreatment may help explain the increasing rates of depression and suicide found in young people. Suicide is currently the fourth leading cause of death among children between the ages of 10 and 14. A study by the Massachusetts Institute of Technology (MIT) found that depression costs the United States economy over $43 billion a year (Sumner, 1998).

Depression is also associated with increased medical costs as somatic complaints lead depressed people to make more visits to health care providers and receive more tests. For instance, a study of over 6,000 primary care patients found that patients diagnosed with depression had significantly higher annual health care costs (including specialty, medical inpatient, pharmacy, laboratory) when compared with other primary care patients. These costs persisted even after the depression was treated (Simon, VonKorff, & Barlow, 1995). In addition, depressed patients with serious medical disorders experience significantly increased morbidity and mortality when compared with controls (Murberg, Bru, Svebak, Tveteras, & Aarsland, 1999).

The total economic impact of PTSD and other anxiety disorders is similar to that of depression. For example, a recent large scale study revealed that anxiety disorders cost the United States economy almost $42 billion a year, with about half of the costs going for nonpsychiatric medical care. Research suggests that individuals with an anxiety disorder are 3 to 5 times more likely to go to a physician, and 6 times more likely to be hospitalized than those without such a disorder (Greenberg et al., 1999).

The costs attributable to childhood maltreatment are also subsumed in the staggering economic burden associated with high-risk behaviors. For example, the combined effects of tobacco, alcohol, and drugs inflict a greater toll on the health and well-being of Americans than any other single preventable factor. For instance, substance abuse is a significant contributor to morbidity, causing approximately 40 million illnesses and injuries each year. Nearly 590,000 deaths -- about a quarter of all deaths in the United States -- are caused by addictive substances. The total costs attributable to addiction are estimated at greater than $400 billion every year, including health care costs, lost worker productivity, and crime (McGinnis & Foege, 1999). Less quantifiable, but equally important, is the emotional toll that addiction exacts on families and communities. Children of substance-abusing parents are more likely to be maltreated and to, as adults, also become addicted (McGinnis & Foege, 1999).

An indication of the enormous socioeconomic costs associated with child maltreatment are provided by a state-level analysis of the costs associated with child abuse and its consequences performed by Michigan Children's Trust Fund. Based on information for 1991, the costs of child abuse in Michigan were estimated at 823 million dollars annually. These costs included those associated with low birthweight babies, infant mortality, special education, protective service, foster care, juvenile and adult criminality, and psychological services. (The impact on adult health was not examined by the study because little research in this area was available at the time of the study.) The costs of prevention programs were estimated to be 43 million dollars annually. It was concluded that child abuse prevention yields a 19 to 1 cost advantage for taxpayers (Caldwell, 1992).

A partial quantification of the health care costs attributable to a history of childhood maltreatment has seen been provided by a recent large-scale study of 1,225 randomly selected female members of a HMO. The investigators compared direct health care costs for women who reported childhood maltreatment to women without such a history. Women with histories of childhood maltreatment were found to have significantly higher primary care and outpatient costs and more frequent emergency department visits than nonabused women. Moreover the researchers found a linear relationship between the amount and type of maltreatment experienced and increased costs. Thus patients who reported no childhood maltreatment had the lowest health care costs, women who reported any abuse or neglect had median annual health care costs that were $97 greater, women who reported sexual abuse had health care costs that were $245 greater, and those who reported the most types of maltreatment had the highest costs -- an average of $439 more annually. These differences persisted after controlling for demographic and chronic disease variables (Walker, Unutzer, et al., 1999). It should be noted that these figures are conservative, as the investigators did not include the cost of treating chronic medical disease in their analysis. In addition, they did not measure the indirect costs related to childhood maltreatment such as disability or lost work productivity.

Conclusion

Maltreatment can alter a child's physical, emotional, cognitive and social development and impact their physical and mental health throughout their lifetime. While we have yet to understand all of the ways which childhood maltreatment effects neurodevelopment, it is clear that the developing brain is exquisitely sensitive to and can be permanently altered by adverse experiences during childhood. Unfortunately, while millions of children are maltreated each year, few resources are dedicated to solving the problem. Costs could be substantially lowered and economic productivity increased through committing more resources to the prevention of childhood maltreatment and providing appropriate psychological therapies when prevention fails. The most obvious savings would be in the lives of the children who will not suffer the devastating effects of neglect and physical, emotional, and sexual abuse. Beyond their benefit, society also profits when its citizens are able to realize their full potential as contributors. Finally, by preventing child maltreatment we save the staggering amounts of money spent annually dealing with its long-term consequences. As this chapter has demonstrated, the cost of doing nothing is simply too great.

References

Ackerman, P. T., Newton, J. E., McPherson, W. B., Jones, J. G., & Dykman, R. A. (1998). Prevalence of post-traumatic stress disorder and other psychiatric diagnoses in three groups of abused children (sexual, physical, and both). *Child Abuse & Neglect, 22*, 759-774.

Adams, J. A., & East, P. L. (1999). Past physical abuse is significantly correlated with pregnancy as an adolescent. *Journal of Pediatric & Adolescent Gynecology, 12*, 133-138.

Anda, R. F, Croft, J. B., Felitti, V. J., Nordenberg, D., Giles, W. H., Williamson, D. F., & Giovino, G. A. (1999). Adverse childhood experiences and smoking during adolescence and adulthood. *JAMA, 282*(17), 1652-1658.

Bifulco, A., Brown, G. W., & Adler, Z. (1991). Early sexual abuse and clinical depression in adult life. *British Journal of Psychiatry, 159*, 115-122.

Bohus, M. J., Landwehrmeyer, G. B., Stiglmayr, C. E., Limberger, M. F., Bohme, R., & Schmahl, C. G. (1999). Naltrexone in the treatment of dissociative symptoms in patients with borderline personality disorder: An open-label trial. *Journal of Clinical Psychiatry, 60*, 598-603.

Boisset-Pioro, M. H., Esdaile, J. M., & Fitzcharles, M. A. (1995). Sexual and physical abuse in women with fibromyalgia syndrome. *Arthritis & Rheumatism, 38*, 235-241.

Boscarino, J. A., & Chang, J. (1999). Higher abnormal leukocyte and lymphocyte counts 20 years after exposure to severe stress: research and clinical implications. *Psychosomatic Medicine, 61*, 378-386.

Boudewyn, A. C., & Liem, J. H. (1995). Childhood sexual abuse as a precursor to depression and self-destructive behavior in adulthood. *Journal of Traumatic Stress, 8*, 445-459.

Bremner, J. D., Narayan, M., Staib, L. H., Southwick, S. M., McGlashan, T., & Charney, D. S. (1999). Neural correlates of memories of childhood sexual abuse in women with and without posttraumatic stress disorder. *American Journal of Psychiatry, 156*, 1787-1795.

Bremner, J. D., Randall, P., Scott, T. M., Capelli, S., Delaney, R., McCarthy, G., & Charney, D.S. (1995). Deficits in short-term memory in adult survivors of childhood abuse. *Psychiatry Research, 59*(1-2), 97-107.

Bremner, J. D., Southwick, S. M., Johnson, D. R., Yehuda, R., & Charney, D. S. Childhood physical abuse and combat-related posttraumatic stress disorder in Vietnam veterans. (1993). *American Journal of Psychiatry, 150*, 235-239.

Bremner, J. D., Staib, L. H., Kaloupek, D., Southwick, S. M., Soufer, R., & Charney, D.S. (1999). Neural correlates of exposure of traumatic pictures and sound in Vietnam combat veterans with and without posttraumatic stress disorder: A Positron Emisson Tomography study. *Biological Psychiatry, 45*, 806-816.

Briere, J. & Runtz, M. (1987). Post sexual abuse trauma: Data and implications for clinical practice. *Journal of Interpersonal Violence, 2*, 367-379.

Brown, J., Cohen, P., Johnson, J. G., & Smailes, E. M. (1999). Childhood abuse and neglect: Specificity of effects on adolescent and young adult depression and suicidality. *Journal of American Academy of Child & Adolescent Psychiatry, 38*, 1490-1496.

Caldwell, R. A. (1992). *The costs of child abuse vs. child abuse prevention: Michigan's experience.* Lansing, MI: Michigan Children's Trust Fund.

Cheasty, M., Clare, A. W., & Collins, C. (1998). Relation between sexual abuse in childhood and adult depression: Case-control study. *British Medical Journal, 316*(7126), 198-201.

Coons, P. M. (1986). Child abuse and multiple personality disorder: Review of the literature and suggestions for treatment. *Child Abuse & Neglect, 19*, 455-462.

De Bellis, M. D., Baum, A. S., Birmaher, B., Keshavan, M. S., Eccard, C. H., Boring, A. M., Jenkins, F. J., & Ryan, N.D. (1999). A.E. Bennett Research Award. Developmental traumatology. Part I: Biological stress systems. *Biological Psychiatry, 45*, 1259-1270.

De Bellis, M. D., Keshavan, M. S., Clark, D. B., Casey, B. J., Giedd, J. N., Boring, A. M., Frustaci, K., & Ryan, N. D. (1999). A. E. Bennett Research Award. Developmental traumatology. Part II: Brain development. *Biological Psychiatry, 45*, 1271-1284.

de Paul, J., & Domenech, L. (2000). Childhood history of abuse and child abuse potential in adolescent mothers: a longitudinal study. *Child Abuse & Neglect, 24*, 701-713.

Diaz, A., Simatov, E., & Rickert, V. I. (2000). The independent and combined effects of physical and sexual abuse on health. Results of a national survey. *Journal of Pediatric & Adolescent Gynecology, 13*, 89.

Dickinson, L. M., deGruy, F. V., Dickinson, W. P., & Candib, L. M. (1999). Health-related quality of life and symptom profiles of female survivors of sexual abuse. *Archives of Family Medicine, 8*, 35-43.

Domino, J. V., & Haber, J. D. (1987). Prior physical and sexual abuse in women with chronic headache: Clinical correlates. *Headache, 27*, 310-314.

Drossman, D. A., Leserman, J., Nachman, G., L,i Z. M., Gluck, H., Toomey, T. C., & Mitchell, C. M. (1990). Sexual and physical abuse in women with functional or organic gastrointestinal disorders. *Annals of Internal Medicine,113*(11), 828-833.

Engel, C. C., Jr., Engel, A. L., Campbell, S. J., McFall, M. E., Russo, J., & Katon, W. (1993). Posttraumatic stress disorder symptoms and precombat sexual and physical abuse in Desert Storm veterans. *Journal of Nervous and Mental Disease, 181*, 683-688.

Felitti, V. J. (1991). Long-term medical consequences of incest, rape, and molestation. *Southern Medical Journal, 84*, 328-331.

Felitti, V. J., Anda, R. F., Nordenberg, D., Williamson, D. F., Spitz, A. M., Edwards, V., Koss, M. P., & Marks, J. S. (1998). Relationship of childhood abuse and household dysfunction to many of the leading causes of death in adults. The Adverse Childhood Experiences (ACE) Study. *American Journal of Preventive Medicine, 14*, 245-258.

Fergusson, D. M., Horwood, L. J., & Lynskey, M. T. (1997). Childhood sexual abuse, adolescent sexual behaviors and sexual revictimization. *Child Abuse & Neglect, 21*, 789-803.

Fukunaga, T., Mizoi, Y., Yamashita, A., Yamada, M., Yamamoto, Y., Tatsuno, Y., & Nishi, K. (1992). Thymus of abused/neglected children. *Forensic Science International, 53*, 69-79.

Garnefski, N., & Arends, E. (1998). Sexual abuse and adolescent maladjustment: Differences between male and female victims. *Journal of Adolescence, 21*, 99-107.

Goldberg, R. T., Pachas, W. N., & Keith, D. (1999). Relationship between traumatic events in childhood and chronic pain. *Disability & Rehabilitation, 21*, 23-30.

Golding, J. M., Cooper, M. L., & George, L. K. (1997). Sexual assault history and health perceptions: Seven general population studies. *Health Psychology, 16*, 417-425.

Greenberg, P. E., Sisitsky, T., Kessler, R. C., Finkelstein, S. N., Berndt, E. R., Davidson, J. R. T., Ballenger, J. C., & Fyer, A. J. (1999). The economic burden of anxiety disorders in the 1990s. *Journal of Clinical Psychiatry, 60*, 427-435.

Harrop-Griffiths, J., Katon, W., Walker, E., Holm, L., Russo, J., & Hickok, L. (1988). The association between chronic pelvic pain, psychiatric diagnoses, and childhood sexual abuse. *Obstetrics & Gynecolology, 71*, 589-594.

Heim, C., Ehlert, U., Hanker, J.P., & Hellhammer, D. H. (1998). Abuse-related posttraumatic stress disorder and alterations of the hypothalamic-pituitary-adrenal axis in women with chronic pelvic pain. *Psychosomatic Medicine, 60*, 309-318.

Heim, C., Ehlert, U., & Hellhammer, D. H. (2000). The potential role of hypocortisolism in the pathophysiology of stress-related bodily disorders. *Psychoneuroendocrinology, 25*, 1-35.

Herman, J. (1992). *Trauma and Recovery*. New York: Basic Books.

Ito, Y., Teicher, M. H., Glod, C. A., & Ackerman, E. (1998). Preliminary evidence for aberrant cortical development in abused children: A quantitative EEG study. *Journal of Neuropsychiatry & Clinical Neurosciences, 10*, 298-307.

Johnsen, L. W., & Harlow, L. L. (1996). Childhood sexual abuse linked with adult substance use, victimization, and AIDS-risk. *AIDS Education & Prevention, 8*, 44-57.

Kellogg, N. D., Hoffman, T. J., & Taylor, E. R. (1999). Early sexual experiences among pregnant and parenting adolescents. *Adolescence, 34*, 293-303.

Lechner, M. E., Vogel, M. E., Garcia-Shelton, L. M., Leichter, J. L., & Steibel, K. R. (1993). Self-reported medical problems of adult female survivors of childhood sexual abuse. *Journal of Family Practice, 36*, 633-638.

Leserman, J., Li, Z., Drossman, D. A., & Hu, Y. J. (1998). Selected symptoms associated with sexual and physical abuse history among female patients with gastrointestinal disorders: the impact on subsequent health care visits. *Psychological Medicine, 28*, 417-425.

McGinnis, M., & Foege, W. H. (1999). Mortality and morbidity attributable to use of addictive substances in the United States. *Proceedings of the Association of American Physicians, 111*(2), 109-18.

Metzger, L. J., Orr, S. P., Berry, N. J., Ahern, C. E., Lasko, N. B., & Pitman, R. K. (1999). Physiologic reactivity to startling tones in women with posttraumatic stress disorder. *Journal of Abnormal Psychology, 108*, 347-352.

Moeller, T. P., & Bachmann, G. A.. (1993). The combined effects of physical, sexual, and emotional abuse during childhood: Long-term health consequences for women. *Child Abuse & Neglect, 17*, 623-640.

Moradi, A. R., Doost, H T., Taghavi, M. R., Yule, W., & Dalgleish, T. (1999). Everyday memory deficits in children and adolescents with PTSD: Performance on the Rivermead Behavioural Memory Test. *Journal of Child Psychology and Psychiatry, 40*, 357-361.

Murberg, T. A., Bru, E., Svebak, S., Tveteras, R., & Aarsland, T. (1999). Depressed mood and subjective health symptoms as predictors of mortality in patients with congestive heart failure: A two-years follow-up study. *International Journal of Psychiatry and Medicine, 29*, 311-326.

Olausson, P. O., Cnattingius, S., & Haglund, B. (1999). Teenage pregnancies and risk of late fetal death and infant mortality. *British Journal of Obstetrics & Gynaecology, 106*, 116-121.

Pao, M., Lyon, M., D'Angelo, L. J., Schuman, W. B., Tipnis, T., & Mrazek, D. A. (2000). Psychiatric diagnoses in adolescents seropositive for the human immunodeficiency virus. *Archives of Pediatric & Adolescent Medicine, 154*, 240-244.

Perry, B. D. (1994). Neurobiological sequelae of childhood trauma: post-traumatic stress disorders in children. In M. Murberg (Ed.), *Catecholamines in Post-traumatic Stress Disorder: Emerging Concepts.* (pp. 253-276). Washington, D.C.: American Psychiatric Press.

Perry, B. D. (2000). Trauma and Terror in Childhood: The neuropsychiatric impact of childhood trauma. In I. Schulz, S. Carella & D.O. Brady (Eds.), *Handbook of Psychological Injuries: Evaluation, Treatment and Compensable Damages.* . Washington, D.C.: American Bar Association Publishing

Perry, B. D., & Azad, I. (1999). Post-traumatic stress disorders in children and adolescents. *Current Opinion in Pediatrics. 11,* 121-132.

Perry, B. D., Pollard, R., Blakely, T., Baker, W., & Vigilante, D. (1995). Childhood trauma, the neurobiology of adaptation and "use-dependent" development of the brain: How "states" become "traits". *Infant Mental Health Journal, 16,* 271-291.

Plihal, W., Krug, R., Pietrowsky, R., Fehm, H. L., & Born, J. (1996). Corticosteroid receptor mediated effects on mood in humans. *Psychoneuroendocrinology, 21,* 515-523.

Pribor, E. F., Yutzy, S. H., Dean, J. T., & Wetzel, R. D. (1993). Birquet's syndrome, dissociation, and abuse. *American Journal of Psychiatry, 150,* 1507-1511.

Putnam, F. W., & Trickett, P. K. (1997). Psychobiological effects of sexual abuse: A longitudinal study. *Annals of the New York Academy of Sciences, 821,* 150-159.

Raj, A., Silverman, J. G., & Amaro, H. (2000). The relationship between sexual abuse and sexual risk among high school students: findings from the 1997 Massachusetts Youth Risk Behavior Survey. *Maternal & Child Health Journal, 4,* 125-134.

Reiter, R. C., Shakerin, L. R., Gambone, J. C., & Milburn, A. K. (1991). Correlation between sexual abuse and somatization in women with somatic and nonsomatic chronic pelvic pain. *American Journal of Obstetrics and Gynecology, 165,* 104-109.

· Resnick, H. S., Acierno, R., & Kilpatrick, D. G. (1997). Health impact of interpersonal violence. Medical and mental health outcomes. *Behavioral Medicine, 23,* 65-78.

Resnick, H. S., Yehuda, R., Pitman, R. K., & Foy, D. W. (1995). Effect of previous trauma on acute plasma cortisol level following rape. *American Journal of Psychiatry, 152*(11), 1675-1677.

Riggs, S., Alario, A. J., & McHorney, C. (1990). Health risk behaviors and attempted suicide in adolescents who report prior maltreatment. *Journal of Pediatrics, 116,* 815-821.

Salmon, P., & Calderbank, S. (1996). The relationship of childhood physical and sexual abuse to adult illness behavior. *Journal of Psychosomatic Research, 40,* 329-336.

Sedlak, A. J., & Broadhurst, D. D. (1996). *Executive summary of the Third National Incidence Study of Child Abuse and Neglect.* Washington, D.C.: U.S. Department of Health and Human Services.

Sexual abuse may affect health for a lifetime. (2000, November 21). Washington, D.C.: Center for the Advancement of Health. Available: http://www.cfah.org/.

Simon, G. E., VonKorff, M., & Barlow, W. (1995). Health care costs of primary care patients with recognized depression. *Archives of General Psychiatry, 52,* 850-6.

Springs, F. E., & Friedrich, W. N. (1992). Health risk behaviors and medical sequelae of childhood sexual abuse. *Mayo Clinic Proceedings, 67,* 527-32.

Stein, M. B., Koverola, C., Hanna, C., Torchia, M. G., & McClarty, B. (1997). Hippocampal volume in women victimized by childhood sexual abuse. *Psychological Medicine, 27,* 951-959.

Stock, J. L., Bell, M. A., Boyer, D. K., & Connell, F. A. (1997). Adolescent pregnancy and sexual risk-taking among sexually abused girls. *Family Planning Perspective, 29,* 200-203, 227.

Sumner, G. (1998, November 11). Untreated depression results in lost workplace productivity. *San Antonio Business Journal.*

U.S. Department of Health and Human Services. (1996). *The third national incidence study of child abuse and neglect.* Washington, D.C.: U.S. Government Printing Office.

Van der Kolk, B. A, Greenberg, M. S., Orr, S. P., & Pitman, R. K. (1989). Endogenous opioids, stress induced analgesia and posttraumatic stress disorder. *Psychopharmacology Bulletin, 25*, 417-420.

Van der Kolk, B. A., Pelcovitz, D., Roth, S., Mandel, F. S., McFarlane, A., & Herman, J. L. (1996). Dissociation, somatization, and affect dysregulation: The complexity of adaptation to trauma. *American Journal of Psychiatry, 153(Suppl)*, 83-93.

Walker, E. A., Gelfand, A., Katon, W. J., Koss, M. P, Von Korff, M., Bernstein, D., & Russo, J. (1999). Adult health status of women with histories of childhood abuse and neglect. *American Journal of Medicine, 107*, 332-339.

Walker, E. A., Katon, W. J., Hansom, J., Harrop-Griffiths, J., Holm, L., Jones, M. L., Hickok, L., & Jemelka, R. P. (1992). Medical and psychiatric symptoms in women with childhood sexual abuse. *Psychosomatic Medicine, 54*, 658-664.

Walker, E. A., Unutzer, J., Rutter, C., Gelfand, A., Saunders, K., VonKorff, M., Koss, M.P., & Katon, W. (1999). Costs of health care use by women HMO members with a history of childhood abuse and neglect. *Archives of General Psychiatry, 56*, 609-613.

Zaidi, L.Y., & Foy, D.W. (1994). Childhood abuse experiences and combat-related PTSD. *Journal of Traumatic Stress, 7*, 33-42.

Zakarian, J. M., Hovellm, M. F., Conway, T. L., Hofstetter, C. R., & Slymen, D. J. (2000). Tobacco use and other risk behaviors: cross-sectional and predictive relationships for adolescent orthodontic patients. *Nicotine & Tobacco Research, 2*(2), 179-186.

Zlotnick, C., Warshaw, M., Shea, M. T., Allsworth, J., Pearlstein, T., & Keller, M. B. (1999). Chronicity in posttraumatic stress disorder (PTSD) and predictors of course of comorbid PTSD in patients with anxiety disorders. *Journal of Traumatic Stress, 12*, 89-100.

The Neuroarcheology of Childhood Maltreatment: The Neurodevelopmental Costs of Adverse Childhood Events

Bruce D. Perry, M.D., Ph.D.

Introduction

Childhood maltreatment has profound impact on the emotional, behavioral, cognitive, social and physical functioning of children. Developmental experiences determine the organizational and functional status of the mature brain and, therefore, adverse events can have a tremendous negative impact on the development of the brain. In turn, these neurodevelopmental effects may result in significant cost to the individual, their family, community and, ultimately, society. In essence, childhood maltreatment alters the potential of a child and, thereby, robs us all.

The present chapter will review some of those costs from a neurodevelopmental perspective. The premise is that when the core principles of neurodevelopment are understood, the costs of adverse childhood events and maltreatment become obvious. Following a brief presentation of the key concepts of neurodevelopment, two primary forms of maltreatment will be considered: (1) neglect and (2) traumatic stress. Maltreatment of children often involves both neglect and trauma; a more complete understanding of the complex neurodevelopmental impact of the combination, however, is best understood after presenting the potential effects of each separately. This chapter presents the current articulation of a neurodevelopmental perspective of childhood maltreatment originally outlined in 1994 (Perry. 1994b) and further elaborated over the last five years (Perry, Pollard, Blakley, Baker, & Vigilante. 1995) (Perry & Pollard. 1998)

This most recent articulation outlines the issue of maltreatment through the lens of developmental neurobiology and coins a descriptive phrase, "neuroarcheology," to capture the impact of adverse events on the developing brain, with the implicit suggestion that experiences leave a 'record' within the matrix of the brain. The nature and location of this record will depend upon the nature of the experience and the time in development when the event took place – much as with the archeological record of the earth. While this phrase may be simplistic to some, it conveys important conceptual principles about the nature of childhood experience, which have been lacking all too often in clinical and research formulations regarding maltreatment. Not a single psychometric instrument measuring traumatic or adverse events, for example, uses time of trauma as a meaningful variable despite the fact that it may be the most important determinant of functional outcome following maltreatment.

The neuroarcheological perspective on childhood experience, therefore, simply posits that the impact of a childhood event (adverse or positive) will be a reflection of (1) the nature, intensity, pattern and duration of the event, and (2) that the resulting strengths (e.g., language) or deficits (e.g., neuropsychiatric symptoms) will be in those functions mediated by the neural systems that are most rapidly organizing (i.e., in the developmental "hot zone") at the time of the experience.

Brain Organization and Function

The human brain is the remarkable organ that allows us to sense, process, perceive, store and act on information from outside and inside the body to carry out the three prime directives required for the survival of our species: (1) survive, (2) affiliate and mate and then, (3) protect and nurture dependents. In order to carry out these core and overarching responsibilities, thousands of inter-related functions have evolved. In the human brain, structure and function have co-evolved. As we have a hierarchy of increasingly complex functions related to our optimal functioning, our brain has evolved a hierarchical structural organization (see Table 1). This hierarchy starts with the lower, simpler brainstem areas and increases in complexity up through the neocortex (Figure 1). In each of these many areas of the brain are neural systems that mediate our many brain-related functions (Figure1; Table1). The 'lower' parts of the brain (brainstem and midbrain) mediate simpler regulatory functions (e.g., regulation of respiration, heart rate, blood pressure, body temperature) while more complex functions (e.g., language and abstract thinking) are mediated by the more complex neocortical structures of the human brain.

This hierarchical structure is the heart of a neuroarcheological understanding of adverse childhood events. This structure becomes the multi-layered soil within which the fossilized evidence of maltreatment can be found – each layer organizing at a different time and each layer reflecting the experiences –good and bad - of that era in the individual's life. Key insights to understanding human functioning, then, will come from understanding neurodevelopment.

Figure 1: Hierarchical Organization of the Human Brain: The brain can be divided into four interconnected areas: brainstem, diencephalons, limbic and neocortex. The complexity of structure, cellular organization and function increases from the lower, simpler areas such as the brainstem to the most complex, the neocortex.

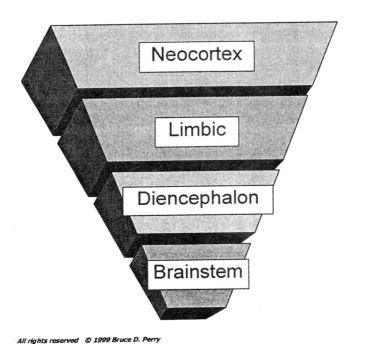

Neocortex — Abstract thought
Concrete Thought
Affiliation
"Attachment"

Limbic — Sexual Behavior
Emotional Reactivity
Motor Regulation

Diencephalon — "Arousal"
Appetite/Satiety
Sleep

Brainstem — Blood Pressure
Heart Rate
Body Temperature

Neurodevelopment

Our brain's complex structure is comprised of 100 billion neurons and ten times as many glial cells – all interconnected by trillions of synaptic connections – and communicating in a non-stop, ever-changing dynamic of neurochemical activity. The brain doesn't just pop into existence. This most complex of all biological systems in the known universe is a product of neurodevelopment – a long process orchestrating billions upon billions of complex chemical transactions. It is through these chemical actions that a human being is created.

The developing child is a remarkable phenomenon of nature. In a few short years, one single cell – the fertilized egg – becomes a walking, talking, learning, loving, and thinking being. This physical transformation is equivalent to a 6-foot tall, 200-pound man growing to the size of Connecticut in three years. In each of the billions and billions of cells in the body, a single set of genes has been expressed in millions of different combinations with precise timing. Development is a breathtaking orchestration of precision micro-construction that allows the healthy development of a human being. And the most remarkable and complex of all the organs in the human body is the human brain. In order to create the brain, a small set of pre-cursor cells must divide, move, specialize, connect and create specialized neural networks that form functional units. The key processes in neurodevelopment are summarized below.

Core Processes of Neurodevelopment

1. Neurogenesis: The brain starts as a few cells present early in the first weeks of life. From a few specialized cells in the unformed brain, come billions of nerve cells and trillions of glia. This, of course, requires that cells be "born." Neurogenesis is the birth of new neurons. The vast majority of neurogenesis takes place in utero during the second and third trimester. At birth, the vast majority of neurons, literally more than 100 billion, used for the remainder of life are present. Few neurons are born after birth, although researchers have demonstrated recently that neurogenesis can and does take place in the mature brain (Gould, Reeves, Graziano, & Gross. 1999). This is a very significant observation and may be one of the important physiological mechanisms responsible for the brain's plasticity (i.e., capacity to restore function) following injury.

Despite being present at birth, these neurons have yet to organize into completely functional systems. Many neurons need to mature themselves and undergo a set of processes that create the functional neural networks of the mature brain (Table 2).

2. Migration: Developing neurons move. Often guided by glial cells and a variety of chemical markers (e.g., cellular adhesion molecules, nerve growth factor: NGF), neurons cluster, sort, move and settle into a location in the brain that will be their final "resting" place. It is the fate of some neurons to settle in the brainstem, others in the cortex, for example. More than one half of all neurons are in the cortex. The processes of cortical cell migration and fate mapping are some of the most studied in all of developmental neuroscience (Rakic. 1981) (Rakic. 1996). It is clear that both genetic and environmental factors play important roles in determining a neuron's final location. Migration takes place primarily during the intrauterine and immediate perinatal period but continues throughout childhood and, possibly, to some degree into adult life. A host of intrauterine and perinatal insults – including infection, lack of oxygen, alcohol and various psychotropic drugs can alter migration of neurons and have profound impact on functioning (Perry. 1988).

3. Differentiation: Neurons mature. Each of the 100 billion neurons in the brain has the same set of genes, yet each neuron is expressing a unique combination of those genes to create a unique identity. Some neurons are large, with long axons; others short. Neurons can mature to use any of a hundred different neurotransmitters such as norepinephrine, dopamine, serotonin, CRF or substance P. Neurons can have dense dendritic fields receiving input from hundreds of other neurons, while other neurons can have a single linear input from one other neuron. Each of these thousands of differentiating "choices" come as a result of the pattern, intensity and timing of various microenvironmental cues which tell the neuron to turn on some genes and turn off others. Each neuron undergoes a series of "decisions" to determine their final location and specialization. These decisions, again, are a combination of genetic and microenvironmental cues. The further along in development, the more differentiated the neuron, the more sensitive it becomes to the environmental signals. From the intrauterine period through early childhood (and to some degree beyond) neurons are very sensitive to experience-based signals, many of which are mediated by patterned neuronal activity in the neural network in which they reside. Neurons are literally designed to change in response to chemical signals. Therefore, any experience or event that alters these neurochemical or microenvironmental signals during development can change the ways in which certain neurons differentiate, thereby altering the functional capacity of the neural networks in which these neurons reside.

Table 1. A Neuroarcheological Chart of Development: Functional Organization

Functional Division	Constituent Parts	Developmental Division	Age of Functional Maturity	Functions
Neocortex	**Cerebral cortex** *Frontal Lobes* ***Temporal Lobes*** *Parietal Lobes* *Occipital Lobes* *Corpus Callosum*	Telencephalon	Puberty Childhood Early childhood	*Abstraction* **Self-image Socialization Affiliation** **Attachment Mood regulation Fine motor Large motor** **Complex state regulation** *(e.g., sleep, appetite)*
Limbic *Cingulate Cortex Amygdala Hippocampus Septum*	**Amygdala**			
	Hippocampus			
	Basal ganglia *Caudate Nucleus Putamen Globus Pallidus*			
Diencephalon	**Thalamus**	**Diencephalon**	**Infancy**	
	Hypothalamus			
Brainstem	**Midbrain** *Superior Colliculus Inferior Colliculus*	**Mesencephalon**	**Six months** *Third trimester*	**Primary state regulation**
	Cerebellum	**Metencephalon**		**Core physiological reflexes and regulatory functions**
	Pons			
	Medulla Oblongata	**Myelencephalon**		
Spinal Cord	**Spinal Cord**		**Third trimester**	

    4. Apoptosis: Some developing neurons die. In many areas of the brain, there are more neurons born than are needed for any given function. Many of these neurons are redundant and when unable to adequately "connect" into an active neural network will die (Kuan, Roth, Flavell, & Rakic. 2000). Research in this area suggests that these neurons may play a role in the remarkable flexibility present in the human brain at birth. Depending upon the challenges of the environment and the potential needs of the individual, some neurons will survive while others will not. Again, this process appears to have genetic and environmental determinants. Neurons that make synaptic connections with others and have an adequate level of activation will survive; those cells that have little activity resorb. This is one example of a general principle of activity-dependence ("use it or lose it") that appears to be important in many neural processes related to learning, memory and development.

5. Arborization: As neurons differentiate, they send out tiny fiber-like extensions from their cell body. These dendrites become the receptive area where other neurons connect. It is in this receptive field that dozens to hundreds of other neurons are able to send neurochemical signals to the neuron. The density of these dendritic branches appears to be related to the frequency and intensity of incoming signals. When there is high activity, the dendritic network extends, essentially branching out in the same fashion as a bush may create new branches. This arborization allows the neuron to receive, process and integrate complex patterns of activity that will, in turn, determine its activity. Again, the arborization process appears to be to some degree activity-dependent. The density of the dendritic arborization appears to be related to the complexity and activity of incoming neural activity. In turn, these neural signals are often dependent upon the complexity and activity of the environment of the animal (Diamond, Law, Rhodes, et al. 1966; Greenough, Volkmar, & Juraska. 1973).

6. Synaptogenesis: Developing neurons make connections with each other. The major mechanism for neuron-to-neuron communication is 'receptor-mediated' neurotransmission that takes place at specialized connections between neurons called synapses. At the synapse, the distance between two neurons is very short. A chemical (classified as a neurotransmitter, neuromodulator or neurohormone) is released from the 'presynaptic' neuron and into the extra-cellular space (called the synaptic cleft) and binds to a specialized receptor protein in the membrane of the 'postsynaptic' neuron. By occupying the binding site, the neurotransmitter helps change the shape of this receptor which then catalyzes a secondary set of chemical interactions inside the postsynaptic neuron that create second messengers. The second messengers such as cyclic AMP, inositol phosphate and calcium will then shift the intracellular chemical milieu, which may even influence the activity of specific genes. This cascade of intracellular chemical responses allows communication from one neuron to another.

A continuous dynamic of synaptic neurotransmission regulates the activity and functional properties of the chains of neurons that allow the brain to do all of its remarkable activities. These neural connections are not random. They are guided by important genetic and environmental cues. In order for our brain to function properly, neurons, during development, need to find and connect with the "right" neurons. During the differentiation process, neurons send fiber-like projections (growth cones) out to make physical contact with other neurons. This process appears to be regulated and guided by certain growth factors and cellular adhesion molecules that attract or repel a specific growth cone to appropriate target neurons. Depending upon a given neuron's specialization, these growth cones will grow (becoming axons) and connect to the dendrites of other cells and create a synapse. During the first eight months of life there is an eight-fold increase in synaptic density while the developing neurons in the brain are "seeking" their appropriate connections (Huttenlocher. 1979) (Huttenlocher. 1994). This explosion of synaptogenesis allows the brain to have the flexibility to organize and function in with a wide range of potential. It is over the next few years, in response to patterned repetitive experiences that these neural connections will be refined and sculpted.

7. Synaptic sculpting: The synapse is a dynamic structure. With ongoing episodic release of neurotransmitter, occupation of receptors, release of growth factors, shifts of ions in and out of cells, laying down of new microtubules and other structural molecules, the synapse is continually changing. A key determinant of change in the synapse appears to be the level of presynaptic activity. When there is a consistent active process of neurotransmitter release, synaptic connections will be strengthened with actual physical changes that make the pre- and postsynaptic neurons come closer and the process of neurotransmission more efficient. When there is little activity, the synaptic connection will literally dissolve. The specific axonal branch to a given neuron will go away. Again, this powerful activity-dependent process appears to be very important for understanding learning, memory and the development. At any given moment – all throughout life – we are making and breaking synaptic connections. For the majority of life we are at equilibrium; the rate of creating new synaptic connections is equal to the rate of resorbing older, unused connections. While somewhat simplistic, it appears that the synaptic sculpting is a "use it or lose it" process. During the first eight months following birth the rate of creating new synapses far outstrips the rate of resorbing unused connections. By age one, however, and from then through early childhood, the rate of resorbing new connections is faster than the rate of creating new synapses. By adolescence, in most cortical areas at least, this process again reaches equilibrium.

8. Myelination: Specialized glial cells wrap around axons and, thereby, create more efficient electrochemical transduction down the neuron. This allows a neural network to function more rapidly and efficiently, thereby allowing more complex functioning (e.g., walking depends upon the myelination of neurons in the spinal cord for efficient, smooth regulation of neuromotor functioning.) The process of myelination begins in the first year of life but continues in many key areas throughout childhood with a final burst of myelination in key cortical areas taking place in adolescence.

All of the neurodevelopmental processes described above are dependent upon both genetic and environmentally determined microenvironmental cues (e.g., neurotransmitters, neuromodulators, neurohormones, ions, growth factors, cellular adhesion molecules and other morphogens). Disruption of the pattern, timing or intensity of these cues can lead to abnormal neurodevelopment and profound dysfunction. The neuroarcheological perspective suggests that the _specific_ dysfunction will depend upon the timing of the insult (e.g., was the insult _in utero_ during the development of the brainstem or at age two during the active development of the cortex), the nature of the insult (e.g., is there a lack of sensory stimulation from neglect or an abnormal persisting activation of the stress response from trauma?), the pattern of the insult (i.e., is this a discreet single event, a chronic experience with a chaotic pattern or an episodic event with a regular pattern?).

While we are only beginning to understand the complexity of neurodevelopment, there are several key principles that emerge from the thousands of studies and years of focused research on these neurodevelopmental processes. These principles, as outlined below, suggest that while the structural organization and functional capabilities of the mature brain can change throughout life, the majority of the key stages of neurodevelopment take place in childhood. Following is a summary of the core principles of neurodevelopment that support a neuroarcheological perspective of childhood adverse events.

Table 2: Key Processes in Neurodevelopment

Key Processes	Age beginning*	Greatest period of activity**	Age of equilibrium**	Other
Neurogenesis	First trimester	*In utero*	99 % of 100 billion neurons born by birth	Evidence of hippocampal cell birth in adult life
Migration	First trimester	*In utero* through first year	Regional specific: majority of migration complete by age three	Some suggestion of migration following brain injury
Differentiation	First-second trimester	Third trimester through year one	Region specific: primary differentiation complete by age three	Continues in some fashion throughout life
Apoptosis	Third trimester	First year	Age one	Majority of programmed death complete by age three
Arborization	Third trimester	First year	Primary dendritic arborization present by age three	Very experience dependent – continued sensitivity throughout life
Synaptogenesis	Third trimester	8 months	Region specific: with most cortical areas by age 10, other areas earlier	Continuous activity-dependent process through life
Synaptic sculpting	Birth	First four years	Region specific: cortical areas by age six	Second phase of activity during puberty
Myelination	Birth	First four years	Region specific: majority complete by 10	Continuing important myelination through adolescence

This refers to the age at which approximately 10% of this specific function is taking place. In most cases, there is evidence that some of these processes have started to some degree. Almost all of these processes continue in some form throughout life, the table is designed to illustrate the relative importance of childhood for the majority of activity in each of these processes.
**These are crude estimates based upon data from multiple sources. The major point it to demonstrate that shifting activity from neurogenesis to myelination.*

Core Principles of Neurodevelopment

1. Nature and nurture: For too many years, any conceptual approach to human behavior has been tainted by the nature versus nurture debate. Do genes cause human behavior or is human behavior a product of learning, education and experience? Ultimately, this debate polarizes and distracts from more complex understandings of human functioning. Genes are designed to work in an environment. Genes are expressed by microenvironmental cues, which, in turn, are influenced by the experiences of the individual. How an individual functions within an environment, then, is dependent upon the expression of a unique combination of genes available to the human species. We don't have the genes to make wings. *And* what we become depends upon how experiences shape the expression – or not - of specific genes we do have. We do have the genes to make forty sounds – and we can have the experiences that turn this genetically determined capacity into a powerful, transforming tool – language. Yet, there are many sad examples of cruel experiments of humanity, where a young child was raised in an environment deprived of language. This child, despite the genetic potential to speak and think and feel in complex humane ways, did not express that potential fully. Genetic potential without appropriately timed experiences can remain unexpressed. Nature and nurture – we are nothing without both; we require both and we are products of both.

The influence of gene-driven processes, however, shifts during development. In the just fertilized ovum, all of the chemical processes that are driving development are very dependent upon a genetically determined sequence of molecular events. By birth, however, the brain has developed to the point where environmental cues mediated by the senses play a major role in determining how neurons will differentiate, sprout dendrites, form and maintain synaptic connections and create the final neural networks that convey functionality. By adolescence, the majority of the changes that are taking place in the brain of that child are determined by experience, not genetics. The languages, beliefs, cultural practices, and complex cognitive and emotional functioning (e.g., self-esteem) by this age are primarily experience-based.

2. Sequential Developmental: The brain develops in a sequential and hierarchical fashion; organizing itself from least (brainstem) to most complex (limbic, cortical areas). These different areas develop, organize and become fully functional at different times during childhood. At birth, for example, the brainstem areas responsible for regulating cardiovascular and respiratory function must be intact for the infant to survive and any malfunction is immediately observable. In contrast, the cortical areas responsible for abstract cognition have years before they will be 'needed' or fully functional.

This means that each brain area will have its own timetable for development. The neurodevelopmental processes described above will be most active in different brain areas at different times and will, therefore, either require (critical periods) or be sensitive to (sensitive periods) organizing experiences (and the neurotrophic cues related to these experiences). The neurons for the brainstem have to migrate, differentiate and connect, for example, before the neurons for the cortex.

The implications of this for a neuroarcheological formulation are profound. Disruptions of experience-dependent neurochemical signals during these periods may lead to major abnormalities or deficits in neurodevelopment. Disruption of critical neurodevelopmental cues can result from 1) lack of sensory experience during sensitive periods (e.g., neglect) or 2) atypical or abnormal patterns of necessary cues due to extremes of experience (e.g., traumatic stress, see below). Insults during the intrauterine period, for example, will more likely influence the rapidly organizing brainstem systems as opposed to the more slowly organizing cortical areas. The symptoms from the intrauterine disruption will alter functions mediated by the brainstem and could include sensory integration problems, hyper-reactivity, poor state regulation (e.g., sleep, feeding, self-soothing), tactile defensiveness and altered regulation of core neurophysiological functions such as respiration, cardiovascular and temperature regulation.

This does not mean that neocortical systems are unaffected by disrupting the development of the brainstem. Indeed, one of the most important aspects of the sequential development is that important organizing signals for any given brain area or system (e.g., patterns of neural activity, neurotransmitters acting as morphogens) come from previously organized brain areas or systems. Due to the sequential development of the brain, disruptions of normal developmental processes early in life (e.g., during the perinatal period) that alter development of the brainstem or diencephalon will necessarily alter the development of limbic and cortical areas. This is so because many of the organizing cues for normal limbic and neocortical organization originate in the lower brain areas.

Any developmental insult can have a cascade effect on the development of all "downstream" brain areas (and functions) that will receive input from the effected neural system.

   3. *Activity-dependent neurodevelopment:* The brain organizes in a use-dependent fashion. As described above, many of the key processes in neurodevelopment are activity dependent. In the developing brain, undifferentiated neural systems are critically dependent upon sets of environmental and micro-environmental cues (e.g., neurotransmitters, cellular adhesion molecules, neurohormones, amino acids, ions) in order for them to appropriately organize from their undifferentiated, immature forms (Lauder. 1988; Perry. 1994b) (Perry & Pollard. 1998). Lack, or disruption, of these critical cues can alter the neurodevelopmental processes of neurogenesis, migration, differentiation, synaptogenesis - all of which can contribute to malorganization and diminished functional capabilities in the specific neural system where development has been disrupted. This is the core of a neuroarcheological perspective on dysfunction related adverse childhood events (Perry. 1994b) (Perry & Pollard. 1998; Perry. 1998). These molecular cues that guide development are dependent upon the experiences of the developing child. The quantity, pattern of activity and nature of these neurochemical and neurotrophic factors depends upon the presence and the nature of the total sensory experience of the child. When the child has adverse experiences – loss, threat, neglect, and injury – there can be disruptions of neurodevelopment that will result in neural organization that can lead to compromised functioning throughout life (see Neglect section, below).

   A neuroarcheological perspective would predict that the dysfunction resulting from a specific adverse event is related to the disrupted (or altered) development of the neural system that is, during the adverse event, most rapidly developing. The degree of disruption is related to the rate of change in the respective neural system. The already organized and functioning neural system is less vulnerable to a developmental insult than the rapidly changing, energy-hungry and microenvironmental cue-sensitive developing system. This is so because of a principle called biological relativity. In any dynamic system, the impact of an event or experience (disruptive or positive) is greatest on the most actively changing or dynamic parts of that system. The power of any experience, therefore, is greatest during the most rapid phases of development. Events taking place during a neural system's most active phase of organization will have more impact than events after the system has organized.

   4. *Windows of Opportunity/Windows of Vulnerability:* The sequential development of the brain and the activity-dependence of many key aspects of neurodevelopment suggest that there must be times during development when a given developing neural system is more sensitive to experience than others (Table 3). In healthy development, that sensitivity allows the brain to rapidly and efficiently organize in response to the unique demands of a given environment to express from its broad genetic potential those characteristics which best fit that child's world. If the child speaks Japanese as opposed to English, for example, or if this child will live in the plains of Africa or the tundra of the Yukon, different genes can be expressed, different neural networks can be organized from that child's potential to best fit that family, culture and environment. We all are aware of how rapidly young children can learn language, develop new behaviors and master new tasks. The very same neurodevelopmental sensitivity that allows amazing developmental advances in response to predictable, nurturing, repetitive and enriching experiences make the developing child vulnerable to adverse experiences.

   Sensitive periods are different for each brain area and neural system, and therefore, for different functions. The sequential development of the brain and the sequential unfolding of the genetic map for development mean that the sensitive periods for neural system (and the functions they mediate) will be when that system is in the developmental 'hot zone' – when that area is most actively organizing. The brainstem must organize key systems by birth; therefore, the sensitive period for those brainstem-mediated functions is during the prenatal period. The neocortex, in contrast, has

23

systems and functions organizing throughout childhood and into adult life. The sensitive periods for these cortically mediated functions are likely to be very long.

With an understanding of the shifting vulnerability of the developing brain to experience, a neuroarcheological perspective becomes apparent. If there are disrupting adverse events during development, they will be mirrored by a matched dysfunctional development in the neural systems whose functioning the adverse experience most altered during the event. If the disruption were the absence of light during the first year of life – the systems most altered would be related to vision. If the disruption activates the stress response, the disruption will be in the neural systems mediating the stress response. The severity and chronicity of the specific dysfunction will be related to the vulnerability of the system affected. Adverse experiences influence the mature brain but in the developing brain, adverse experiences literally play a role in organizing neural systems. It is much easier to influence the functioning of a developing system than to reorganize and alter the functioning of a developed system. Adverse childhood events, therefore, can alter the organization of developing neural systems in ways that create a lifetime of vulnerability.

Table 3: Shifting Developmental Activity across Brain Regions

Brain Region	Age of greatest developmental activity	Age of functional maturity**	Key functions
Neocortex	Childhood	Adult	Reasoning, problem solving, abstraction, secondary sensory integration
Limbic	Early childhood	Puberty	Memory, emotional regulation, attachment, affect regulation, primary sensory integration
Diencephalon	Infancy	Childhood	Motor control, secondary sensory processing
Brainstem	In utero	Infancy	Core physiological state regulation, primary sensory processing

The simple and unavoidable conclusion of these neurodevelopmental principles is that the organizing, sensitive brain of an infant or young children is more malleable to experience than a mature brain. While experience may alter the behavior of an adult, experience literally provides the organizing framework for an infant and child. Because the brain is most plastic (receptive to environmental input) in early childhood, the child is most vulnerable to variance of experience during this time. In the second half of this chapter two primary forms of extreme childhood adverse experience will be discussed in context of the neuroarcheological perspective of adverse childhood events.

The Neurodevelopmental Impact of Neglect in Childhood

Neglect is the absence of critical organizing experiences at key times during development. Despite its obvious importance in understanding child maltreatment, neglect has been understudied. Indeed, deprivation of critical experiences during development may be the most destructive yet the least understood area of child maltreatment. There are several reasons for this. The most obvious is that neglect is difficult to "see." Unlike a broken bone, maldevelopment of neural systems mediating empathy, for example, resulting from emotional neglect during infancy is not readily observable. Another important, yet poorly appreciated, aspect of neglect is the issue of timing. The needs of the child shift during development; therefore, what may be neglectful at one age is not at another. The very same experience that is essential for life at one stage of life may be of little significance or even inappropriate at another age. We would all question the mother who held, rocked and breastfed her pubescent child. Touch, for example, is essential during infancy. The untouched newborn may literally die; in Spitz' landmark studies, the mortality rates in the institutionalized infants was near thirty percent (Spitz. 1945; Spitz. 1946). If one doesn't touch an adolescent for weeks, however, no significant adverse effects will result. Creating standardized protocols, procedures and "measures" of neglect, therefore, are significantly confounded by the shifting developmental needs and demands of childhood. Finally, neglect is understudied because it is very difficult to find large populations of humans where specific and controlled neglectful experiences have been well documented. In some cases, these cruel experiments of humanity have provided unique and promising insights (see below). In general, however, there will never be – and there never should be – the opportunity to study neglect in humans with the rigor that can be applied in animal models.

With these limitations, however, what we do know about neglect during early childhood supports a neuroarcheological view of adverse childhood experience. The earlier and more pervasive the neglect is, the more devastating the developmental problems for the child. Indeed, a chaotic, inattentive and ignorant caregiver can produce pervasive developmental delay (PDD) in a young child (Rutter, Andersen-Wood, Beckett, et al. 1999). Yet the very same inattention for the same duration if the child is ten will have very different and less severe impact than inattention during the first years of life.

There are two main sources of insight to childhood neglect. The first is the indirect but more rigorous animal studies and the second is a growing number of descriptive reports with severely neglected children.

Environmental Manipulation and Neurodevelopment: Animal Studies

Some of the most important studies in developmental neurosciences in the last century have been focusing on various aspects of experience and extreme sensory experience models. Indeed, the Nobel Prize was awarded to Hubel and Weisel for their landmark studies on development of the visual system using sensory deprivation techniques (Hubel & Wiesel. 1963). In hundreds of other studies, extremes of sensory deprivation (Hubel & Wiesel. 1970; Greenough, Volkmar, & Juraska. 1973) or sensory enrichment (Greenough & Volkmar. 1973; Diamond, Krech, & Rosenzweig. 1964; Diamond, Law, Rhodes, et al. 1966) have been studied. These include disruptions of visual stimuli (Coleman & Riesen. 1968), environmental enrichment (Altman & Das. 1964; Cummins & Livesey. 1979), touch (Ebinger. 1974; Rutledge, Wright, & Duncan. 1974), and other factors that alter the typical experiences of development (Uno, Tarara, Else, & et.al. 1989; Plotsky & Meaney. 1993; Meaney, Aitken, van Berkal, Bhatnagar, & Sapolsky. 1988). These findings generally demonstrate that the brains of animals reared in enriched environments are larger, more complex and functional more flexible than those raised under deprivation conditions. Diamond's work, for example, examining the relationships between experience and brain cytoarchitecture has demonstrated a relationship between density of dendritic branching and the complexity of an environment (for a good review of this and related data see (Diamond & Hopson. 1998)). Others have shown that rats raised in environmentally enriched environments have higher density of various neuronal and glial microstructures, including a 30% higher synaptic density in cortex compared to rats raised in an environmentally deprived setting (Bennett, Diamond, Krech, & Rosenzweig. 1964; Altman & Das. 1964). Animals raised in the wild have from 15 to 30% larger brain mass than their offspring who are domestically reared (Darwin. 1868; Rohrs. 1955; Rohrs & Ebinger. 1978; Rehkamper, Haase, & Frahm. 1988).

Animal studies suggest that critical periods exist during which specific sensory experience was required for optimal organization and development of the part of the brain mediating a specific function (e.g., visual input during the development of the visual cortex). While these phenomena have been examined in great detail for the primary sensory modalities in animals, few studies have examined the issues of critical or sensitive periods in humans. What evidence there is would suggest that humans tend to have longer periods of sensitivity and that the concept of critical period may not be useful in humans. It is plausible, however, that abnormal micro-environmental cues and atypical patterns of neural activity during sensitive periods in humans could result in malorganization and compromised function in a host of brain-mediated functions. Indeed, altered emotional, behavioral, cognitive, social and physical functioning has been demonstrated in humans following specific types of neglect. The majority of this information comes from the clinical rather than the experimental disciplines.

<u>The Impact of Neglect in Early Childhood: Clinical Findings</u>

Over the last sixty years, many case reports, case series and descriptive studies have been conducted with children neglected in early childhood. The majority of these studies have focused on institutionalized children. As early as 1833, with the famous Kaspar Hauser, feral children had been described (Heidenreich. 1834). Hauser was abandoned as a young child and raised from early childhood (likely around age two) until seventeen in a dungeon, experiencing relative sensory, emotional and cognitive neglect. His emotional, behavioral and cognitive functioning was, as one might expect, very primitive and delayed. At autopsy, Hauser's brain was noted to have a small cerebrum (cortex) with few and non-distinct cortical gyri. These findings are consistent with cortical atrophy (or underdevelopment), a condition we have reported in children following severe total global neglect in childhood (Perry & Pollard. 1997).

In the early forties, Spitz described the impact of neglectful caregiving on children in foundling homes (orphanages). Most significant, he was able to demonstrate that children raised in fostered placements with more attentive and nurturing caregiving had superior physical, emotional and cognitive outcomes (Spitz. 1945; Spitz. 1946). Some of the most powerful clinical examples of this phenomenon are related to profound neglect experiences early in life.

In a landmark report of children raised in a Lebanese orphanage, the Creche, Dennis (1973) described a series of findings supporting a neuroarcheological model of maltreatment. These children were raised in an institutional environment devoid of individual attention, cognitive stimulation, emotional affection or other enrichment. Prior to 1956 all of these children remained at the orphanage until age six, at which time they were transferred to another institution. Evaluation of these children at age 16 demonstrated a mean IQ of approximately 50. When adoption became common, children adopted prior to age 2 had a mean IQ of 100 by adolescence while children adopted between ages 2 and 6 had IQ values of approximately 80 (Dennis. 1973). This graded recovery reflected the neuroarcheological impact of neglect. A number of similar studies of children adopted from neglectful settings demonstrate this general principle. The older a child was at time of adoption, (i.e., the longer the child spent in the neglectful environment) the more pervasive and resistant to recovery were the deficits.

Money and Annecillo (1976) reported the impact of change in placement on children with psychosocial dwarfism (failure to thrive). In this preliminary study, 12 of 16 children removed from neglectful homes recorded remarkable increases in IQ and other aspects of emotional and behavioral functioning. Furthermore, they reported that the longer the child was out of the abusive home the higher the increase in IQ. In some cases IQ increased by 55 points (Money & Annecillo. 1976).

A more recent report on a group of 111 Romanian orphans (Rutter & English and Romanian Adoptees study team. 1998; Rutter, Andersen-Wood, Beckett, et al. 1999) adopted prior to age two from very emotionally and physically depriving institutional settings demonstrate similar findings. Approximately one half of the children were adopted prior to age six months and the other half between six months and 2 years old. At the time of adoption, these children had significant delays. Four years after being placed in stable and enriching environments, these children were re-evaluated. While both groups improved, the group adopted at a younger age had a significantly greater improvement in all domains.

These observations are consistent with the experiences of our clinic research group working with maltreated children. Over the last ten-year we have worked with more than 1000 children neglected in some fashion. We have recorded increases in IQ of over 40 points in more than 60 children following removal from neglectful environments and placed in consistent, predictable, nurturing, safe and enriching placements (Perry et al., in preparation). In addition, in a study of more than 200 children under the age of 6 removed from parental care following abuse and neglect we demonstrated significant developmental delays in more than 85% of the children. The severity of these developmental problems increased with age, suggesting, again, that the longer the child was in the adverse environment - the earlier and more pervasive the neglect - the more indelible and pervasive the deficits.

The impact of deprivation can be approximated by sensory chaos. Indeed, sensory deprivation is much less clinically significant than sensory chaos. The vast majority of children suffering from neglect do so because their experiences are chaotic, dysynchronous, inconsistent and episodic rather than consistent, predictable and continuous. The organizing brain requires patterns of sensory experience to create patterns of neural activity that, in turn, play a role in guiding the various neurodevelopmental processes involved in healthy development. When experience is chaotic or sensory patterns are not consistent and predictable, the organizing systems in the brain reflect this chaos and, typically, organize in ways that result in dysregulation and dysynchronous. Imagine trying to learn a language if you only heard random words without the context, grammar and syntax of the language (i.e., the patterns of use). Even if you heard and perceived all words, you could not develop language. *Random exposure to words absent an organizing pattern leads to abnormal development of speech and language.* Our clinical group has evaluated many children capable of parroting advertising phrases from television but incapable of simple verbal communication.

This requirement for consistent, repetitive and patterned stimuli holds for all experience – cognitive, emotional, social and physical. Repetitive, patterned, consistent experience allows the brain to create an internal representation of the external world. A child growing up in the midst of chaos and unpredictability will develop neural systems and functional capabilities that reflect this disorganization.

The Impact of Neglect in Early Childhood: Neurobiological Findings

All of these reported developmental problems – language, fine and large motor delays, impulsivity, disorganized attachment, dysphoria, attention and hyperactivity, and a host of others described in these neglected children – are caused by abnormalities in the brain. Despite this obvious statement, very few studies have examined directly any aspect of neurobiology in neglected children. The reasons include a lack of capacity, until the recent past, to examine the brain in any non-invasive fashion.

Our group has examined various aspects of neurodevelopment in neglected children (Perry & Pollard. 1997). Neglect was considered global neglect when a history of relative sensory deprivation in more than one domain was obtained (e.g., minimal exposure to language, touch and social interactions). Chaotic neglect is far more common and was considered present if history was obtained that was consistent with physical, emotional, social or cognitive neglect. When possible history was obtained from multiple sources (e.g., investigating CPS workers, family, police). The neglected children (n= 122) were divided into four groups: Global Neglect (GN; n=40); Global Neglect with Prenatal Drug Exposure (GN+PND; n=18); Chaotic Neglect (CN; n=36); Chaotic Neglect with Prenatal Drug Exposure (CN+PND; n=28). Measures of growth were compared across group and compared to standard norms developed and used in all major pediatric settings.

Dramatic differences from the norm were observed in FOC (the frontal-occipital circumference, a measure of head size and in young children a reasonable measure of brain size). In the globally neglected children the lower FOC values suggested abnormal brain growth. For these globally neglected children the group mean was below the 8th percentile. In contrast, the chaotically neglected children did not demonstrate this marked group difference in FOC. Furthermore in cases where MRI or CT scans were available, neuroradiologists interpreted 11 of 17 scans as abnormal from the children with global neglect (64.7 %) and only 3 of 26 scans abnormal from the children with chaotic neglect (11.5 %). The majority of the readings were "enlarged ventricles" or "cortical atrophy." While the actual size of the brain in chaotically neglected children did not appear to be different from norms, it is reasonable to hypothesize that organizational abnormalities exist and that with function MRI studies these abnormalities will be more readily detected.

These findings strongly suggest that when early life neglect is characterized by decreased sensory input (e.g., relative poverty of words, touch and social interactions) there will be a similar effect on human brain growth as in other mammalian species. The human cortex grows in size, develops complexity, makes synaptic connections and modifies as a function of the quality and quantity of sensory experience. Lack of type and quantity of sensory-motor and cognitive experiences lead to underdevelopment of the cortex – in rats, non-human primates and humans.

Studies from other groups are beginning to report similar altered neurodevelopment in neglected children. In the study of Romanian orphans described above, the 38 % had FOC values below the third percentile (greater than 2 SD from the norm) at the time of adoption. In the group adopted after six months, fewer than 3 % and the group adopted after six months 13 % had persistently low FOCs four years later (Rutter & English and Romanian Adoptees study team. 1998; O'Connor, Rutter, & English and Romanian Adoptees study team. 2000). Strathearn (submitted) has followed extremely low birth weight infants and shown that when these infants end up in neglectful homes they have a significantly smaller head circumference at 2 and 4 years, but not at birth. This is despite having no significant difference in other growth parameters. Finally in a related population, maltreated children and adolescents with post-traumatic stress disorder (PTSD), De Bellis and colleagues found that subject children have significantly smaller intracranial and cerebral volumes than matched controls on MRI scan. Brain volume in these children correlated "robustly and positively" with the age of onset of PTSD trauma, and negatively with the duration of abuse, suggesting that traumatic childhood experiences may adversely affect brain development. Specific brain areas were affected differentially, in reflection of their importance in the stress response, further support of a neuroarcheological formulation of adverse childhood experience (De Bellis, Keshavan, Clark, et al. 1999).

While deprivations and lack of specific sensory experiences are common in the maltreated child, the traumatized child experiences developmental insults related to discrete patterns of over-activation of neurochemical cues. Rather than a deprivation of sensory stimuli, the traumatized child experiences over-activation of important neural systems during sensitive periods of development.

The Neurodevelopmental Impact of Traumatic Stress in Childhood

Each year in United States more than five million children are exposed to some form of extreme traumatic stressor. These traumatic events include natural disasters (e.g., tornadoes, floods, hurricanes), motor vehicle accidents, life threatening illness and associated painful medical procedures (e.g., severe burns, cancer), physical abuse, sexual assault, witnessing domestic or community violence, kidnapping and sudden death of a parent, among others (Pfefferbaum. 1997; Anonymous. 1998). These events, posing an actual or perceived threat to the individual, activate a stress response. During the traumatic event, the child's brain mediates the adaptive response. Brainstem and diencehpalic stress-mediating neural systems are activated. These systems include the hypothalamic-pituitary-adrenal (HPA) axis, central nervous system (CNS) noradrenergic (NA), dopaminergic (DA) systems and associated CNS and peripheral systems that provide the adaptive emotional, behavioral, cognitive and physiological changes necessary for survival (Perry. 1994a; Perry & Pollard. 1998).

Individual neurobiological responses during traumatic stress are heterogeneous (Perry, Pollard, Blakley, Baker, & Vigilante. 1995). The specific nature of a child's responses to a given traumatic event may vary with the nature, duration and the pattern of traumatic stressor and the child's constitutional characteristics (e.g., genetic predisposition, age, gender, history of previous stress exposure, presence of attenuating factors such as supportive caregivers). Whatever the individual response, however, the extreme nature of the external threat is matched by an extreme and persisting internal activation of the neurophysiological systems mediating the stress response and their associated functions (Perry, Pollard, Blakley, Baker, & Vigilante. 1995; Perry & Pollard. 1998).

As described above, neural systems respond to prolonged, repetitive activation by altering their neurochemical and sometimes, microarchitectural (e.g., synaptic sculpting) organization and functioning. This is no different for the neural systems mediating the stress response. Following any traumatic event children will likely experience some persisting emotional, behavioral, cognitive and physiological signs and symptoms related to the, sometimes temporary, shifts in the activity of these neural systems originating in the brainstem and diencephalon. In general, the longer the activation of the stress-response systems (i.e., the more intense and prolonged the traumatic event), the more likely there will be a 'use-dependent' change in these neural systems (for review see (Perry & Pollard. 1998)). In some cases, then, the stress-response systems do not return to the pre-event homeostasis. In these cases, the signs and symptoms become so severe, persisting and disruptive that they reach the level of a clinical disorder (Perry. 1998). In a new context and in the absence of any true external threat, the abnormal persistence of a once adaptive response becomes maladaptive.

Post traumatic stress-related clinical syndromes

Post traumatic stress disorder (PTSD) is a clinical syndrome that may develop following extreme traumatic stress (DSM IV). Like all other DSM IV diagnoses, it is likely that heterogeneous pathophysiologies underlie the cluster of diagnostic signs and symptoms labeled PTSD. There are six diagnostic criteria for PTSD: 1) extreme traumatic stress accompanied by intense fear, horror or disorganized behavior; 2) persistent re-experiencing of the traumatic event such as repetitive play or recurring intrusive thoughts; 3) avoidance of cues associated with the trauma or emotional numbing; 4) persistent physiological hyper-reactivity or arousal; 5) signs and symptoms present for more than one month following the traumatic event and 6) clinically significant disturbance in functioning.

Posttraumatic stress disorder has been studied primarily in adult populations, most commonly combat veterans and victims of sexual assault. Despite high numbers of traumatized children, the clinical phenomenology, treatment and neurophysiological correlates of childhood PTSD remain under studied. The clinical phenomenology of trauma-related neuropsychiatric sequelae is poorly characterized (Terr. 1991; Mulder, Fergusson, Beautrais, & Joyce. 1998). Most of the studies of PTSD have been following single discreet trauma (e.g., a shooting). The least characterized populations are very young children and children with multiple or chronic traumatic events.

Clinical presentations

If during development, this stress response apparatus is required to be persistently active, the stress response apparatus in the central nervous system will develop in response to constant threat. These stress-response neural systems (and all functions they mediate – including sympathetic-parasympathetic tone, level of vigilance, regulation of mood, attention and sleep) will be poorly regulated, often overactive and hypersensitive. It is highly adaptive for a child growing up in a violent, chaotic environment to be hypersensitive to external stimuli, to be hypervigilant, and to be in a persistent stress-response state. It is important to realize that children exposed to traumatic stress during development literally organize their neural systems to adapt to this kind of environment. In contrast, an adult with no previous traumatic stress can develop PTSD. The cardiovascular reactivity and physiological hypersensitivity that the adult develops, however, is cue specific. This means that they will demonstrate increased heart rate, startle response and other neurophysiological symptoms when exposed to a cue from the original trauma (e.g., the Vietnam vet hearing a helicopter). In contrast, young children will develop a generalized physiological hyper-reactivity and hypersensitivity to all cues that activate the stress response apparatus. This generalized change results when the traumatic stress literally provides the organizing cues for their developing stress response neurobiology (Perry. 1999).

Clinically, this is very easily seen in children who are exposed to chronic neurodevelopmental trauma. These children are frequently diagnosed as having attention deficit disorder (ADD-H) with hyperactivity (Haddad & Garralda. 1992). This is somewhat misleading, however. These children are hypervigilant; they do not have a core abnormality of their capacity to attend to a given task. These children have behavioral impulsivity, and cognitive distortions, all of which result from a use-dependent organization of the brain (Perry, Pollard, Blakley, Baker, & Vigilante. 1995). During development, these children spent so much time in a low-level state of fear (mediated by brainstem and diencehpalic areas) that they consistently were focusing on non-verbal but not verbal cues. In our clinical population, children raised in chronically traumatic environments demonstrate a prominent V-P split on IQ testing (n = 108; WISC Verbal = 8. 2; WISC Performance = 10.4, Perry et al., in preparation). Often these children are labeled as learning disabled. We have seen these V-P splits in children in the juvenile justice system, child protective system and in the specialized clinical populations referred to our Child Trauma clinic.

These children are also characterized by persisting physiological hyperarousal and hyperactivity (Perry, Pollard, Baker, Sturges, Vigilante, & Blakley. 1995; Perry. 1994b; Perry. 2000). These children are observed to have increased muscle tone, frequently a low grade increase in temperature, an increased startle response, profound sleep disturbances, affect regulation problems and anxiety (Kaufman. 1991; Ornitz & Pynoos. 1989; Perry. 2000). In addition, our studies indicate that·a significant portion of these children have abnormalities in cardiovascular regulation (Perry, Pollard, Baker, Sturges, Vigilante, & Blakley. 1995; Perry. 2000). All of these symptoms are the result of a use-dependent organization of the brain stem nuclei involved in the stress response apparatus.

Children with PTSD may present with a combination of problems including impulsivity, distractibility and attention problems (due to hypervigilance), dysphoria, emotional numbing, social avoidance, dissociation, sleep problems, aggressive (often re-enactment) play, school failure and regressed or delayed development. In most studies examining the development of PTSD following a given traumatic experience, twice as many children suffer from significant post-traumatic signs or symptoms (PTSS) but lack all of the criteria necessary for the diagnosis of PTSD (Friedrich. 1998). In these cases, the clinician may identify the trauma-related symptom as being part of another neuropsychiatric syndrome.

The clinician is often unaware of ongoing traumatic stressors (e.g., domestic or community violence) or the family makes no association between the present symptoms and past events (e.g., car accident, death of a relative, exposure to violence) and may provide no relevant history to aid the clinician in the differential. As a result, PTSD is frequently misdiagnosed and PTSS are under recognized. Children with PTSD as a primary diagnosis are often labeled with Attention Deficit Disorder with Hyperactivity (ADHD), major depression, oppositional-defiant disorder, conduct disorder, separation anxiety or specific phobia. Ackerman and colleagues examined the prevalence of PTSD and other neuropsychiatric disorders in 204 abused children (ages 7 to 13) (Ackerman, Newton, McPHerson, Jones, & Dykman. 1998). Thirty four percent of these children met criteria for PTSD. Over fifty percent of the children in this study suffering both physical and sexual abuse had PTSD. Using structured diagnostic interview, the majority of these children met diagnostic criteria for three or more Axis I diagnoses in addition to PTSD. Indeed, only 6 of 204 children met criteria for only PTSD. The broad co-morbidity reported in this study echoes previous studies.

Incidence and prevalence

Children exposed to various traumatic events have much higher incidence (from 15 to 90+ %) and prevalence rates than the general population (Pfefferbaum. 1997). Furthermore, the younger a child is the more vulnerable they appear to be for the development of trauma-related symptoms. The percentage of children developing PTSD following a traumatic event is significantly higher than the percentage of adults developing PTSD following a similar traumatic stress. Several studies published in 1998 confirm previous reports of high prevalence rates for PTSD in child and adolescent populations. Thirty five percent of a sample of adolescents diagnosed with cancer met criteria for lifetime PTSD (Pelcovitz, Kaplan, Goldenberg, Mandel, Lehane, & Guarrera. 1994); 15 % of children surviving cancer had moderate to severe PTSS (Stuber, Kazak, Meeske, et al. 1997); 93 % of a sample of children witnessing domestic violence had PTSD (Kilpatrick & Williams. 1998); over 80 % of the Kuwaiti children exposed to the violence of the Gulf Crisis had PTSS (Hadi & Llabre. 1998); 73 % of juvenile male rape victims develop PTSD (Ruchkin, Eisemann, & Hagglof. 1998); 34 % of a sample of children experiencing sexual or physical abuse and 58 % of children experiencing both physical and sexual abuse all met criteria for PTSD (Ackerman, Newton, McPHerson, Jones, & Dykman. 1998). In all of these studies, clinically significant symptoms, though not full PTSD, were observed in essentially all of the children or adolescents following the traumatic experiences.

Vulnerability and resilience

Not all children exposed to traumatic events develop PTSD. A major research focus has been identifying factors (mediating factors) that are associated with increased (vulnerability) or decreased (resilience) risk for developing PTSD following exposure to traumatic stress (Kilpatrick & Williams. 1998). Factors previously demonstrated to be related to risk can be summarized in these broad categories: 1) characteristics of the child (e.g., subjective perception of threat to life or limb, history of previous traumatic exposures, coping style, general level of anxiety, gender, age); 2) characteristics of the event (e.g., nature of the event, direct physical harm, proximity to threat, pattern and duration); 3) characteristics of family/social system (e.g., supportive, calm, nurturing vs. chaotic, distant, absent, anxious) (Briggs & Joyce. 1997; Stuber, Kazak, Meeske, et al. 1997; Winje & Ulvik. 1998). Each of these mediating factors can be related to the degree to which they either prolong or attenuate the child's stress-response activation resulting from the traumatic experience. Factors that increase stress-related reactivity (e.g., family chaos) will make children more vulnerable while factors that provide structure, predictability, nurturing and sense of safety will decrease vulnerability. Persistently activated stress-response neurophysiology in the dependent, fearful child will predispose the child to use-dependent change in the neural systems mediated by the stress response, thereby resulting in post-traumatic stress symptoms (see Table 4).

Long-term costs of childhood trauma

PTSD is a chronic disorder. Untreated, PTSS and PTSD remit at a very low rate. Indeed the residual emotional, behavioral, cognitive and social sequelae of childhood trauma persist and appear to contribute to a host of neuropsychiatric problems throughout life (Fergusson & Horwood. 1998) including attachment problems (Bell & Belicki. 1998; Alexander, Anderson, Brand, Schaeffer, Grelling, & Kretz. 1998), eating disorders (Rorty & Yager. 1996), depression (Winje & Ulvik. 1998; Fergusson & Horwood. 1998), suicidal behavior (Molnar, Shade, Kral, Booth, & Watters. 1998), anxiety (Fergusson & Horwood. 1998), alcoholism (Fergusson & Horwood. 1998; Epstein, Saunders, Kilpatrick, & Resnick. 1998), violent behavior (O'Keefe. 1995), mood disorders (Kaufman. 1991) and, of course, PTSD (Ford & Kidd. 1998; Schaaf & McCanne. 1998).

Childhood trauma impacts other aspects of physical health throughout life, as well (Hertzman & Wiens. 1996; Orr, Lasko, Metzger, Berry, Ahern, & Pitman. 1998; Felliti, Anda, Nordenberg, et al. 1998). Adults victimized by sexual abuse in childhood are more likely to have difficulty in childbirth, a variety of gastrointestinal and gynecological disorders and other somatic problems such as chronic pain, headaches and fatigue (Rhodes & Hutchinson. 1994). The Adverse Childhood Experiences study (Felliti, Anda, Nordenberg, et al. 1998) examined exposure to seven categories of adverse events during childhood (e.g., sexual abuse, physical abuse, witnessing domestic violence: events associated with increase risk for PTSD). This study found a graded relationship between the number of adverse events in childhood and the adult health and disease outcomes examined (e.g., heart disease, cancer, chronic lung disease, and various risk behaviors). With four or more adverse childhood events, the risk for various medical conditions increased 4- to 12-fold. Clearly studies of this sort will help clarify the true costs of childhood maltreatment.

Table 4. Post-traumatic Stress Disorder: Risk and Attenuating Factors

	Event	*Individual*	*Family and Social*
Increase Risk *(Prolong the intensity or duration of the acute stress response)*	" Multiple or repeated event (e.g., domestic violence or physical abuse) " Physical injury to child " Involves physical injury or death to loved one, particularly mother " Dismembered or disfigured bodies seen " Destroys home, school or community " Disrupts community infrastructure (e.g., earthquake) " Perpetrator is family member " Long duration (e.g., flood)	" Female " Age (Younger more vulnerable) " Subjective perception of physical harm " History of previous exposure to trauma " No cultural or religious anchors " No shared experience with peers (experiential isolation) " Low IQ " Pre-existing neuropsychiatric disorder (especially anxiety related)	" Trauma directly impacts caregivers " Anxiety in primary caregivers " Continuing threat and disruption to family " Chaotic, overwhelmed family " Physical isolation " Distant caregiving " Absent caregivers
Decrease Risk *(Decrease intensity or duration of the acute stress response)*	" Single event " Perpetrator is stranger " No disruption of family or community structure " Short duration (e.g., tornado)	" Cognitively capable of understanding abstract concepts " Healthy coping skills " Educated about normative post-traumatic responses " Immediate post-traumatic interventions " Strong ties to cultural or religious belief system	" Intact, nurturing family supports " Non-traumatized caregivers " Caregivers educated about normative post-traumatic responses " Strong family beliefs " Mature and attuned parenting skills

Summary and Future Directions

The remarkable property of the human brain, unlike any other animal species, is that it has the capacity to take the accumulated experience of thousands of previous generations and absorb it within one lifetime. This capability is endowed by the design of our neural systems. Neurons and neural systems are designed to change in response to microenvironmental events. In turn, our experiences influence the pattern and nature of these microenvironmental signals, allowing neural systems to create a biological record of our lives. The brain, then, becomes an historical organ. In its organization and functioning are memorialized our accumulated, synthesized and transformed experiences. And there is no greater period of sensitivity to experience than when the brain is developing. Indeed, as described above, the neuroarcheological record of maltreatment has pervasive and chronic impact on the child. An event that lasts a few months in infancy can rob a child's potential for a lifetime. The true costs of childhood maltreatment will never be appreciated, and can never be avoided, until clinicians, researchers and policy makers become aware of the core concepts of neurodevelopment and the neuorarcheology of child maltreatment.

Acknowledgements

This work was supported, in part, by the Brown Family Foundation, the Hogg Foundation for Mental Health, Children's Justice Act/Court Improvement Act, Texas Department of Protective and Regulatory Services, Maconda O'Connor and the Pritzker Cousins Foundation.

References

Ackerman, P.T., Newton, J.E., McPHerson, W.B., Jones, J.G., & Dykman, R.A. (1998). Prevalence of post traumatic stress disorder and other psychiatric diagnoses in three groups of abused children (sexual, physical, and both). *Child Abuse & Neglect, 22,* 759-774.

Alexander, P.C., Anderson, C.L., Brand, B., Schaeffer, C.M., Grelling, B.Z., & Kretz, L. (1998). Adult attachment and longterm effects in survivors of incest. *Child Abuse & Neglect, 22,* 45-61.

Altman, J., & Das, G.D. (1964). Autoradiographic examination of the effects of enriched environment on the rate of glial multipication in the adult rat brain. *Nature, 204,* 1161-1165.

Bell, D., & Belicki, K. (1998). A community-based study of well being in adults reporting childhood abuse. *Child Abuse & Neglect, 22,* 681-685.

Bennett, E.L., Diamond, M.L., Krech, D., & Rosenzweig, M.R. (1964). Chemical and anatomical plasticity of the brain. *Science, 146,* 610-619.

Briggs, L., & Joyce, P.R. (1997). What determines post-traumatic stress disorder symptomatology for survivors of childhood sexual abuse? *Child Abuse & Neglect, 21,* 575-582.

Coleman, P.D., & Riesen, A.H. (1968). Environmental effects on cortical dendritic fields: I. rearing in the dark. *Journal of Anatomy (London), 102,* 363-374.

Cummins, R.A., & Livesey, P. (1979). Enrichment-isolation, cortex length, and the rank order effect. *Brain Research, 178,* 88-98.

Darwin, C. (1868). *The variations of animals and plants under domestication.* London:J. Murray.

De Bellis, M.D., Keshavan, M.S., Clark, D.B., Casey, B.J., Giedd, J.N., Boring, A.M., Frustaci, K., & Ryan, N.D. (1999). Developmental traumatology part II: brain development. *Biol Psychiat, 45,* 1271-1284.

Dennis, W. (1973). *Children of the Creche.* New York: Appleton-Century-Crofts.

Diamond, M.C., & Hopson, J. (1998). *Magic Trees of the Mind: How to nurture your child's intelligence, creativity, and healthy emotions from birth through adolescence.* New York: Dutton.

Diamond, M.C., Krech, D., & Rosenzweig, M.R. (1964). The effects of an enriched environment on the histology of the rat cerebral cortex. *Comparative Neurology, 123,* 111-119.

Diamond, M.C., Law, F., Rhodes, H., Lindner, B., Rosenzweig, M.R., Krech, D., & Bennett, E.L. (1966). Increases in cortical depth and glia numbers in rats subjected to enriched environments. *Comparative Neurology, 128,* 117-126.

Diagnostic and Statistical Manual of Mental Disorders: Fourth Edition (DSM IV). (1994). Washington, DC: American Psychiatric Association.

Ebinger, P. (1974). A cytoachitectonic volumetric comparison of brains in wild and domestic sheep. *Z.Anat.Entwicklungsgesch*, *144*, 267-302.

Epstein, J.N., Saunders, B.E., Kilpatrick, D.G., & Resnick, H.S. (1998). PTSD as a mediator between childhood rape and alcohol use in adult women. *Child Abuse & Neglect*, *22*, 223-234.

Felliti, V.J., Anda, R.F., Nordenberg, D., Wiallamson, D.F., Spitz, A.M., Edwards, V., Koss, M.P., & Marks, J.S. (1998). Relationship of childhood abuse and household dysfunction to many of the leading causes of death in adults: the Adverse Childhood Experiences (ACE) Study. *American Journal of Preventive Medicine*, *14*, 245-258.

Fergusson, D.M., & Horwood, L.J. (1998). Exposure to interparental violence in childhood and psychological adjustment in young adulthood. *Child Abuse & Neglect*, *22*, 339-357.

Ford, J.D., & Kidd, P. (1998). Early childhood trauma and disorders of extreme stress and predictors of treatment outcome with chronic posttraumatic stress disorder. *Journal of Traumatic Stress*, *11*, 743-761.

Friedrich, W.N. (1998). Behavioral manifestations of child sexual abuse. *Child Abuse & Neglect*, *22*, 523-531.

Gould, E., Reeves, A.J., Graziano, M.S.A., & Gross, C.G. (1999). Neurogenesis in the neocortex of adult primates. *Science*, *286*, 548-552.

Greenough, W.T., & Volkmar, F.R. (1973). Pattern of dendritic branching in occipital cortex of rats reared in complex environments. *Experimental Neurology*, *40*, 491-504.

Greenough, W.T., Volkmar, F.R., & Juraska, J.M. (1973). Effects of rearing complexity on dendritic branching in frontolateral and temporal cortex of the rat. *Experimental Neurology*, *41*, 371-378.

Haddad, P., & Garralda, M. (1992). Hyperkinetic syndrome and disruptive early experiences . *British Journal of Psychiatry*, *161*, 700-703.

Hadi, F.A., & Llabre, M.M. (1998). The Gulf crisis experience of Kuwaiti children: Psychological and cognitive factors. *Journal of Traumatic Stress*, *11*, 45-56.

Heidenreich, F.W. (1834). Kaspar Hausers verwundung, krankeit und liechenoffnung. *Journal der Chirurgie und Augen-Heilkunde*, *21 (1834)*, 91-123.

Hertzman, C., & Wiens, M. (1996). Child development and long-term outcomes: a population health perspective and summary of successful interventions. *Soc.Sci.Med.*, *43*, 1083-1095.

Hubel, D.H., & Wiesel, T.N. (1963). Receptive fields of cells in striate cortex of very young, visually inexperienced kittens. *Journal of Neurophysiology*, *26*, 994-1002.

Hubel, D.H., & Wiesel, T.N. (1970). The period of susceptibility to the physiological effects of unilateral eye closure in kittens. *Journal of Physiology*, *206*, 419-436.

Huttenlocher, P.R. (1979). Synaptic density in human frontal cortex: developmental changes and effects of aging. *Brain Research*, *163*, 195-205.

Huttenlocher, P.R. (1994). Synaptogenesis in human cerebral cortex. In G. Dawson & K.W. Fischer (Eds.), *Human Behavior and the Developing Brain.* (pp. 35-54). New York: Guilford.

Kaufman, J. (1991). Depressive disorders in maltreated children. *Journal of the American Academy of Child and Adolescent Psychiatry*, *30 (2)*, 257-265.

Kilpatrick, K.L., & Williams, L.M. (1998). Potential mediators of post-traumatic stress disorder in child witnesses to domestic violence. *Child Abuse & Neglect*, *22*, 319-330.

Kuan, C.-Y., Roth, K.A., Flavell, R.A., & Rakic, P. (2000). Mechanisms of programmed cell death in the developing brain . *Trends in Neuroscience*, *23*, 291-297.

Lauder, J.M. (1988). Neurotransmitters as morphogens. *Progress in Brain Research*, *73*, 365-388.

Meaney, M.J., Aitken, D.H., van Berkal, C., Bhatnagar, S., & Sapolsky, R.M. (1988). Effect of neonatal handling on age-related impairments associated with the hippocampus. *Science*, *239*:766-768.

Molnar, B.E., Shade, S.B., Kral, A.H., Booth, R.E., & Watters, J.K. (1998). Suicidal behavior and sexual/physical abuse among street youth. *Child Abuse & Neglect*, *22*, 213-222.

Money, J., & Annecillo, C. (1976). IQ changes following change of domicile in the syndrome of reversible hyposomatotropinism (psychosocial dwarfism): pilot investigation . *Psychoneuroendocrinology*, *1*, 427-429.

Mulder, R.T., Fergusson, D.M., Beautrais, A.L., & Joyce, P.R. (1998). Relationship between dissociation, childhood sexual abuse, childhood physical abuse, and mental illness in a general population sample. *American Journal of Psychiatry*, *155*, 806-811.

O'Connor, C., Rutter, M., & English and Romanian Adoptees study team. (2000). Attachment disorder behavior following early severe deprivation: extension and longitudinal follow-up. *J.Am.Acad.Child Adolesc.Psychiatry*, *39*, 703-712.

O'Keefe, M. (1995). Predictors of child abuse in maritally violent families. *Journal of Interpersonal Violence*, *10*, 3-25.

Ornitz, E.M., & Pynoos, R.S. (1989). Startle modulation in children with post-traumatic stress disorder. *American Journal of Psychiatry*, *147*, 866-870.

Orr, S.P., Lasko, N.B., Metzger, L.J., Berry, N.J., Ahern, C.E., & Pitman, R.K. (1998). Psychophysiologic assessment of women with posttraumatic stress disorder resulting from childhood sexual abuse. *Journal of Consulting and Clinical Psychology*, *66*, 906-913.

Pelcovitz, D., Kaplan, S., Goldenberg, B.A., Mandel, F., Lehane, J., & Guarrera, J. (1994). Post-traumatic stress disorder in physically abused adolescents. *Journal of the American Academy of Child and Adolescent Psychiatry*, *33:* (305). 312

Perry, B.D. (1988). Placental and blood element neurotransmitter receptor regulation in humans: potential models for studying neurochemical mechanisms underlying behavioral teratology. *Progress in Brain Research*, *73*, 189-206.

Perry, B.D. (1994). Neurobiological sequelae of childhood trauma: post-traumatic stress disorders in children. In M. Murberg (Ed.), *Catecholamines in Post-traumatic Stress Disorder: Emerging Concepts*. (pp. 253-276). Washington, D.C.: American Psychiatric Press.

Perry, B.D. (1998). Anxiety Disorders. In C.E. Coffey & R.A. Brumback (Eds.), *Textbook of Pediatric Neuropsychiatry*. (pp. 579-594). Washington, D.C: American Psychiatric Press, Inc.

Perry, B.D. (1999). The memories of states: how the brain stores and retrieves traumatic experience. In J.M. Goodwin & R. Attias (Eds.), *Splintered Reflections: Images of the Body In Trauma*. (pp. 9-38). New York: Basic Books.

Perry, B.D. (2000). The neurodevelopmental impact of violence in childhood. In D. Schetky & E. Benedek (Eds.), *Textbook of Child and Adolescent Forensic Psychiatry*. Washington, D.C.: American Psychiatric Press, Inc.

Perry, B.D., & Pollard, R. (1997). Altered brain development following global neglect in early childhood. *Proceedings from the Society for Neuroscience Annual Meeting (New Orleans)*, (abstract)

Perry, B.D., & Pollard, R. (1998). Homeostasis, stress, trauma, and adaptation: A neurodevelopmental view of childhood trauma. *Child and Adolescent Psychiatric Clinics of North America*, *7*, 33-51.

Perry, B.D., Pollard, R.A., Baker, W.L., Sturges, C., Vigilante, D., & Blakley, T.L. (1995). Continuous heartrate monitoring in maltreated children. *Annual Meeting of the American Academy of Child and Adolescent Psychiatry, New Research,* (abstract)

Perry, B.D., Pollard, R.A., Blakley, T.L., Baker, W.L., & Vigilante, D. (1995). Childhood trauma, the neurobiology of adaptation and use-dependent development of the brain: How states become traits. *Infant Mental Health Journal, 16,* 271-291.

Pfefferbaum, B. (1997). Posttraumatic stress disorder in children: A review of the past 10 years. *J.Am.Acad.Child Adolesc.Psychiatry, 36,* 1503-1511.

Pfefferbaum, B. (Ed.) (1998). *Stress in Children.* Philadelphia: W.B. Saunders Company.

Plotsky, P.M., & Meaney, M.J. (1993). Early, postnatal experience alters hypothalamic corticotropin releasing factor (CRF) mRNA, median eminence CRF content and stress-induced release in adult rats. *Molec Brain Res, 18,* 195-200.

Rakic, P. (1981). Development of visual centers in the primate brain depends upon binocular competition before birth. *Science, 214,* 928-931.

Rakic, P. (1996). Development of cerebral cortex in human and non-human primates. In M. Lewis (Ed.), *Child and Adolescent Psychiatry: A Comprehensive Textbook.* (pp. 9-30). New York: Williams and Wilkins.

Rehkamper, G., Haase, E., & Frahm, H.D. (1988). Allometric comparison of brain weight and brain structure volumes in different breeds of the domestic pigeon, columbia livia f. d. *Brain Behav.Evol., 31,* 141-149.

Rhodes, N., & Hutchinson, S. (1994). Labor experiences of childhood sexual abuse survivors. *Birth, 21,* 213-220.

Rohrs, M. (1955). Vergleichende untersuchungen an wild- und hauskatzen. *Zool.Anz., 155,* 53-69.

Rohrs, M., & Ebinger, P. (1978). Die beurteilung von hirngrobenunterschieden zwischen wild- und haustieren. *Z.zool.Syst.Evolut.-forsch, 16,* 1-14.

Rorty, M., & Yager, J. (1996). Histories of childhood trauma and complex post-traumatic sequelae in women with eating disorders. *The Psychiatric Clinics of North America, 19,*

Ruchkin, V.V., Eisemann, M., & Hagglof, B. (1998). Juvenile male rape victims: Is the level of post-traumatic stress related to personality and parenting. *Child Abuse & Neglect, 22,* 889-899.

Rutledge, L.T., Wright, C., & Duncan, J. (1974). Morphological changes in pyramidal cells of mammalian neocortex associated with increased use. *Experimental Neurology, 44,* 209-228.

Rutter, M., Andersen-Wood, L., Beckett, C., Bredenkamp, D., Castle, J., Grootheus, C., Keppner, J., Keaveny, L., Lord, C., O'Connor, T.G., & English and Romanian Adoptees study team. (1999). Quasi-autistic patterns following severe early global privation. *J.Child Psychol.Psychiat., 40,* 537-49.

Rutter, M., & English and Romanian Adoptees study team. (1998). Developmental catch-up, and deficit, following adoption after severe global early privation. *J.Child Psychol.Psychiat., 39,* 465-476.

Schaaf, K.K., & McCanne, T.R. (1998). Relationship of childhood sexual, physical and combined sexual and physical abuse to adult victimization and posttraumatic stress disorder. *Child Abuse & Neglect, 22,* 1119-1133.

Spitz, R.A. (1945). Hospitalism: An inquiry into the genesis of psychiatric conditions in early childhood. *Psychoanalytic Study of the Child, 1:*53-74.

Spitz, R.A. (1946). Hospitalism: A follow-up report on investigation described in Volume I, 1945. *Psychoanalytic Study of the Child, 2:*113-117.

Stuber, M.L., Kazak, A.E., Meeske, K., Barakat, L., Guthrie, D., Garnier, H., Pynoos, R., & Meadows, A. (1997). Predictors of posttraumatic stress symptoms in childhood cancer survivors . *Pediatrics*, *100*, 958-964.

Terr, L. (1991). Childhood traumas: an outline and overview. *American Journal of Psychiatry*, *148*, 1-20.

Uno, H., Tarara, R., Else, J., & et.al. (1989). Hippocampal damage associated with prolonged and fatal stress in primates . *Journal of Neuroscience*, *9*, 1705-1711.

Winje, D., & Ulvik, A. (1998). Long-term outcome of trauma in children: The psychological consequences of a bus accident. *J.Child Psychol.Psychiat.*, *39*, 635-642.

The Cost of Family Violence: Risk for Impaired Development

**Martha L. Coulter, Dr., P.H., Kathryn Kuehnle, Ph.D.,
Brenda Morissette Joly, & Lynette Menezes**

Introduction

Family violence creates a devastating and ever expanding cost to our society. Annually, over one million children experience injury or harm from some form of abuse or neglect perpetrated by their parent or parent-substitute, with the rate of neglect increasing more rapidly than abuse (Sedlak & Broadhurst, 1996). Additionally, between 3 and 10 million children each year are witnesses to domestic violence (Straus, 1992; Thormaehlen & Bass-Field, 1994). Growing up in a violent family is associated with increased risk for learning problems and school failure (Davies & Cummings, 1994; Dyson, 1990; Kendall-Tackett, Williams, & Finkelhor, 1993), early pregnancy (Children's Defense Fund, 1998), and substance abuse (Henning, Leitenberg, Coffey, Turner, & Bennett, 1996), as well as the development of children's behavior problems, aggression, violence, and delinquency (Graham-Berman, 1998; Herrenkohl, Egolf, & Herrenkohl, 1997; Jouriles et al., 1996; Kolbe, Blakely, & Englemann, 1996; McCloskey, Figueredo, & Koss, 1995; O'Keef, 1994). Chronic stress or trauma caused by family violence has the potential of altering physical brain structures, which impact the integration of the maltreated child's biological, cognitive, emotional, and social domains (Cicchetti & Cohen, 1995; Kendall-Tackett, 1999; Putnam, 1997).

Although it is unknown how many different forms of violence coexist in families; multiple forms of violence may frequently co-occur in families where one form is identified. The finding of a 30% to 70% co-occurrence between spouse and child abuse (Strauss, Gelles, & Steinmetz, 1980) lends evidence to this possibility. While husbands who abuse their partners may also attempt to control their children through physical abuse, their battered spouses may become depressed, unprotective of their children, and inconsistent or abusive in their parenting (Holden & Ritchie, 1991). Furthermore, children often are not just witnesses to a parent's abuse but may be involved in the incident by seeking help, being the focus of an argument that led to violence, or becoming the alternative target for physical abuse (Fantuzzo, Boruch, Beriama, Atkins, & Marcus, 1997).

The chronicity of the spouse abuse witnessed by a child is found to impact the child's psychological outcome. When the effects of a large number of variables (e.g., mother-child violence, father-child violence, socioeconomic status, stressful life events, and formal and informal support systems) were controlled, children's adjustment was related to the amount of violence between parents observed by the child (O'Keef, 1994). The current study investigates mothers' reports of partner violence, mothers' stress, and children's behavior problems. Furthermore, this study examines child reports of partner to mother violence and the presence of child to mother violence in chronically violent families.

Method

Participants

Participants were women and their children who entered a domestic violence shelter from a violent relationship, between July 1998 and February 2000. The shelter is located in a west central Florida county, with a population of over 900,000 people. The facility has a hundred bed capacity and provides residential, outreach, and offender treatment services. Seventy-five percent of the shelter population has an annual income of under $10,000. Eighty-five consenting female victims and 56 children 4 to 16 years old participated in this study. Mothers ranged in age from 19 to 52 years with a mean age of 31. Forty-nine percent of the mothers were White, 37% percent African American, 9% Latino, 1% Native American, and 4% other (see Figure 1). Mothers' education ranged from less than four years of high school to four years of college. Mothers signed a written consent form for themselves and their children to participate in the study. Children ages 4 to 9 years old assented and children 10 and older signed a written consent form.

Figure 1

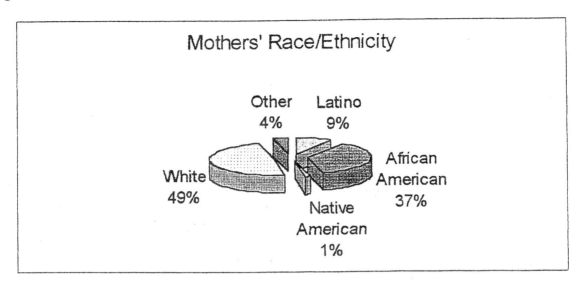

Procedures

Questionnaires and checklists were administered to participating domestic violence victims and their children within 72 hours after arrival at the domestic violence shelter, when possible. Due to ongoing crises at the shelter not all participants completed the instruments within 72 hours of admission. Mothers were administered instruments regarding their history/circumstances (Global History Questionnaire) and instruments related to stress in parenting (Parenting Stress Index; Abidin, 1995) and their child's emotional and behavioral problems (Child Behavior Checklist; Achenbach, 1991). For each participating mother with more than one child, the shelter staff randomly selected the identified child on whom the mother completed the latter two instruments.

Three months after the study the Conflict Tactics Scale-2 was added. Forty mothers and their children participated in this phase of the study and completed instruments measuring chronicity of partner to parent domestic violence (Conflict Tactics Scale-2; Straus, Hamby, Boney-McCoy, & Sugarman, 1996) and violence perpetrated against mothers by their child (Conflict Tactics Scale-2, modified- child to parent). The shelter staff continued the procedure of randomly selecting a child subject from each participating mother with more than one child. The mother completed instruments only on the child randomly selected. Eighteen of the randomly selected children were ages 7 and older. These children completed instruments regarding their history/circumstances (Child Global History Questionnaire), knowledge of partner to parent violence (Conflict Tactics Scale-2, modified-child as witness), and report of child to parent violence (Conflict Tactics Scale-2, modified- child as assailant). Randomly selected children younger than age 7 were not administered the modified versions of the Conflict Tactics Scale-2 due to their cognitive immaturity.

In addition to the randomly selected children, all participating children ages 4 to 16 years old were administered the Child Global History Questionnaire for Children and all participating 7 to 16 year old children were administered the Conflict Tactics Scale-2, modified-child as witness, and Conflict Tactics Scale-2, modified- child as assailant. Due to the potential conflict of confidentiality for the participants and the state law requiring information on child abuse and neglect to be reported to a central abuse registry, mothers and their children were not questioned about parent to child sexual, physical, or verbal abuse.

Instruments

The five instruments administered to the mothers and three instruments administered to the children are described below (see Table 1):

Global History Questionnaire for Mother. The questionnaire was developed for this study to collect information on factors related to overall life stability including homelessness, employment, transportation, health insurance, child-care, and psychological support systems for the mother.

Parenting Stress Index. This standardized instrument includes 120 items designed to measure four main areas related to stress. The four areas of focus are the child; the parent, or in this case, the mother; total parenting stress; and the life stress. One underlying assumption of the PSI is that stressors are multidimensional as to source and kind (Abidin, 1995).

Achenbach Child Behavior Checklist (Age 4 to 18). This standardized instrument for 4 to 18 year old children includes 113 items that complete the eight subscales reflecting internalized and externalized problems: Withdrawn, Somatic Complaints, Anxious/Depressed, Social Problems, Thought Problems, Attention Problems, Delinquent Behavior, and Aggressive Behavior. The instrument also provides total scores for Internalized Behavior, Externalized Behavior, and Total problem behaviors.

Conflict Tactics Scale-2. This 39 item standardized instrument measures both the extent to which partners in a dating, cohabiting, or marital relationship engage in psychological and physical attacks on each other, as well as their use of reasoning or negotiation to deal with conflicts.

Conflict Tactics Scale-2- (CTS-2; modified- child as aggressor). The CTS-2 was modified by changing the word "partner" to "my child." The purpose of this modification was to create a measure to evaluate the child's engagement in aggressive psychological and physical attacks on his or her mother, as well as to evaluate the child's use of reasoning or negotiation to deal with parent-child conflicts. The eight items from the Sexual Assault Domain (e.g., used force like hitting, holding down, or using a weapon to make me have sex) were removed on the modified version of the CTS-2. This left a total of 31 items.

Global History Questionnaire for Children (Two versions for ages 4 to 6 & 7 to 18). These questionnaires were developed for this study to collect information on factors related to overall life stability including: school attendance, homelessness, and psychological support systems for the child. Two versions were created in order to match questionnaire language with the developmental abilities of the children.

Conflict Tactics Scale-2 (CTS-2; modified- child as witness to partner to parent violence). The CTS-2 was modified by changing the word "I" to "Father or Mother's Boyfriend" and the word "partner" to "Mother." The purpose of this modification was to create a measure to evaluate the child's knowledge of the extent to which the partner of the mother in a dating, cohabiting, or marital relationship engaged in psychological and physical attacks on the mother, as well as the parent's use of reasoning or negotiation to deal with conflicts. Eight items (e.g., used force like hitting, holding down, or using a weapon to make me have sex) were deleted from the modified CTS-2 due to the respondent being a child. This left a total of 31 items.

Conflict Tactics Scale-2- (CTS-2; modified- child as aggressor). The CTS-2 was modified by leaving the word "I" and changing the word "partner" to "my mother." The purpose of this modification was to create a measure to evaluate the child's engagement in aggressive psychological and physical attacks on his or her mother, as well as to evaluate the child's use of reasoning or negotiation to deal with parent-child conflicts. Eight items (e.g., used force like hitting, holding down, or using a weapon to make me have sex) were deleted from the modified CTS-2 due to the aggressor being a child. This left a total of 31 items.

On the Conflict Tactic Scale-2, for those respondents with one missing item in the Negotiation, Psychological Aggression, Injury, and Sexual Coercion scales, a mean value was imputed for the missing item. If respondents had more than one missing item in any of these four scales, they were dropped from the analysis. For those respondents with two missing items in the Physical Assault scale mean values were imputed for missing items. For the Physical Assault scale, respondents with more than two missing items were dropped. The chronicity (mean number of acts in a year for each individual) was derived by adding the total number of items in each scale.

Table 1
Instruments and Subject Sample

Instrument	Number of Participants Administered Instrument	Dropped Protocol: Missing Data	Number of Protocols used in Data Analysis
Parent (N=85*)			
Global History Parent	77	0	77
PSI	85	4	81
Achenbach CBC 4-18	70	1	69
CTS-2 (partner to parent)	40	2	38
CTS-2 (child to parent)	40	0	40
Child (N=56*)			
Global History Age 4 to 6	25	0	25
Global History Age 7 to 16	25	0	25
CTS-2 (partner to parent)	26	0	26
CTS-2 (child to parent)	26	4	22
*These instrument numbers may represent different individuals			

Results

A total of 77 mothers completed the Global History Checklist. Mothers were almost equally divided between employment (54.5%) and unemployment (45.5%). Forty-five percent received Aid For Dependent Children (AFDC) or some other support. Only 48% of the mothers owned a car and 52% reported having difficulty getting to where they needed to go. Almost one-half (47%) reported that they had a hard time getting childcare and over one-fourth (28%) reported that the lack of adequate childcare interfered in their keeping a job. Over one- half of the mothers (54%) reported moving between two and seven times in the past year. Approximately one-third (30%) of the mothers reported that their children had learning problems and an equal percentage (31%) reported that their children missed school often. Over one-half (56%) of the mothers reported that they were not involved in any of their children's school activities (see Figure 2). Thirty percent of the mothers reported difficulty in acquiring healthcare for themselves and twenty-three percent reported difficulty in getting healthcare for their children. Approximately, one-fourth (23%) reported that they were taking medication for depression.

Figure 2

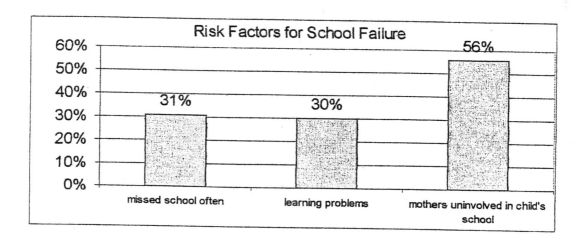

Four percent of the mothers reported problems with alcohol and 5% reported problems with drugs. Eighty-five percent of the mothers reported that one of the reasons they left their assailant was the safety of their children and 96% reported their own safety as a reason. Over one-half (55%) of the mothers reported experiencing physical abuse more than once in the past year and one-third (36%) reported experiencing physical abuse more than once a week in that same time period. Ninety-four percent of the mothers reported experiencing verbal abuse more than once in the past year and 86% reported experiencing verbal abuse more than once a week. Approximately 5% to 10% of the mothers did not complete the questions on physical and verbal abuse, respectively.

A total of 81 mothers completed the Parenting Stress Index. Fifty-nine percent of the mothers with children under age 7 and 53% of the mothers with children age 7 and above scored within the clinically significant range on Total Parenting Stress. Ninety-four percent of the mothers with children under age 7 and an equivalent percentage (94%) of the mothers with children age 7 and above scored within the clinically significant range for Life Stress. Forty-nine percent of the mothers with children under age 7 and 38% of the mothers with children age 7 and above scored within the clinically significant range on the Child Domain. These mothers endorsed items on the Child Domain scale that revealed higher levels of stress related to the characteristics of their child compared to the stress children cause parents in the general population. Approximately, one-half of the mothers with children under 7 (53%) and those with children 7 and above (47%) obtained scores on the Parent Domain subscale that fell in the clinically significant range. These mothers endorsed items on the Parent Domain scale that revealed higher levels of stress related to their parent functions compared to the stress of other parents in the general population. Only 1% of the 81 mothers obtained a significantly elevated defensive score, which indicates that the majority of the mothers were open and forthright with their answers.

Sixty-nine mothers completed the Achenbach Child Behavior Checklist 4-18. Over three-fourths (83%) of these mothers endorsed problem behaviors that culminated in a clinically significant Total score. Eighty-seven percent of the mothers endorsed items that aggregated into a clinically significant elevation on the Internalizing scale, while 84% obtained a clinically significant score for their children on the Externalizing Scale. There were no significant differences at the .05 level between the profiles obtained for boys and girls, with these mothers as the respondents. Statistically significant correlations were found between all domains on the Parenting Stress Index and the Child Behavior Checklist ($p > .01$; see Table 2).

Table 2
Statistically Significant Associations Between the Parenting Stress Index (PSI) and Child Behavior Checklist (CBC)

Instrument Subscales and Total Scores	Total Problems	Internalizing	Externalizing
Life Stress	.42 $p = .0003$	.34 $p=.0035$	.34 $p=.0035$
Total Stress	.69 $p=.001$	.60 $p=.0001$	.68 $p=.001$
Child Domain	.74 $p=.0001$	.63 $p=.001$	.73 $p=.0001$
Parent Domain	.57 $p=.0001$	.51 $p=.0001$	.55 $p=.0001$

Thirty-eight mothers completed the Conflict Tactics Scale-2 for partner to parent conflict. Their scores on Negotiation ranged from 0 to 115 ($\bar{x}= 44$), Psychological Aggression from 1 to 179 ($\bar{x}=90$), Physical Assault ranged 3 to 231 ($\bar{x}=70$), Injury from 0 to 93 ($\bar{x}=23$), Sexual Coercion from 0 to 154 ($\bar{x}=41$). Ninety-seven percent of the mothers reported that their husbands or boyfriends negotiated with them two or more times within the past year, with an equal number (97%) reporting that their husbands or boyfriends were psychologically aggressive with them. One hundred percent of these women reported that their husbands or boyfriends were physically assaultive with them two or more times in the past year. Sexual Coercion was also experienced by 93% of the mothers and 95% of the mothers reported that they were injured two or more times in the past year.

Forty mothers completed the child to parent version, with the child identified as the aggressor. Their scores on Negotiation ranged from 17 to 101 (x=64), Psychological Aggression from 0 to 93 (x=28), Physical Assault from 0 to 130 (x=9), and Injury from 0 to 43 (x=2; see Figure 3). One hundred percent of the mothers reported that their child negotiated with them two or more times within the past year. Eighty percent of the mothers reported their child was psychologically aggressive with them and 40% reported their child was physically assaultive with them two or more times in the past year. Eight percent of the mothers reported that their children physically injured them two or more times in the past year.

Twenty-five 4 to 6 year old children completed the Global History instrument. These children's responses to questions regarding chronicity and severity of violence in the home confirm the mothers' reports and indicate that the majority of children living in homes with partner to parent abuse have knowledge of the violence. Three-fourths (75%) of the children reported that someone hurt their mother and approximately two-thirds (68%) reported that the person who hurt their mother was their father or mother's boyfriend. To the question "Why are you and your mom here?," children's responses reflected violence to their mother, violence to themselves, and homelessness (see Table 3).

Figure 3

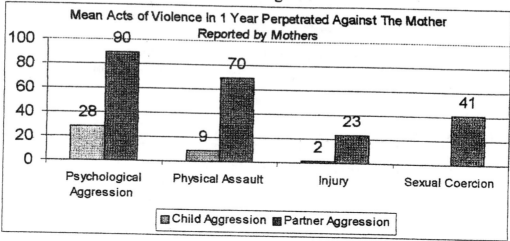

Figure 3

Table 3
Children's Understanding of Why They Were at the Shelter

Question: "Why are you and your mom here?"	Category	% of Children Responding to Category
"Because one night we had a fight-my dad threw grease at my mom's eyes on accident..." "...My dad thinks my mom lies and on Christmas he threatened to cut her hands off." "Because my dad-my dad hit my mom in one eye"	Violence to their mother	36%
"Because I got hit by my daddy with a board- the board's broken right now" "...My dad hurt my head and stuff"	Violence to themselves	8%
"Cause we didn't have no house- our house was all tore up" "Because we moved from our grandma's house because she don't let us stay"	Homelessness	16%
"Because this is the place mom wants to live"	Other Don't Know No Response	28% 12% 0%

When queried if someone "hurt your mommy because she was naughty," 12% of the preschoolers answered in the affirmative. Approximately two-thirds of the preschool-age children (64%) reported that they saw or heard their mother being hurt; twelve percent of the children did not respond to this question. Examples of 4 to 6 year old children's responses to what they saw or heard:
   "My daddy had a knife and was putting it at my mommy's head- my mommy was screaming"
   "I saw her bleeding on her mouth"
   "Busts through the glass door and hit my mom with a knife"
   "I hear my mom slam the door and dad hitting her"
   "My dad almost threw an ashtray at my mom- my mom almost hit my dad with a fan"
   "Saw him chokin' her, punchin' her, harrassin' her, cussin', sayin' the F word"

When these preschool-age children were asked "What does your mother say or do when someone starts to hurt her?" they reported a range of responses: "She says, 'but I didn't do nothing'", "Calls the cops-calls the bad person bad words-now my sister says bad words", "She shouts, 'don't hurt me'", "She calls for help and I be calling 911-and I got in trouble from my dad", "Screamed and screamed and yelled and yelled- and had nightmares- sometimes mom is bonkers and bonkers out of her mind". When the preschool-age children were asked how they respond when their mother is being hurt their responses reflected that they sought help, tried to intervene, or attempted to avoid the violence (see Table 4).

Table 4
Examples of 4 to 6 Year Old Children's Responses to What They Do

Question: "What do you do when someone starts to hurt your mommy?"	Category	% of Children Responding to Category
"I just call the police-911" "We shut the door or I call the police" "Call the cops on the one that is being bad"	Seek help	12%
"I say stop that's it" "Tell them to stop" "I just run to him and hit him"	Try to intervene	12%
"Watch TV." "Go to my room" "Run away and go fast" "I run to my room"	Try to avoid the violence or do nothing	44%
"We didn't have a phone and it was at night and my mom kicked him out of the apartment"	Other Don't Know No Response	12% 12% 8%

Twenty-five 7 to 16 year old children completed the Global History instrument. Approximately, three-fourths (72%) of these children reported that they had seen someone hurting their mother and an almost equal percentage (76%) reported that they heard someone hurting their mother. Examples of 7 to 16 year old children's responses to what they heard:
> "My dad was beating up my mom"
> "I heard my dad stomping her"
> "I heard pushing, shouting, choking, and pulling hair"
> "Her screaming"
> "Heard fighting, yelling, stuff breaking"
> "All the beating"
> "I heard a bang, mom crying"

Examples of 7 to 16 year old children's responses to what they saw:
> "My dad twisted mom's back and pulled her hair"
> "Punches, slamming her on the ground, kicking"
> "Pushing shoving, and pulling-he was doing all that"
> "I've seen him hit her with a belt"
> "Punching, throwing mom"
> "I've seen him pushing her into the window and hitting her; he stole all our stuff"

To the question "What does your mom say or do when someone starts to hurt her?, 20% of the children reported that their mothers told them to get help. Almost one-half (46%) of the 7 to 16 year old children thought that children could do something to stop their mothers from being hurt. When queried, "What do you do when someone starts to hurt your mom?" 28% of these same children reported that they called the police. Other responses reflected trying to intervene in the violence or avoid the violence (see Table 5).

Table 5
Examples of 7 to 16 Year Old Children's Responses to What They Do

Question: "What do you do when someone starts to hurt your mommy?"	Category	% of Children Responding to Category
"Call the police and wait outside 'cause the police tell us to wait outside" "Call 911" "I call the police"	Seek help	36%
"Tell him to stop hurting my mom" "I defend her" "Tell them to stop or cry" "Hit whoever it is or call the police	Try to intervene	20%
"Watch TV because we can't do anything else- he won't let us get up" "Nothing -just watch" "Go to my room "I don't do nothing"	Try to avoid the violence or do nothing	32%
"cry"	Other Don't know No Response	8% 4% 0%

Over one-half (56%) of the 7 to 16 year old children reported moving between 2 and 10 times in the last year. One-third (32%) of the children reported that they had missed a lot of school and almost one-half (48%) reported they had failed a grade. When asked if anyone in their family gets drunk or uses drugs one-half (52%) answered in the affirmative. Of these same children approximately half (46%) reported that the people in their family fight when they drink or use drugs.

Twenty-six children, 7 to 16 years old, completed the Conflict Tactics Scale-2 modified for the child as witness to partner to parent conflict. Their scores for partner to mother on Negotiation ranged from 0 to 66 ($\bar{x}$ = 19), Psychological Aggression from 2 to 175 ($\bar{x}$=49), Physical Assault from 0 to 140 ($\bar{x}$=31), and Injury from 0 to 30 ($\bar{x}$=7). Eighty-one percent of the children observed their father or mother's boyfriend negotiate with the mother two or more times within the past year. One hundred percent of the children observed their father or mother's boyfriend become psychologically aggressive with their mother and 91% observed their father or mother's boyfriend to be physically assaultive with their mother two or more times in the past year. Twenty-six percent of the children saw their mother injured two or more times in the past year. Children did not complete items on the Sexual Coercion scale.

Twenty-two children completed the Conflict Tactics Scale-2 modified for the child as the aggressor toward the mother. Their scores for child to mother on Negotiation ranged from 4 to 150 ($\bar{x} = 78$), Psychological Aggression from 0 to 62 ($\bar{x}=10$), Physical Assault from 0 to 25 ($\bar{x}=2$), and Injury from 0 to 15 ($\bar{x}=1$) (see Figure 4). All of the children reported that they had negotiated with their mother two or more times within the past year. Fifty percent of the children reported they were psychologically aggressive with their mother and 36% reported they were physically assaultive with their mother two or more times in the past year. Only two children acknowledged injuring their mother. One of these children reported injuring his mother 15 times and the other child reported injuring his mother 4 times within the past year. Children did not complete items on the Sexual Coercion scale.

Figure 4

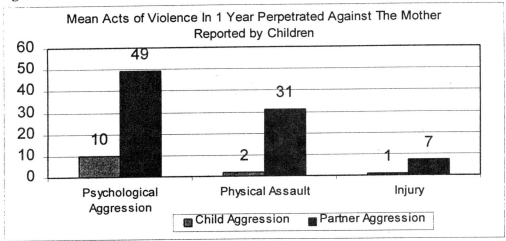

The problems in this study regarding the inability to match mothers and their children will be discussed later when study limitations are addressed. Only 18 mothers and their randomly selected child were matched on the Conflict Tactics Scale-2. Mother's and children's responses were not found to be significantly correlated for partner to parent violence and child to mother violence on any of the four subscales (i.e., Negotiation, Psychological Aggression, Physical Aggression, Injury). Furthermore, mothers' responses on the Parenting Stress Index (PSI) and mother and children's responses on the Conflict Tactics Scale-2 were not found to be significantly correlated.

Discussion

The mothers in this sample lived in homes with chronic and severe violence. Ninety-seven percent of the mothers in this study reported that their husbands or boyfriends were psychologically aggressive with them and 100% reported that their husbands or boyfriends were physically assaultive with them two or more times in the past year, with an average of 70 assaults a year. Ninety-five percent of the mothers reported that they were injured two or more times in the past year, with an average of 23 injuries a year. Because it is important to understand how the violence a mother experiences at the hands of her partner may affect her overall level of stress, especially related to parenting, the mothers in this sample were administered the Parenting Stress Index (PSI). Results indicated that the majority of mothers were experiencing clinically significant stress in their parenting role and almost one-half of the mothers found the specific characteristics of their children stressful. The results of a child behavior checklist also showed the majority of mothers to observe clinically significant problems, both internalizing and externalizing behavior problems, in their 4 to 18 year old children. The PSI and Achenbach results were found to be strongly associated, suggesting that children's behavior problems may be a source of the mothers' stress or the mothers' stress may be a source of the children's problems. However, the mothers' responses on the PSI and the Conflict Tactics Scale-2 (CTS-2) were not found to be associated, which suggests that factors other than partner violence and poor conflict resolution may be related to the mothers' stress.

The current study further underscores the chronic instability in the lives of children living in violent homes and the impact that this chaos has on their school attendance and achievement. Over one-half of the mothers reported moving between two and seven times in the past year. Approximately one-third of the mothers reported that their children had learning problems and an equal percentage reported that their children missed school often. It is of grave concern that over one-half of these mothers were not involved in any of their children's school activities. Also distressing are the results that over one-half of the school age children in this study had failed a grade.

The children participating in this study were exposed to chronic and severe violence. Approximately, two-thirds of the 4 to 6 year old and three-fourths of the 7 to 16 year old children reporting exposure through seeing or hearing their mother being hurt by her partner. Twenty-five percent of the older age group children also reported witnessing their mother injured two or more times in the past year. This older age group of children witnessed an average of 31 physical assaults on their mother, with an average of 7 injuries per year. Consistent with earlier studies, there was a lack of correlation between mother and children's reports, which supports the need to have multiple reporters because of their varying perspectives.

A unique finding of this study is children's involvement with seeking help by either initiating a call to the police or being told by their mother to seek help for her by calling the police. Twenty-eight percent of the 7 to 16 year old children reported that they called the police in an attempt to help their mother when they were aware that she was being hurt. Interestingly, children reported that they called the police or were asked to call the police by their mother more frequently than they reported their mother called the police in response to the violence.

An alarming finding of this study was the high percentage of the children who were exposed to partner to parent violence also were perpetrating violence against their mothers. Over three-fourths of the mothers reported their child was psychologically aggressive, with an average number of 28 incidents per year. Over one-third of the mothers reported their child was physically assaultive with them two or more times in the past year, with average number 9 of incidents. Three of the mothers reported that their children physically injured them two or more times in the past year. Children's responses confirmed that a high percentage of children living in violent families also psychologically and physically assault their mothers. Half of the children reported that they were psychologically aggressive with their mothers, with an average of 10 incidents per year. Over one-third reported that they were physically assaultive with their mothers over the past year, with a mean of 2 incidents a year. Two children reported that their assaults resulted in physical injury to their mother. Although the children and mothers are not matched, these results suggest that children may under report the violence they direct at their mothers.

The impact of family violence on children frequently is reported to have an effect on children's future behavior with their own adult partners. However, there has been little research investigating children's exposure to partner to parent violence and the impact on children's violence directed toward their mother. The findings of this research show that the children in violent families are adding to the abuse of their mothers through their own aggressive and violent behaviors. These findings have important implications for developing public policy and highlight the need for domestic violence intervention programs to include the provision of services for the batterer and victim's children. Future interventions must have a broader scope and include learning modules for the batterers and victims, which focus them on the effect of domestic violence on their children. Interventions such as group therapy must routinely be offered to child witnesses if the intergenerational transmission of violence is to be curbed. Group therapy for children not only needs to focus on verbally processing exposure to parent partner violence but also must intervene in the early intergenerational transmission of violence as a tool of power and control with women. The current study indicates the transmission of intergeneration violence and acting out witnessed or experienced violence is not delayed until the adult years.

The weaknesses in this study include a non-random selection of the mothers and children in the sample and a delay in the administration of some of the instruments used in the study. Furthermore, there was a broad age range for children, which created variability in the number of instruments administered to children in the younger and older age groups. Although chronic and severe levels of aggression were reported by both mothers and children in the subject sample, the small sample size of matched mothers and their children did not allow for a correlation analysis because of low statistical power.

Further research should compare the agreement between mother-victims and batterers' reports of domestic violence with their children's reports for both batterer to victim and child to victim events. The chronicity and severity of domestic violence witnessed by children should also be compared to the children's developmental history of violence against their mother-victim. Longitudinal research is needed to explore the association between violence by children against their mothers and the developmental progression of this violence, both intrafamilial and extrafamilial. This should include violence against siblings and peers, and later violence directed by these children toward their girlfriends or boyfriends. Although the high frequency of sexual coercion experienced by the women in study was not investigated relative to children's exposure, future research may find an important link between children's exposure and the development of sexual violence and/or other sexual disorders.

References

Achenbach, T. M. (1991). *Manual for the child behavior checklist/4-18 and 1991 profile.* Burlington, VT: University of Vermont, Department of Psychiatry.

Abidin, R.R. (1995). *Parenting stress index (third edition) professional manual.* Odessa, Fl: Psychological Assessment Resources, Inc.

Cicchetti, D. & Cohen, D.J. (1995). Perspectives on developmental psychopathology. In D. Cicchetti and D. Cohen (Eds.), *Developmental Psychopathology: Vol. 1* (pp. 3-20). New York: Wiley.

Children's Defense Fund. (1998). *The State of America's Children.* Boston, MA: Beacon Press.

Davies, P.T., & Cummings, E.M. (1994). Martial conflict and child adjustment: An emotional security hypothesis. *Psychological Bulletin, 116,* 387-411.

Dyson, J.L. (1990). The effect of family violence on children's academic performance and behavior. *Journal of National Medical Association, 82,* 17-22.

Fantuzzo, J., Boruch, R., Beriama, A., Atkins, M., & Marcus, S. (1997). Domestic violence and children: Prevalence and risk in five major U.S. cities. *Journal of the American Academy of Child and Adolescent Psychiatry, 36,* 116-122.

Graham-Berman, S.A. (1998). The impact of woman abuse on children's social development: Research and theoretical perspectives. In G.W. Holden, R. Geffner, & E.N. Jouriles (Eds.) *Children exposed to marital violence* (pp. 21-54). Washington DC: American Psychological Association.

Henning, K., Leitenberg, H., Coffey, P., Turner, T., & Bennett, R.T. (1996). Long-term psychological and social impact of witnessing physical conflict between parents. *Journal of Interpersonal Violence, 11,* 35-51.

Herrenkohl, R.C., Egolf, B.P., & Herrenkohl, E.C. (1997). Preschool antecedents of adolescent assaultive behavior: A longitudinal study. *American Journal of Orthopsychiatry, 67,* 422-432.

Holden, G.W., & Ritchie, K.L. (1991). Linking extreme martial discord, child rearing, and child behavior problems: Evidence from battered women. *Child Development, 62,* 311-327.

Jouriles, E.N., Norwood, W.D., McDonald, R., Vincent, J.P., & Mahoney, A. (1996). Physical violence and other forms of marital aggression: Links with children's behavior problems. *Journal of Family Psychology, 10*, 223-234.Hampshire.

Kendall-Tackett, K.A. (1999, July). *Chronic hyperarousal in three sequelae of child abuse: PTSD, depression, and irritable bowel syndrome.* Paper presented at the 6th International Family Violence Research Conference, Durham, New Hampshire.

Kendall-Tackett, K.A, Williams, L.M., & Finkelhor, D. (1993). Impact of sexual abuse on children: A review and synthesis of recent empirical studies. *Psychological Bulletin, 113*, 164-180.

Kolbe, J.R., Blakely, E.H., Englemann, D. (1996). Children who witness domestic violence: A review of the empirical literature. *Journal of Interpersonal Violence, 11*, 281-293.

McCloskey, L.A., Figueredo, A.J., & Koss, M.P. (1995). The effects of systematic family violence on children's mental health. *Child Development, 66*, 1239-1261.

O' Keefe, M. (1994). Linking marital violence, mother-child/father-child aggression, and child behavior problems. *Journal of Family Violence, 9*, 63-78.

Putnam, F.W. (1997). *Dissociation in children and adolescents.* Guilford Press.

Sedlak, A.J., & Broadhurst, D.D. (1996). *The third national incidence study of child abuse and neglect.* Washington DC: U.S. Department of Health and Human Services.

Straus, M.A. (1992). Children as witnesses to marital violence: A risk factor for life long problems among a nationally representative sample of American men and women. In D. Schwarz (Ed.), *Children and violence: Report of the twenty-third Ross Roundtable on critical approaches to common pediatric problems* (pp. 98-109). Columbus, OH: Ross Laboratories.

Straus, M.A., Hamby, S.L., Boney-McCoy, S., & Sugarman, D.B. (1996). The revised conflict tactics scales (CTS2). *Journal of Family Issues, 17*, 283-316.

Straus, M. A., Gelles, R. J., & Steinmetz, S. K. (1980). *Behind closed doors: Violence in the American Family.* Garden City, NY: Doubleday.

Thormaehlen, D.J., & Bass-Field, E.R. (1994). Children: The secondary victims of domestic violence. *Maryland Medical Journal, 43*, 355-359.

Relationship of Childhood Abuse and Household Dysfunction to Many of the Leading Causes of Death in Adults

The Adverse Childhood Experiences (ACE) Study*

Vincent J. Felitti, MD, FACP, Robert F. Anda, MD, MS, Dale Nordenberg, MD, David F. Williamson, MS, PhD, Alison M. Spitz, MS, MPH, Valerie Edwards, BA, Mary P. Koss, PhD, James S. Marks, MD, MPH

Introduction

Only recently have medical investigators in primary care settings begun to examine associations' between childhood abuse and adult health risk behaviors and disease.[1-5] These associations are important because it is now clear that the leading causes of morbidity and mortality in the United States [6] are related to health behaviors and lifestyle factors; these factors have been called the "actual" causes of death .[7] Insofar as abuse and other potentially damaging childhood experiences contribute to the development of these risk factors, then these childhood exposures should be recognized as the basic causes of morbidity and mortality in adult life.

Although sociologists and psychologists have published numerous articles about the frequency[8-12] and long-term consequences [13-15] of childhood abuse, understanding their relevance to adult medical problems is rudimentary. Furthermore, medical research in this field has limited relevance to most primary care physicians because it is focused on adolescent health, [11-20] mental health in adults [20], or on symptoms among patients in specialty clinics.[22, 23] Studies of the long-term effects of childhood abuse have usually examined single types of abuse, particularly sexual abuse, and few have assessed the impact of more than one type of abuse. [5,24-21] Conditions such as drug abuse, spousal violence, and criminal activity in the household may co-occur with specific forms of abuse that involve children. Without measuring these household factors as well, long-term influence might be wrongly attributed solely to single types of abuse and the cumulative influence of multiple categories of adverse childhood experiences would not be assessed. To our knowledge, the relationship of adult health risk behaviors, health status, and disease states to childhood abuse and household dysfunction [29-35] has not been described.

We undertook the Adverse Childhood Experiences (ACE) Study in a primary care setting to describe the long-term relationship of childhood experiences to important medical and public health problems. The ACE Study is assessing, retrospectively and prospectively, the long-term impact of abuse and household dysfunction during childhood on the following outcomes in adults: disease risk factors and incidence, quality of life, health care utilization, and mortality. In this initial paper we use baseline data from the study to provide an overview of the prevalence and interrelation of exposures to childhood abuse and household dysfunction. We then describe the relationship between the number of categories of these deleterious childhood exposures and risk factors and those diseases that underlie many of the leading causes of death in adults.[6,7,36,37]

*As previously published in: Am J Prev Med 1998; 14 (4) @ 1998 American journal of Preventive Medicine
0749-3797/98/$19.00 24S P11 S0749-3797(98)00017-8

Methods

Study Setting

The ACE Study is based at Kaiser Permanente's San Diego Health Appraisal Clinic. More than 45,000 adults undergo standardized examinations there each year, making this clinic one of the nation's largest freestanding medical evaluation centers. All enrollees in the Kaiser Health Plan in San Diego are advised through sales literature about the services (free for members) at the clinic; after enrollment, members are advised again of its availability through new member literature. Most members obtain appointments by self-referral; 20% are referred by their health care provider. A recent review of membership and utilization records among Kaiser members in San Diego continuously enrolled between 1992 and 1995 showed that 81 % of those 25 years and older had been evaluated in the Health Appraisal Clinic.

Health appraisals include completion of a standardized medical questionnaire that requests demographic and biopsychosocial information, review of organ systems, previous medical diagnoses, and family medical history. A health care provider completes the medical history, performs a physical examination, and reviews the results of laboratory tests with the patient.

Survey Methods

The ACE Study protocol was approved by the Institutional Review Boards of the Southern California Permanente Medical Group (Kaiser Permanente), the Emory University School of Medicine, and the Office of Protection from Research Risks, National Institutes of Health. All 13,494 Kaiser Health Plan members who completed standardized medical evaluations at the Health Appraisal Clinic between August-November of 1995 and January-March of 1996 were eligible to participate in the ACE Study. Those seen at the clinic during December were not included because survey response rates are known to be lower during the holiday period.[38]

In the week after visiting the clinic, and hence having their standardized medical history already completed, members were mailed the ACE Study questionnaire that included questions about childhood abuse and exposure to forms of household dysfunction while growing up. After second mailings of the questionnaire to persons who did not respond to the first mailing, the response rate for the survey was 70.5% (9,508/13,494).

Survey Wave I-complete

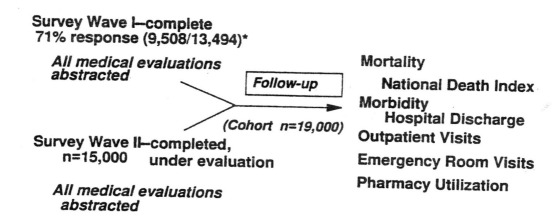

Figure 1. ACE Study design. *After exclusions, *59.7% of* the original wave I sample *(8,056/13,494)* were included in this analysis.

A second survey wave of approximately the same number of patients as the first wave was conducted between June and October of 1997. The data for the second survey wave is currently being compiled for analysis. The methods for the second mail survey wave were identical to the first survey wave as described above. The second wave was done to enhance the precision of future detailed analyses on special topics and to reduce the time necessary to obtain precise statistics on follow-up health events. An overview of the total ACE Study design is provided in Figure 1.

Comparison of Respondents and Nonrespondents

We abstracted the completed medical evaluation for every person eligible for the study; this included their medical history, laboratory results, and physical findings. Respondent (n = 9,508) and nonrespondent (n = 3,986) groups were similar in their percentages of women (53.7% and 51.0%, respectively) and in their mean years of education (14.0 years and 13.6 years, respectively). Respondents were older than nonrespondents (means 56.1 years and 49.3 years) and more likely to be white (83.9% vs. 75.3%) although the actual magnitude of the differences was small.

Respondents and nonrespondents did not differ with regard to their self-rated health, smoking, other substance abuse, or the presence of common medical conditions such as a history of heart attack or stroke, chronic obstructive lung disease, hypertension, or diabetes, or with regard to marital status or current family, marital, or job-related problems (data not shown). The health appraisal questionnaire used in the clinic contains a single question about childhood sexual abuse that reads "As a child were you ever raped or sexually molested?" Respondents were slightly more likely to answer affirmatively than nonrespondents (6.1% vs. 5.4%, respectively).

Questionnaire Design

We used questions from published surveys to construct the ACE Study questionnaire. Questions from the Conflicts Tactics Scale [39] were used to define psychological and physical abuse during childhood and to define violence against the respondent's mother. We adapted four questions from Wyatt[40] to define contact sexual abuse during childhood. Questions about exposure to alcohol or drug abuse during childhood were adapted [41] All from the 1988 National Health Interview Survey. All of the questions we used in this study to determine childhood experiences were introduced with the phrase "While you were growing up during your first 18 years of life". Questions about health-related behaviors and health problems were taken from health surveys such as the Behavioral Risk Factor Surveys'2 and the Third National Health and Nutrition Examination Survey, [43] both of which are directed by the Centers for Disease Control and Prevention. Questions about depression came from the Diagnostic Interview Schedule of the [41] National Institute of Mental Health (NIMH). Other information for this analysis such as disease history was obtained from the standardized questionnaire used in the Health Appraisal Clinic. (A copy of the questionnaires used in this study may be found at *www.elsevier.com/locate/amepre.)*

Defining Childhood Exposures

We used three categories of childhood abuse: psychological abuse (2 questions), physical abuse (2 questions), or contact sexual abuse (4 questions). There were four categories of exposure to household dysfunction during childhood: exposure to substance abuse (defined by 2 questions), mental illness (2 questions), violent treatment of mother or stepmother (4 questions), and criminal behavior (1 question) in the household. Respondents were defined as exposed to a category if they responded "yes" to 1 or more of the questions in that category. The prevalence of positive responses to the individual questions and the category prevalences are shown in Table 1.

We used these 7 categories of childhood exposures to abuse and household dysfunction for our analysis. The measure of childhood exposure that we used was simply the sum of the categories with an exposure; thus the possible number of exposures ranged from 0 (unexposed) to 7 (exposed to all categories).

Table 1. Prevalence of childhood exposure to abuse and household dysfunction

Category of childhood exposure[a]	Prevalence (%)	Prevalence (%)
Abuse by category		
Psychological	**11.1**	
(Did a parent or other adult in the household ...		
Often or very often swear at, insult. or put you down?		10.0
Often or very often act in a way that made you afraid that you would be physically hurt?		4.8
Physical	**10.8**	
(Did a parent or other adult in the household ...		
Often or very often push, grab, shove, or slap you?		4.9
Often or very often hit you so hard that you had marks or were injured?		9.6
Sexual	**22.8**	
(Did an adult or person at least 5 years older ever...		
Touch or fondle you in a sexual way?		19.3
Have you touch their body in a sexual way?		8.7
Attempt oral, anal, or vaginal intercourse with you?		8.9
Actually have oral, anal, or vaginal intercourse with you?		6.9
Household dysfunction by category		
Substance abuse	**25.6**	
Live with anyone who was a problem drinker or alcoholic?		23.5
Live with anyone who used street drugs?		4.9
Mental illness	**18.8**	
Was a household member depressed or mentally ill?		17.5
Did a household member attempt suicide?		4.0
Mother treated violently	**12.5**	
Was your mother (or stepmother)		
Sometimes, often, or very often pushed, grabbed, slapped, or had something thrown at her?		11.9
Sometimes, often, or very often kicked, bitten, hit with a fist, or hit with something hard?		6.3
Ever repeatedly hit over at least a few minutes?		6.6
Ever threatened with, or hurt by, a knife or gun?		3.0
Criminal behavior in household	**3.4**	
Did a household member go to prison?		3.4
Any category reported	**52.1%**	

[a] An exposure to one or more items listed under the set of questions for each category.

Risk Factors and Disease Conditions Assessed

Using information from both the study questionnaire and the Health Appraisal Clinic's questionnaire, we chose 10 risk factors that contribute to the leading causes of morbidity and mortality in the United States.[6, 7, 36, 17] The risk factors included smoking, severe obesity, physical inactivity, depressed mood, suicide attempts, alcoholism, any drug abuse, parental drug abuse, a high lifetime number of sexual partners (>50), and a history of having a sexually transmitted disease.

We also assessed the relationship between childhood exposures and disease conditions that are among the 6 leading causes of mortality in the United States. The presence of these disease conditions was based upon medical histories that patients provided in response to the clinic questionnaire. We included a history of ischemic heart disease (including, heart attack or use of nitroglycerin for exertional chest pain), any cancer, stroke, chronic bronchitis, or emphysema (COPD), diabetes, hepatitis or jaundice, and any skeletal fractures (as a proxy for risk of unintentional injuries). We also included responses to the following question about self-rated health: "Do you consider your physical health to be excellent, very good, good, fair, or poor-" because it is strongly predictive of mortality.[45]

Definition of Risk Factors

We defined severe obesity as a body mass index (kg/ *meter 2*) $\geq$35 based on measured height and weight; physical inactivity as no participation in recreational physical activity in the past month; and alcoholism as a 'Yes" response to the question "Have you ever considered yourself to be an alcoholic?" The other risk factors that we assessed are self-explanatory.

Exclusions from Analysis

Of the 9,508 survey respondents, we excluded 51 (0.5%) whose race was unstated and 34 (0.4%) whose educational attainment was not reported. We also excluded persons who did not respond to certain questions about adverse childhood experiences. This involved the following exclusions: 125 (1.3%) for household substance abuse, 181 (1.9%) for mental illness in the home, 148 (1.6%) for violence against mother, 7 (0.1%) for imprisonment of a household member, 109 (1.1%) for childhood psychological abuse, 44 (0.5%) for childhood physical abuse, and 753 (7.9%) for childhood sexual abuse. After these exclusions, 8,056 of the original 9,508 survey respondents (59.7% of the original sample of 13,494) remained and were included in the analysis. Procedures for insuring that the findings based on complete data were generalizable to the entire sample are described below.

The mean age of the 8,506 persons included in this analysis was 56.1 years (range: 19 -92 years); 52.1 % were women; 79.4% were white. Forty-three percent had graduated from college; only 6.0% had not graduated from high school.

Statistical Analysis

We used the Statistical Analysis System (SAS) [46] for our analyses. We used the direct method to age-adjust the prevalence estimates. Logistic regression analysis was employed to adjust for the potential confounding effects of age, sex, race, and educational attainment on the relationship between the number of childhood exposures and health problems.

To test for a dose-response relationship to health problems, we entered the number of childhood exposures as a single ordinal variable (0, 1, 2, 3, 4, 5, 6, 7) into a separate logistic regression model for each risk factor or disease condition.

Assessing the Possible Influence of Exclusions

To determine whether our results were influenced by excluding persons with incomplete information on any of the categories of childhood exposure, we performed a separate sensitivity analysis in which we included all persons with complete demographic information but assumed that persons with missing information for it category of childhood exposure did not have an exposure in that category.

Results

Adverse Childhood Exposures

The level of positive responses for the 17 questions included in the seven categories of childhood exposure ranged from 3.0% for a respondent's mother (or stepmother) having been threatened with or hurt by a gun or knife to 23.5% for having lived with a problem drinker or alcoholic (Table 1). The most prevalent of the 7 categories of childhood exposure was substance abuse in the household (25.6%); the least prevalent exposure category was evidence of criminal behavior in the household (3.4%). More than half of respondents (52%) experienced $\geq$ 1category of adverse childhood exposure; 6.2% reported $\geq$4 exposures.

Relationships between Categories of Childhood Exposure

The probability that persons who were exposed to any single category of exposure were also exposed to another category is shown in Table 2. The relationship between single categories of exposure was significant for all comparisons (P < .00 1; chi-square). For persons reporting any single category of exposure, the probability of exposure to any additional category ranged from 65%-93% (median: 80%); similarly, the probability of ≥2 additional exposures ranged from 40%-74% (median: 54.5%).

The number of categories of childhood exposures by demographic characteristics is shown in Table 3. Statistically, significantly fewer categories of exposure were found among older persons, white or Asian persons and college graduates (P < .001). Because age is associated with both the childhood exposures as well as many of the health risk factors and disease outcomes, all prevalence estimates in the tables are adjusted for age.

Relationship between Childhood Exposures and Health Risk Factors

Both the prevalence and risk (adjusted odds ratio) increased for smoking, severe obesity, physical inactivity, depressed mood, and suicide attempts as the number of childhood exposures increased (Table 4). When persons with 4 categories of exposure were compared to those with none, the odds ratios ranged from 1.3 for physical inactivity to 12.2 for suicide attempts (Table 4).

Similarly, the prevalence and risk (adjusted odds ratio) of alcoholism, use of illicit drugs, injection of illicit drugs, ≥50 intercourse partners, and history of a sexually transmitted disease increased as the number of childhood exposures increased (Table 5). In comparing persons with ≥ 4 childhood exposures to those with none, odds ratios ranged from 2.5 for sexually transmitted diseases to 7.4 for alcoholism and 10.3 for injected drug use.

Childhood Exposures and Clustering of Health Risk Factors

We found a strong relationship between the number of childhood exposures and the number of health risk factors for leading causes of death in adults (Table 6). For example, among persons with no childhood exposures, 56% had none of the 10 risk factors whereas only 14% of persons with ≥4 categories of childhood exposure had no risk factors. By contrast, only 1 % of persons with no childhood exposures had four or more risk factors, whereas 7% of persons with ≥4 childhood exposures had four or more risk factors (Table 6).

Table 2. Relationships between categories of adverse childhood exposure

| | | Percent (%) Exposed to Another Category | | | | | | | | |
First Category of Childhood Exposure	Sample Size*	Psychological Abuse	Physical Abuse	Sexual Abuse	Substance Abuse	Mental Illness	Treated Violently	Imprisoned Member	Any One Additional Category	Any Two Additional Categories
Childhood Abuse:										
Psychological	898	—	52*	47	51	50	39	9	93	74
Physical abuse	874	54	—	44	45	38	35	9	86	64
Sexual abuse	1770	24	22	—	39	31	23	6	65	41
Household dysfunction:										
Substance abuse	2064	22	19	34	—	34	29	8	69	40
Mental illness	1512	30	22	37	46	—	26	7	74	47
Mother treated violently	1010	34	31	41	59	38	—	10	86	62
Member imprisoned	271	29	29	40	62	42	37	—	86	64
median		29.5	25.4	40.5	48.5	38	32	8.5	80	54.5
range		(22–54)	(19–52)	(34–47)	(39–62)	(31–50)	(23–39)	(6–10)	(65–93)	(40–74)

*Number exposed to first category. For example, among persons who were psychologically abused, 52% were also physically abused. More persons were a second category than would be expected by chance (P < .001; chi-square).

Relationship between Childhood Exposures and Disease Conditions

When persons with 4 or more categories of childhood exposure were compared to those with none, the odds ratios for the presence of studied disease conditions ranged from 1.6 for diabetes to 3.9 for chronic bronchitis or emphysema (Table 7). Similarly the odds ratios for skeletal fractures, hepatitis or jaundice, and poor self-rated health were 1.6, 2.3, respectively (Table 8).

Significance of Dose-Response Relationships

In logistic regression models (which included age, gender, race, and educational attainment as covariates) we found a strong, dose-response relationship between the number of childhood exposures and each of the 10 risk factors for the leading causes of death that we studied ($P < .001$). We also found a significant ($P < .05$) dose-response relationship between the number of childhood exposures and the following disease conditions: ischemic heart disease, cancer, chronic bronchitis or emphysema, history of hepatitis or jaundice, skeletal fractures, and poor self-rated health. There was no statistically significant dose-response relationship for a history of stroke or diabetes.

Table 3. Prevalence of categories of adverse childhood exposures by demographic characteristics

Characteristic	Sample size (N)	Number of categories (%)*				
		0	1	2	3	4
Age group (years)						
19-34	807	35.4	25.4	17.2	11.0	10.9
35-49	2,063	39.3	25.1	15.6	9.1	10.9
50-64	2,577	46.5	25.2	13.9	7.9	6.6
≥ 65	2,610	60.0	24.5	8.9	4.2	2.4
Gender [b]						
Women	4,197	45.4	24.0	13.4	8.7	8.5
Men	3,859	53.7	25.8	11.6	5.0	3.9
Race [b]						
White	6,432	49.7	25.3	12.4	6.7	6.0
Black	385	38.8	25.7	16.3	12.3	7.0
Hispanic	431	42.9	24.9	13.7	7.4	11.2
Asian	508	66.0	19.0	9.9	3.4	1.7
Other	300	41.0	23.5	13.9	9.5	12.1
Education [b]						
No HS diploma	480	56.5	21.5	8.4	6.5	7.2
HS graduate	1,536	51.6	24.5	11.3	7.4	5.2
Any college	2,541	44.1	25.5	14.8	7.8	7.8
College graduate	3,499	51.4	25.1	12.1	6.1	5.3
All participants	8,056	49.5	24.9	12.5	6.9	6.2

*The number of categories of exposure was simply the sum of each of the seven individual categories that were assessed (see Table 1)
[b]Prevalence estimates adjusted for age.

Assessment of the Influence of Exclusions

In the sensitivity analysis where missing information for a category of childhood exposure was considered as no exposure, the direction and strength of the associations between the number of childhood exposures and the risk factors and disease conditions were nearly identical (data not shown). Thus, the results we present appear to be unaffected by our decision to exclude persons for whom information on any category of childhood exposure was incomplete.

Discussion

We found a strong dose response relationship between the breadth of exposure to abuse or household dysfunction during childhood and multiple risk factors for several of the leading causes of death in adults. Disease conditions including ischemic heart disease, cancer, chronic lung disease, skeletal fractures, and liver disease, as well as poor self-rated health also showed a graded relationship to the breadth of childhood exposures. The findings suggest that the impact of these adverse childhood experiences on adult health status is strong and cumulative.

The clear majority of patients in our study who were exposed to one category of childhood abuse or household dysfunction were also exposed to at least one other. Therefore, researchers trying to understand the long-term health implications of childhood abuse may benefit from considering a wide range of related adverse childhood exposures. Certain adult health outcomes may be more strongly related to unique combinations or the intensity of adverse childhood exposures than to the total breadth of exposure that we used for our analysis. However, the analysis we present illustrates the need for an overview of the net effects of a *group* of complex interactions on a wide range of health risk behaviors and diseases.

Several potential limitations need to be considered when interpreting the results of this study. The data about adverse childhood experiences are based on self-report, retrospective, and can only demonstrate associations between childhood exposures and health risk behaviors, health status, and diseases in adulthood. Second, some persons with health risk behaviors or diseases may have been either more, or less, likely to report adverse childhood experiences. Each of these issues potentially limits inferences about causality. Furthermore, disease conditions could be either over- or under-reported by patients when they complete the medical questionnaire. In addition, there may be mediators of the relationship between childhood experiences and adult health status other than the risk factors we examined. For example, adverse childhood experiences may affect attitudes and behaviors toward health and health care, sensitivity to internal sensations, or physiologic functioning in brain centers and neurotransmitter systems. A more complete understanding of these issues is likely to lead to more effective ways to address the long-term health problems associated with childhood abuse and household dysfunction.

However, our estimates of the prevalence of child hood exposures are similar to estimates from nationally representative surveys, indicating that the experiences of our study participants are comparable to the larger population of U.S. adults. In our study, 23.5% of participants reported having grown up with an alcohol abuser; the 1988 National Health Interview Survey estimated that 18.1 % of adults had lived with an alcohol abuser during childhood.[41] Contact sexual abuse was reported by 22% of respondents (28% of women and 16% of men) in our study. A national telephone survey of adults in 1990 using similar criteria for sexual abuse estimated that 27% of women and 16% of men had been sexually abused.[12]

There are several reasons to believe that our estimates of the long-term relationship between adverse childhood experiences and adult health are conservative. Longitudinal follow-up of adults whose childhood abuse was well documented has shown that their retrospective reports of childhood abuse are likely to underestimate actual occurrence.[47,18] Underestimates of childhood exposures would result in downwardly biased estimates of the relationships between childhood exposures and adult health risk behaviors and diseases. Another potential source of underestimation of the strength of these relationships is the lower number of childhood exposures reported by older persons in our study. This may be an artifact caused by premature mortality in persons with multiple adverse childhood exposures; the clustering of multiple risk factors among persons with multiple childhood exposures is consistent with this hypothesis. Thus, the true relationships between adverse childhood exposures and adult health risk behaviors, health status, and diseases may be even stronger than those we report.

An essential question posed by our observations is "Exactly how are adverse childhood experiences linked to health risk behaviors and adult diseases?" The linking mechanisms appear to center on behaviors such as smoking, alcohol or drug abuse, overeating, or sexual behaviors that may be consciously or unconsciously used because they have immediate pharmacological or psychological benefit as coping devices in the face of the stress of abuse, domestic violence, or other forms of family and household dysfunction. High levels of exposure to adverse childhood experiences would expectedly produce anxiety, anger, and depression in children. To the degree that behaviors such as smoking, alcohol, or drug use are found to be effective as coping devices, they would tend to be used chronically. For example, nicotine is recognized as having beneficial psychoactive effects in terms of regulating affect [19] and persons who are depressed are more likely to smoke. [50,51] Thus, persons exposed to adverse childhood experiences may benefit from using drugs such as nicotine to regulate their mood [41,12]

Consideration of the positive neuroregulatory effects of health-risk behaviors such as smoking may provide biobehavioral explanations[53] for the link between adverse childhood experiences and health risk behaviors and diseases in adults. In fact, we found that exposure to higher numbers of categories of adverse childhood experiences increased the likelihood of smoking by the age of 14, chronic smoking as adults, and the presence of smoking-related diseases. Thus, smoking, which is medically and socially viewed as a "problem" may, from the perspective of the user, represent an effective immediate solution that leads to chronic use. Decades later, when this "solution" manifests as emphysema, cardiovascular disease, or malignancy, time and the tendency to ignore psychological issues in the management of organic disease make improbable any full understanding of the original causes of adult disease (Figure 2). Thus, incomplete understanding of the possible benefits of health risk behaviors leads them to be viewed as irrational and having solely negative consequences.

Because adverse childhood experiences are common and they have strong long-term associations with adult health risk behaviors, health status, and diseases, increased attention to primary, secondary, and tertiary prevention strategies is needed. These strategies include prevention of the occurrence of adverse childhood experiences, preventing the adoption of health risk behaviors as responses to adverse experiences during childhood and adolescence, and, finally, helping change the health risk and ameliorating the disease burden among adults whose health problems may represent a long-term consequence of adverse childhood experiences.

Primary prevention of adverse childhood experiences has proven difficult and will ultimately require societal changes that improve the quality of family and household environments during childhood. Recent research on the long-term benefit of early home visitation on reducing the prevalence of adverse childhood experiences is promising. In fact, preliminary data from the ACE Study provided the impetus for the Kaiser Health Plan to provide funding to participate at 4 locations (including San Diego County, California) in the Commonwealth Fund's "Healthy Steps" program. This program extends the traditional practice of pediatrics by adding one or more specialists in the developmental and psychosocial dimensions of both childhood and parenthood. Through a series of office visits, home visits, and a telephone advice line for parents, these specialists develop close relationships between children and their families from birth to 3 years of age. This approach is consistent with the recommendation of the U.S. Advisory Board on Child Abuse and Neglect that a universal home visitation program for new parents be developed and provides an example of a family-based primary prevention effort that is being explored in a managed care setting. If these types of approaches can be replicated and implemented on a large scale, the long-term benefits may include, somewhat unexpectedly, substantial improvements in over-all adult health.

Table 4. Number of categories of adverse childhood exposure and the adjusted odds of risk factors including current smoking, severe obesity, physical inactivity, depressed mood, and suicide attempt

Health problem	Number of Categories	Sample size (N)[a]	Prevalence (%)[b]	Adjusted odds ratio[c]	95% confidence interval
Current smoker [d]	0	3,836	6.8	1.0	Referent
	1	2,005	7.9	1.1	(0.9 -1.4)
	2	1,046	10.3	1.5	(1.1-1.8)
	3	587	13.9	2.0	(1.5-2.6)
	4 or more	544	16.5	2.2	(1.7-2.9)
	Total	8,018	8.6	----	-----------
Severe obesity [d] (BMI ≥ 35)	0	3,850	5.4	1.0	Referent
	1	2,004	7.0	1.1	(0.9-1.4)
	2	1,041	9.5	1.4	(1.1-1.9)
	3	590	10.3	1.4	(1.0-1.9)
	4 or more	543	12.0	1.6	(1.2-2.1)
	Total	8,028	7.1	-----	------------
No leisure-time physical activity	0	3,634	18.4	1.0	Referent
	1	1,917	22.8	1.2	(1.1-1.4)
	2	1,006	22.0	1.2	(1.0-1.4)
	3	559	26.6	1.4	(1.1-1.7)
	4 or more	523	26.6	1.3	(1.1-1.6)
	Total	7,639	21.0	----	------------
Two or more weeks of depressed mood in the past year	0	3,799	14.2	1.0	Referent
	1	1,984	21.4	1.5	(1.3-1.7)
	2	1,036	31.5	2.4	(2.0-2.8)
	3	584	36.2	2.6	(2.1-3.2)
	4 or more	542	50.7	4.6	(3.8-5.6)
	Total	7,945	22.0	----	-----------
Ever attempted suicide	0	3,852	1.2	1.0	Referent
	1	1,997	2.4	1.8	(1.2-2.6)
	2	1,048	4.3	3.0	(2.0-4.6)
	3	587	9.5	6.6	(4.5-9.8)
	4 or more	544	18.3	12.2	(8.5-17.5)
	Total	8,028	3.5	-----	-----------

[a] Sample sizes will vary due to incomplete or missing information about health problems. [b] Prevalence estimates are adjusted for age. [c] Odds ratios adjusted for age, gender, race, and educational attainment. [d] Indicates information recorded in the patient's chart before the study questionnaire was mailed.

Health problem	Number of Categories	Sample size (N)[a]	Prevalence (%)[b]	Adjusted odds ratio[c]	95% confidence interval
Considers self an alcoholic	0	3,841	2.9	1.0	Referent
	1	1,993	5.7	2.0	(1.6–2.7)
	2	1,042	10.3	4.0	(3.0-5.3)
	3	586	11.3	4.9	(3.5-6.8)
	4 or more	540	16.1	7.4	(5.4-10.2)
	Total	8,002	5.9	---	---
Ever used illicit Drugs	0	3,856	6.4	1.0	Referent
	1	1,998	11.4	1.7	(1.4-2.0)
	2	1,045	19.2	2.9	(2.4-3.6)
	3	589	21.5	3.6	(2.8-4.6)
	4 or more	541	28.4	4.7	(3.7-6.0)
	Total	8,029	11.6	---	---
Ever injected drugs	0	3,855	0.3	1.0	Referent
	1	1,996	0.5	1.3	(0.6-3.1)
	2	1,044	1.4	3.8	(1.8-8.2)
	3	587	2.3	7.1	(3.3-15.5)
	4 or more	540	3.4	10.3	(4.9-21.4)
	Total	8,022	0.8	---	---
Had 50 or more intercourse Partners	0	3,400	3.0	1.0	Referent
	1	1,812	5.1	1.7	(1.3-2.3)
	2	926	6.1	2.3	(1.6-3.2)
	3	526	6.3	3.1	(2.0-4.7)
	4 or more	474	6.8	3.2	(2.1-5.1)
	Total	7,138	4.4	---	---
Ever had a sexually Transmitted disease [d]	0	3,848	5.6	1.0	Referent
	1	2,001	8.6	1.4	(1.1-1.7)
	2	1,044	10.4	1.5	(1.2-1.9)
	3	588	13.1	1.9	(1.4-2.5)
	4 or more	542	16.7	2.5	(1.9-3.2)
	Total	8,023	8.2	----	----------

Table 5. Number of categories of adverse childhood exposure and the prevalence and risk (adjusted odds ratio) of health risk factors including alcohol or drug abuse, high lifetime number of sexual partners, or history of sexually transmitted disease

[a] Sample sizes will vary due to incomplete or missing information about health problems. [b] Prevalence estimates are adjusted for age. [c] Odds ratios adjusted for age, gender, race, and educational attainment. [d] Indicates information recorded in the patient's chart before the study questionnaire was mailed.

Table 6. Relationship between number of categories of childhood exposure and number of risk factors for the leading causes of death'							
Number of categories	Sample Size	% with number of risk factors					
		0	1	2	3	4	
0	3,861	56	29	10	4	1	
1	2,009	42	33	16	6	2	
2	1,051	31	33	20	10	4	
3	590	24	33	20	13	7	
4	545	14	26	28	17	7	
Total	8,056	44	31	15	7	3	

'Risk factors include: smoking, severe obesity, physical inactivity, depressed mood, suicide attempt, alcoholism, any drug use, injected drug use, >50 lifetime sexual partners, and history of a sexually transmitted disease.

Table 7. Number of categories of adverse childhood exposure and the prevalence and risk (adjusted odds ratio) or heart attack, cancer, stroke, COPD, and diabetes					
Disease condition [d]	Number of categories	Sample size (N)[a]	Prevalence (%)[b]	Adjusted odds ratio[c]	95% confidence interval
Ischernic heart disease	0	3,859	3.7	1.0	Referent
	1	2,009	3.5	0.9	(0.7-1.3)
	2	1,050	3.4	0.9	(0.6-1.4)
	3	590	4.6	1.4	(0.8-2.4)
	4 or more	545	5.6	2.2	(1.3-3.7)
	Total	8,022	3.8	---	---
Any cancer	0	3,842	1.9	1.0	Referent
	1	1,995	1.9	1.2	(1.0-1.5)
	2	1,043	1.9	1.2	(1.0-1.5)
	3	588	1.9	1.0	(0.7-1.5)
	4 or more	543	1.9	1.9	(1.3-2.7)
	Total	8,011	1.9	---	---
Stroke	0	3,832	2.6	1.0	Referent
	1	1,993	2.4	0.9	(0.7-1.3)
	2	1,042	2.0	0.7	(0.4-1.3)
	3	588	2.9	1.3	(0.7-2.4)
	4 or more	543	4.1	2.4	(1.3-4.3)
	Total	7,998	2.6	---	---
Chronic bronchitis or emphysema	0	3,758	2.8	1.0	Referent
	1	1,939	4.4	1.6	(1.2-2.1)
	2	1,009	4.4	1.6	(1.1-2.3)
	3	565	5.7	2.2	(1.4-3.3)
	4 or more	543	8.7	3.9	(2.6-5.8)
	Total	7,783	4.0	---	---
Diabetes	0	3,850	4.3	1.0	Referent
	1	2,002	4.1	1.0	(0.7-1.3)
	2	1,046	3.9	0.9	(0.6-1.3)
	3	587	5.0	1.2	(0.8-1.9)
	4 or more	542	5.8	1.6	(1.0-2.5)
	Total	8,027	4.3	---	---

[a]Sample sizes will vary due to incomplete or missing information about health problems.
[b]Prevalence estimates are adjusted for age.
[c]Odds ratios adjusted for age, gender, race, and educational attainment.
[d]Indicates information recorded in the patient's chart before the study questionnaire was mailed.

Table 8. Number of categories of adverse childhood exposure and the prevalence and risk (adjusted odds ratio) of skeletal fracture, hepatitis or jaundice, and poor self-rated health

Disease condition[d]	Number of categories	Sample size (N)[a]	Prevalence (%)[b]	Adjusted odds ratio[c]	95% confidence interval
Ever had a skeletal fracture	0	3,843	3.6	1.0	Referent
	1	1,998	4.0	1.1	(1.0-1.2)
	2	1,048	4.5	1.4	(1.2-1.6)
	3	587	4.0	1.2	(1.0-1.4)
	4 or more	544	4.8	1.6	(1.3--2.0)
	Total	8,020	3.9	---	---
Ever had hepatitis or jaundice	0	3,846	5.3	1.0	Referent
	1	2,006	5.5	1.1	(0.9-1.4)
	2	1,045	7.7	1.8	(1.4-2.3)
	3	590	10.2	1.6	(1.2-2.3)
	4 or more	543	10.7	2.4	(1.8-3.3)
	Total	8,030	6.5	---	---
Fair or poor self-rated health	0	3,762	16.3	1.0	Referent
	1	1,957	17.8	1.2	(1.0-1.4)
	2	1,029	19.9	1.4	(1.2-1.7)
	3	584	20.3	1.4	(1.1-1.7)
	4 or more	527	28.7	2.2	(1.8-2.7)
	Total	7,859	18.2	---	---

[a] Sample sizes will vary due to incomplete or missing information about health problems.
[b] Prevalence estimates are adjusted for age and gender.
[c] Odds ratios adjusted for age, gender, race, and educational attainment.
[d] Indicates information recorded in the patient's chart before the study questionnaire was mailed.

Secondary prevention of the effects of adverse childhood experiences will first require increased recognition of their occurrence and second, an effective understanding of the behavioral coping devices that commonly are adopted to reduce the emotional impact of these experiences. The improbability of giving up an immediate "solution" in return for a nebulous long term health benefit has thwarted many well-intended preventive efforts. Although articles in the general medical literature are alerting the medical community to the fact that childhood abuse is common, adolescent health care is often inadequate in terms of psychosocial assessment and anticipatory guidance. Clearly, comprehensive strategies are needed to identify and intervene with children and families who are at risk for these adverse experiences and their related outcomes. Such strategies should include increased communication between and among those involved in family practice, internal medicine, nursing, social work, pediatrics, emergency medicine, and preventive medicine and public health. Improved understanding is also needed of the effects of childhood exposure to domestic violence. Additionally, increased physician training is needed to recognize and coordinate the management of all persons affected by child abuse, domestic violence, and other forms of family adversity such as alcohol abuse or mental illness.

In the meantime, tertiary care of adults whose health problems are related to experiences such as childhood abuse will continue to be a difficult challenge. The relationship between childhood experiences and adult health status is likely to be overlooked in medical practice because the time delay between exposure during childhood and recognition of health problems in adult medical practice is lengthy. Moreover, these childhood exposures include emotionally sensitive topics such as family alcoholism and sexual abuse. Many physicians may fear that discussions of sexual violence and other sensitive issues are too personal even for the doctor-patient relationship. For example, the

American Medical Association recommends screening of women for exposure to violence at every entrance to the health system; however, such screening appears to be rare. By contrast, women who are asked about exposure to sexual violence say they consider such questions to be welcome and germane to routine medical care, which suggests that physicians' fears about patient reactions are largely unfounded.

Figure 2. Potential influences throughout the lifespan of adverse childhood experiences.

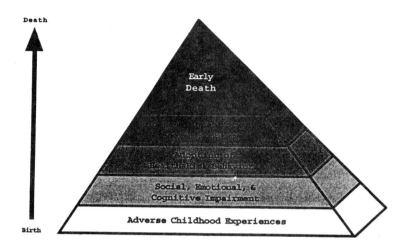

Clearly, further research and training are needed to help medical and public health practitioners understand how social, emotional, and medical problems are linked throughout the lifespan (Figure 2). Such research and training would provide physicians with the confidence and skills to inquire and respond to patients who acknowledge these types of childhood exposures. Increased awareness of the frequency and long-term consequences of adverse childhood experiences may also lead to improvements in health promotion and disease prevention programs. The magnitude of the difficulty of introducing the requisite changes into medical and public health research, education, and practice can be offset only by the magnitude of the implications that these changes have for improving the health of the nation.

We thank Naomi Howard for her dedication to the ACE Study. This research is supported by the Centers for Disease Control and Prevention via cooperative agreement TS-44-10/12 with the Association of Teachers of Preventive Medicine.

References

1   Springs F, Friedrich WN. Health risk behaviors and medical sequelae of childhood sexual abuse. *Mayo Clin Proc* 1992;67:527-32.

2.   Felitti,V.J.. Long-term medical consequences of incest, rape, and molestation. *South Med J 1991;84*:328-31.

3.   Felitti NJ. Childhood sexual abuse, depression and family dysfunction in adult obese patients: a case control study. *South Med J* 1993;86:732-6.

4. Gould DA, Stevens NG, Ward NG, Carlin AS, Sowell HE, Gustafson B. Self-reported childhood abuse in an adult population in a primary care setting. *Arch Fam Med* 1994;3:252-6.

5. McCauley J, Kern DE, Kolodner K, Schroeder AF, et al. Clinical characteristics of women with a history of childhood abuse. *JAMA* 1997;277:1362-8.

6. Mortality patterns: United States, 1993. *Morb Mortal Wkly Rep* 1996;45:161-4.

7. McGinnis JM, Foege WH. Actual causes of death in the United States. *JAMA* 1993;270:2207-12.

8. Landis J. Experiences of 500 children with adult sexual deviation. *Psychiatr Q* 1956;30(Suppi):91-109.

9. Straus MA, Gelles RJ. Societal change and change in family violence from 1975 to 1985 as revealed by two national surveys. *J. Marriage Family* 1986;48:465-79.

10. Wyatt GE, Peters SD. Methodological considerations in research on the prevalence of child sexual abuse. *Child Abuse Negl* 1986;10:241-51.

11. Berger AM, Knutson JF, Mehm JG, Perkins KA. The self-report of punitive childhood experiences of young adults and adolescents. *Child Abuse Negl* 1988;12:25162.

12. Finkelhor D, Hotaling G, Lewis IA, Smith C. Sexual abuse in a national survey of adult men and women: prevalence, characteristics, and risk factors *Child Abuse Negl* 1990; 14:19-28.

13. Egelend B Sroufe LA, Erickson M. The developmental consequence of different patterns of maltreatment. *Child Abuse Negl* 1983;7:459-69.

14. Finkelhor D, Browne A. The traumatic impact of child sexual abuse *Am J Orthopsychiatry*. 1985;55:530 - 4 1.

15. Beitchman JH, Zucker KJ, Hood JE, DaCosta GA, Akman D, Cassa E. A review of the long-term effects of sexual abuse. *Child Abuse Negl* 1992;16:101-18.

16. Hibbard RA, Ingersoll GM, Orr DP. Behavioral risk, emotional risk, and child abuse among adolescents in a nonclinical setting. *Pediatrics* 1990;86:896-901.

17. Nagy S, Adcock AG, Nagy MC. A comparison of risky health behaviors of sexually active, sexually abused , and abstaining adolescents. *Pediatrics* 1994;93:570-5.

18. Cunningham RM, Stiffman AR, Dore P. The association of physical and sexual abuse with HIV risk behaviors in adolescence and young adulthood: implications for public health. *Child Abuse Negl* 1994;18:233-45.

19. Council on Scientific Affairs. Adolescents as victims of family violence. *JAMA* 1993;270:1850-6.

20. Nelson DE, Higginson Gls~ Grant-Worley JA. Physical abuse among high school students. Prevalence and correlation with other health behaviors. *Arch Pediatr Adolesc Med* 1995;149:1254-8.

21. Mullen PE, Roman-Clarkson SE, Walton VA, Herbison GP. Impact of sexual and physical abuse on women's mental health. *Lancet* 1988;1:841-5.

22. Drossman DA, Lesermanj, Nachman G, Li Z, et al. Sexual and physical abuse in women with functional or organic gastrointestinal disorders. *Ann Intern Med* 1990;113: 828-33.

23. Harrop-GriffithsJ, Katon W, Walker E, Holm L, RussoJ, Hickok L. The association between chronic pelvic pain, psychiatric diagnoses, and childhood sexual abuse. *Obstet Gynecol* 1988;71:589-94.

24. Briere J Runtz M. Multivariate correlates of childhood psychological and physical maltreatment among university women. *Child Abuse Negl* 1988;12:331-41.

25. Briere J Runtz M. Differential adult symptornatology associated with three types of child abuse histories. *Child Abuse Negl* 1990;14:357-64.

26. Claussen AH, Crittenden PM. Physical and psychological maltreatment: relations among types of maltreatment. *Child Abuse Negl* 1991;15:5-18.

27. Moeller TP, Bachman GA, Moeller JR. The combined effects of physical, sexual, and emotional abuse during childhood: long-term health consequences for women. *Child Abuse Negl* 1993;17:623-40.

28. Bryant SL, Range LM. Suicidality in college women who were sexually and physically punished by parents. *Violence Vict* 1995;10:195-201.

29. Zeitlen H. Children with alcohol misusing parents. *Br Med Bull* 1994;50:139-51.

30. Dore MM, Doris JM, Wright P. Identifing substance abuse in maltreating families: a child welfare challenge. *Child Abuse Negl* 1995;19:531-43.

31. Ethier LS, Lacharite C, Couture G. Childhood adversity, parental stress, and depression of negligent mothers. *Child Abuse Negl* 1995;19:619-32.

32. Spaccarelli S, Coatsworth JD, Bowden BS. Exposure to family violence among incarcerated boys; its association with violent offending and potential mediating variables. *Violence Vict* 1995;10:163-82.

33. McCloskey LA, Figueredo AJ, Koss MP. The effects of systemic family violence on children's mental health. *Child Dev* 1995;66:1239-61.

34. Brent DA, Perper JA, Moritz G, Schweers J Balach L, Roth C. Familial risk factors for adolescent suicide: a case-control study. *Acta Psychiatr Scand* 1994;89:52-8.

35. Shaw DS, VondraJI, Hommerding KD, Keenan K, Dunn M. Chronic family adversity and early child behavior problems: a longitudinal study of low income families. *J Child Psychol Psychiatry* 1994;35:1109-22.

36. U.S. Department of Health and Human Services. *Physical activity and health: A report of the Surgeon General*. Atlanta, Georgia. U.S. Department of Health and Human Services, Centers for Disease Control and Prevention, National Center for Chronic Disease Prevention and Health Promotion; 1996.

37. Rivara FP, Mueller BA, Somes G, Mendoza CT, Rushforth NB, Kellerman AL. Alcohol and illicit drug abuse and the risk of violent death in the home. *JAMA* 1997;278:56975.

38. Dillman DA. *Mail and telephone surveys: the total design method.* New York: John Wiley & Sons; 1978.

39. Straus M, Gelles RJ. *Physical violence in American families: risk factors and adaptations to violence in 8,145 families.* New Brunswick: Transaction Press; 1990.

40. Wyatt GE. The sexual abuse of Afro-American and WhiteAmerican women in childhood. *Child Abuse Negl* 1985; 9:507-19.

41. National Center for Health Statistics. *Exposure to alcoholism in the family*: United States, 1988. Advance Data, No. 205. U.S, Department of Health and Human Services, Washington, DC; September 30, 1991.

42. Siegel PZ, Frazier EL, Mariolis P, et al. Behaviorial risk factor surveillance, 1991; Monitoring progress toward the Nation's Year 2000 Health Objectives. *Morb Mortal Wkly Rep* 1992;42(SS-4).1-15.

43. Crespo CJ, Keteyian SJ, Heath GW, Sempos CT. Leisure time physical activity among US adults: Results from the Third National Health and Nutrition Examination Survey. *Arch Intern Med* 1996;156:93-8.

44. Robins LN, Helzer JE, Groughan J, Ratliff K National Institute of Mental Health Diagnostic Interview Schedule: its history, characteristics, and validitv. *Arch Gen Psychiatry* 1981;38:381-9.

45. Idler E, Angel RJ. Self-rated health and mortality in the NHAINES I Epidemiologic Follow-up Study. *Am J Pub Health* 1990;80:446-52.

46. *SAS Procedures Guide.* SAS Institute Inc. Version 6, 3rd edition, Cary, NC: SAS Institute; 1990

47. Femina DD, Yeager CA, Lewis DO. Child abuse: adolescent records vs. adult recall, *Child Abuse Negl* 1990;14: 227-31.

48. Williams LM. Recovered memories of abuse in women with documented child sexual victimization histories.*J Traumatic Stress* 1995;8:649-73.

49. Carmody TP. Affect regulation, nicotine addiction, and smoking cessation. *J Psychoactive Drugs* 1989;21:331-42.

50. Anda RF, Williamson DF, Escobedo-LG, Mast EE, Giovino GA, Remington PL. Depression and the dynamics of smoking. A national perspective. *JAMA* 1990;264:1541-5.

51. Glassman AH, HelzerJE, Covey LS, Cottler LB, Stemer F, Tipp JE, Johnson J. Smoking, smoking cessation, and major depression. *JAMA* 1990;264:1546-9.

52. Hughes JR. Clonidine, depression, and smoking cessation. *JAMA* 1988;259:2901-2.

53. Pomerlau O.F, Pomerlau CS. Neuroregulators and the reinforcement of smoking: towards a biobehavioral explanation. *Neurosci Biobehav Rev* 1984;8:503-13.

54. Hardy JB, Street R. Family support and parenting education in the home: an effective extension of clinic-based preventive health care services for poor children. *J Pediatr* 1989;115:927-31.

55. Olds DL, Henderson CR, Chamberlin R, Tatelbaum R. Preventing child abuse and neglect: a randomized trial of nurse home visitation. *Pediatrics* 1986;78:65-78.

56. Olds DL, Eckenrodej, Henderson CR, Kitzman H, et al. Long-term effects of home visitation on matemal life course and child abuse and neglect: Fifteen-year follow-up of a randomized trial. *JAMA* 1997;278:637-43.

57. U.S. Advisory Board on Child Abuse and Neglect. *Child abuse and neglect: critical first steps in response to a national emergency.* Washington, DC: U.S. Government Printing Office; August 1990; publication no. 017-09200104-5.

58. U.S. Advisory Board on Child Abuse and Neglect. *Creating caring communities: blueprint for an effective federal policy on child abuse and neglect.* Washington, DC: U.S. Government Printing Office; September 1991.

59. MacMillan HL, Fleming JE, Trocme N, Boyle MH, et al. Prevalence of child physical and sexual abuse in the community. Results from the Ontario Health Supplement. *JAMA* 1997;278:131-5.

60. Rixey S. Family violence and the adolescent. *Maryland MedJ* 1994;43:351-3.

61. Chamberlin RW. Preventing low birth weight, child abuse, and school failure: the need for comprehensive, community-wide approaches. *Pediatr Rev* 1992;13:64-71.

62. KashaniJH, Daniel AE, Dandoy AC, Holcomb WR. Family violence: impact on children. *J Am Acad Child Adolesc Psychiatry* 1992;31:181-9.

63. Dubowitz H. Child abuse programs and pediatric residency training. *Pediatrics* 1988;82:477-80.

64. Tabachnick J, Henry F, Denny L. Perceptions of child sexual abuse as a public health problem. Vermont, September 1995. *Morb Mortal Wkly Rep* 1997;46:801-3.

65. Sugg NK, Inui T. Primary care physicians' response to domestic violence. Opening Pandora's box. *JAMA* 1992; 267:3157-60.

66. Council on Scientific Affairs. American Medical Association Diagnostic and Treatment Guidelines on Domestic Violence. *Arch Fam Med* 1992;1:38-47.

67. Hamberger L& Saunders DG, Hovey M. Prevalence of domestic violence in community practice and rate of physician inquiry. *Fam Med* 1992;24:283-7.

68. Friedman LS, Samet JH, Roberts MS, Hans P. Inquiry about victimization experiences. A survey of patient preferences and physician practices. *Arch Int Med* 1992;152: 1186-90.

Victimization and Diabetes: An Exploratory Study*

Kathleen A. Kendall-Tackett, Ph.D.
and
Roberta Marshall, MSN, ARNP

Introduction

In recent years, researchers have documented higher rates of health problems in adult survivors of abuse than in the general population. These problems include diffuse soft tissue pain (Boisset-Pioro, Esdaile & Fitzcharles, 1995), irritable bowel syndrome (Leserman, Drossman, Li, Toomey, Nachman & Glogau, 1996), and chronic pelvic pain (Walling, Reiter, O'Hara, Milburn, Lilly & Vincent, 1994). While this past research has done much to increase our understanding, it is somewhat limited. For example, the samples are typically drawn from populations with specific medical problems (e.g., those presenting at a gastroenterology clinic), which influences the choice of illness studied (Laws, 1993).

In the present study, we focus on diabetes. Diabetes has not been examined with regard to past victimization, but we believe that it is potentially fruitful. Chronic stress can lead to an elevation in blood levels of triglycerides, free fatty acids, cholesterol, glucose, and insulin (Lovallo, 1997; Meaney, 1997; Sapolsky, 1994). When glucose and insulin levels are chronically elevated, the body responds by becoming less sensitive to insulin. The person then becomes "insulin resistant," a hallmark symptom of diabetes (American Diabetes Association, 1997). We propose that child and domestic abuse are chronic stressors, and as such they can create an even wider variety of health problems than ones already studied.

To summarize, the present study considers diabetes and symptoms of diabetes in patients with a past history of victimization. Since our sample is from primary care and essentially healthy, we expect relatively low incidence of illness but we do expect a greater reporting of both illness and symptoms in members of the abused group.

Method

Subjects.

A sample of 130 patients (65 abused, 65 non-abused controls) was drawn from an adult primary-care practice in a small, affluent, predominantly Caucasian community in northern New England. All questionnaires were completed from 1994 to 1997. The total practice was 1,005 patients. Of these, 905 patients completed the questionnaire; one hundred patients did not. Those who did not were either seen as inpatients only, or on an on-call or emergency basis.

We first identified all patients who answered "yes" to at least one of two questions about either child or domestic abuse (N=65; 9 males, 56 females). We then gathered our control group from among the remaining patients by matching for age and sex with members of the abused group. The subjects ranged in age from 18 to 88 (M=47).

*Reprinted from : Child Abuse & Neglect, Vol 23, 1999, pp 593-596; Victimization and Diabeties: An Exploratory Study, Kathleen A. Kendall-Tackett, Ph.D. and Roberta Marshall, MSN , ARNP With permission from Elsevier Science

Key words: diabetes, victimization, childhood abuse

Of the 65 patients in the abused group, 33 indicated that they had experienced physical or sexual abuse as children, 21 indicated that they had experienced domestic abuse as adults, and I I indicated that they had experienced both child and domestic abuse. Among the abused group, preliminary analyses revealed no significant differences between patients abused as adults and those abused as children. Therefore, data were combined for subsequent analyses, as in to previous studies (see Golding, Cooper & George, 1997; Leserman et al., 1996).

Questionnaire

The questionnaire was a five-page, 169 item, closed-ended (yes-no), self administered form, and was designed to be used clinically. The questionnaire included demographic information; self-rated health; past medical history (yes-no questions about 20 illnesses including diabetes: "Do you presently suffer, or have you ever suffered in the past, from any of the following illnesses?"); family history of illness; victimization history ("Were you sexually or physically abused as a child?" and "Have you been the victim of domestic abuse as an adult?"), and a "review of systems."

The review of systems was designed to serve as a screening device for a wide variety of physical conditions that might present in a primary-care practice. In order to select relevant symptoms for this analysis, we referred to the American Diabetes Association (1997) list of symptoms. This list included both type I and type 11 diabetes. We found a match for nine out of ten of these symptoms on our patient questionnaire: excessive fatigue or weakness; excessive hunger or thirst; recent weight loss or gain; problems with vision; bleeding gums; frequent urinary tract infections; sores that will not heal; increase or decrease in frequency or urination; and loss of sensation, tingling or "pins and needles." The only symptom for which we had no match was "irritability."

Data Analysis

The data were analyzed by comparing the abused group with the non-abused group using A' or one-way ANOVA.

Results

As predicted, patients with a history of abuse were significantly more likely to report diabetes ($X2=4.13$, $p <. 042$). There were four patients in the abused group who reported diabetes, and none in the control group. Interestingly, those patients in the abused group did not have a significantly higher family history of diabetes than those in the non-abused group ($X2=2.94$, $p<.09$). Further, there was no significant difference in physician-rated obesity between the groups ($X2=2.68$, $p<. 102$). (There was no self-report measure of obesity.)

Also as predicted, those with a history of victimization reported significantly more symptoms of diabetes ($M=2.4 1$) than those without a history ($M= 1.04$; $F(1,99)=15.97$, $p<.0001$). Further, a higher percentage of patients in the abused group reported three or more symptoms (39%) than did those in the control group (10%).

Discussion

Diabetes is the seventh leading cause of death in the U.S., and is responsible for a number of life-threatening complications including blindness, kidney disease, neuropathy, amputations, heart disease and stroke (American Diabetes Association, 1997). The present study indicates that patients with a history of victimization were significantly more likely to be diabetic or to have symptoms of diabetes than were their non-abused counterparts.

Although only four people identified themselves as having diabetes, this number should be interpreted in the broader context of incidence of diabetes in the general population. The Centers for Disease Control and Prevention (1997) have estimated the percentage of diagnosed cases in the state where our data were collected as 2.8% of the population. In comparison, 6.3% of the abused patients in the present study reported diabetes-more than twice the percentage that we would expect in a sample from our region. In spite of this, we do not want to oversell our case. Our finding on reported diabetes could be due to chance. Similarly, many of the symptoms are non-specific and could be related to other diseases. We hope that this preliminary study inspires future research.

The patients who did not identify themselves as having diabetes but reported symptoms are also of concern. According to the American Diabetes Association (1997), an additional 5.4 million people have the disease but are not aware that they have it. In the present study, 39% of the those in the victims' group indicated that they had three or more symptoms of diabetes, compared with 10% of the control group. While there are many other factors that put people at risk for diabetes, a history of past victimization should also be considered.

One intriguing finding was that three of the diabetic patients were victims of domestic abuse alone, and the fourth was a victim of both child and domestic abuse. It is possible that diabetes risk increases with a more proximal stressor (i.e., abuse as an adult); a question that should be considered in future studies.

There were several limitations to our study. First, the question about child abuse does not differentiate between physical and sexual abuse. Second, for both abuse questions, we do not know the identity of the perpetrator, the type and severity of abuse that occurred, the frequency and duration of the abuse experience, and whether force was involved. Each of these factors has been found to contribute to the severity of the abuse experience and the severity of subsequent symptoms (Boisset-Pioro, et al., 1995; Kendall-Tackett, Williams & Finkelhor, 1993; Leserman et al., 1996).

Our question about diabetes is also limited. We do not know about the type or severity of the diabetes, or even such a basic distinction as type I versus type 11. Type 11 is by far the most common (American Diabetes Association, 1997), but we cannot assume that the four patients who identified themselves as diabetic had type 11 diabetes. They ranged in age from 52 to 76, ruling out gestational diabetes and leaning toward type 11, but we cannot be certain. Further, we have no way of ruling out response bias, either the tendency to over report among the abused group, or under-report in the nonabused group.

Even with these limitations, the present study suggests that past victimization may put people at risk for a wide variety of future health problems. By anticipating the potential influence effects of past abuse, practitioners can educate patients who have been abused about possible health consequences they might face and empower them to seek appropriate levels of care.

We wish to thank members of the Family Research Laboratory's seminar group and two anonymous reviewers for their helpful comments and suggestions. Requests for reprints can be sent to Kathleen Kendall-Tackett, Ph.D., 34 Western Avenue, Henniker NH 03242 (603) 428-8716, FAX (603) 428-7852, kkendallt@aol.com.

References

American Diabetes Association (1997). *Diabetes facts and figures.* Alexandria, VA: Author.

Boisset-Pioro MH, Esdaile JM, & Fitzcharles MA. (1995). Sexual and physical abuse in women with fibrornyalgia syndrome. *Arthritis & Rheumatism, 38,* 235-24 1.

Centers for Disease Control and Prevention (1997). *Estimated number of adults with diagnosed diabetes by age, sex and state, United States, 1994.* Atlanta, GA: Author.

Golding, JM, Cooper, ML, & George, LK. (1997). Sexual assault history and health perceptions: Seven general population studies. *Health Psychology, 16,* 417-425.

Kendall-Tackett KA, Williams LM & Finkelhor D. (1993). The effects of sexual abuse on children: A review and synthesis of recent empirical findings. *Psychological Bulletin, 113,* 164-181.

Laws, A. (1993). Sexual abuse history and women's medical problems. *Journal of General Internal Medicine,* 8, 441-443.

Leserman J, Drossman DA, Li Z, Toomey TC, Nachman G & Glogau L. (1996). Sexual and physical abuse history in gastroenterology practice: How types of abuse impact health status. *Psychosomatic Medicine,* 58, 4-15.

Lovallo, W.R. (1997). *Stress and health: Biological and psychological interactions.* Newbury Park, CA: Sage.

Meaney M. (1997). *Stress and disease.* Palo Alto, CA: Institute for CorText Research and Development.

Sapolsky, RM (1994). *Why zebras don't get ulcers: A guide to stress, stress related diseases, and coping.* New York: WH Freeman.

Walling, MK, Reiter, RC, O'Hara, MW, Milburn, AK, Lilly, G, & Vincent, SD. (1994). Abuse history and chronic pain in women: 1. Prevalences of sexual abuse and physical abuse. *Obstetrics & Gynecology,* 84: 193-199.

The Cumulative Impact of Abuse Across the Life Span: Child Sexual Abuse and Adult Revictimization

Elizabeth Frenkel and Margaret O'Dougherty Wright

Introduction

In 1996, child protective service agencies in the United States identified almost 1 million children as victims of abuse or neglect, based on over 2 million reports alleging maltreatment of over 3 million children (United States Department of Health and Human Services [USDHHS], 1998a). This is almost a 20% increase since 1990, resulting in an incidence rate of slightly over 1% of the child population of the United States. Of these, about 12% experienced sexual abuse. Seventy-seven percent of sexual abuse victims were female, while 71% of the perpetrators were male, compared to a more even division between male and female victims and perpetrators of other types of child maltreatment (USDHHS, 1998a). Child sexual abuse occurred 17 times more frequently in families living in poverty (income less than $15,000/year) than in middle or upper SES families (income over $30,000/year; USDHHS, 1998b). However, there was no relationship between family structure or family size and occurrence of abuse (USDHHS, 1998b).

Sexual abuse is defined as "fondling a child's genitals, intercourse, incest, rape, sodomy, exhibitionism, and commercial exploitation through prostitution or the production of pornographic materials" (National Clearinghouse on Child Abuse and Neglect Information, 1998 [On-line]). This definition is based on the Child Abuse Prevention and Treatment Act (CAPTA) that was amended in 1996. Although child sexual abuse is often reported - and studied-separately from other types of abuse, it often occurs together with physical or emotional abuse or neglect (Masten & Wright, 1998). A disturbing finding of the studies on the long-term effects of child sexual abuse is that children who were sexually abused have higher rates of abuse in adulthood than children who were not abused. This phenomenon is called revictimization. Child abuse survivors' who are revictimized in adulthood tend to experience a wide-range of victimizations. Regardless of type of abuse they experienced in childhood, they may experience stranger, acquaintance, or marital rape; stranger assault; or battering from intimate partners in adulthood (Messman & Long, 1996). On the other hand, a large percentage of child sexual abuse survivors do not experience any abuse in adulthood. The mechanisms that contribute to this recovery process need to be better understood in order for professionals to be able to provide services to cultivate the long-term well-being of these children and to reduce the long-term costs of childhood abuse.[1]

This chapter focuses on factors promoting resilience or contributing to later revictimization in childhood sexual abuse survivors. A transactional, interpersonal model focusing on risk and protective factors is employed. In this model, child sexual abuse is seen as an interpersonal stressor that increases the child's vulnerability to future victimization. However, it is not a necessary or sufficient condition for adult victimization to occur. Instead, the occurrence of revictimization is thought to be the result of interactions between multiple risk factors and protective factors.

Footnote'
This chapter focuses exclusively on female victims. This is not meant to deny the existence of sexual abuse of boys. However, while boys are also the victims of child sexual abuse, studies have shown that boys are as likely to become perpetrators as to be revictimized in adulthood, while girls are more likely to be revictimized (Stevenson & Gajarsky, 1991). The explanations for these two phenomena are likely to be quite different and based heavily in differential socialization of females and males in our society (see, for example, Levant, 1995; Thorne, 1990). Boys and girls may also react differently to child sexual abuse experiences because they tend to experience different kinds of child sexual abuse.

A child sexual abuse survivor with many risk factors and few protective factors would be seen as highly vulnerable to revictimization, while another survivor with many protective factors and few other risk factors would be expected to be resilient (Masten & Wright, 1998). Revictimization is also considered within an ecological framework, which broadens the study of critical factors beyond the individual child victim and adult perpetrator to the family, community, and culture (Belsky, 1993; Cicchetti & Lynch, 1993; Heise, 1998).

One of the important realizations that comes from using transactional, ecological models is that child abuse is multiply determined (Belsky, 1993; Cicchetti & Lynch, 1993; Masten & Wright, 1998; Wright & Masten, 1997). This has the advantage of identifying many possible interventions for abusive families. However, the disadvantage is that there are no necessary or sufficient conditions whose elimination would prevent child abuse (Belsky, 1993). Instead, there appears to be cumulative risk, that is, the more risk factors in place in a child/family/system, the more likely it will be for abuse to occur (Wright & Masten, 1997). Cicchetti and Rizley (1981) theorized that these risk factors fall into two categories: transient challengers, which can be thought of as acute stressors whose effects will fade over time, and enduring vulnerability factors, which can be thought of as chronic conditions that increase the vulnerability of a child. These latter factors are particularly critical to identify since they may contribute strongly to persisting difficulties for victims of child sexual abuse.

Psychological Sequelae of Sexual Abuse

In a comprehensive review of the literature in this area, Kendall-Tackett and colleagues (1993) reported that children display a wide range of symptoms in response to sexual abuse-including none at all. Some children will never be symptomatic. Others will display different symptoms, with varying severity, over time. Some children's symptoms will improve over time, while other children's symptomology will get worse. The types of symptoms displayed by children range across the entire spectrum of emotional disturbance (see Table 1; Beitchman, Zucker, Hood, daCosta, & Akman, 1991; Kendall -Tackett, Williams, & Finkelhor, 1993). The symptoms are virtually indistinguishable from the symptoms of emotionally disturbed children who were not abused, with two exceptions: children who have been sexually abused display more specific symptoms of post-traumatic stress disorder (PTSD) and more sexualized behavior than other children (Beitchman et al., 1991; Kendall-Tackett et al., 1993). Otherwise, there seems to be little consistency in the occurrence and pattern of symptoms in children who have been abused (Beitchman et al., 1991; Kendall-Tackett et al., 1993).

Table 1   Symptoms Displayed by Sexually Abused Children

Symptoms Displayed by Sexually Abused Children
Aggressive behavior
Anxiety
Fears
Depression
Derealization
Dissociation
Hyperactivity
Isolation
Low self-esteem
Post-traumatic stress disorder
School problems
Self-injurious behavior
Sexualized behavior
Sleep disturbance/nightmares
Somatic complaints
Substance abuse
Suicidality

A number of studies have investigated the relationship between characteristics of sexual abuse and the severity of symptoms. A number of abuse characteristics have been studied, usually with contradictory or inconclusive results. For example, different studies looking at age of onset of abuse have found that: (a) it is not related to severity; (b) younger children display more severe symptoms; and (c) older children display more severe symptoms (Beitchman et al., 1991; Kendall-Tackett et al., 1993). Studies examining the number of perpetrators and the time elapsed since the abuse have found similarly inconclusive evidence (Kendall-Tackett et al., 1993).

Stronger evidence exists for links between other abuse variables and severity of symptoms. Older age at assessment, more frequent abuse, longer lasting abuse, more severe abuse (i.e., penetration), a close relationship to the perpetrator, lack of maternal support, and use of force during the abuse have all been found to predict greater symptomology consistently, but not universally (Beitchman et al., 1991; Kendall-Tackett et al., 1993). There are a number of reasons for inconsistent findings. Abuse itself is defined differently in different studies, and symptom measures vary widely. In a meta-analysis of studies examining these factors, Rind, Tromovitch, and Bauserman (1998) found that force, incest, and in one case a composite measure of abuse characteristics (paternal incest, force, and penetration) were associated with poorer subsequent adjustment. Duration, penetration, and frequency did not moderate outcome. These results need to be viewed cautiously, however, since they were based on a small number of samples in which these factors had been recorded. Also, there are often strong correlations between many of the abuse statistics so that it may be difficult to parcel out main effects, if they exist (Kendall-Tackett et al., 1993). The inconsistency with which composite measures of sexual abuse characteristics predicted adult outcome might also be attributable to the additive nature of composite variables (Rind et al., 1998).

Numerous prior studies comprised of clinical, community, and college student samples have documented the deleterious effects of incest on survivors. Adult survivors of incest often display the same range of symptoms displayed by children in the immediate aftermath of abuse: depression, dissociation, low self-esteem, PTSD, etc. (Briere & Runtz, 1987; Kinzl & Biebl, 1992; Rew, 1989). In addition, adult incest survivors are more likely than adults without abuse histories to develop sexual dysfunctions, eating disorders, Dissociative Identity Disorder, and Borderline Personality Disorder, and to become involved in prostitution (Briere & Runtz, 1987; Goodwin, Cheeves, & Connell, 1990; Kinzl & Biebl, 1992; Rew, 1989). Finally, an increasingly large number of studies have made one fact clear: girls who are sexually abused in childhood are vulnerable to victimization in adulthood at approximately three to four times the rate of girls who were not abused in childhood (Messman & Long, 1996).

Revictimization

Revictimization has become a well-documented phenomenon. One of the earliest studies to document revictimization is Russell's (1986) study of 930 women sampled from the San Francisco phone book (cited in Messman & Long, 1996). Russell found that over 60% of child sexual abuse survivors were raped as adults, compared to 35% of women who were not abused as children, while 27% of prior victims were battered by a partner, compared to 7% of nonvictims (Messman & Long, 1996). In their review of studies of child sexual abuse survivors, Messman and Long (1996) found strong support for the phenomenon of revictimization. Very few studies did not find statistical significance for higher rates of rape or battery in adulthood of child abuse victims than nonvictims. The studies they reviewed found revictimization rates ranging from 16% to 72% and found that women who were revictimized had higher levels of symptomology and psychological distress than other women.

In the only prospective study to date, Gidycz, Coble, Lathan, and Layman (1993) found that child sexual abuse could predict adult sexual assault. College women filled out measures assessing for child sexual assault and emotional distress at the beginning of a quarter. At the end of the quarter, they filled out measures assessing for adult sexual assault during the quarter and repeated the measures of emotional distress. Even over a period as short as three months, childhood sexual assault predicted adult sexual assault. It also predicted distress at the beginning of the study. While it did not directly predict distress at the end of the three months, adult sexual assault did predict distress after three months, so there was an indirect link between childhood sexual assault and distress at the end of the three months. The combination of a prospective design and significant results over such a brief time period demonstrated the power of the revictimization phenomenon.

Revictimization is a poorly understood phenomenon. While the existence of revictimization has been well documented, there is little consensus about the mechanism that put women in danger to be revictimized. In the last decade, several studies have addressed the phenomenon of revictimization from a model-testing perspective. These studies have focused primarily on coping skills, attributions, and risky lifestyles and have had varied results.

In 1990, Ames studied 584 women working at health-care facilities in the Midwest. Ames theorized that child abuse leads to learned helplessness, which in turn leads to risky behaviors and revictimization. Ames found a strong relationship between child abuse and adult revictimization for both physical and sexual abuse. Women who were abused as children were 3.64 times more likely to be victimized in adulthood than women who were not. The women who were revictimized were almost exclusively victims of familial abuse in childhood. Furthermore, women who were not abused in childhood were indistinguishable symptomatically, whether or not they had been abused in adulthood. Ames's model was only partially supported. Adult physical abuse was best predicted by child physical abuse, low self-esteem (one of the correlates of learned helplessness), and likelihood of leaving a bar with a stranger. Adult sexual abuse was predicted by self-blame, low self-esteem, and depression (correlates of learned helplessness) but not by child abuse.

Wyatt, Guthrie, and Notgrass (1992) also examined the role of risky behavior in 248 abused and nonabused African-American and Caucasian women. Wyatt et al. (1992) hypothesized that sexual abuse would be related to frequency of sexual behavior, use of birth control, multiple sexual partners, and unwanted and aborted pregnancies. They found that child sexual abuse victims were 2.4 times more likely to be sexually victimized in adulthood than women who were not child abuse victims. Wyatt et al. (1992) did not find any relationship between the above factors using a definition of abuse that included only rape and attempted rape. However, when they expanded the definition to include noncontact experiences, they did find relationships between child sexual abuse and higher numbers of pregnancies and sexual partners and more brief sexual relationships. This finding is consistent with findings that survivors of sexual abuse engage in higher levels of (risky) sexual activity both in the short- and long-term. Wyatt et al.'s (1992) findings are contradictory to other findings in that they only found significant relationships when they included noncontactual abuse. However, their definition of contactual sexual abuse is not typical, in that it is limited to rape and attempted rape and did not include other unwanted forms of contact.

In Bryant, Gidycz, and Appel's (1997) study of factors differentiating abuse victims who are revictimized from those who are not, sexualization factors also emerged. Women who were revictimized placed a greater emphasis on the role that sex plays in their relationships. In addition, women who were revictimized became sexually active at an earlier age and had a greater number of sexual partners than those women who did not become revictimized.

Two studies have examined the role of coping strategies in recovery from sexual abuse and found inconsistent results. Knowles (1992) examined the relationships between adult rape and degree of child sexual abuse, symptom severity, cognitive attributions, coping strategies, and risky behaviors in a sample of 595 college women. She found a small but significant relationship between childhood and adult sexual assault. She also found a small but significant relationship between degree of child sexual abuse and revictimization. Knowles (1992) did not find any differences between abused, revictimized, and nonabused women in coping strategies or attributions.

Proulx, Koverola, Fedorowicz, and Kral (1995) did find significant differences in current coping strategies used by college women who were sexually abused in childhood, revictimized, and never abused. All women who had been victimized used more escapism than women who had never been victimized. Women who had been revictimized used higher levels of negotiation, instrumental action, and self-blame than women who had never been victimized. Use of coping strategies predicted distress in all three groups, but particularly in the revictimized group; however, there was no direct link between revictimization and distress. Use of escapism was particularly predictive of distress.

Several problems make these data difficult to interpret. First, general recent coping was assessed, not coping specific to the stressor of sexual abuse. Second, since coping was assessed only once, it is not possible to determine causality. These data may only reflect the connection between experiences of significant stress or trauma and an increased use of (all or any) coping mechanisms. Another problem is that Proulx et al. (1995) defined childhood abuse to only include children who were victimized a single time. Incest victims who were abused more than a single time were included in the revictimization group, even if they were only abused by a single perpetrator and only in childhood. Therefore, significant relationships between coping and revictimization might have been hidden by grouping together long-term child abuse victims who both were and were not abused in adulthood.

Mayall and Gold (1995) studied the relationship between different definitions of sexual abuse and revictimization as well as testing a model of lack of parental support; severe sexual abuse; nonexpressive coping strategies; internal, global, and stable cognitive attributions; and not receiving therapy as risk factors for revictimization. Mayall and Gold (1995) found that definitions of abuse that required physical contact were related to revictimization, but noncontactual definitions were not. Their model of revictimization was not supported, but a discriminant analysis found that a model of sexual experience (number of sexual partners and range of sexual experiences); lack of maternal support; global, stable, internal attributions; and child sexual abuse could correctly classify 67% of the subjects.

A few studies have looked at the role of dissociation in revictimization. Whetsell (1990) studied 99 women who were identified by their therapists as survivors of child abuse. She failed to find any predictive ability of abuse characteristics for revictimization, but she did find that abuse by primary caretakers was related to dissociation. Whetsell's (1990) sample was fairly homogenous on abuse characteristics: 60% were abused by primary caretakers; 67% experienced force; 47% had an age of onset before 6 years old; 82% experienced penetration; and 100% were currently in therapy. There may not have been enough variability of abuse characteristics within her sample to be predictive.

Becker-Lausen, Sanders, and Chinsky (1995) found that dissociation mediated revictimization of childhood sexual abuse survivors, but depression did not. In their study, depression differentially predicted difficulties in interpersonal relationships. They took this as support of Kluft's "sitting duck syndrome," which posits that dissociation leaves abuse victims vulnerable through their failing to integrate, learn from, or be able to recognize dangerous cues in the environment or behavior of others (Becker-Lausen et al., 1995).

Overall, the research to date has not provided a clear picture of the causes of revictimization, either in terms of ongoing cumulative environmental risk or with respect to increases in vulnerability resulting from victimization. The evidence to date is fairly consistent in showing that revictimized women engage in more risky sexual behavior and experience higher levels of dissociation. However, the rest of the evidence is less clear. Research on coping strategies and attributions of abuse survivors shows inconsistent and conflicting results. Similarly, there is inconsistent evidence for the role of self-esteem, self-blame, depression, and submissive behaviors in revictimization.

Resilience

Psychologists are very interested in what distinguishes child abuse survivors who are revictimized from those who are not, in other word, those who are resilient. Resilience has been defined as "successful adaptation or development during or following adverse conditions that challenge or threaten adaptive functioning or healthy development" (Masten & Wright, 1998, p. 10).

Resilience is of particular interest because we hope to discover the mechanisms through which adulthood victimization can be avoided. Researchers studying the effects of a wide range of traumatic experiences in children have found both intrapsychic (such as intelligence) and interpersonal (such as supportive relationships in childhood and adulthood) factors as important in fostering resilience (Masten & Wright, 1998).

One study found that women who had been abused in childhood, but not revictimized in adulthood, could not be distinguished from women who had never been abused on any measures of current symptomology (Ames, 1990). This is very promising for children who have been abused, but we need to better understand what has made the difference between those who recover from child abuse and those who are revictimized. Some factors that have been found to foster resilience in traumatized children include: having a close relationship with a parent or an adult outside the family (sometimes a therapist), having protective and supportive parents, being in a good school system or having a good teacher, having a supportive social network, having high self-esteem, having non-self-blaming attributions for the abuse, and having maternal support after disclosure of abuse (Kaufman & Zigler, 1989; Masten & Wright, 1998; Wright & Masten, 1997).

An Interpersonal Multisystems Perspective

The interpersonal theory of Harry Stack Sullivan (1953) focuses on the psychological development of human beings over time and through relationships. According to Sullivan (1953), most key psychological defense mechanisms are not innate, but develop in infancy and childhood through crucial interpersonal relationships; primarily, but not solely, parent-child relationships. Sullivan explains how dysfunctional parenting can have long-term and far-reaching effects on both interpersonal and intrapsychic factors for children. This model can be extremely useful in understanding the processes through which incest victims are shaped by their abuse.

Interpersonal theory suggests that the presence of traumatic emotions leads to the use of dissociative defense mechanisms, which "protect" the individual by blocking from memory the disturbing experiences that rouse the emotions, as well as blocking the experiencing of the emotions themselves. However, this "protection" contributes to long-term difficulties by keeping important experiences from being processed and integrated, which then prevents learning from these experiences and adopting protective behaviors in the future. The presence of dissociative symptoms and disorders among abuse survivors has been well documented and is thought to be crucial in their later experiences (Kluft, 1990; Putnam, 1990).

Sullivan (1953) developed the concept of "uncanny emotions," which encompass shame, guilt, humiliation, and anxiety. These emotions cause intense distress, lower self-esteem, and leave the person who experiences them interpersonally vulnerable. Sullivan's (1953) concept of "uncanny emotions" fits well with Finkelhor and Browne's (1985) widely accepted model of the traumatic emotions associated with child sexual abuse, which are: traumatic sexualization, stigmatization, betrayal, and powerlessness. Traumatic sexualization refers to the process by which a child's beliefs about sexuality are malformed and a tendency to respond to others sexually is inappropriately conditioned. Stigmatization refers to various processes that induce feelings of shame and guilt in the child and foster beliefs in the child's worthlessness. Betrayal refers to the child learning that she cannot depend on others for protection and that significant others are not trustworthy. Powerlessness refers to processes through which the child learns that she is unable to control her environment or protect herself. Each of these factors is believed to be connected to different patterns of subsequent symptomology. Thus, childhood sexual abuse can have pervasive effects on the victim's ability to interact appropriately with others through formation of dangerous defense mechanisms and unhealthy patterns of interpersonal behavior.

One of the central themes of interpersonal theories is that people develop patterns of interacting that tend to elicit reciprocal behavior (Benjamin, 1996). Victims of abuse may have learned to engage in behaviors that they are not able to recognize as reciprocal to abusive behavior, and they may need to have certain types of corrective experiences through supportive relationships in order to do so. The closer the relative who is the perpetrator and the longer the abuse, the more likely the child will be to learn dangerous patterns of behavior and the more difficult it will be to correct those patterns. Children who are not abused for long periods of time or by close relatives are less likely to develop dangerous patterns, especially if they have close and supportive relationships with their parents.

Early explanations of revictimization focused on ideas like "repetition compulsion" or "addiction to trauma" (van der Kolk, 1989). These explanations can lead to victim-blaming, as they posit that the victim seeks out the victimization experiences, even if it is unconscious on her part. Interpersonal theory provides an alternative explanation. From this perspective the abuse survivor does not want, enjoy, or derive anything positive from the victimization experience. Rather, the survivor has maladaptive patterns of interpreting her own experience and interacting with and interpreting the behavior of others. If the survivor were capable of recognizing the dangerousness of potential perpetrators' behavior, she would not elect to stay in the situation. The problem is that, due to self-blame, dissociative defense mechanisms, and lack of knowledge of and experience in healthy relationships, the survivors who are most at risk for revictimization are not capable of recognizing the potential dangerousness of others' behavior and therefore acting to remove themselves from it. It is critical to note that the evocation of reciprocal behaviors is neither conscious nor recognized. The victim does not choose to act in these ways deliberately; they are the only ways she knows, and they have been molded by her abusive family of origin. She does not recognize that these patterns are likely to lead to further abuse.

Benjamin (1996) identified relevant dysfunctional patterns in the families of women with Borderline Personality Disorder, the vast majority of whom were abused in childhood. These included: a chaotic family life, in which abuse is the most common denominator, but many other crises occur (such as alcoholism, marital fighting, financial difficulties, etc.); traumatic abandonment, in which enforced isolation of the child, because the child is "bad," is (often) the context in which the abuse occurs; and attacks against the child's self-definition and happiness. The child is given messages that separation from the family is bad and to be feared because she could not survive on her own. There is a pattern of cumulative and chronic stress, and these multiple problems play key roles in the psychological development of most victims of chronic incest.

Women who are abused as children are likely to experience isolation that is interrupted by abuse and receive messages about incompetence and the need to stay close to the family (Benjamin, 1996; Herman, 1992). The isolation can be both physical and/or psychological (Finkelhor, 1979; Herman, 1992). Families in which abuse occurs often keep to themselves in order to keep the abuse a secret and sometimes because the abuser enforces isolation in order to maintain control (Herman, 1992). On the other hand, these families are enmeshed with one another; there are not appropriate boundaries of roles or of physical space (Finkelhor, 1979; Herman, 1992). Abused children are given messages that they are worthless or worse and are kept away from anybody who might contradict that message (Benjamin, 1996; Briere, 1992). They are raised in an environment in which abuse shapes their perceptions of the world (as dangerous), of others (as demanding complete submission and as only giving "love" with abuse), and of themselves (as deserving of abuse), as well as shaping their patterns of communication and behavior (Benjamin, 1996; Herman, 1992).

Benjamin's (1996) model has three levels: focus on other; focus on self, and introjects, which are messages that have been internalized from important others. Child abuse survivors engage in behaviors in adulthood based not only on the actual behavior of the other person with whom they interact, but also based on their internalized expectations from childhood (the introject). The woman's wishes and fears are significant in shaping her future relationships. She is seeking protection, not just because she has never been protected but because she believes she needs protection - - she is not capable of surviving on her own. She fears being ignored because she has no sense of self; who she is has always been defined by the acts, emotions, and needs of others. These wishes and fears have been shaped by constant messages of her worthlessness and evil nature, which get internalized as self-hate and self-neglect. These conditions lead the woman to a position of submitting herself to the control of another, who would presumably protect her. The woman tries to protect herself by putting trust in a protector. However, her judgment in choosing such a person has been deleteriously influenced by her past abusive experiences.

These concepts tie closely to Herman's (1992) concept of doublethink. According to Herman (1992), the incest victim "must find a way to form primary attachments to caretakers who are either dangerous or, from her perspective, negligent" (p. 101). The way the abuse victim does this is through significant cognitive distortions. The child receives powerful messages from our culture that parents are loving and protective of their children. She is also completely dependent on her parents. In order to reconcile their abusive or negligent behavior with a belief system that says parents are always loving and benevolent, the child convinces herself that she is evil and deserving of punishment, which is why her parents treat her this way. In order not to be overwhelmed by feelings of powerlessness and betrayal, the child stigmatizes herself to justify the situation.

Sullivan's (1953) and Benjamin's (1996) theories, through their focus on the development of dysfunctional patterns of behavior and self-system operations in important relationships, contribute significantly to the understanding of revictimization of child abuse survivors in adult intimate relationships. The above explanations are particular to a certain subset of child abuse victims. The repeated use of the word "pattern" is important; it takes numerous experiences for these types of dangerous patterns to develop (Sullivan, 1953). Women who were only victimized once (or a few times) would be in significantly less danger of developing a self system that relies on dissociation or the dangerous types of distorted communication shaped by child abuse. According to this model, the longer the abuse and the higher the degree of intimacy with the abuser, the more likely a child would be to develop this dangerous combination. Girls who are abused over a period of years by a parent or sibling would be at the highest risk. Indeed, studies that have examined the relationship of the victim to the perpetrator have found that incest victims are more vulnerable to revictimization than women who were abused by nonrelatives (Ames, 1990; Whetsell, 1990).

Implications for Intervention

Research to date has demonstrated that even though abuse survivors are at a higher risk for revictimization, most survivors, in fact, avoid revictimization in adulthood (Messman & Long, 1996; Wyatt et al., 1992). The interpersonal model holds implications for understanding possible mechanisms that might lead to resilience. Even girls who are at the highest level of risk could avoid patterns likely to lead to revictimization if they have other, "corrective" experiences. Sullivan (1953) discussed the importance of the juvenile and pre-adolescent stages in the development of human relationships. If an abused child developed a friendship or a mentoring relationship during those formative years that modeled nonabusive relating and healthy intimacy, that child would be at a much lower risk for revictimization. Also, if the abuse were discovered and stopped and corrective measures aimed at protecting the child and modeling more appropriate relationships were taken by a trusted other, the child would be at less risk. Any experiences that raise the child's self-esteem also foster the development of the self-system and reduce the need for reliance on dissociation as the primary defense mechanism (Kluft, 1990; Putnam, 1990, 1995; Sullivan, 1953).

Studies have found the existence of supportive relationships to mediate distress and dangerous behavior in women who have been abused, both in childhood and adulthood (Masten & Wright, 1998). For example, Egeland, Jacobvitz, and Sroufe (1988) found that women who were abused as children but did not abuse their children differed from women who were abused and committed abuse in that the resilient women were more likely to have a supportive relationship with an adult during childhood, extended psychotherapy, and a supportive, nonabusive partner. Kaslow et al. (1988) found that African-American women who had been abused by a partner were less likely to become suicidal if they had higher levels of perceived social support.

Using this model, there are several clear messages about reducing the long-term costs of childhood sexual abuse. The first is that certain types of childhood sexual experiences are more likely to lead to reliance on harmful dissociative defense mechanisms and the development of dangerous interpersonal patterns. Children who are victims of incest from close relatives over long periods of time are more likely to develop harmful patterns and need interventions specifically aimed at counteracting the interpersonal effects of sexual abuse, as well as the effects of the sexual trauma. The mechanisms that have been proposed suggest that the factors resulting in the initial abuse may subsequently create personal vulnerabilities in the victim that heighten her risk for continued abuse or later revictimization. In particular, some sexually abused girls may develop or learn sexualized behaviors and patterns of interacting that put them at continued risk for abuse. They may fail to learn self-protection skills that reduce the risk of subsequent victimization and may have difficulty assessing trustworthiness in relationships (Herman, 1992; Masten & Wright, 1998; Meiselman, 1990). Change in these critical areas of communication, interpersonal relationships, and self-worth will require the establishment of caring, positive relationships, and this process will take time. There is no single, short-term target for change that will dramatically alter risk for those most vulnerable.

The second message is that other healthy relationships (within the home, school, neighborhood, and community) should mediate the effects of incest. Having high levels of social support or receiving therapy should help survivors develop more appropriate interpersonal relationships that would increase their likelihood of engaging in safer behavior in adulthood. Mental health practitioners need to identify strengths as well as difficulties in the child's life, identifying assets as well as risk factors. Social isolation from neighborhood networks, support groups, and extended family blocks critical access to both emotional and material support during times of stress. Although intrapsychic factors can, and do, play an important role in resilience, in the case of recovery from sexual abuse, it seems clear that a wider range of supportive factors need to be in place for a child to be resilient. These factors encompass the family unit and broader community systems.

Finally, the risk of revictimization among victims of childhood sexual abuse is likely to be particularly high for those children exposed to chronic stressors within their home and community. To the extent that stress within the family is already high (due to poverty, parental conflict, neglect, and physical abuse) and/or compounded by exposure to community violence, the child's risk increases significantly (Masten & Wright, 1998). Under these stressful circumstances children already at risk experience significantly higher levels of poor communication and witness modeling of inappropriate behavior and coping responses. Economic, sociocultural, and interpersonal factors combine to create situations of economic hardship and interpersonal stress that threaten adequate family functioning (Cicchetti & Lynch, 1993). Thus, effective intervention programs must consider not only personal vulnerabilities within the child and interpersonal dynamics within the family, but potentiating factors within the broader community that heighten risk for abuse. In the case of sexual abuse, these factors might include lack of social support, victim-blaming messages from society, lack of serious judicial attention to the problem, and limited access to appropriate therapeutic resources. Attention to these multiple factors, operating at different systemic levels, may significantly enhance our ability to impact long-term developmental outcomes for victims of child sexual abuse.

References

Ames, M.A. (1990) Indiana University. Childhood abuse, learned helplessness and risky lifestyle: A model of revictimization in women. *Dissertation Abstracts International*. Vol 52 (5-B) November 1991, 2764

Becker-Lausen, E., Sanders, B., & Chinsky, J. M. (1995). Mediation of abusive childhood experiences: Depression, dissociation, and negative life outcomes. *American Journal of Orthopsychiatry, 65,* 560-573.

Beitchman, J. H., Zucker, K. J., Hood, J. E., daCosta, G. A., & Akman, D. (1991). A review of the short-term effects of child sexual abuse. *Child Abuse & Neglect, 15,* 537-556.

Belsky, J. (1993). Etiology of child maltreatment: A developmental ecological analysis. *Psychological Bulletin, 114,* 413-434.

Benjamin, L. S. (1996). *Interpersonal diagnosis and treatment of personality disorders* (2nd ed.). New York: Guilford.

Briere, J. (1992). *Child abuse trauma: Theory and treatment of the lasting effects.* Newbury Park, CA: Sage Publications.

Briere, J. N., & Runtz, M. (1987). Post sexual abuse trauma: Data and implications for clinical practice. *Journal of Interpersonal Violence, 2.* 367-379.

Bryant, N. L., Gidycz, C. A., & Appel, M. A. (1997). *Factors differentiating child sexual abuse victims who are revictimized from those who are not revictimized,* Paper presented at the meeting of the Midwest Psychological Association, Chicago, IL.

Cicchetti, D., & Lynch, M. (1993). Toward an ecological transactional model of community violence and child maltreatment: Consequences for children's development. *Psychiatry 56,* 96-118.

Cicchetti, D., & Rizley, R. (198 1). Developmental perspectives on the etiology, intergenerational transmission, and sequelae of child maltreatment. *New Directions for Child Development, 11,* 31-55.

Egeland, B., Jacobvitz, D., & Sroufe, L. A. (1988). Breaking the cycle of abuse. *Child Development, 59,* 1080-1088.

Finkelhor, D. (1979). *Sexually victimized children.* New York: The Free Press.

Finkelhor, D., & Browne, A. (1985). The traumatic impact of child sexual abuse: A conceptualization. *American Journal of Orthopsychiatry. 55,* 530-541.

Goodwin, J. M., Cheeves, K., & Connell, V. (1990). Borderline and other severe symptoms in adult survivors of incestuous abuse. *Psychiatric Annals, 20,* 22-32.

Herman, J. (1992). Child abuse. *Trauma and recovery* (pp. 96-114). New York: Basic Books.

Heise, L. L. (1998). Violence against women: An integrated, ecological framework. *Violence Against Women, 4.* 262-290.

Kaslow, N. J., Thompson, M. P., Meadows, L. A., Jacobs, D., Chance, S., Gibb, B., Bornstein, H., Hollins, L., Rashid, A., & Phillips, K. (1988). Factors that mediate and moderate the link between partner abuse and suicidal behavior in African-American women. *Journal of Consulting and Clinical Psychology. 66,* 533-540.

Kaufman, J., & Zigler, E. (1989). The intergenerational transmission of child abuse. In D.Cicchetti & V. Carlson (Eds.), *Child maltreatment: Theory and research on the causes and consequences of child abuse and neglect* (pp. 129-150). Cambridge: Cambridge University Press.

Kendall-Tackett, K. A., Williams, L. M., & Finkelhor, D. (1993). Impact of sexual abuse on children: A review and synthesis of recent empirical studies. *Psychological Bulletin, 113,* 164-180.

Kinzl, J., & Biebl, W. (1992). Long-term effects of incest: Life events triggering mental disorders in female patients with sexual abuse in childhood. *Child Abuse & Neglect, 16,* 567-573.

Kluft, R. P. (1990). Dissociation and subsequent vulnerability: A preliminary study. *Dissociation,* 3(3), 167-173.

Knowles, K.B. (1992) Auburn University. Sexual Revictimization: A Comparison of single-incident versus recidivistic rape victims on symptom severity, definitions, attributions, coping strategies and precautionary behaviors. *Dissertation Abstracts International.* Vol 53 (8-B) February, 1993, 4376

Levant, R. F. (1995). Male violence against female partners: Roots in male socialization and development. In C. D. Spielberger, 1. G. Sarason, J. M. T. Brebner, E. Greenglass, P. Laungani, & A. M. O'Roark (Eds.), *Stress and emotion: Anxiety. anger, and curiosity* (pp. 91 100). Washington, DC: Taylor & Francis.

Masten, A. S., & Wright, A 0. (1998). Cumulative risk and protection models of child maltreatment. In B. B. R. Rossman & M. S. Rosenberg, *Multiple victimization of children: Conceptual, developmental, research, and treatment* issues (pp. 7-30). Binghamton, NY: Haworth Press, Inc.

Mayall, A., & Gold, S. R. (1995). Definitional issues and mediating variables in the sexual revictimization of women sexually abused as children. *Journal of Interpersonal Violence., 10*(1), 26-42.

Meiselman, K. C. (1990). *Resolving the trauma of incest.* San Francisco: Jossey-Bass Publishers.

Messman, T. L., & Long, P. J. (1996). Child sexual abuse and its relationship to revictimization in adult women: A review. *Clinical Psychology Review, 16,* 397-420.

National Clearinghouse on Child Abuse and Neglect Information. 1998. [On-line] www.calib.com/necanch/pubs/factsheets/whatis.htm

Proulx, J., Koverola, C., Fedorowicz, A., & Kral, M. (1995). Coping strategies as predictors of distress in survivors of single and multiple sexual victimization and nonvictimized controls. *Journal of Applied Social Psychology, 26,* 1464-1483.

Putnam, F. W. (1990). Disturbances of "self' in victims of childhood sexual abuse. In R. P. Kluft (Ed.), *Incest-related syndromes of adult psychopathology* (pp. 113 -131). Washington, DC: American Psychiatric Press, Inc.

Putnam, F. W. (1995). Development of dissociative disorders. In D. Cicchetti & D. J. Cohen (Eds.), *Developmental psychopathology* (pp. 581-608). New York: John Wiley & Sons, Inc.

Rew, L. (1989). Long-term effects of childhood sexual exploitation. *Issues in Mental Health Nursing, 10,* 229-244.

Rind, B., Tromovitch, P., & Bauserman, R. (1998). A meta-analytic examination of assumed properties of child sexual abuse using college samples. *Psychological Bulletin, 124,22-53.*

Russell, D. E. (1986). *The secret trauma: Incest in the lives of girls and women.* New York: Basic Books, Inc.

Stevenson, M. R., & Gajarsky, W. M. (199 1). Unwanted childhood sexual experiences relate to later revictimization and male perpetration. *Journal of Psychology and Human Sexuality*, 4(4), 57-70.

Sullivan, H. S. (1953). *The interpersonal theory of psychiatry.* New York: W. W. Norton.

Thorne, B. (1990). Children and gender: Constructions of difference. In D. Rhode (Ed.), *Theoretical perspectives on sexual difference.* New Haven: Yale University Press.

United States Department of Health and Human Services, Children's Bureau. (I 998a). *Child maltreatment 1996: Reports from the states from the National Child Abuse and Neglect Data System.* Washington, DC: United States Government Printing Office.

United States Department of Health and Human Services, Children's Bureau. (I 998b). *Third national incidence study of child abuse and neglect (NIS-3).* Washington, DC: United States Government Printing Office.

van der Kolk, B. A. (1989). The compulsion to repeat the trauma: Reenactment, revictimization, and masochism. *Treatment of Victims of Sexual Abuse, 12(2),* 389-411.

Whetsell, M.S. (1990) University of Kentucky. The relationship of abuse factors and revictimization to the long-term effects of childhood sexual abuse in women. Dissertation Abstracts International. Vol 51 (10-B), April, 1991, 5047

Wright, M. 0., & Masten, A. S. (1997). Vulnerability and resilience in young children. In J. D. Noshpitz, S. Greenspan, S. Weider, & J. Osofsky (Eds.), *Handbook of child and adolescent psychiatry. Volume one. Infants and preschoolers: Development and syndromes* (pp. 202-224). New York: John Wiley & Sons.

Wyatt, G. E., Guthrie, D., & Notgrass, C. M. (1992). Differential effects of women's child sexual abuse and subsequent sexual revictimization. *Journal of Consulting and Clinical Psychology. 60,* 167-173.

Adversity and its Outcomes: The Measurement of Childhood Trauma

Evvie Becker*

Introduction

Adversity has many faces in the United States. In addition to physical and sexual abuse, childhood trauma takes a variety of forms (Rickel & Becker, 1997). Children in our poorest cities and rural areas suffer a broad range of difficulties. Jonathan Kozol (2000), in his book, *Ordinary Resurrections* (2000), describes children in one such urban neighborhood in the South Bronx:

> All are very poor; statistics tell us that they are the poorest children in New York.
>
> Some know hunger several times a month. Many have respiratory problems.
>
> Most have lost a relative or grown-up friend to AIDS.
>
> Some have previously lived in homeless shelters.
>
> A large number see their fathers only when they visit them in prison.
>
> (p. 4)

These and other traumatic conditions, such as racism and violence-ridden neighborhoods, go hand-in-hand with poverty in the United States. Yet only rarely are they the subject of child protective investigations, and when they are, blame is most likely to be assigned to a parent. Far rarer are serious analyses of the social conditions that created these situations, or of the society that created the social conditions.

A recent report from UNICEF's research center, titled "Child Poverty in Rich Nations" (2000), indicated that, of 29 "rich" nations participating, the same six countries had the worst child poverty rates, regardless of how poverty was measured (i.e., "relative" to the rest of the country's wealth, or "absolute" poverty, based on U.S. poverty guidelines). The United States was one of these six countries. The four countries with the lowest child poverty rates, by both definitions, were Sweden, Denmark, Norway and Finland. The report notes that these four countries have continuously kept in place strong, supportive child and family policies, through good and bad economic times.

In this chapter, the many aspects of trauma and its outcomes are explored. Victimization and exposure to violence are linked to a range of negative outcomes for survivors. A series of research studies are presented, designed to document childhood trauma in the lives of high-risk youth and adults who represent some of the potentially negative consequences (e.g., psychiatric inpatients, high-school drop-outs, incarcerated young men). These studies also demonstrate the validity and usefulness of several measures of childhood trauma and its consequences.

Adversity and Resiliency

A few youth manage to survive and even succeed despite the most devastatingly negative circumstances. In the spring of 1999, six students were awarded *New York Times* scholarships, chosen from 3,000 applicants citywide (Kennedy, 1999). The scholarships provide $12,000 per year for four years, more per year than many of the students' parents' salaries.

All of these students had overcome extreme adversity to succeed. For example, one 18-year-old recipient, who was about to graduate at the top of her class in a magnet school, had done her homework in littered Bronx hallways and stairwells. Her mother died of AIDS, and her drug-addicted father also had AIDS. After her mother died, she often slept on park benches and in hallways:

*The author is a senior analyst at the US Department of Health and Human Services, Office of the Assistant Secretary for Planning and Evaluation. The views expressed herein are those of the author and should not be attributed to the Department.

"I started to grasp the value of the lessons I was learning living on the streets," she said. "I knew after overcoming these obstacles, next to nothing could hold me down" (p. B10). She finished high school in just two years.

Another recipient of the *Times* award graduated with a 90 percent average, after she dropped out for more than 2 years, fighting with her drug-addicted mother for money to feed her younger brothers. She was eventually sent to New York to live with her grandmother. Other winners were from poor and working class families; many families were recent immigrants to the United States. None of the parents had attended college.

While these are inspirational tales illustrating both the extent of hardship encountered and the degree of resiliency required for some youth, caution must be exercised in interpreting the lessons of these stories. First, resiliency is not without its costs for survivors (D'Imperio, Dubow, & Ippolito, 2000), and resilient young people may face negative consequences of childhood trauma at later stages and in other arenas of their lives.

Further, the danger of anecdotal stories, such as these of resilient New York youth, is the impression that <u>anyone</u> can do well in such circumstances, that it is merely a matter of "pulling oneself up by one's bootstraps" (as American folklore would have it) -- what Reich (1987) has termed the "myth of the triumphant individual" (p. 105).

Often we overlook the <u>extraordinary</u> talents of those who do well in the face of such adverse situations, as well as the specific circumstances that may have supported and promoted their resiliency. We then expect or demand that the more ordinary child, regardless of the severity of the trauma, should be able to thrive despite the degree of damage they have suffered.

In fact, research confirms that those most likely to overcome adversity are blessed with greater intelligence, with a problem-solving orientation, and, generally, with at least one caring adult who was there for them somewhere along life's way (Herman, 1992). Recently, the concept of "emotional intelligence" has also begun to show evidence of being a protective factor (Vaillant & Davis, 2000).

The Other Side

For every brilliant, resilient child like these scholarship winners, there are many more children who fall victim to the circumstances and situations to which they are subjected. Poverty, socioeconomic status, and living in a poor neighborhood have each been shown to independently predict lower scores on intelligence tests, as well as decreased school achievement and higher levels of socioemotional problems, even when family and parental factors are controlled (McLoyd, 1998). Long-standing, chronic poverty has greater negative effects on intelligence scores, on school achievement, and on socioemotional functioning than does intermittent or temporary poverty. In addition, the primary mediators of the relationship between poverty and children's socioemotional functioning have been found to be harsh, inconsistent parenting and higher levels of exposure to both acute and chronic stressors.

All too often, such extreme adversity overwhelms the child's or youth's ability to cope and spills out as violence into the community, touching the lives of others. A young 6-year-old shoots a 6-year-old classmate; the child found the gun where he was living -- with an uncle -- in what might be termed "kinship care." The home was, in fact, a crack house, where the child did not even have a bed.

Such violence is never an isolated incident that comes unpredictably out of nowhere -- although at first it may seem so (Rickel & Becker, 1997). After such tragedies, we often hear television newscasters questioning community members and experts, asking anxiously, "who is to blame"? But such occurrences of child or youth violence generally follow months or years of neglect and denial on the part of all the adults around the child, at all levels of society and across all systems. Until we understand and accept that we all bear responsibility, as a society, for these tragic outcomes, we will continue to look for a specific person to take the fall, someone to bear the brunt of our frustration and anger, someone we can lock up.

Below is an outline of some of what is known about the transmission of violence.

A Violent Society

By now it is fairly well known that the United States has the highest homicide rate of any industrialized country, far above the country with the next highest rate (American Psychological Association, 1993; Rickel & Becker, 1997).

Exposure to Violence and Post-traumatic Stress

In a study of 96 Miami low-income, multiethnic youth in alternative high schools, Berman, Kurtines, Silverman, and Serafini (1996) found that more than 93 percent had witnessed at least one violent event, 44 percent were victims of at least one of these events, and 41.6 percent had witnessed a murder. Post-traumatic stress disorder (PTSD) symptoms were common: subjects showed an average of 10 symptoms; 34.5 percent met criteria for PTSD diagnosis; 48.8 percent were symptomatic only; and another 16.7 percent were without symptoms. Similar findings have been reported for low-income, African American youth aged 7 to 18: both victimization and witnessing violence were significantly related to PTSD symptoms (Fitzpatrick and Boldizar, 1993).

Trauma and the Development of Violent Behavior

A decade ago, Widom (1989a; 1989b) documented the relationship between a history of child maltreatment and criminal activity in youth or adulthood, finding a strong relationship between physical abuse or neglect and later violent behavior. Other studies have reported a relationship between a history of sexual abuse and sexual offending by youth; however, neglect, physical abuse, and witnessing family violence were all more prevalent among adolescent sexual offenders than was sexual victimization (Kaplan, Becker, & Cunningham-Rathner, 1989; Pierce & Pierce, 1987).

While the link is certainly not inevitable between maltreatment and later violent behavior, it does appear that the greater the violence and victimization, the more likely a child will engage in violent or abusive behavior (American Psychological Association, 1996).

Studies have also continued to document relationships among violence exposure, victimization and delinquency (Rickel & Becker-Lausen, 1995). For example, one study of 50 abused women and 80 of their children, aged 11-12 years, revealed that among youth exposed to family violence, the earlier the abuse began in the lives of the children, the more frequent and severe was the youth's own participation in offending behavior (Kruttschnitt and Dornfeld, 1993).

One study of 536 inner-city children in grades 2 to 8, witnessing a shooting or stabbing and being exposed to family fighting were both linked to involvement in fighting (Bell & Jenkins, 1991; 1993). Among 1,035 youth aged 10-19, perpetrators of violence were more likely to have been witnesses and victims of violence (Bell & Jenkins, 1994). Common among these youth were post-traumatic stress disorder (PTSD) symptoms, lowered self-esteem, decline in cognitive performance, anger, despair and psychic numbing related to exposure to chronic and repeated trauma. The authors note that these youth will be unlikely to benefit from interventions unless and until trauma symptoms are addressed.

Recent studies have linked adolescent PTSD with substance use, finding interactional effects and severe psychological impairment for youth with these co-occurring disorders (Giaconia, et al., 2000). Others have identified factors that mediate the exposure to community violence and the development of PTSD symptoms, such as family conflict and neighborhood safety (Overstreet & Braun, 2000).

The latter study supports earlier research with 225 African American youth, aged 11-19 (44 percent male), living in or near public housing projects (DuRant, Cadenhead, Pendergrast, Slavens, and Linder, 1994; DuRant, Pendergrast, and Cadenhead, 1994). DuRant and colleagues found the strongest results for relationships among the youth's self-reported use of violence and 1) exposure to violence (particularly victimization); 2) family conflict; and 3) severity of punishment or discipline.

Recently, Dulmus and Wodarski (2000) expanded the findings on exposure to violence by examining 30 6-to-12-year-old African-American children whose parents had been victimized by community violence, comparing them to 30 similar children, living in the same community, whose parents had not been victimized. Children of victimized parents were significantly more distressed. Although the children's prior exposure to community violence accounted for 22.7 to 44.8 percent of their symptoms, the victimization of their parents added substantially to the explanation, accounting for another 11.5 to 13.7 percent of the variance.

Family Disruption, Delinquency and Drug Use
Data from a national study of 4,000 youth (Thornberry, Smith, Rivera, Huizinga, & Stouthamer-Loeber, 1999) have demonstrated that, in urban samples, where populations were poor and ethnically diverse, youth experience a high number of family transitions and at earlier ages than youth in other settings. In this sample of poor, urban youth, 67 percent reported at least one family transition before age 15, indicating a very high level of instability. In general, Thornberry, et al, found a consistent, positive relationship between the number of family transitions and increased levels of delinquency and drug use.

Other studies have continued to document the intergenerational nature of violence. In interviews with 439 injection drug users, Clarke, Stein, Sobota, Marisi, and Hanna (1999) found 51 percent of the women and 31 percent of the men reported a history of childhood physical or sexual abuse. Those who reported a history of abuse were more likely to admit to having abused or assaulted others; 28 percent of abuse survivors reported they had victimized others, compared to 10 percent of those who did not report abuse in their own childhood.

Further Exploration of Childhood Trauma and Its Outcomes

A series of research studies have supported the premise that sequelae of childhood trauma appear across domains of functioning, resulting in a variety of negative outcomes and behaviors among survivors (Becker, Rankin, & Rickel, 1998; Becker-Lausen, Sanders & Chinsky, 1995). For example, for adults abused as children, disturbances have been noted in their sense of trust, esteem, safety, intimacy, and control (Becker-Lausen & Mallon-Kraft, 1997; Briere, 1992; Pearlman & Saakvitne, 1995).

Earlier work with college students and with pregnant teens suggested relationships among childhood trauma, psychopathology, and adolescent problem behavior, as shown in Figure 1. (Becker-Lausen, Sanders, & Chinsky, 1995; Becker-Lausen and Rickel, 1995; Becker, Rankin, & Rickel, 1998).

From that starting point, we set out to measure and examine the effects of childhood trauma on the functioning of individuals in a variety of circumstances, particularly those already experiencing negative outcomes, such as dropping out of high school, psychiatric hospitalization, or serving time in jail.

Study 1 -- Mothers in a Clinical Setting
The first study (Prinos, Becker-Lausen, & Rickel, 1997; Prinos, 1996) assessed 53 low-income mothers and their children in a community child guidance center (31 mother-son dyads; 22 mother-daughter dyads). The mothers' ages ranged from 28 to 54, with a median of 35. Two-thirds of the mothers reported their ethnicity: 53 percent were white, 6 percent were black, and 7 percent were Hispanic. The children's ages ranged from 9.5 to 15 years, with the boys' median age at 12 and the girls' median age at 13. About 21 percent of these children were born when their mothers were in their teens, and 38 percent of the mothers reported an intact relationship with the child's father.

Measures

- The <u>Child Abuse and Trauma</u> (CAT) scale (Sanders & Becker-Lausen, 1995), a 38-item self-report measure of childhood maltreatment, includes factor-analyzed subscales for Sexual Abuse (SA), Punishment (PUN), and Neglect/Negative Home Environment (NEG). The CAT has a Cronbach's alpha of .9, and a test-retest reliability of .89.
- The <u>Trauma Symptom Inventory</u> (TSI; Briere, 1996), a self-report checklist, consists of 10 subscales measuring trauma-related symptomatology in adults (e.g., intrusive experiences, dissociation, depression).
- The <u>Trauma Symptom Checklist for Children</u> (TSCC; Briere, 1996), a self-report inventory for children aged 8-15, contains six subscales that measure anxiety, depression, post-traumatic stress disorder (PTSD) symptoms, dissociation, anger, and sexual concerns.
- Two measures of parenting styles were used, including the Rickel Modified Child-Rearing Practices Report (R-CRPR; Rickel & Biasetti, 1982), and the Schwarz/Zuroff Love Inconsistency Scale (Schwarz, J.C., & Zuroff, D., 1994).

Results

Clinic mothers in this study scored significantly higher on the Child Abuse and Trauma (CAT) scale than either college students or inpatient adolescents (Sanders & Becker-Lausen, 1995), as shown in Table 1. In addition, for the mothers, the CAT was significantly correlated with all of the Trauma Symptom Inventory (TSI) subscales, with the exception of sexual concerns, sexual dysfunction, and tension reduction subscales.

One of the most important findings emerged not from the study's predictions, but from the demographic data on the mothers. Mothers were asked questions about their history of child protective services (CPS) involvement. Mothers who said they had been substantiated for abuse and neglect, compared to mothers who reported no CPS involvement, reported significantly higher levels of:

- maltreatment in their own childhoods, on the CAT and each of its subscales; and
- trauma symptoms, as measured by the TSI.

In addition, substantiated mothers were rated by their children as less consistently affectionate than those who reported no CPS involvement. On the other hand, children's symptoms, as measured by the TSCC, did not reveal any differences when analyzed by their mother's reported history of CPS involvement.

Table 1. <u>Comparison of Mean Scores on CAT Scale</u>

AUTHORS	SAMPLE	TOTAL CAT	NEG (Subscales)	PUN	SA
Sanders & Becker-Lausen (1995)	MPD/DID patients	2.70 (.84)			
Prinos, Becker-Lausen, & Rickel (1996)	Clinic Mothers	1.87 (.64)	1.70 (.99)	1.82 (.81)	.39 (.66)
Matthews, K.E., Becker, E., & Laviage (1999)	Violent Offenders	1.67	1.60	2.51	.60
Price, Rankin, Becker, & Rickel (1998)	Adolescent Inpatients	1.56 (.87)	1.73 (.93)	1.72 (.85)	1.00 (1.20)
Laviage, Becker, & Britner (1999)	Incarcerated Men	1.47 (.58)	1.38 (.85)	2.40 (.51)	.45 (.51)
Sanders & Giolas (1991)	Adolescent Inpatients	1.40			
Ganter, Becker, & Schmidt (1999)	College Students from Divorced Families Only	.98 (.46)	1.23 (.72)	1.36 . (.58)	12 (.24)
Rankin, Price, & Becker (1998)	College Students	.94 (.58)	1.07 (.73)	1.36 (.70)	.20 (.43)
Sanders & Becker-Lausen (1995; data collected 1990-91)	College Students	.73 (.41)	.80 (.59)	1.16 (.53)	.11 (.29)
Ganter, Becker, & Schmidt (1999)	College Students from Intact Families Only	.72 (.44)	.69 (.59)	1.27 (.63)	.08 (.21)

(Subscales reported where available.)

Studies 2 and 3 -- College Students and Inpatient Adolescents

Two studies (Price, Rankin, Becker, & Rickel, 1998; Rankin, Price & Becker, 1998) specifically tested the assumptions of the model shown in Figure 1.

Figure 1. <u>**Model of Child Maltreatment and High-Risk Sexual Behavior**</u>

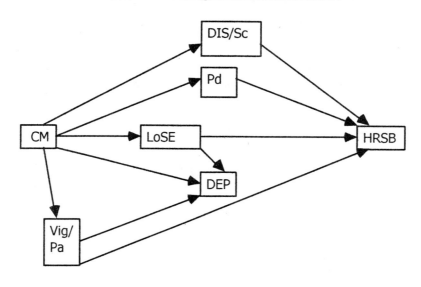

CM = Child Maltreatment   Pd = Psychopathic scale
DEP = Depression   Vig/Pa = Vigilance/Paranoia scale
LoSE = Low Self-Esteem   HRSB = High-Risk Sexual Behavior
DIS/Sc = Dissociation/Schizophrenia scale

(Modified from Becker-Lausen & Rickel, 1995)

Subjects were:

- 30 adolescents in a local psychiatric facility (20 girls; 10 boys), aged 12-17
- 102 college students (66 women; 36 men)

Measures used included:

- Child Abuse and Trauma (CAT) scale (Sanders & Becker-Lausen, 1995), described above in Study 1;
- Minnesota Multiphasic Personality Inventory (MMPI-2 and MMPI-A), a standardized personality test, the adult and adolescent versions (Greene, 1991);
- Dissociative Experiences Scale (DES; Bernstein & Putnam, 1986), a 28-item measure of dissociation.

These studies provided some initial support for the specific predictions of the model.

College Students

    For college students, significant relationships were found between the MMPI-2 Scale 4 (Psychopathic Deviate) and the CAT and each of its subscales. After a Bonferroni correction for multiple correlations, Scale 4 of the MMPI-2 remained correlated with the overall CAT; but among the subscales, only the Neglect/Negative Home Environment (NEG) was still significant. Elevated scores on Scale 4 have been associated with poor judgment and engaging in risky behavior; individuals with these elevations may also be antisocial (Graham, 1993).

    Likewise, the MMPI-2 Scale 8 (Schizophrenia) was correlated with the CAT and two of its subscales (NEG; Punishment), and also with the DES. After the Bonferroni correction, only the DES and the NEG subscale of the CAT were still correlated with Scale 8. Graham (1993) describes Scale 8 elevations as indicative of confusion, disorientation, and feelings of detachment. The link here to scores on a measure of dissociation lends support to our suggestion that these Scale 8 characteristics are consistent with dissociation.

After the Bonferroni correction, the DES also remained inversely correlated with Scale K of the MMPI-2 (indicating lower levels of defensiveness associated with higher levels of dissociation), and correlated with Scale 9 (Social Introversion).

Inpatient Youth

For inpatient youth, significant relationships were found among the MMPI-A Scale 5 (Male/Female), the CAT and its NEG subscale. The MMPI-A Scale 6 (Paranoia) was correlated with the DES; and the MMPI-A scale L with the Punishment subscale of the CAT. In addition, the CAT and its NEG and Punishment subscales were correlated with the number of foster homes a youth had experienced, providing construct validity for the CAT.

The adolescent study was particularly hampered by the small sample size. For the associations among the MMPI-A Scale 4, the CAT and all its subscales, and the DES, the Pearson R's were .3 or higher; yet the CAT and the NEG Subscale only approached significance ($p<.10$) with this sample. Likewise, the MMPI-A Scale 8 and the Sexual Abuse subscale were correlated at .368, and approached significance ($p<.10$).

In addition, we found that the average number of out-of-home placements for these youth was 6.5, indicating considerable disruption in their family situation. As in the study by Thornberry, et al (1999), described earlier, the high rate of family disruption in our study was associated with negative outcomes for these youth. In fact, as with the link to delinquency in the Thornberry, et al, study, some of the youth in our study reported at least one placement in a state juvenile detention facility. Juvenile detention placement was correlated with Scale 4 of the MMPI-A, as would be expected. On the other hand, juvenile detention placement was also significantly correlated ($r=.537$; $p < .01$) with the youth's number of psychiatric hospitalizations, as well as with their residential placements.

Our data suggest these adolescents often bounce from one system to another (e.g., psychiatric hospital to group home to juvenile detention), with no one system fully capable of providing adequate resources or interventions that could change the course of the young person's life.

Study 4: Trauma and Disrupted Beliefs -- High School Students

In a subsequent study (Laviage, Becker, & Cillessen, 1998), we again examined the psychological symptoms of trauma, using the TSCC (Briere, 1996). We also began to look at disrupted beliefs associated with traumatic experiences (Pearlman & Saakvitne, 1995).

Based on their studies of trauma survivors, Pearlman and her colleagues (McCann & Pearlman, 1990; Pearlman & MacIan, 1995) developed a theory of trauma and its outcomes that melds cognitive-behavioral and psychodynamic perspectives with a constructivist explanation for the difficulties survivors often encounter long after the traumatic experience has ended. Constructivist self-development theory (CSDT; Pearlman & Saakvitne, 1995) holds that trauma affects the internal self-structure in specific ways, and that the survivor's beliefs about his or her self and others are disrupted in predictable ways as a result of the traumatic experience. The particular beliefs disrupted by trauma are those related to trust, intimacy, safety, control and esteem, with regard to self and to others (e.g., self-esteem; other-esteem).

In study 4, trauma symptoms and disrupted beliefs were examined among high school students and dropouts from a large suburban high school (Laviage, Becker & Cillessen, 1998).

Subjects

The study involved three groups of students:
1. Control group: 40 randomly chosen students from the junior class at the high school (22 girls, 18 boys; mean age=16.5 years);

2. High-risk group: 25 students currently enrolled in alternative programs because of attendance and behavior problems (10 girls, 15 boys; mean age=17.0 years);
3. Drop-out group: 25 students who had dropped out of the high school within the past two years (12 girls, 13 boys; mean age=17.6 years).

The total sample involved 44 girls and 46 boys, with a mean age of 16.9 years. While the student population at the high school is 73 percent Caucasian, 15.6 percent African-American, 7.9 percent Hispanic, and 3.3 percent Asian; the study sample was 90 percent Caucasian, 8.9 percent African-American, and 1.1 percent Asian. In fact, there were slightly more white students in the at-risk and dropout groups than in the control group; however, there were no significant differences in ethnic composition by group within the study sample.

Measures

- Measures used included the <u>Trauma Symptom Checklist for Children - Alternate Version</u> (TSCC-A; Briere, 1996). The alternate version of the full TSCC (described above) does not include the subscale made up of items related to sexual concerns. It was designed to be used in settings where such questions might raise objections. In this study, the school board did object to the use of the sexual concerns subscale items, and so the alternative version was employed.

- The Traumatic Stress Institute (TSI) Belief Scale - Adolescent Version was developed from the TSI Belief Scale (Pearlman, 1996), adult version. An 80-item, self-report questionnaire, the Belief Scale assesses disruptions of the five cognitive schemas posited by CSDT: safety, trust, esteem, intimacy, and control. Each of these constructs is measured as related to beliefs about "self" and "other," yielding two scores for each of the five belief subscales. The Belief Scale has been shown to discriminate between clinical and nonclinical samples (McCann & Pearlman, 1990), and between sexual abuse survivors and survivors of other trauma (Mas, 1992).

In consultation with Pearlman, the wording of items was altered slightly for the adolescent version. For example, "I generally feel safe from danger" was changed to "I feel safe." In this study, Cronbach's alpha for the adolescent version was .95.

Results

Both the high-risk and dropout teens reported significantly more trauma symptoms and higher level of disrupted beliefs associated with trauma than their control group peers. The latter two groups scored higher than controls on measures of symptomatology, including depression, dissociation, posttraumatic stress, and anger. They also showed significantly more disrupted beliefs than controls, including problematic beliefs regarding self-esteem, esteem for others, self-control, control by others, safety with others, trust of others, and intimacy with others.

Gender differences were found as well: across all groups, girls indicated more anxiety and depression and more problems with self-safety, self-trust, control by others, and intimacy with others than their male peers.

Study 5: Incarcerated Young Men

The final study reviewed here documents trauma symptoms and negative life outcomes in a sample of incarcerated young men (Laviage, Becker, & Britner, 1999). We collected data on 169 incarcerated men aged 18-25, in a large, urban correctional facility in the Northeastern United States.

As in most correctional settings, the subjects were predominantly men of color: 37 percent were African-American, 34 percent were Hispanic, 21 percent Caucasian, 4 percent Asian, and 2.4 percent were of other ethnic backgrounds.

Less than half of these young men (about 47 percent) had a high school diploma, a GED or any higher levels of education. Half (50.9 percent) were reared in a mother-only household, and only 26 percent were reared by both parents. By contrast, our studies of college students in the same state and of similar ages indicated from 76 to 79 percent of them were reared by both biological parents (Ganter, Becker, & Schmidt, 1999; Mallon-Kraft, 1997).

About half of these young men had been arrested for the first or second time; the other half had been arrested from three to twelve times (11.2 percent had five or more arrests). Just 21.9 percent were incarcerated for violent crimes, compared to 78.1 percent who were in jail for nonviolent crimes.

More than half of these men had never received any mental health services, although 16.6 percent had taken or were taking psychotropic drugs. Many inmates were arrested for drug-related offenses, but just 22.5 percent had received any treatment for substance abuse.

Table 2. Violent and Repeat Offenders in a Jail Population

CATEGORY	N	PERCENT OF TOTAL SAMPLE
Current Incarceration		
Violent Offense	37	21.9%
Nonviolent Offense	132	78.1%
Prior Incarcerations		
Violent Offense	28	16.6%
Nonviolent Offense	65	38.5%
Violence: Current or Prior Offense		
Ever Violent	56	33.1%
Never Violent	113	66.9%
Repeat Offenders (Violent and Nonviolent)		
Repeaters	93	55.0%
First Offenders	76	45.0%

COMBINED CATEGORIES	N	PERCENTAGES BY CATEGORY	
(No significant size differences by category)		VIOLENCE/ NO VIOLENCE	REPEAT/ FIRST TIME
Repeat Offenders:			
Ever Violent Repeaters	35	63% of Violent	38% of Repeat
Never Violent Repeaters	58	51% of Nonviolent	62% of Repeat
First-Time Offenders			
First-time, Violent Offense	21	38% of Violent	28% of First
First-time, Nonviolent Offense	55	49% of Nonviolent	72% of First

In this study, as in the studies presented above, the following measures were administered (all are described above):

- The Child Abuse and Trauma (CAT) scale (Sanders & Becker-Lausen, 1995)
- The Trauma Symptom Inventory (TSI; Briere, 1996)
- The TSI Belief Scale (Pearlman, 1996)

Results

Inmates reported levels of childhood maltreatment, as measured by the CAT scale (mean = 1.47), that were nearly double those of college students in the same state and of similar ages (see Table 1). The inmates' CAT scores were similar to those of adolescent psychiatric inpatients, but were somewhat lower than those of mothers in a low-income clinic setting.

On the TSI Belief Scale, inmates scored significantly higher on all subscales for disrupted beliefs than did college students, with the exception of Self-Esteem, where they actually scored significantly lower than college students, indicating the inmates reported higher levels of self-regard. Subscale scores for inmates' Self-Intimacy and for inmates' sense of Other-Control were significantly higher than those of psychiatric outpatients, but significantly lower than scores of chronic mental patients.

On Other-Esteem and on Other-Safety, inmates' scores were significantly higher than those of outpatients, but did not differ significantly from scores of chronic mental patients. In addition, inmates' scores on Other-Trust were significantly higher than the scores of chronic mental patients, indicating they are the least trusting of any population sampled. In general, the subscale findings and specifically, the latter finding regarding trust of others, provide evidence of construct validity for the TSI Believe Scale.

Finally, on the Trauma Symptom Inventory, incarcerated men scored higher than normative samples of men aged 18 to 54.

Comparing this group to the population of hospitalized adolescents (Price, et al, 1998), described above, we note that this sample of inmates may represent the future for some of the youth in the Price, et al study. The endpoint for a childhood of trauma and disrupted family life can already be seen in the multiple placements in adolescence, which for the same youth sometimes included a mix of foster homes, psychiatric settings, group homes, and juvenile justice facilities.

Referral for Mental Health Services

In the correctional institution studied, inmates were referred for mental health services only if they reported a prior history of treatment or were taking psychotropic drugs. Yet, consistent with our predictions, men referred to mental health services showed no significant differences in trauma histories, symptoms or disrupted beliefs when compared to those not referred to mental health.

Although we had not included it in our predictions, we also found, consistent with other studies, that the only other predictor of mental health services referrals (besides a history of services) was ethnicity: 44.4 percent of Caucasian inmates were referred, nearly double the 22.4 percent of African-Americans who were referred for services; while just 17.2 percent of Hispanic inmates were sent for service. Given the requirement of a history of services, these findings are no doubt confounded by cultural issues that affect who seeks mental health services, in addition to issues of access to such services in our poorest communities.

First-time and Violent Offenders

Further analyses of the data were undertaken to explore differences between men incarcerated for violent versus nonviolent offenses, and for first time versus repeat offenses (Matthews, Becker, & Laviage, 1999). For these analyses, we used only the CAT scale and the TSI Belief Scale, where we expected to see the biggest differences between these groups.

As mentioned above, 78.1 percent of the sample were currently incarcerated for a nonviolent offense; 21.9 percent were in jail for a violent offense. When prior incarcerations were included, 33.1 percent of the men had served time for a violent offense; two-thirds had not. For repeat offenses, 55 percent were serving time for at least the second time; 45 percent were first-time offenders. Table 2 shows the breakdown when these groups are combined; there were no significant differences by group.

No interaction effects were found for violent/nonviolent offenders by repeat/first-time offenders for the CAT and the TSI Belief Scale or for any of the subscales for either measure. However, there were main effects for Violence and for Repeat Offending for the CAT mean and for the total score on the TSI Belief Scale. For the subscales of the CAT and the Belief Scale, there was a main effect for Violence, but not for Repeat offending.

These findings suggest critical points for intervention when men first enter the criminal justice system. Violent offenders, who are likely to have the most severe trauma histories and the most disrupted beliefs, should be assessed and referred to the best intervention programs available. However, we need further studies of repeat offenders not incarcerated for violence, as they also appear to have more traumatic histories than other offenders. These men may, in fact, represent the link between substance abuse and traumatic experiences, mentioned earlier in this chapter.

Summary and Conclusions

Cohen (1998) calculated "The Monetary Value of Saving a High-Risk Youth" by figuring the costs to society of career criminal behavior, drug use, and high-school dropouts, discounted for duplication among these categories (i.e., drug user who commits crimes). He concluded the value of saving such a youth is $1.7 to $2.3 million. He noted that even if we disregard the cost of non-monetary losses (such as pain and suffering or quality of life), one youth saved still results in a savings of $1.2 to $1.5 million in "tangible benefits" (p. 27).

The research presented above documents the incidence and significance of trauma and its symptoms in a range of populations, including inpatient adolescent psychiatric patients, high school dropouts, college students, and young men in jail. The levels of trauma and the symptoms and beliefs associated with it, including dissociation, depression, and distrust of others, remind us of the many pathways by which traumatic histories lead to negative life outcomes.

The growing body of literature described here provides data useful for the design of programs to prevent a variety of negative outcomes (Rickel & Becker, 1997). However, unless and until issues of poverty, racism, and inequality are addressed, children will continue to be subjected to multiple and cumulative forms of trauma.

The UNICEF report on child poverty in wealthy nations (2000) cited at the beginning of this chapter, states:

> The persistence of child poverty in rich countries undermines both equality of opportunity and commonality of values. It therefore confronts the industrialized world with a test both of its ideals and of its capacity to resolve many of its most intractable social problems. (Frontispiece)

On the other hand, there is evidence we may be moving toward some consensus among policy makers of the causes and consequences of violence. In a bipartisan report on youth violence from the 106th Congress, issued in November 1999, members concluded:

> Although there is no single cause for youth violence, the most common factor is family dysfunction. Domestic violence and conflict/tension within the family are often associated with troubled youth. Abuse, neglect and hostility are prevalent in cases of youth violence. Exposure to violence leads to acceptance of violence as a means to solve problems. Research demonstrates that this develops into the cycle of violence. (p. 8)

When as a society we understand that poverty, deprivation, and racial discrimination affect the levels of violence and trauma in the lives of children, and in turn, affect the outcome for these children, then there may truly be -- to borrow from the title of the American Psychological Association's (Eron, Gentry, & Schlegal, 1994) report on youth violence -- "reason to hope."

References

American Psychological Association. (1996). *Violence and the family*. Report of the APA Presidential Task Force on Violence and the Family. Washington, DC:.

American Psychological Association Commission on Violence and Youth (1993). *Violence and youth: Psychology's response*. Washington, DC: American Psychological Association.

Becker, E., Rankin, E., & Rickel, A.U. (1998). *High-risk sexual behavior: Interventions with vulnerable populations*. New York: Plenum Press.

Becker-Lausen, E., & Rickel, A.U. (1995). Integrating research on child abuse and teen pregnancy: Identifying mediator variables for pregnancy outcome. *Journal of Primary Prevention, 16*, 39-53.

Becker-Lausen, E., Sanders, B., and Chinsky, J.M. (1995). The mediation of abusive childhood experiences: Depression, dissociation, and negative life outcomes. *American Journal of Orthopsychiatry, 65,* 560-573.

Becker-Lausen, E., and Mallon-Kraft, S. (1997). Pandemic outcomes: The intimacy variable. In G. Kaufman Kantor and J. Jasinski (Eds.), *Out of the darkness: Contemporary research perspectives on family violence* (pp. 49-57). Thousand Oaks, CA: Sage.

Bell, C.C., & Jenkins, E.J. (1991). Traumatic stress and children. *Journal of Health Care for the Poor and Underserved, 2*, 175-185.

Bell, C.C., & Jenkins, E.J. (1993). Community violence and children on Chicago's southside. *Psychiatry Interpersonal and Biological Processes, 56* (1), 46-54.

Bell, C.C., & Jenkins, E.J. (1994). Effects of child abuse and race. *Journal of the National Medical Association, 86*, 165, 232.

Berman, S.L., Kurtines, W.M., Silverman, W.K., & Serafini, L.T. (1996). The impact of exposure to crime and violence on urban youth. *American Journal of Orthopsychiatry, 66*, 329-336.

Bernstein, E.M., & Putnam, F.W. (1986). Development, reliability, and validity of a dissociation scale. *Journal of Nervous and Mental Disease, 174*, 727-735.

Bipartisan Working Group on Youth Violence. (1999). *Final report: 106th Congress*. Washington, DC: U.S. House of Representatives. (http://www.house.gov/frost/youthviol.htm)

Briere, J.N. (1992). *Child abuse trauma: Theory and treatment of lasting effects*. Newbury Park, CA: Sage.

Briere, J.N. (1996). *Trauma symptom inventory professional manual*. Odessa, FL: Psychological Assessment Resources.

Clarke, J., Stein, M.D., Sobota, M., Marisi, M., & Hanna, L. (1999). Victims as victimizers: Physical aggression by persons with a history of childhood abuse. *Archives of Internal Medicine, 159*, 1920-1924.

Cohen, M.A. (1998). The monetary value of saving a high-risk youth. *Journal of Quantitative Criminology, 14* (1), 5-33.

D'Imperio, R.L., Dubow, E.F., & Ippolito, M.F. (2000). Resilient and stress-affected adolescents in an urban setting. *Journal of Clinical Child Psychology, 29*, 129-142.

Dulmus, C.N., & Wodarski, J.S. (2000). Trauma-related symptomatology among children of parents victimized by urban community violence. *American Journal of Orthopsychiatry, 70*, 272-277.

DuRant, R.H., Cadenhead, C., Pendergrast, R.A., Slavens, G., & Linder, C.W. (1994). Factors associated with the use of violence among urban Black adolescents. *American Journal of Public Health, 84*, 612-617.

DuRant, R.H., Pendergrast, R.A., & Cadenhead, C. (1994). Exposure to violence and victimization and fighting behavior by urban Black adolescents. *Journal of Adolescent Health, 15*, 311-318.

Eron, L.D., Gentry, J.H., & Schlegel, P. (1994). *Reason to hope: A psychosocial perspective on violence and youth*. Washington, DC: American Psychological Association.

Fitzpatrick, K.M., & Boldizar, J.P. (1993). The prevalence and consequences of exposure to violence among African American youth. *Journal of the American Academy of Child and Adolescent Psychiatry, 32*, 424-430.

Ganter, J., Becker, E, & Schmidt, C. (1999, June). *College students at the turn of the century: Divorce, childhood trauma, and interpersonal outcomes.* Poster presentation, 7th Biennial Conference on Community Research and Action (Division 27, American Psychological Association), New Haven, CT.

Giaconia, R.M., Reinherz, H.Z., Hauf, A.C., Paradis, A.D., Wasserman, M.S., & Langhammer, D.M. (2000). Comorbidity of substance use and post-traumatic stress disorders in a community sample of adolescents. *American Journal of Orthopsychiatry, 70*, 253-262.

Graham, J. (1993). *MMPI-2: Assessing personality and psychopathology* (2nd Edition). New York: Oxford.

Greene, J.L. (1991). *The MMPI-2/MMPI: An interpretive manual.* Odessa, FL: Psychological Assessment Resources.

Herman, J. (1992). *Trauma and recovery.* New York: Basic Books.

Kaplan, M.S., Becker, J.V., & Cunningham-Rathner, J. (1988). Characteristics of parents of adolescent incest perpetrators: Preliminary findings. *Journal of Family Violence, 3*, 183-191.

Kennedy, R. (1999, March 3). Six whose path to excellence was on the mean streets of adversity. *New York Times*, pp. B1, B10.

Kozol, J. (2000). *Ordinary resurrections: Children in the years of hope.* New York: Crown Publishers.

Kruttschnitt, C., & Dornfeld, M. (1993). Exposure to family violence: A partial explanation for initial and subsequent levels of delinquency? *Criminal Behaviour and Mental Health, 3* (2), 61-75.

Laviage, M., Becker, E., & Britner, P. (1999, August*). Childhood trauma and young incarcerated men: Treatment, prevention, and policy.* Poster presentation, 107th Annual Convention of the American Psychological Association, Boston

Laviage, M., Becker, E., & Cillessen, A. (1998, August). *Failures in high school: Psychological effects of childhood trauma.* Poster presentation, 106th Annual Convention of the American Psychological Association, San Francisco.

Mallon-Kraft, S.D. (1997). *Child maltreatment history, perceived parental child rearing styles, and intimacy functioning in college students.* Unpublished master's thesis, University of Connecticut, Storrs.

McCann, I.L., & Pearlman, L.A. (1990). *Psychological trauma and the adult survivor: Theory, therapy, and transformation.* New York: Bruner/Mazel.

Mas, K. (1992). *Disrupted schema in psychiatric patients with a history of childhood sexual abuse on the McPearl Belief Scale.* Unpublished doctoral dissertation, California School of Professional Psychology, Fresno.

Matthews, K.E., Becker, E., & Laviage, M. (1999, August). *Childhood maltreatment and self-versus-other esteem in incarcerated offenders.* Poster presentation, 107th Annual Convention of the American Psychological Association, Boston.

McLoyd, V.C. (1998). Socioeconomic disadvantage and child development. *American Psychologist, 53*, 185-204.

Overstreet, S., & Braun, S. (2000). Exposure to community violence and post-traumatic stress symptoms: Mediating factors. *American Journal of Orthopsychiatry, 70*, 263-271.

Pearlman, L.A. (1996). Psychometric review of the TSI Belief Scale, Revision L. In B.H. Stamm (Ed.), *Measurement of stress, trauma, and adaptation* (pp. 415-417). Lutherville, MD: Sidran Press.

Pearlman, L.A., & Maclan, P.S. (1995). *The TSI Belief Scale: Normative data from four criterion groups.* Paper presented at the annual conference of the International Society for Traumatic Stress Studies, Los Angeles, CA.

Pearlman, L.A., & Saakvitne, K. (1995). *Trauma and the therapist: Countertransference and vicarious traumatization in psychotherapy with incest survivors.* New York: W.W. Norton.

Pierce, L.H., & Pierce, R.L. (1987). Incestuous victimization by juvenile sex offenders. *Journal of Family Violence, 2*, 351-364.

Price, K., Rankin, E., Becker, E., & Rickel, A.U. (1998, August). *Trauma, MMPI profiles, and high-risk sexual behavior: Policy implications.* Poster presentation, 106th Annual Convention of the American Psychological Association, San Francisco.

Prinos, M.J. (1996). *Intergenerational patterns of psychological maltreatment, child rearing practices, and trauma-related symptomatology in a clinical population.* Doctoral dissertation, University of Connecticut, Storrs.

Prinos, M.J., Becker-Lausen, E., & Rickel, A.U. (1997, August). *Measurement of parental practices: Nurturance, restrictiveness, inconsistency, and child maltreatment.* Poster presentation, 105th Annual Convention of the American Psychological Association, Chicago.

Rankin, E., Price, K., & Becker, E. (1998, August*). Child maltreatment and psychopathology: Evidence from two diverse* populations. Poster presentation, 106th Annual Convention of the American Psychological Association, San Francisco.

Reich, R.B. (1987). *Tales of a new America.* New York: Vintage Books.

Rickel, A.U., & Becker, E. (1997). *Keeping children from harm's way: How national policy affects psychological development.* Washington, DC: American Psychological Association.

Rickel, A. U., & Becker-Lausen, E. (1995). Intergenerational influences on child outcomes: Implications for prevention and intervention. In B.A. Ryan, G.R. Adams, T.P. Gullotta, R.P. Weissberg, and R.L. Hampton (Eds.), *The family-school connection: Theory, research, and practice* (pp. 315-340). Thousand Oaks, CA: Sage.

Rickel, A.U., & Biasetti, L.L. (1982). Modification of the Block Child Rearing Practices Report. *Journal of Clinical Psychology, 38*, 129-134.

Sanders, B., & Becker-Lausen, E. (1995). The measurement of psychological maltreatment: Early data on the Child Abuse and Trauma scale. *Child Abuse and Neglect, 19* (3), 315-323.

Schwarz, J.C., & Zuroff, D. (1994). *Development and validation of the Schwarz/Zuroff Love Inconsistency Scale.* Unpublished manuscript, University of Connecticut, Storrs.

Thornberry, T.P., Smith, C.A., Rivera, C., Huizinga, D., & Stouthamer-Loeber, M. (1999, September). *Family disruption and delinquency.* OJJDP Juvenile Justice Bulletin, NCJ 178285. Washington, DC: Department of Justice.

UNICEF Innocenti Research Centre. (2000, June). A league table of child poverty in rich nations. *Innocenti Report Card, 1.* (http://www.unicef-icdc.org/new/poverty.htm)

Vaillant, G.E., & Davis, J.T. (2000). Social/emotional intelligence and midlife resiliency in schoolboys with low tested intelligence. *American Journal of Orthopsychiatry, 70*, 215-222.

Widom, C.S. (1989a). The cycle of violence. *Science, 244*, 160-166.

Widom, C.S. (1989b). Does violence beget violence? A critical examination of the literature. *Psychological Bulletin, 1*, 3-28.

CHILD ABUSE AND SEVERITY OF DISTURBANCE AMONG ADULT PSYCHIATRIC INPATIENTS*

JOHN READ

Introduction

The long-term effects of child abuse are now well documented. They include depression, anxiety disorders, eating disorders, sexual dysfunction, dissociative disorders, personality disorders, post traumatic stress disorder, and substance abuse (Beitchman et al., 1992; Finkelhor, 1990; Kluft, 1990). It has also been established that the more severe the abuse, the greater the probability of psychiatric disorder in adulthood (Fergusson, Horwood, & Lynskey, 1996; Mullen Martin, Anderson, Romans, & Herbison, 1993). In the last decade it has been repeatedly demonstrated that psychiatric inpatients frequently have histories of abuse as children. A recent review of 15 studies from 1984 to 1996 (Read, 1997a) has calculated that 64% of women inpatients report either physical or sexual childhood abuse. Child sexual abuse was reported by 50% of the women, child physical abuse was reported by 44%, and 29% reported both physical and sexual abuse.

Male inpatients report similar rates of childhood physical abuse but lower rates of childhood sexual abuse than female inpatients (Jacobson & Richardson, 1987). Differences for sexual abuse among inpatients have been reported as 38% female versus 24% male (Sansonnet-Hayden, J Haley Marriage, & Fine, 1987), 52% versus 39% (Wurr & Partridge, 1996), and 54% versus 26% (Jacobson & Herald, 1990). Nevertheless, prevalence rates for male inpatients are at least twice as high as rates for men in general in both the USA (Jacobson & Herald, 1990) and England (Palmer, Bramble, Metcalfe, Oppenheimer, & Smith, 1994).

A recent study, including abuse as an adult, found that among patients with "severe mental illness" 76% of women and 72% of men had been sexually or physically abused (Ritscher, Coursey, & Farrell, 1997). Even before the more recent studies, Herman (1992, p. 122) concluded:

> Many or even most psychiatric patients are survivors of child abuse. The data on this point are beyond contention. On careful questioning, 50-60% of psychiatric inpatients and 40-60% of outpatients report childhood histories of physical or sexual abuse or both.

Such consistently high prevalence rates among inpatients might be expected to generate hypotheses about the causative or contributory role of child abuse in the probability of developing a psychotic psychiatric disorder in adulthood, in the same way that similar or weaker findings among the less seriously disturbed clinical populations have done. However, psychiatric hospitals also treat people with less severe problems for which child abuse is acknowledged to have a causal role. Is it possible that it is within this subgroup of inpatients, and not within the psychotic subgroup, that the high prevalence of child abuse is present?

Two approaches to answering this question have emerged. The first is to examine the relationship between child abuse and those diagnostic categories or symptoms indicative of more severe disturbance, such as psychosis in general or schizophrenia in particular. Read (1997a) summarizes studies demonstrating relationships between child abuse and actual diagnoses of psychosis or schizophrenia (Beck & Van der Kolk, 1987; Friedman & Harrison, 1984), measures of

*Reprinted From: Child Abuse & Neglect, Vol 22, no5, 1998 Child Abuse And Severity of Disturbance Among Adult Psychiatric Inpatients John Read, Pages 359-368 With Permission from Elsevier Science LTD PII S0145-2134(98)00009-X

psychoticism and schizophrenia using standardized assessment scales (Bryer, Nelson, Miller, & Krol, 1987; Carlin & Ward, 1992; Lundberg-Love, Marmion, Ford, Geffner, & Peacock, 1992; Swett, Surrey, & Cohen, 1990) and the presence of psychotic symptoms usually considered indicative of schizophrenia, such as hallucinations and delusions (Ellenson, 1985; Goff, Brotman, Kindlon, Waites, & Amico, 1991a; Heins, Gray, & Tennant, 1990; Ross, Anderson, & Clark, 1994; Sansonnet-Hayden et al., 1987; Shearer, Peters, Quaytman, & Ogden, 1990). Not only are abused patients more likely to show psychotic symptoms as adults, those symptoms appear at an earlier age than in nonabused patients (Goff et al., 1991b). Livingston (1987), reporting on 100 consecutive inpatient admissions of children aged 6-12, found that 77% of those who had been sexually abused were diagnosed as psychotic compared to just 10% of the nonabused children (p < .0005).

The second approach, adopted by the present study, involves measures based not on diagnosis or symptomatology but on those variables traditionally considered indicative of global severity of disturbance. Psychiatric patients who have been abused as children compared to other psychiatric patients enter a psychiatric hospital at a younger age (Darves-Bornoz, Lemperiere, Degiovanni, & Gaillard, 1995; Margo & McLees, 1991), have longer and more frequent hospitalizations (Carlilen, Ricker, & Mills, 1984; Rose, 1991; Sansonnet-Hayden et al., 1987; Shearer et al., 1990), spend more time in seclusion (Beck & Van der Kolk, 1987), are more likely to receive psychotropic medication (Briere & Runtz, 1988; Bryer et al., 1987; Sansonnet-Hayden et al., 1987), relapse more frequently (Goff- et al., 199 1 a), and are more likely to attempt suicide and deliberately self harm (Beitchnian, et al. 1992; Briere & Runtz, 1988; Brown & Anderson, 1991, Darves-Bornoz et al., 1995; Rose, 1991; Sansonnet-Hayden et al., 1987).

The current study seeks to contribute to this small but growing body of literature which suggests that even within the most disturbed populations (i.e., inpatients) child abuse is positively related to higher levels of severity of disturbance as measured, here, by suicidality, length of hospitalization, use of the Mental Health Act and seclusion, and history of previous admissions. The hypotheses tested were that of each of these variables, subjects who had been either physically or sexually abused as children would show higher levels of disturbance than those who had not.

Method

The medical records of 100 consecutive admissions (excluding repeat admissions) to an acute psychiatric inpatient unit of an urban general hospital in New Zealand were read in their entirety and disclosures of sexual or physical abuse as a child were recorded. For the purposes of this study a "disclosure" included first disclosures (spontaneous or as a result of being asked) and mention in the file of disclosures prior to the current admission.

To provide an indication of reliability, 15 randomly selected files were re-examined without reference to the data already gathered. One example of abuse was found in the "Clinical Notes" section (predominantly used by nurses) which had been missed on first examination. All disclosures recorded in the study were confirmed during the blind reexamination.

Four indicators of the degree of current severity of disturbance were recorded: suicidality on admission, length of admission, use of Mental Health Act, and use of Intensive Care Unit (ICU). Suicidality was categorized on a 4 point scale: (1) nil ideation, past or present; (2) some ideation, past or present, but no plans or attempts; (3) either past attempts with no current ideation, or no previous attempt but currently considered at risk; (4) previous attempt(s) and currently considered high risk. Whether or not the subjects had been admitted at least once in the 12 months preceding the current admission and age of first admission were also recorded as indicators of recent and past levels of severity of disturbance.

Of the 100 subjects, 57 were men and 43 women. The mean age was 37.6 years (range, 20-67 years). Sixty-eight were of European descent, 15 were Maori, 11 Pacific Islanders, and 6 classified as "Other." The most frequent diagnoses were schizophrenia-34, major depressive disorder-19, bipolar affective disorder-17, and substance abuse-16.

Results

Current Severity

Table 1 shows the relationships of four measures of current severity of disturbance to childhood abuse, analyzed by gender.

Table 1. Relationships Between Abuse and Measures of Current Disturbance Severity

	No Abuse Disclosed (n = 78)	Physical or Sexual (n = 22)	Sexual (n = 17)	Physical (n = 12)
Suicidal	17(22%)	14 (64%)****	11 (65%)****	8(67%)***
Female (n - 43)	3(10%)	4(33%)	2 (25%)	3(43%)*
Male (n = 57)	14(30%)	10 (100)******	9 (100%)*****	5(100%)**
Days in Hospital	24.6	33.7	33.6	39.8*
Female	23.5	31.6	40.0**	24.6
Male	25.3	36.3	27.9	61.2***
Mental Health Act	53(68%)	14(64%)	11 (65%)	7(58%)
Female	22(71%)	9(75%)	7(87.5%)	4(57%)
Male	31(66%)	5(50%)	4(44%)	3(60%)
Intensive Care Unit	36(46%)	10(45%)	8(47%)	5(42%)
Female	12(39%)	6(50%)	5(62.5%)	3(43%)
Male	24(51%)	4(40%)	3(33%)	2(40%)

$*p < .05;$ $**p < .01;$ $***p < .005;$ $****p < .001;$ $*****p < .0001;$ $******p < .00001.$ (Levels of probability determined by Phi, except for Days in Hospital for which one-tailed t-tests were utilized.)

Suicidality

The relationship between having been physically or sexually abused as a child and being rated at the highest point on the 4 point Suicidality scale (previous attempt(s) and currently considered high risk) was significant at the $p < .001$ level (chi-square-Phi). When analyzed by gender and type of abuse the strongest relationship was with men who had been sexually abused. All nine sexually abused men were highly suicidal, compared to 15 of the 48 (31%) who had not been sexually abused ($p < .0001$). For women the relationships between suicidality and sexual or physical abuse and between suicidality and sexual abuse did not reach statistical significance. However the difference between three of the seven physically abused women (43%) and four of the 36 women who were not physically abused (11%) being highly suicidal was significant ($p < .05$).

Length of Admission

The difference in length of admission between the 22 subjects who had been either sexually or physically abused (33.7 days) and the 78 who had not (24.6) was in the predicted direction but not statistically significant. However the mean of 39.8 days for the 12 physically abused subjects was significantly greater than the mean of 24.8 for the 88 nonphysically abused subjects ($p < .05$, one-tailed, $df = 98$). Furthermore significant differences were found between women who had been sexually abused and those who had not ($p < .01$; $df = 41$) and men who had been physically abused and those who had not ($< .005$; $df = 55$).

Mental Health Act

No significant relationships were found, overall or by gender, between childhood abuse and the likelihood of an admission being to some degree nonvoluntary by virtue of the use of various sections of the Mental Health Act. The strongest nonsignificant trend (p= .028) in the predicted direction was the finding that the admissions of seven of the eight women who had been sexually abused (87.5%) but only 24 of the 35 who had not (69%) had involved the Mental Health Act.

Seclusion

No significant relationships were found, overall or by gender, between childhood abuse and use of the Intensive Care Unit (a part of the ward used for separating particularly distressed or distressing patients from other patients and for providing specialized attention). Again, the strongest nonsignificant trend (p = .19) in the predicted direction was the finding that five of the eight women who had been sexually abused (62.5%) and 13 of the 35 who had not (37%) had spent time in the ICU.

Previous Admissions

Table 2 and Table 3 show the findings from two measures of previous severity, admission during preceding 12 months and age at first admission.

Table 2. Admission During 12 Months Preceding Current Admission

	No Abuse Disclosed (n = 56)	Physical or Sexual (n = 14)	Sexual (n = 10)	Physical (n = 9)
All (n = 70)	24 (43%)	8 (57%)	6 (60%)	6 (67%)
Female (n = 33)	10 (40%)	4 (50%)	3(60%)	3 (60%)
Male (n = 37)	14 (45%)	4 (67%)	3 (60%)	3 (75%)

Admission in previous 12 months.

Data was available on 70 of the 100 subjects regarding admissions in the preceding 12 months. Although all differences were in the predicted direction no significant relationships, overall or by gender were found between child abuse and having had one or more admissions in the year prior to the current admission. Twenty-four of the 56 nonabused (43%), six of the 10 who had been sexually abused (60%) and six of the nine physically abused patients (67%) had been hospitalized in the past year.

Table 3. Age at First Admission

First Admission[1]

	No Abuse Disclosed (n = 73)	Physical or Sexual (n = 21)	Sexual (n = 16)	Physical (n = 11)
Age	28.0	24.8	24.9	26.2
Female (n = 40)	30.7	24.6*	23.6	26.7
Male (it = 54)	26.2	25.0	26.0	25.6
18 or under	6(8%)	8 (38%)****	6 (37.5%) **	5 (45%)***
Female	2(7%)	3 (27%)	2 (29%)	2 (33%)
Male	4(9%)	5 (50%)***	4 (44%)*	3 (60%)**

[1] Data available on 94 subjects.

*p < .05; **p < .01; ***p < .005; ****p < .001. (Levels of probability determined by one-tailed t-tests for mean ages at first admission and by Phi for differences in percentages admitted before age 18).

Age at first admission.

Data was available on 94 of the 100 subjects with regard to age at first admission to a psychiatric hospital. The mean age for the 73 nonabused patients was 28.0 years, while the mean for the 21 abused as children was 24.8. Although in the predicted direction, this difference did not reach statistical significance (p = 0.085). The difference for women, (30.7 vs. 24.6) was significant at the p < .05 level. The difference for women was more marked among those women who had been sexually abused (30.2 vs. 23.6) than among the physically abused (29.4 vs. 26.7).

When analyzed in terms of being admitted at or before age 18, a different picture emerged. First, the overall difference between abused and nonabused was significant at the p < .001 level, with eight of the 21 abused patients (38%) but only six of the 73 nonabused (8%) having been first admitted at or before age 18. Moreover it was now the men, rather than the women, who were primarily contributing to this overall difference. Five of the 10 abused males (50%) but only four the 44 nonabused males (9%) had been admitted at or before age 18 (p < .005 level) whereas the corresponding difference among the women (27% vs. 7%) was not statistically significant.

Discussion

Methodological Limitations

Clearly, a prospective study would have been preferable to the retrospective approach adopted here. The small Subgroup numbers could be avoided, in replications, either by studying a larger overall sample or by inquiring about abuse with all subjects within a sample of similar size. Numerous studies have demonstrated that routine clinical practice within psychiatric settings assessed by examination of medical records, produces significantly lower abuse rates than those elicited by questioning all patients (Goodwin, Attias, McCarty, Chandler, & Romanik 1988; Jacobson, Koehler, & Jones-Brown, 1987; Rosenfeld, 1979). Briere and Zaidi (1989), for instance reported that while the records of women attending a psychiatric emergency room recorded that 6% had been abused, 70% disclosed abuse when asked. Most recently, Wurr and Partridge (1996) found that while inpatient case notes suggested a prevalence rate for childhood sexual abuse 01 14% (male and female combined), direct investigation produced a rate of 46%.

It must therefore, be acknowledged that the abuse prevalence rates produced by this study are almost certainly underestimates. Consequently the positive relationships between abuse and measures of severity of disturbance found in the current study are likely to be underestimates of the strength of that relationship, since a significant number of the abused patients will actually be in the nonabused group for statistical analysis. This renders even more noteworthy the findings that years, or decades, after the occurrence of childhood abuse the abused patients are significantly more likely to be suicidal, and that sexually abused women and physically abused men spent significantly longer in the hospital.

An additional factor potentially contributing to underestimation of the relationship between child abuse and those variables involving categorical data, such as suicidality, admission during previous 12 months and first admission at or before age 18, is the fact that Phi, like all chi-square analyses, is a nondirectional test. Unlike the one-tailed t-tests used for the two ratio scale variables, days in hospital and age at first admission Phi is a test for significance in either direction and not only in the direction hypothesized, that is, that abuse would be positively related to disturbance severity. Because of its bi-directionality Phi necessarily reduces the chances of rejecting the null hypothesis that child abuse is not positively related to, for instance, admission during the previous year. When all four points on the suicidality scale are taken into consideration it becomes possible to utilize a Spearman Correlation Coefficient which allows for one-tailed levels of significance. The correlation between child abuse (physical or sexual) and suicidality among women, .324, is significant (p < .05) level, whereas this relationship was nonsignificant when using Phi (Table 1).

Furthermore, analyses involving one specific category of child abuse compared patients who had experienced that particular form of abuse with those who had not. Thus when testing for significance with the sexually abused group, the comparison was made not with nonabused patients but with nonabused and physically abused combined. This might also have underestimated the significance of these particular analyses.

Finally, it must be pointed out that those significant findings emerging from this study involved comparisons of abused and nonabused groups within the most severely disturbed sub-population in the mental health field, inpatients. The finding here that child abuse is related to suicidality, for instance, does not merely demonstrate the existence of such a relationship but suggests that even within a particularly suicidal sub-population child abuse partially determines, statistically if not necessarily causatively, suicidality.

Theoretical Implications

The pattern of findings emerging from this Study confirms the small but growing body of literature that child abuse is related not only to relatively mild or moderate dysfunction in adulthood but to the most severe levels of dysfunction. This study suggests that inpatients who have been abused as children are more likely to he acutely suicidal on admission than those who were not abused and that this relationship is particularly strong for men who were sexually abused as boys. Women who were sexually abused as girls and men who were physically abused as boys seem to spend longer in the hospital when admitted. Inpatients who have been abused as children, especially men, tend to be admitted to the hospital for the first time at or before age 18.

The mechanisms by which the relationship between child abuse and psychotic conditions such as schizophrenia is minimized by researchers and clinicians have been reviewed elsewhere (Read, 1997a). They include rediagnosis from "psychotic" to "nonpsychotic" if abuse is identified, with the result that simplistic biological explanations of psychosis remain unchallenged by the high numbers of abused individuals in inpatient settings. Of relevance to the emerging debate concerning whether child abuse may have a causative role in conditions such as schizophrenia is the finding that men who have been abused as boys were significantly more likely to be admitted at or before age 18 than those who have not been abused, and that there was no such significant difference for women. One of the most consistent findings in schizophrenia research, from Bleuler to the present, is that the onset of this "illness" occurs at a slightly earlier age for men than for women. Loranger (1984) for instance found that 30% of male "schizophrenics" but only 17%, of women "schizophrenics" first receive this diagnosis between the ages of 15 and 19. Is it possible that the explanations of the dominant paradigm, concerning hypothetical but undemonstrated gender differences in hormonal or genetic triggering or suppression of the "illness," might be replaced by a more parsimonious explanation? If the tentative finding of this study were to be replicated with larger numbers, the question to be next addressed is: Why is abuse of boys followed more quickly, or more often, by psychosis than abuse of girls? One hypothesis worthy of exploration may be the relatively low disclosure rate of sexual abuse by males, possibly compounded by fears around sexual identity, and the consequential low level of support received by boys concerning such abuse.

Also worthy of further research are the various gender differences, found here, in the relationships of specific types of abuse (physical and sexual) with long-term sequelae such as suicidality and length of hospitalization. Is there, for instance, a connection between the high rate of suicidality for sexually abused males and the high rate of suicidality among schizophrenics in general and male schizophrenics in particular (Breier & Astrachan, 1984)?

Future research may demonstrate that the frequently documented relationships of child abuse to inpatient status, psychosis, suicidality, and length and frequency of admissions are of a causal nature. The relationships may be found to be mediated by other environmental variables. Recently, however, when researchers have controlled for the most likely such factors, using various measures of family dysfunction as well as demographic variables, the relationship between severity of abuse and severity of psychiatric disturbance remains (Fergusson et al., 1996; Mullen et al., 1993). The New Zealand research team which found that women whose childhood abuse involved intercourse were 16 times more likely than nonabused women to enter psychiatric hospital as adults, concluded that "CSA [child sexual abuse] emerged from logistic regression, which took these potentially confounding variables into account, as a substantial and direct contributor to adult psychopathology" (Mullen et al., 1993, p. 721).

Those interpreting the data from the more biological perspective currently dominating inpatient mental health services may conclude, nevertheless, that the relationship is mediated by genetic predisposition to both being abused and becoming psychotic (Palmer et al., 1994). A variation on this theme, also awaiting empirical support, is the hypothesis that disorders such as schizophrenia, assumed to involve genetic predisposition, produce families in which schizophrenic parents are more likely, because of their "illness," to abuse their children who themselves are already predisposed to develop psychosis if traumatized. Others, of course, continue to see the relationships under discussion here as purely coincidental.

Clinical Implications

In the meantime our various interpretations of the proven relationship between severity of child abuse and severity of adult psychopathology (which for many of us may currently he based as much on our professional or paradigmatic biases as on methodologically sound data) should not prevent us, any longer, from introducing policies of routine inquiry about abuse histories in all mental health settings, including and especially inpatient units. Such a recommendation has been repeatedly made (Bryer et al., 1987; Jacobson & Richardson, 1987; Herman, 1986; Leserman & Drossman, 1995; Sansonnet-Hayden et al., 1987; Read 1997a; Read & Fraser, 1998a Swett et al., 1990). The extent to which the advice has been acted on can be gauged from the studies, reviewed earlier, demonstrating that only a small proportion of child abuse is currently being identified in inpatient settings. The introduction of policies of routine inquiry, however, are likely to be ineffective unless those policies include training on how and when to ask and how to respond to affirmative responses (Read & Fraser 1998a). Even when inpatients do disclose abuse, the response of staff can be inadequate (Read & Fraser, 1998b). The differential and complimentary roles of the different professions also need to be delineated (Read, 1997b).

When dealing with the most severely disturbed populations even community-based models which focus on the role of the family can ignore the importance of abuse histories (Allen & Read, 1997). Even when dealing with constructs traditionally acknowledged to have a clear psychosocial component, such as depression, the biological model has tended to mask the importance of those factors, including child abuse (Read & Towns, 1995). The assumption of the biological paradigm that the more severe the psychiatric condition the less important the psychosocial factors is increasingly challenged by the body of literature apparently demonstrating the contrary, to which this study has contributed.

Conclusion

Further evidence that child abuse is related to several measures of disturbance severity, even within a highly disturbed population, raises the possibility that child abuse may have a causative role in the most severe psychiatric conditions, including those currently thought to be primarily biological in aetiology. Regardless of the outcome of future research in this regard, there is an urgent need for review of current policies in inpatient settings regarding child abuse.

References

Allen, R. E. S., & Read, J. (1997). integrated mental health care: Practitioners' perspectives. *Australian and New Zealand Journal of Psychiatry, 31,* 534-541.

Beck, J. C., & van der Kolk, B. A. (1987). Reports of childhood incest and current behavior of chronically hospitalized psychotic women. *American Journal of Psychiatry* 144, 1474-1476.

Beitchman, J. H., Zucker, K. J., Hood, J. E., daCosta, G. A., Ackman, D., & Cassavia, F. (1992). A review of the long-term effects of child sexual abuse. *Child Abuse & Neglect,* 16, 101-118.

Breier, A., & Astrachan, B. M. (1984). Characterization of schizophrenic patients who commit suicide. *American Journal of Psychiatry,* 141, 206-209.

Briere, J., & Runtz, M. (1988). Post sexual abuse trauma. In G. Wyatt, & G. Powell (Eds.), *Lasting effects of child sexual abuse* (pp. 85-99). Newbury Park, CA: Sage Publications.

Briere J., & Zaidi, L Y. (1989). Sexual abuse histories and sequelae in female psychiatric emergency room patients. *American Journal of Psychiatry,* 146, 1602-1606.

Brown, G. R., & Anderson, B. (1991). Psychiatric morbidity in adult inpatient,, with childhood histories Of Sexual and physical abuse. *American Journal of Psychiatry,* 148, 55-61.

Bryer J. B., Nelson, B. A., Miller, J. B., & Krol P. A. (1987). Childhood sexual and physical abuse as factors in psychiatric illness. *American Journal of Psychiatry,* 144, 1426-1430.

Carlin, A. S., & Ward, N. G (1992). Subtypes of- psychiatric inpatient women who have been sexually abused. *The Journal of Nervous and Mental Disease,* 180, 392-397.

Carmen, E, Rieker, P., & Mills, T. (1984). Victims of violence and psychiatric illness. *American Journal of Psychiatry,* 141, 378-383.

Darves-Bornoz, J. Ivl., Lemperiere T., Degiovanni A., & Gaillard, 1'. (1995). Sexual victimization in women with schizophrenia and bipolar disorder. *Social Psychiatry and Psychiatric Epidemiology,* 30, 78 - 84.

Ellenson G. S. (1985). Detecting a history of incest: A predictive syndrome. Social Casework *The Journal of Contemporary Social Work,* November, 525-532.

Fergusson, D.M., Horwood J., & Lynskey M.T. (1996). Childhood sexual abuse and psychiatric disorder in young adulthood: 11. Psychiatric outcomes of childhood sexual abuse. *Journal of the American Academy of Child and Adolescent Psychiatry,* 34, 1165-1374.

Finkelhor, D. (1990). Early and long-term effects of child sexual abuse: An update. *Professional Psychology: Research and Practice,* 21, 325-330.

Friedman, S., & Harrison G. (1984). Sexual histories, attitudes and behavior of schizophrenic and normal women. *Archives of Sexual Behavior,* 13, 555-567.

Goff, D.C., Brotman A. W., Kindlon D., Waites, M., & Amico, E. (1991a). The delusion of possession in chronically psychotic patients. *The Journal of Nervous and Menial Disease,* 179, 567-571.

Goff, D.C., Brotman A.W., Kindlon, D., Waites, M., & Amico, E. (1991b). Self-Reports of childhood abuse in chronically psychotic patients. *Psychiatry Research,* 37, 73 - 80,

Goodwin, J., Attias, R., McCarty, T., Chandler S., & Romanik R. (1988). Reporting by adult psychiatric patients of childhood sexual abuse. *American Journal of Psy chiatry,* 145, 1183.

Heins, T., Gray, A., & Tennant. M. (1990). Persisting hallucinations following childhood sexual abuse. *Australian and New Zealand Journal of Psychiatry,* 24, 561-565.

Herman, J. L. (1992). *Trauma and recovery: The aftermath of violence front domestic abuse to political terror* . New York: Basic Books.

Herman, J. L. (1986). Histories of violence in an outpatient population: An exploratory study. *American Journal of Orthopsychiatry,* 56, 137-141.

Jacobson, A., & Herald, C. (1990). The relevance of childhood sexual abuse to adult psychiatric inpatient care. *Hospital and Community Psychiatry,* 41, 154-158.

Jacobson, A., Koehler, B. S., & Jones-Brown, C. (1987). The failure of routine assessment to detect histories of assault experienced by psychiatric patients. *Hospital and Community Psychiatry, 38,* 386-389.

Jacobson, A., & Richardson, B. (1987). Assault experiences of 100 psychiatric inpatients: Evidence of the need for routine inquiry. *American Journal of Psychiatry, 144,* 508-513.

Kluft, R. P. (Ed.) (1990). *Incest-related syndromes of adult psychopathology* Washington, DC: American Psychiatric Press.

Leserman, J., & Drossman, D. A. (1995). Sexual and physical abuse history and medical practice. *General Hospital Psychiatry, 17,* 71-74.

Livingston, R. (1987). Sexually and physically abused children. *Journal of the American Academy of Child and Adolescent Psychiatry, 26,* 413-415.

Loranger, A. W. (1984). Sex difference in age at onset of schizophrenia. *Archives of General Psychiatry, 41,* 157-161.

Lundberg-Love, P. K., Marmion, S., Ford, K., Geffner, R., & Peacock, L. (1992). The long-term consequences of childhood incestuous victimization upon adult women's psychological symptomatology. *Journal of Child Sexual Abuse, 1,* 81-102.

Margo, G. M., & McLees, E. M. (1991). Further evidence for the significance of a childhood abuse history in psychiatric inpatients. *Comprehensive Psychiatry, 32,* 362-366.

Mullen, P. E., Martin, J. L., Anderson, J. C., Romans, S. E., & Herbison, P. (1993). Child sexual abuse and mental health in adult life. *British Journal of Psychiatry, 163,* 721-732.

Palmer, R. L., Bramble, D., Metcalfe, M., Oppenheimer, R., & Smith, J. (1994). Childhood sexual experiences with adults: Adult male psychiatric patients and general practice attenders *British Journal of Psychiatry, 165,* 675-679.

Read, J. (1997a). Child abuse and psychosis: A literature review and implications for professional practice. *Professional Psychology: Research and Practice, 28,* 448-456.

Read, J. (1997b). The role of psychologists in the assessment of psychosis. In H. Love & W. Whittaker (Eds.), *Professional guidelines for New Zealand clinical and other applied psychologists* (pp. 277-292). Wellington, New Zealand: New Zealand Psychological Society,

Read, J., & Fraser, A. (1998a). Abuse histories of psychiatric inpatients: To ask or not to ask. *Psychiatric Services, 49,* 355-359.

Read, J., & Fraser, A. (1998b). Staff response to abuse histories of psychiatric inpatients. *Australian and New Zealand Journal of Psychiatry, 32,* 157-164.

Read, J., & Towns, A. (1995). De-medicalising the construct of depression. *Bulletin of the New Zealand Psychological Society, 87,* 9-12.

Ritscher, J. E. B., Coursey, R. B., & Farrell, E. W. (1997). A survey on issues in the lives of women with severe mental illness. *Psychiatric Services, 48,* 1273-1282.

Rose, S. M. (1991). Acknowledging abuse backgrounds of intensive case management clients. *Community Mental Health Journal, 27,* 255-263.

Rosenfeld, A. A. (1979). Incidence of a history of incest among 18 female psychiatric patients. *American Journal of Psychiatry, 136,* 791-795.

Ross, C. A., Anderson, G., & Clark, P. (1994). Childhood abuse and the symptoms of schizophrenia. *Hospital and Community Psychiatry, 45,* 489-491.

Sansonnet- Hayden, H., Haley, G., Marriage, K. & Fine, S. (1987). Sexual abuse and psychopathology in hospitalized adolescents. *Journal of the American Academy of Child and Adolescnet Psychiatry, 26,* 753-757.

Shearer, S. L., Peters, C. P., Quaytman, M. S., & Ogden R. L. (1990). Frequency and correlates of childhood sexual and physical abuse histories in adult female borderline inpatients. *American Journal of Psychiatry, 147, 214-216.*

Swett, C., Jr., Surrey, J., & Cohen, C. (1990). Sexual and physical abuse histories and psychiatric symptoms among male psychiatric outpatients. *American Journal* of *Psychiatry, 147, 632 - 636.*

Wurr, J.C., & Partridge, I.M. (1996). The prevalence of a history of childhood sexual abuse in an acute adult inpatient population. *Child Abuse & Neglect, 20, 867-872.*

TYPE AND SEVERITY OF CHILD ABUSE AND COLLEGE STUDENTS' LIFETIME SUICIDALITY*

SUSAN L. BRYANT AND LILLIAN M. RANGE

Introduction

Individuals who experience both physical and sexual abuse as children are at greater risk than singly and nonabused individuals for short and long-term pathology (i.e., Wind & Silvern, 1992). However, research on sexual and physical abuse typically errs by focusing on one or the other, even though they often occur together (Brown & Anderson. 1991; Bryer, Nelson, Miller, & Krol, 1987: Wind & Silvern, 1992). Reviewing long-term effects of sexual abuse, Beitchman and colleagues (1992) stressed studying the concomitant effects of sexual and physical abuse on suicidality, and criticized several studies for drawing conclusions about sexual abuse and suicidality are independent of physical abuse.

Only a few studies on suicidality compare mutually exclusive multiple and single abuse groups. In one well-designed study, pregnant teenagers were divided into four groups: sexually abused only (n = 52), physically abused only (n = 39) sexually and physically abused (n = 11) and nonabused (n = 272). Those who experienced physical or sexual abuse were four times more likely to have suicidal thoughts compared to nonabused teens. Those who experienced sexual and physical abuse were seven times more likely to have suicidal thoughts and attempts than nonabused teens (Bayatpour, Wells, & Holford, 1992). This study was strengthened by classifying participants into discrete groups. A weakness, however, was failing to clarify the questions used to establish abuse and suicide, suggesting that these instruments were nonstandardized. Further, results from this high risk population may not generalize to other populations.

In another study using mutually exclusive abuse groups, Mills, Reiker, and Carmen (1985) used hospital records to categorize adolescent and adult inpatients as sexually and physically abused, only sexually abused, only physically abused, and nonabused. Multiply abused patients were more likely to be actively suicidal than singly abused patients, who were more likely to be actively suicidal than those not abused. A limitation of these results is the blend of adolescent and adult abuse, so the abuse might have been physical child abuse, incest, martial violence, or rape.

Thus, the present purpose was to (a) use mutually exclusive sexual and physical abuse groups: (b) examine severity as a potential moderator: (c) utilize clear definitions of sexual and physical abuse before age 18 and (d) employ multiple standardized suicidality measures. We expected those multiply abused as children to he more suicidal than those singly or not abused, those singly abused to be more suicidal than those not abused, and those severely abused to be more suicidal and lower in reasons for living, than all others. Also, consistent with past research, we expected women to report more sexual abuse than men, but greater reasons for living.

Method

Participants

Participants were 486 undergraduates at a mid-sized southeastern university who received extra credit. Most were women (74%) and Caucasian (72%), and the average age was 23.6 (range = 18 – 51). A 3 (Physical Abuse) x 4 (Sexual Abuse) ANOVA on age was not significant. Chi-squares were

*Reprinted From: Child Abuse & Neglect, Vol 21, no 12, 1997 Type And Severity Of Child Abuse And College Students' Lifetime Suicidality Susan L. Bryant And Lillian M. Range Pages 1169-1176 With Permission from Elsevier Science LTD 0145-2134/97

nonsignificant on class and race, but significant on gender and marital status. More women (33%) reported sexual abuse than men (15%), $X^2 (3)=16.53$, p<.01, more single people than expected reported no physical abuse (75%) and more married people than expected reported severe physical abuse (22%) x2(6) = 187, p<.01.

Instruments

The self-report version of the *Scale for Suicide Ideation* (SSI; Beck, Steer, & Ranieri, 1988) consists of 19 suicide-related items scored on a 3-point Likert scale where higher scores indicate more suicidal ideation. The SSI has three factors: Active Suicidal Desire, Passive Suicidal Desire, and Specific Plans for Suicide. It is internally consistent (alpha = 93) and highly correlated with the original SSI (r =. 90) (Beck et al, 1988).

The shortened *Suicidal Behaviors Questionnaire* (SBQ; Linehan & Nielsen, 1981) consists of four items about suicidal thoughts, expressions and probability (Cole, 1988) where scores range from 0 (no suicidality) to 16 (very suicidal). The 4-item SBQ has test-restest reliability over 2 weeks (r=.95) internal consistency (alpha = .81) and validity as evidenced by a moderate correlation with the SSI (r = .69; Cotton, Peters, & Range, 1995).

The *Brief Reasons for Living Inventory* (BRFL; Ivanoff, Jang, Smyth, & Linehan, 1994) adapted from the Reasons For Living Inventory, (RFL; Linehan, Goodstein, Nielsen, and Chiles, 1983) consists of 12 possible reasons for not committing suicide. The BRFL, is internally consistent (alpha = .86). Evidence of validity are high correlations with RFL subscales (rs = .73 to .58, total = .94), and its accounting for significant variance in inmates SSI scores over hopelessness, depression, and social desirability (Ivanoff et al, 1994).

The *Child Sexual Abuse Questionnaire* (CASQ; Bendixen, Muus & Schei, 1994) is a question about abuse followed by 13 items referring to type of sexual abuse (Finkelhor, 1979). Respondents indicate the age at first incidence and the relationship to the offender for each item. The CSAQ has been used to ascertain sexual abuse (Bendixen et al, 1994), and in the present sample was internally consistent (alpha = .91).

The *Child Abuse Questionnaire* (CAQ; Gross & Keller, 1992) consists of seven questions about physical abuse by parents or primary guardians. Questions are rated on a likert scale from 1 (never), 2 (rarely, once or twice in a lifetime), 3 (sometimes, one to five times a year), 4 (often, once a month) or 5 (frequently, more than once a month). The CAQ has satisfactory internal consistency (alpha = .77; Gross & Keller, 1992; present sample =. 80).

Procedure

Participants were recruited during or after class for a study about childhood experiences and suicide, and those consenting anonymously completed, in order, demographic questions, the BRFL, SSI, CAQ, CSAQ, and SBQ. Students were recruited from a variety of psychology classes including a large introductory course taken by a broad cross-section of students and more advanced courses typically taken by majors. In most classes there were more women than men students. In addition, women typically enroll for extra credit opportunities outside class more so than men (Range, Turzo, & Ellis, 1992). Thus, it was not surprising that more women than men students participated. Students had many opportunities to earn extra credit, those who chose to participate in the present project typically did so because the time was convenient for them (most common), or because of personal interest.

Because the questions were sensitive, free counseling was offered to anyone who needed assistance dealing with these issues. No one took advantage of this offer. At the end of the battery, each participant checked yes to a final question, "I have answered these questions to the best of my ability. You may use my responses in the study.

As in Bendixen and colleagues (1994), participants who answered "yes" to any CSAQ items were considered sexually abused (n=137). Of these, participants were categorized as severely abused (n = 54) if they endorsed one or more of 9 – 13; moderately abused (n = 45) if they endorsed one or more of 6-8 and none higher; mildly abused (n = 38) if they endorsed one or more of 1-5 and none higher; and nonsexually abused (n = 347) if they endorsed no CSAQ items.

As in Gross and Keller (1992), participants who endorsed frequently, often, or sometimes, to any of CAQ items 2. 4. 6 and 7 OR often or frequently on question 3, OR frequently, often, sometimes, or rarely on question 5 were considered physically abused (n = 186). Of these participants who endorsed any CAQ items involving sequelae were categorized as severely abused (n = 65): participants who endorsed no sequelae items but any nonsequelae were categorized as moderately abused (n = 121); and participants who endorsed only item 1 (about spanking) and/or no physical abuse items were categorized as nonphysically abused (n = 300).

At this point, the sexual abuse groups included those who reported physical abuse and the physical abuse groups included those who reported sexual abuse. For the MANOVA and to avoid overlap, they were further categorized into 12 mutually exclusive groups based on the above criteria yielding a total sample of 483 (three missing observations) (see Table I).

Results

See Table I for means and standard deviations. A 4 (Sexual Abuse) X 3 (Physical Abuse) MANOVA yielded significant main effects for *sexual abuse* F (9. 1413) = 4.50~ p = < .001 and *physical abuse*,. F (6, 940) = 3.23. p < .01, but no significant interaction. In follow-up ANOVAs and Tukeys, on the SSI those severely sexually abused (M = 6.78) had significantly more suicidal ideas than those not sexually abused (M=2.61), F (3, 471) = 7.70, p<. 001.

Table 1. Means and Standard Deviations of Mutually Exclusive Groups

		Physical Abuse		
		None	Moderate	Severe
Sexual Abuse				
None	**n**	**234**	**78**	**34**
	SSI	2.59 (5.49)	2.06 (4.53)	4.06 (6.41)
	SBQ	1.52 (2.26)	1.72 (2.37)	2.29 (2.60
	BRFL	4.61 (0.88)	4.64 (0.83)	4.33 (1.01)
Mild	**n**	**21**	**12**	**5**
	SSI	2.62 (4.93)	5.33 (7.54)	7.40 (7.92
	SBQ	2.52 (2.54)	3.42 (2.78)	4.20 (3.11)
	BRFL	4.40 (1.03)	4.34 (0.92)	4.78 (0.77)
Moderate	**n**	**20**	**15**	**10**
	SSI	1.70 (4.52)	6.40 (9.85)	5.60 (5.85)
	SBQ	1.70 (1.84)	3.13 (3.23)	2.80 (2.94)
	BRFL	4.77 (0.92)	4.42 (0.67)	4.97 (0.72
Severe	**n**	**22**	**16**	**16**
	SSI	3.91 (8.78)	7.50 (8.69)	10.31 (7.62)
	SBQ	2.82 (3.23)	4.44 (3.48)	4.94 (3.30)
	BRFL	4.65 (0.90)	4.13(0.98)	4.13 (1.08)

On the SBQ those severely (M= 3.93), moderately (M=2.42) and mildly (M=3.03) sexually abused were significantly more suicidal than those not sexually abused (M=2.64), F (3, 471)= 12.36, p<. .001; and those severely sexually abused were significantly more suicidal than those moderately sexually abused. An additional MANOVA on the BRFL subscales yielded significant main effects for sexual abuse, F (24, 1293) = 2.58. p<.0001. and physical abuse, F (16, 860) = 2.07, p<.01 but no significant interaction. On follow-ups, those severely sexually abused (M=5.08) had significantly lower BRFL survival and coping beliefs than those moderately sexually abused (M=5.59), F (3, 436)= 3.22. p<.05.

On the SSI those severely physically abused (M=6.09) had significantly more suicidal ideas than those moderately (M=3.64) and not physically abused (M=2.61), F (2, 471) = 8.52. p < .001. On the SBQ, those severely physically abused (M=3.17) were significantly more suicidal than those not physically abused (M=1.70), F (2, 471) = 6.37, p<.01. Follow-up ANOVAs on BRFL subscales were significant on the Survive, F (2,436) = 3.48, p< .05 and Family subscale F (2, 436) = 3.64, p< .05, but Tukey tests were not.

Those severely sexually and severely physically abused (n=16) were significantly worse than all other abuse groups (n=235) on SSI, t(249) = 4.32, p < .05; SBQ, t (249) = 3.98, p < .05; and BRFL Total, t (249) = 1.74, p <.05 as well as BRFL Social subscale scores, t(249) = 2.41, p < .05. Family, t(484) = 2.35, p< .05, Fear t(484) = 1.66, p <.05, and Moral, t(484) = 2.59, p< .05.

A multiple regression indicated that sexual and physical abuse entered together accounted for the most variance in SBQ scores (14%), F92, 480) = 40.55, p < .0001, followed by SSI scores (10% additional variance), F (2, 480) = 26.76, p < .0001, and BRFL total scores (2% additional variance), F (2, 480) = 5.13, p <. 01. No other variables accounted for significant and unique variance in SBQ scores.

Women had significantly higher CSAQ scores than men, t (459) = 2.48, p < .05. Women also had significantly higher BRFL Total scores than men, t (459) = 5.61, p < .001, as well as significantly higher scores on all but one BRFL subscale; Survive, t(459) = 4.73, p < .001; Family t (457) = 3.57, p < .001; Child, t (428) = 3.06, p < .01; Fear, t (457) = 5.51, p < .001; and Moral t (458) = 2.61, p < .01. Men and women did not differ significantly on CAQ, SSI or SBQ scores.

Discussion

Present results indicate that, contrary to expectations, there was no interaction between childhood sexual and physical abuse in terms of lifetime suicidality or suicidal ideas. Past research suggests that individuals who report both types of abuse as children are more likely to be suicidal as adults than those who report single or no abuse (Bayatpour, et al., 1992; Brown & Anderson, 1991; Bryer et al., 1987), but these studies do not address whether it is the sexual or physical abuse, or the combination that increase suicidality. In this study, absence of an interaction between sexual and physical abuse suggests that one type of abuse does not interact with the other to heighten suicidality. Sexual abuse and physical abuse apparently have additive rather than multiplicative effects on lifetime suicidality.

Present results also indicate that severity of both sexual and physical abuse made a difference in later suicidality. Consistent with other research, students who reported both severe sexual and severe physical abuse were more suicidal than students who reported moderate sexual and/or physical abuse (Bayatpour et al., 1992; Bryant & Range, 1995b).

The severity factor held true in terms of sexual abuse alone. The severe sexual abuse group was more suicidal than the no sexual abuse group on both measures of suicidality. This finding is consistent with previous findings that participants who report intrusive sexual acts are more likely to be suicidal than nonabused participants (Bendixen, et al., 1994; Mullen, Martin, Anderson, Romans, & Herbison, 1993). Also, on SBQ scores, all sexual abuse groups were more suicidal than the no sexual abuse group. In addition, the severe sexual abuse group was more suicidal than the moderate sexual abuse group. This result is somewhat different from a previous study in which sexually abused college students (touched or forced to touch others) but not sexually exploited students (unwanted kissing, hugging, sexual invitations) were more suicidal than the nonabused group (Peters & Range, 1995). Perhaps sexual abuse involving genital touching and/or penetration is more likely to be associated with suicidality than sexual abuse involving less invasive sexual acts.

The severity factor also held true in terms of physical abuse alone. The severe physical abuse group was more suicidal than moderate and no physical abuse groups on SSI scores, and the severe physical abuse group was more suicidal than the no physical abuse group on SBQ scores. These results are consistent with other research (Bryant & Range, 1995b; Milner, Robertson & Rogers, 1990). It is also not surprising that there were no differences between the moderate and no physical abuse groups because participants who endorsed that their parents hit them with objects such as belts or brushes were included in the moderate physical abuse group. Using a belt to discipline children is a culturally condoned form of punishment, and may account for the low suicidality scores among participants who reported moderate and no physical abuse. An implication is that actions viewed as discipline, even if they involve hitting or leaving bruises, may have no with connection with later suicidality, unlike actions viewed as unjustified abuse.

Apparently the negative ramifications of the abuse extended to reasons for living. Those severely physically and severely sexually abused had fewer overall reasons for living and fewer social concerns as a reason for not committing suicide than all other abuse groups. Those severely sexually abused had fewer survival and coping beliefs than those moderately sexually abused, which is consistent with Peters and Range (1995). Apparently, participants who reported severe sexual and physical abuse endorsed less cognitive deterrents to suicide than participants who reported moderate sexual and/or physical abuse and no abuse. Sexual and/or physical abuse may hinder the development of cognitive suicide inhibitions. Or, cognitive deterrents to suicide may hinder remembering sexual and/or physical abuse. Alternatively, people who remember abuse may, be poor at producing cognitive deterrents to suicide. Finally, another factor may influence reporting of sexual and/or physical abuse as well its cognitive deterrents to suicide.

Severity of physical and sexual abuse accounted for 14% of variance in SBQ scores, 10% of variance in SSI scores, and only 2% of variance in BRFL scores, findings which are consistent with other research in which low variance in SSI scores was accounted for by sexual abuse (12%) and physical abuse (3%) (Bryant & Range, 1995a). Thus, the variance from sexual and physical abuse scores was statistically significant, but these findings are of little clinical significance.

Gender differences in present results sometimes favored women and at other times favored men. Consistent with Finkelhor and Browne (1985), women reported significantly more sexual abuse than men. Consistent with Peters and Range (1995), women reported more Survival and Coping Beliefs, Fear Of Suicide, Responsibility to Family, Child-related Concerns, and Moral Objections, as reasons for not committing suicide than men. Further, women and men were about the same in suicidality. Women college students apparently endorse more reasons for living than men and about the same level of suicidality despite a greater likelihood of having been abused.

In terms of demographic variables, a disproportionate number of single participants (75% overall) reported no physical abuse, and a disproportionate number of married participants reported severe physical abuse. However, age was unrelated to abuse in the present sample. Marriage may influence or help people to remember past abuse; or, abused people may be more likely to marry, or, some third factor may have influenced how participants responded to these two items. Whatever the explanation, this demographic difference is a limitation of present results.

Another limitation was voluntary rather than random participation. Also, the proportion of women (n=342) to men (n =120) is consistent with other research indicating that women are more likely to participate in extra credit activities than men (Range et al., 1992), but means that the present sample is more generalizable to college women than college men. In addition, the average age of 24 may have accounted for the large number of participants who expressed some suicidal ideas or global suicidality because suicide is the third leading cause of death 15- 24-year-olds and the fourth leading cause of death for 25- 44-year-olds (Centers for Disease Control, 1986). Other limitations include self-report and retrospective measures that may limit the reliability of participant responses due to the desire to look good or an inability to remember accurately. In contrast, the subject matter was sensitive, so participants may have hesitated to answer certain questions because of painful memories or feelings.

Finally, present results are limited by the failure to control for psychological abuse. Psychological abuse almost always accompanies all other forms of maltreatment, is probably the most prevalent form of abuse, and is often considered the most destructive form of abuse (Hart & Brassard, 1987). By omitting psychological abuse, we may have neglected the most damaging type of abuse. Future research is recommended to develop a standardized measure of psychological abuse, so that possible links to suicidality can be examined.

Despite these limitations, the present study indicated that college students who reported any sexual or physical abuse were more suicidal and had fewer cognitive deterrents to suicide than college students who reported no abuse. Further, severity made a difference. Apparently, sexual abuse involving invasive sexual acts such as rape and physical abuse involving behaviors that result in physical injury to the child are the most damaging, at least in terms of suicidality. However, the absence of an interaction between sexual and physical abuse on all dependent measures suggests that the ramifications of abuse are additive rather than multiplicative. An implication is, first, that college counseling personnel need to be aware of the suicide risk of those students reporting sexual and/or physical abuse, particularly in individuals who report histories of severe sexual and physical abuse.

References:

Bayatpour, M., Wells, R., & Holford, S. (1992). Physical and sexual abuse as predictors of substance use and suicidality among pregnant teenagers. *Journal of Adolescent Health*. 13. 128-132..

Beck, A.T.., Steer, R.A., & Ranieri, W.F (1988). Scale for Suicide Ideations: Psychometric properties of a self-report version. *Journal of Clinical Psychology*. 44, 499 – 505.

Betchman, J., Zucker, K., Hood, J. daCosta, G., Akman. D., & Cassavia, E.,:(1992). A review of the long-term effects of child sexual abuse. *Child Abuse and Neglect* 16 101- 118.

Bendixen, M., Muus, K.M. & Schei, B., (1994). The impact of child abuse: A study of a random sample of Norwegian students. *Child Abuse and Neglect* 18. 837-847.

Brown, G.R., & Anderson B.,.(1991). Psychiatric morbidity in adult inpatients with childhood histories of sexual and physical abuse. *American Journal of Psychiatry* 148. 55-61.

Bryant, S.L. & Range, L. M. (1995a). Suicidality in college women who were sexually, physically or psychologically maltreated by parents. *Journal of Child Sexual Abuse*. 4 87 -94,

Bryant, S.L. & Range, L. M. (1995b) Suicidality in college women who were sexually and physically abused and physically punished by parents. *Violence and Victims*. 10, 125-131.

Bryer,J., Nelson. B. A., Miller, J. B. & Krol, P.A. (1987) Childhood sexual and physical abuse as factors in adult psychiatric illness. *American Journal of Psychiatry* 144. 1426- 1430.

Centers for Disease Control. (1986). *Youth suicide in the United States, 1970 – 1980.* Atlanta, GA: Department of Health and Human Services.

Cole, D.A., (1988). Hopelessness, social desirability, depression, and parasuicide in two college student samples. *Journal of Consulting and Clinical Psychology*. 56, 131 136.

Cotton,. R.C., Peters,. D. K. & Range. L. M. (1995) Psychometric properties of the Suicide Behaviors Questionnaire. *Death Studies*. 19, 391-397.

Finkelhor, D. (1979) *Sexually victimized children.* New York Free Press

Finkelhor, D & Browne, A. (1985). The traumatic impact of child sexual abuse: A conceptualization. *American Journal of Orthopsychiatry,* 55, 530-541.

Gross, A. B.,. & Keller, H. R. (1992). Long-term consequences of childhood physical and psychological maltreatment. *Aggressive Behavior*. 18 171-185.

Hart, S. N., & Brassard M. R. (1987) A major threat to children's mental health: Psychological maltreatment. *American Psychologist,* 42 160-165.

Ivanoff, A., Jang, S., Smyth., N., & Linehan,, M. (1994). Fewer reasons for staying alive when you are thinking of killing yourself: A brief reasons for living inventory. *Journal of Psychopathology and Behavioral Assessment*. 16. 1-13

Linehan, M. M., & Nielsen, S. L. (1981). Assessment of suicide ideation and parasuicide: Hopelessness and social desirability. *Journal of Consulting and Clinical Psychology*. 49, 773-775.

Linehan, M., Goodstein, J., Nielsen, S., & Chiles, J. (1983). Reasons for staying alive when you are thinking of killing yourself: The reasons for living inventory. *Journal of Consulting and Clinical Psychology*. 51. 276-286.

Mills T., Reiker, P. P., & Carmen. E. H. (1985). Hospitalization experiences of victims of abuse. *Victimology: An International Journal*, 9. 436-449.

Milner, K/ S/. Robertson, K. R., & Rogers, D. L. (1990). Childhood history of abuse and adult child abuse potential. *Journal of Family Violence*, 5. 15-33.

Mullen, P. E., Martin, J. L., Anderson, J., Romans, S., & Herbison. G. (1993). Childhood sexual abuse and mental health in adult life. *British Journal of Psychiatry*. 163. 721-732.

Peters, D., & Range, L. M. (1995). Childhood sexual abuse and current suicidality in college women and men. *Child Abuse, & Neglect*, 19. 335-341.

Range, L. M., Turzo, P., & Ellis, J. B. (1992). On the difficulties of recruiting men as undergraduate subjects. *College Student Journal*, 23. 340-342.

Wind, T. W., & Silvern, L. (1992). Type and extent of child abuse as predictors of adult functioning. *Journal of Family Violence*, 7. 261-281.

Immediate and Long-Term Impacts of Child Sexual Abuse*

John N. Briere, Ph.D.
and
Diana M. Elliott Ph.D.

Introduction

Research conducted over the past decade indicates that a wide range of psychological and interpersonal problems are more prevalent among those who have been sexually abused than among individuals with no such experiences. Although a definitive causal relationship between such difficulties and sexual abuse cannot be established using current retrospective research methodologies, [1] the aggregate of consistent findings in this literature has led many researchers and clinicians to conclude that childhood sexual abuse is a major risk factor for a variety of problems, both in the short term and in later adult functioning.[2] Further, longitudinal studies currently under way[3] suggest that sexual abuse, as well as other forms of child maltreatment, does in fact lead to subsequent psychological difficulties in the short and longer term. As a result, the contention of some earlier clinicians[4] that childhood sexual abuse is a neutral or even benign event has little current acceptance in the field.

This article summarizes what is currently known about the potential impacts of child molestation. The long-term impacts in adults have been documented across a wide variety of samples, including university, general population, psychiatric inpatient, psychotherapy outpatient, and professional subjects. Although individual studies may not include a fully representative sample of adults abused as children, a confluence of findings suggests that there are predictable sequelae to sexual abuse in the long term. In contrast to the study of adult survivors, the scientific study of the impact of sexual abuse on children is a relatively recent endeavor. Many of the studies on children have relied on clinical or forensic samples and may not be generalizable to all sexually abused children. These studies may underrepresent the impact of abuse in children who are motivated to deny their abuse[5] or children whose reaction to abuse is significantly delayed.[6]

These various issues decrease the likelihood that there is a "sexual abuse syndrome" present in all those molested as children. A substantial minority of sexually abused children (10% to 28%) report no psychological distress.[7, 8] This may be because the term "sexual abuse" covers a range of abusive behaviors of varying intensity and duration. Survivors who experience, for example, a single incident of less intrusive sexual abuse that is disclosed to a supportive parent who takes protective action may be more likely to report minimal or none of the typical sequelae documented in research studies and outlined in this paper. Thus, it cannot be assumed that the relative presence or absence of a given symptom or symptom complex is indicative of a sexual abuse history in any given individual.

This paper highlights some of the key studies on the potential psychological and interpersonal impacts of childhood molestation. While literally hundreds of studies have been completed in the past decade, the authors have included only those with larger sample sizes and those with similar behavioral definitions of sexual abuse (that is, sexual contact prior to the age of 16 or 18 either [a] with someone five or more years older or [b] by the use of force). Unless specifically stated, all studies cited are retrospective in nature.

*As previously printed in: The Future of Children SEXUAL ABUSE OF CHILDREN Vol. 4 - No. 2 - Summer/Fall 1994 Reprinted with the permission of The David and Lucile Packard Foundation.

With these precautions in mind, the primary psychological impacts of sexual abuse are thought to occur in at least three stages: (1) initial reactions to victimization, involving posttraumatic stress, disruptions of normal psychological development, painful emotions, and cognitive distortions; (2) accommodation to ongoing abuse, involving coping behaviors intended to increase safety and/or decrease pain during victimization; and (3) the more long-term consequences, reflecting the impacts of initial reactions and abuse related accommodations on the individual's ongoing psychological development and personality formation.[9] Although some initial reactions of victims to their abuse may abate with time, other reactions, along with abuse-specific coping behaviors, appear to generalize and elaborate over the long term.

The various problems and symptoms described in the literature on child sexual abuse can be divided into a series of broad categories or spheres of impact that the authors have found useful in understanding sexual abuse sequelae. These are posttraumatic stress, cognitive distortions, emotional pain, avoidance, an impaired sense of self and interpersonal difficulties.

Posttraumatic Stress

Posttraumatic stress refers to certain enduring psychological symptoms that occur in reaction to a highly distressing, psychically disruptive event. A diagnosis of posttraumatic stress disorder (PTSD) requires the occurrence of a traumatic event, as well as (1) frequent reexperiencing of the event through nightmares or intrusive thoughts, (2) a numbing of general responsiveness to, or avoidance of, current events, and (3) persistent symptoms of increased arousal, such as jumpiness, sleep disturbance, or poor concentration.[10]

Although PTSD was initially associated with adult response to disasters, accidents' and combat experiences, more recent research has linked short- and long-term posttraumatic symptoms to childhood sexual abuse.[11] For example, children who have been abused exhibit more posttraumatic fear, anxiety, and concentration problems than do their nonabused peers.[12] Research focusing on assessing sexually abused children has found that these children are more likely to receive the diagnosis of PTSD than their nonabused peers, at rates of up to 48%.[13] Although most child sexual abuse victims do not meet the full diagnostic criteria for PTSD, more than 80% are reported to have some posttraumatic symptoms.[14]

Both clinical and nonclinical groups of adult sexual abuse survivors have been found to display more intrusive, avoidant, and arousal symptoms of PTSD than those not abused as children.[15] Especially prominent for adult survivors are PTSD related flashbacks-sudden, intrusive sensory experiences, often involving visual, auditory, olfactory, and/or tactile sensations reminiscent of the original assault, experienced as though they were occurring in the present rather than as a memory of a past event. Triggers of flashbacks include sexual stimuli or interactions, abusive behavior by other adults, disclosure of one's abuse experiences to others, and reading or seeing sexual or violent media depictions.[16]

Other PTSD symptoms involve repetitive, intrusive thoughts and/or memories of childhood sexual victimization-difficulties that many survivors of sexual abuse find both distressing and disruptive. These differ from flashbacks in that they are thoughts and recollections rather than sensory experiences. Typically, intrusive thoughts center around themes of danger, humiliation, spontaneous sexual contact, guilt, and "badness," whereas intrusive memories involve unexpected recall of specific abusive events. Nightmares with violent abuse-related themes are also commonly associated with sexual abuse related PTSD.

Cognitive Distortions

People make significant assumptions about themselves, others, the environment, and the future based upon childhood learning. Because the experiences of children who are abused are often negative, these assumptions and self-perceptions typically reflect an overestimation of the amount of danger or adversity in the world and an underestimation of the abuse survivor's self-efficacy and self-worth. A variety of studies document chronic self-perceptions of helplessness and hopelessness, impaired trust, self-blame, and low self-esteem in abused children. [17] These cognitive alterations often continue on into adolescence and adulthood. [18]

Such negative thoughts probably arise from multiple sources, including psychological reactions to abuse-specific events, stigmatization of the victim by the abuser and society, and the victim's attempt to make sense of his or her maltreatment. [9, 19] Chronic perceptions of helplessness and danger are thought to result from the fact that the child abuse occurred when the victim was physically and psychologically unable to resist or defend against the abuser. This expectation of injury may lead to hyperreactivity or "overreaction" to real, potential, or imagined threats. The most predictable impact of this dynamic is the victim's growing assumption that he or she is without recourse or options under a widening variety of circumstances. Because such experiences are often chronic and ongoing, feelings of hopelessness regarding the future are also likely. Similarly, the child may make assumptions about his or her inherent badness, based on misinterpretation of maltreatment as, in fact, punishment for unknown transgressions. [9]

As would be predicted from the above, the study of cognition in the adjustment of victims of sexual molestation has linked such abuse to subsequent guilt, low self-esteem, self-blame, and other dysfunctional or inaccurate attributions. [20] Gold found that women with a history of child sexual abuse were more likely to attribute the cause of negative events to internal, stable, and global factors, as well as to their character and to their behavior (that is, "this negative event occurred because I am an inherently bad person and I will never change"). [21] These same women tended to attribute the cause of good events to external factors. Such cognitive distortions may contribute to or, alternatively, act as mediators of the emotional distress evident among many adult survivors of child sexual abuse. [22]

Emotional Distress

Clinicians have long noted the emotional pain reported by many survivors of sexual abuse. [23] This distress is also well documented in the research literature, primarily in terms of increased depression, anxiety, and anger.

Depression

Browne and Finkelhor note that, "in the clinical literature, depression is the symptom most commonly reported among adults molested as children. [11, 24] A variety of studies have documented greater depressive symptomatology among child victims, [25] as well as adult survivors. [26] Lanktree, Briere, and Zaidi found that child victims in outpatient therapy were more than four times as likely to have received a diagnosis of major depression than were nonabused patients. [27] Similarly, adults with a history of sexual abuse may have as much as a four-time greater lifetime risk for major depression than do individuals with no such abuse history. [28] These findings are supported by a wide variety of other studies documenting greater depressive symptomatology in adolescents and adults with sexual abuse histories. [29]

Anxiety

Child abuse is, by its nature, threatening and disruptive, and may interfere with the child's developing sense of security and belief in a safe Just world. [9] Thus, it should not be surprising that victims of such maltreatment are prone to chronic feelings of fearfulness or anxiety. Elevated anxiety has been documented in child victims of sexual abuse, [6,30] as well as in adults who were molested as children. [31] In the general population, survivors are more likely than nonabused individuals to meet the criteria for generalized anxiety disorder, phobias, panic disorder, and/or obsessive compulsive disorder, with sexual abuse survivors having up to five times greater likelihood of being diagnosed with at least one anxiety disorder than their nonabused peers. [28,32]

Clinical experience suggests that the anxiety frequently has a conditioned component, in that sexual abuse usually takes place in human relationships where closeness and nurturance is expected, yet intrusion, abandonment, devaluation, and/or pain occur. As a result, a learned association may form between various social or environmental stimuli and danger, such that a variety of otherwise relatively neutral interpersonal events elicit fear. [33] For example, the formerly abused individual may become anxious in the presence of intimate or close relationships, especially fearful of evaluation, or frightened when interacting with authority figures.

Perhaps the most obvious example of conditioned, abuse-related fear among adult survivors is that of sexual dysfunction. Because childhood sexual molestation is likely to create an association between sexual stimuli and invasion or pain, many adults molested as children report fear or anxiety-related difficulties during sexual contact. Meiselman, for example, reported that 87% of her clinical sample of adults molested as children had "serious" sexual problems, as opposed to 20% of those clients without a sexual abuse history. [34] Similarly, Maltz and Holman found that 60% of the incest survivors they studied reported pain during sexual intercourse, and 48% were unable to experience orgasms during sex. [35] A number of other studies also report an empirical connection between childhood sexual abuse and sexual problems or dysfunction in childhood, adolescence, and adulthood. [36]

Abuse-related anxiety can also be expressed physically, resulting from the impacts of sustained fearfulness on bodily functioning or perception. These somatic difficulties arise as a natural extension of hyperarousal of the sympathetic ("fight or flight") nervous system. Physical problems that have been associated with child sexual abuse histories include headaches, stomach pain, asthma, bladder infections, and chronic pelvic pain. [37] Such findings suggest that some proportion of medical complaints presented to physicians and other health care practitioners may less reflect inherent bodily dysfunction than somatic equivalents of anxiety that arise from unresolved childhood maltreatment experiences. [38]

Anger

Another common emotional sequel of child sexual abuse is that of anger. Chronic irritability, unexpected or uncontrollable feelings of anger, and difficulties associated with the expression of anger have been reported by child victims. [5, 39] Such feelings can become internalized as self-hatred and depression, or be externalized and result in the perpetration of abuse against others. [40]

In children, anger is frequently expressed in behavioral problems, with abused children and adolescents displaying significantly more difficulties in this area than what is found typically in the general population. [41] These data suggest that children's aggressiveness toward others-commonly expressed as fighting, bullying, or attacking other children-is a frequent short-term sequel of sexual molestation. Although such behavior may represent an externalization of children's distress from their own abuse trauma, and, perhaps, a cry for help, the net effect of this angry aggression is often increased social isolation and unpopularity. [42]

Less research has been done on the extent of anger experienced by adolescent and adult survivors, although the data available suggest that difficulties in this area are also a long-term sequel of sexual abuse. [43] In these studies, adult sexual abuse survivors score higher on measures of anger and irritability than do adults without childhood sexual abuse histories. One possible form of abuse-related anger is that of sexually aggressive behavior toward others. As a group, adolescent and adult sexual abuse survivors are more prone than others to victimize children and women sexually. [44] It should be noted, however, that most studies in this area indicate that the majority of survivors do not go on to perpetrate such abuse against others. [45]

Impaired Sense of Self

The development of a sense of self is thought to be one of the earliest developmental tasks of the infant and young child, typically unfolding in the context of early relationships.[46] How a child is treated (or maltreated) early in life influences his or her growing self-awareness. As a result, severe child maltreatment-including early and sustained sexual abuse-may interfere with the child's development of a sense of self.[47]

Without such an internal base, individuals may lack the ability to soothe or comfort themselves adequately, leading to what appear to be overreactions to stress or painful effects. This impairment can also cause difficulties in separating self from others. Adults molested early in life have more problems understanding or relating to others independent of their own experiences or needs, and they may not be able to perceive or experience their own internal states independent of the reactions or demands of others.[48] These difficulties may translate into a continuing inability to define one's own boundaries or reasonable rights when faced with the needs or demands of others in the interpersonal environment. Such problems, in turn, are associated with subsequent psychosocial difficulties, including increased suggestibility or gullibility, inadequate self-protectiveness, and a greater likelihood of being victimized or exploited by others.

Avoidance

Avoidant behavior among victims of sexual abuse may be understood as attempts to cope with the chronic trauma and dysphoria induced by childhood victimization. Among the dysfunctional activities associated with avoidance of abuse-specific memories and feeling are dissociation, substance abuse, suicidality, and various tension-reducing activities.[9] In each instance, the problem behavior may represent a conscious or unconscious choice to be involved in seemingly dysfunctional and/or self-destructive behaviors rather than fully experience the considerable pain of abuse-specific awareness. Unfortunately, although sometimes immediately effective in reducing distress, avoidance and self-destructive methods of coping with child abuse experiences may lead ultimately to higher levels of symptomatology, lower self-esteem, and greater feelings of guilt and anger.[49]

Dissociative Phenomena

Dissociation can be defined as a disruption in the normally occurring linkages between subjective awareness, feelings, thoughts, behavior, and memories, consciously or unconsciously invoked to reduce psychological distress.[9] Examples of dissociation include: (1) derealization and depersonalization, that is, the experience of self or the environment as suddenly strange or unreal; (2) periods of disengagement from the immediate environment during times of stress, for example via "spacing out" or excessive daydreaming; (3) alterations in bodily perception; (4) emotional numbing; (5) out-of-body experiences; (6) amnesia for painful abuse-related memories; and (7) multiple personality disorder.[50] Dissociative symptomatology has been linked to sexual trauma in children [5,51] and adults.[52] Such symptoms are apt to be prevalent among child and adult survivors because they reduce or circumvent the emotional pain associated with abuse-related experiences or recollections, permitting superficially higher levels of psychological functioning.[53]

Dissociation is thought to underlie many individuals' reports of periods of amnesia for their childhood abuse in that such memories are believed to have been defensively excluded from conscious awareness.[54] Two studies suggest that adults in psychotherapy quite commonly report some period in their lives when they had incomplete or absent memories of their childhood abuse. Herman and Schatzow found that 64% of 53 women undergoing group therapy for sexual abuse trauma had some period of time prior to treatment when they had incomplete or absent memories of their molestation.[55] Among 450 men and women in psychotherapy to deal with abuse-related difficulties, 59% reported having had some period before age 18 when they had no memory of being abused.[56] In both of these studies, self-reported abuse-related amnesia was associated with more severe and extensive abuse that occurred at a relatively earlier age. Loftus, Polonsky, and Fullilove found that 19% of more than 50 sexual abuse survivors in treatment for chemical dependency stated that, at some point in the past, they had no sexual abuse memories and that an additional 12% had only partial memories of their childhood sexual victimization.[57] Interestingly, in the latter study, the authors interpreted their data as not necessarily supporting the notion of psychogenic amnesia, per se, but rather referred to this process, at least in some instances, as "forgetting."

In a methodological improvement (over the above retrospective studies, Williams followed up 129 women who, as children, had been seen in an urban emergency room with a primary complaint of having been sexually abused.[58] These subjects were interviewed approximately 18 to 20 years later-without knowledge that the interviewers were aware of their childhood ER visit-and asked whether they had ever been sexually abused as children. Thirty-eight percent of this sample reported no memory of having been sexually abused, despite records that sexual abuse had, in fact, taken place. Unlike previous investigations, this new study cannot be faulted in terms of potential biases to recall, because the original abuse had been verified and the subjects were currently denying (as opposed to alleging) a sexual abuse history. Assuming that their nonreport was not caused by inhibition, modesty, or other conscious influences (a doubtful explanation because many reported other painful or upsetting childhood events, including other sexual abuse experiences), Williams's subjects appear to provide data that childhood abuse experiences can, in fact, be excluded from current memory.[59]

Substance Abuse and Addiction

A number of studies have found a relationship between sexual abuse and later substance abuse among adolescent[60] and adult survivors.[61] Briere and Runtz report that sexually abused female crisis center clients had ten times the likelihood of a drug addiction history and two times the likelihood of alcoholism relative to a group of nonabused female clients.[62] It seems likely that sustained drug or alcohol abuse allows the abuse survivor to separate psychologically from the environment, anesthetize painful internal states, and blur distressing memories. Thus, some significant proportion of those currently addicted to drugs or alcohol may be attempting to self-medicate severe abuse related depression, anxiety, or posttraumatic stress. From this perspective, treatment or forensic interventions that merely detoxify and/or punish substance abuse are unlikely to be effective - - especially in the longer term. Instead, addicted survivors may respond more definitively to therapeutic or self-help interventions that reduce the abuse-related internal distress motivating chemical dependency.

Suicide

The ultimate avoidance strategy may be suicide. As noted by Schneidman, Farberow, and Litman, escape from extreme psychic pain-that is, depression, anxiety, or extreme hopelessness-is a commonly expressed motivation for suicide.[63] Thus, it should not be surprising that increased suicidal ideation and behaviors have been linked to sexual abuse in child victims.[27, 64] Similarly, several studies of adults who were molested as children document more frequent suicidal behavior and/or greater suicidal ideation among survivors relative to their nonabused peers. Rates of a previous suicide attempt, for example, were 51 % in a subsample of 67 sexually abused female crisis clients[65] and 66% in a subgroup of 50 sexually abused female psychiatric emergency room patients,[66] as compared with an average rate of 27% for nonabused patients in these studies. In a community sample, approximately 16% of survivors had attempted suicide, whereas fewer than 6% of their nonabused cohorts had made a similar attempt.[32]

Tension- Reducing Activities

Certain behaviors reported by adult survivors of child sexual abuse, such as compulsive and indiscriminate sexual activity, bingeing or chronic overeating, and self-mutilation, can be seen as fulfilling a need to reduce the considerable painful affect that can accompany unresolved sexual abuse trauma. Often these activities are seen as "acting-out," "impulsivity," or, most recently, as arising from "addictions." For the abuse survivor, however, such behaviors may best be understood as problem solving behaviors in the face of extreme abuse-related dysphoria.

Chronic abuse-related distress may be reduced by activities that provide temporary distraction, interrupt dysphoric states, anesthetize psychic pain, restore a sense of control, temporarily "fill" perceived emptiness, and/or relieve guilt or selfhatred.[9] These behaviors are frequently effective in creating a temporary sense of calm and relief, at least for some period of time. Ultimately, the use of tension reducing mechanisms in the future is reinforced through a process of avoidance learning: behavior that reduces pain is likely to be repeated in the presence of future pain.

Indiscriminate Sexual Behavior

It is widely noted by clinicians that adolescents and adults molested as children are prone to episodes of frequent, short-term sexual activity, often with a number of different sexual partners.[34, 67] This may explain why, compared with their nonabused peers, survivors of sexual abuse are at greater risk for unintended and terminated pregnancies, as well as for contracting sexually transmitted diseases.[68]

In addition to temporarily addressing the need for closeness and intimacy arising from deprivation in these areas during childhood-indiscriminate sexual behavior by some sexual abuse survivors may provide distraction and avoidance of distress for some adults molested as children. Sexual arousal and positive sexual attention can temporarily mask or dispel chronic abuse-related emotional pain by providing more pleasurable or distress-incompatible experiences. For such individuals, frequent sexual activity may represent a consciously or unconsciously chosen coping mechanism, invoked specifically to control painful internal experience.

Bingeing and Purging

Specialists in eating disorders have suggested recently that both adolescent and adults with bulimia (episodes of bingeing on food, then purging via vomiting or laxatives) may be especially likely to report child sexual abuse histories.[69] Although this is a relatively new area of research related to sexual abuse, it appears that childhood molestation is associated specifically with bulimic bingeing and purging, whereas (nonbingeing) anorexia nervosa is less relevant to sexual molestation history, per se.[70] It should be noted, however, that at least one review of the literature questions the validity of a sexual abuse-bulimia relationship.[71] Root and Fallon suggest that binge-purge behaviors can operate as "both a reaction to and a method of coping with physical and sexual abuse.[72] The tension-reducing aspects of bulimia include self-soothing, distraction from non-food-related concerns, and a (literal) filling of perceived emptiness.

Self-Mutilation

Self-mutilation is defined by Walsh and Rosen as "deliberate, non-life-threatening, self-effected bodily harm or disfigurement of a socially unacceptable nature.[1, 73] It most typically involves repetitious cutting or carving of the body or limbs, burning of the skin with cigarettes, or hitting of the head or body against or with objects.[74] Each of these forms of self-injury has been found to occur among recent or former victims of child sexual abuse.[74,75] Various authors have hypothesized that self-mutilatory behavior serves to temporarily reduce the psychic tension associated with extremely negative affect, guilt, intense depersonalization, feelings of helplessness, and/or painfully fragmented thought processes-states all too common among survivors of severe sexual abuse.[76] Although often immediately effective, such behavior is rarely adaptive in the long term, leading to repeated cycles of self-injury, subsequent calm, the slow building of further tension, and, ultimately, further self-mutilation.

Interpersonal Difficulties

Research and clinical observation have long suggested that child sexual abuse is associated with both initial and long-term alterations in social functioning.[9,77] Interpersonal difficulties arise from both the immediate cognitive and conditioned responses to victimization that extend into the long term (for example, distrust of others, anger at and/or fear of those with greater power, concerns about abandonment, perceptions of injustice), as well as the accommodation responses to ongoing abuse (for example, avoidance, passivity, and sexualization).

Sexual abuse usually occurs in the context of human relationships, with as many as 85% of cases perpetrated by individuals known to the victim.[78] The violation and betrayal of boundaries in the context of developing intimacy can create interpersonal difficulties in many survivors. These intimacy problems appear to center primarily on ambivalence and fear regarding interpersonal vulnerability. Although interpersonal difficulties are commonly reported by survivors, they are more prominent when the victimization begins at an especially early age, lasts over an extended period of time, or occurs within the nuclear family.[48]

It has been observed that sexually abused children tend to be less socially competent, more aggressive, and more socially withdrawn than nonabused children.[79] These children, as a group, tend to perceive themselves as different from others and tend to be less trusting of those in their immediate environment.[80] They have fewer friends during childhood, less satisfaction in relationships, and report less closeness with their parents than do nonvictims.

A specific interpersonal effect of sexual abuse among children is that of increased sexual behavior. Sexually abused children are consistently reported to have more sexual behavior problems than nonabused children or children whose abuse was restricted to (nonsexual) physical or emotional maltreatment.[30,81] Although some kinds of sexual behaviors are quite common among nonabused children (for example, kissing, touching genitals manually), sexually abused children tend to engage in a greater number of sexual behaviors than their nonabused peers, many of which are developmentally precocious and seemingly imitative of adult sexual activity.[82] Such behavior not only may result in interpersonal rejection or stigmatization by the victim's peer milieu, but also may lead to social sanctions and punishments when it escalates into the victimization of other children.[83]

As adults, survivors report a greater fear of both men and women.[84] They are more likely to remain single and, once married, are more likely to divorce or separate from their spouses than are those without sexual abuse histories.[85] Sexual abuse survivors typically report having fewer friends,[21] less interpersonal trust,[84] less satisfaction in their relationships, more maladaptive interpersonal patterns,[48] and greater discomfort, isolation, and interpersonal sensitivity.

Conte and Schuerman speculate that adults victimized as children may see themselves as unworthy of relationships with people they consider good or healthy, and that some victims may attempt to gain mastery over the abuse experience by recreating it in the form of involvement in poor or abusive relationships.[86] In this regard, sexual or physical revictimization (that is, rape or spousal abuse) has been associated with prior child sexual abuse in a number of studies.[87]

Adults who were sexually abused as children are particularly likely to report difficulties with sexual intimacy. Such problems may present as: (1) sexual dysfunction related to fears of vulnerability and revictimization,[35] (2) as noted earlier, a tendency to be dependent upon or to overidealize those with whom they form close relationships,[16,88] and (3) also as previously noted, a history of multiple, superficial, or brief sexual relationships that quickly end as intimacy develops. The effects of abuse on the survivor's later sexuality is thought to contribute to the high incidence of sexual abuse histories found among adolescent and adult prostitutes,[89] many of whom appear to view their current occupation as an extension of their childhood experiences.[90]

Mitigating Factors

Because the literature summarized above is relatively unanimous with regard to the potential negative psychological impacts of childhood sexual abuse, there is a risk that the reader will assume that such victimization has an inevitable, uniform, and massive impact on victims. This impression results in part from the way in which most sexual abuse research is done: A group of subjects with childhood sexual abuse histories are compared with another group who were not abused on a variety of psychological measures. This nomothetic approach (that is, an approach involving the comparison of groups of subjects) is well known for glossing over individual differences and producing generalizations that, although valid for the group, may not be accurate for any given individual subject. In the present context, this approach tends to mask individual protective or pathogenic factors in the abuse symptom relationship. A careful examination of the data suggests that, although child and adult survivors tend, as groups, to have more problems than their nonabused peers, there is no single universal or uniform impact of sexual abuse, and no certainty that any given person will develop any posttraumatic responses to sexual abuse (for example, sexual concerns and dissociation).

As previously stated, as many as one fourth of all sexually abused children either report no initial abuse-related problems or may no longer present with demonstrable symptomatology within two years of their abuse.[7,8] However, as reported in an 18-month longitudinal study, children who were initially asymptomatic had more problems at an 18-month follow-up than did children who were initially highly symptomatic.[6] Additionally, it is likely that some abuse-related problems are overlooked by research that utilizes measures of general psychological distress rather than abuse-specific measures. Studies that use generic nonabuse-specific measures potentially overestimate the number of "asymptomatic" abuse victims in a given sample.[91] This occurs because such measures do not tap the effects most often associated with sexual abuse (for example, sexual concerns and dissociation).

Although research on mediators of sexual abuse effects is in its infancy, a number of factors appear to be associated with increased distress for survivors. Significant, yet modest, correlations have been demonstrated between specific aspects of a sexual abuse event and subsequent symptomatology. Variables associated with increased distress include molestation at an especially early age, extended and frequent abuse, incest by a biological parent, the presence of force, and a greater number of perpetrators.[92] More extreme psychological problems are also predicted by the presence of other concomitant forms of child maltreatment, including physical and psychological abuse or neglect, and/or subsequent revictimization in adulthood.[93]

Family characteristics and response to abuse disclosure also tend to predict subsequent levels of distress. Child victims and adult survivors are often more distressed if their families are characterized by greater dysfunction, especially in terms of conflict and low intrafamilial cohesion.[94] Additionally, parental response to a child's disclosure is significantly associated with the survivor's symptomatic outcome. Belief in the victim's disclosure and support for his or her experience are associated with decreased symptomatology, whereas disclosures that were met with disbelief or punishment appear to be associated with increased psychological disturbance.[95]

Most parents appear to believe their children when they disclose sexual abuse and often take some protective action.[61, 96] However, at least for sexual abuse perpetrated by males, the closer the relationship of the offender to the mother (for example, if he is her spouse or boyfriend), the more likely it is that support will be compromised.[5,6] This is especially unfortunate because enjoying maternal support or having a supportive relationship with an adult tends to decrease the impact of the abuse on the survivor.[6,86]

Finally, it is the impression of clinicians and researchers in the field that a child's pre-abuse functioning may have significant impacts on how he or she responds to subsequent abuse events and the extent to which abuse-related symptoms persist over time. These may include inborn temperamental differences and antecedent psychological disorder or distress. Especially intriguing at this juncture is the possibility that problems in the early infant caregiver attachment ("bonding") relationship may exacerbate or complicate the impacts of later sexual abuse, [97] leading to subsequent difficulties in the victim's developing sense of self.[9]

Directions for Future Research

This first wave of scientific inquiry has demonstrated the wide variety of psychological problems that can be associated with childhood sexual abuse. However, the data on both adult and child victims have certain limitations. As indicated in the previous section, certain pre- and post-abuse variables may affect the victim and his or her response to the abuse in either a positive or a negative direction. Studies often do not have large enough samples to examine these variables while, at the same time, controlling for the potential impact of other forms of concomitant child abuse. As a result, it is not always clear to what extent a given study has identified the *unique* effects of sexual abuse.[9]

Only a second wave of research-focusing on potential ameliorating or exacerbating variables in the genesis of abuse effects-can provide a more complete picture of the complexities of childhood sexual victimization and its psychological impacts. Such research should continue to examine the impacts of abuse in a variety of large samples (for example, general population, clinical samples, university studies) and to utilize multivariate approaches to the study of sexual abuse. Ultimately, the issues will be best addressed with longitudinal and prospective studies, rather than with the heavy reliance on retrospective studies in the work described in this paper.

Conclusion

This paper outlines the results of a decade of research on the association between childhood sexual victimization experiences and a variety of later psychological symptoms and difficulties. Taken together, the data provide strong support for the negative psychological effects of sexual abuse. Childhood sexual abuse appears both to have sustained impacts on psychological functioning in many survivors and to have the potential for motivating the development of behaviors that, while immediately adaptive, often have long-term self-injurious consequences. At the same time, these data suggest that the extent to which a given individual manifests abuse related symptomatology and distress is a function of an undetermined number of abuse-specific variables, as well as individual and environmental factors that existed prior to, or occurred subsequent to, the incidents of sexual abuse.

References

1. Briere, J. Methodological issues in the study of sexual abuse effects. *Journal of Consulting and Clinical Psychology* (1992) 60:196-203.
2. Browne, A., and Finkelhor, D. Impact of child sexual abuse: A review of the research. *Psychological Bulletin* (1986) 99:66-77; Finkelhor, D. Early and long-term effects of child sexual abuse: An update. *Professional Psychology* (1990) 21:325-30.
3. Erickson, M.F., Egeland, B., and Pianta, R. The effects of maltreatment on the development of young children. In *Research and theory: Child maltreatment.* D. Cicchetti and V Carlson, eds. London: Cambridge, 1989; Everson, M.D., Hunter, W.M., Runyon, DX, et al. Maternal support following disclosure of incest. *Americanjournal of Orthopsychiatry* (1989) 59:198-207.
4. See, for example, Constantine, L.L. Effects of early sexual experiences: A review and synthesis of research. In *Children and sex: Newfindings, new perspectives.* L.L. Constantine and F.M. Martinson, eds. Boston: Little, Brown, 1980; Henderson, DJ. Is incest harmful? *Canadian Journal of Psychiatry* (1983) 28:34-39.
5. Elliott, D.M., and Briere, J. Forensic sexual abuse evaluations in older children: Disclosures and symptomatology. *Behavioral Sciences and the Law.* In press.

6.   Gomes-Schwartz, B., Horowitz, J.M., and Cardarelli, A.P. *Child sexual abuse: The initial effects*. Newbury Park, CA: Sage, 1990.

7.   Conte, J.R., and Berliner, L. The impact of sexual abuse on children: Empirical findings. In *Handbook on sexual abuse of children: Assessment and treatment issues*. L.E. Walker, ed. New York: Springer, 1988, pp. 72-93.

8.   Kendall-Tackett, KA., Williams, L.M., and Finkelhor, D. Impact of sexual abuse on children: A review and synthesis of recent empirical studies. *Psychological Bulletin* (1993) 113:164-80.

9.   Briere, J. *Child abuse trauma: Theory and treatment of the lasting effects*. Newbury Park, CA: Sage, 1992.

10.   American Psychiatric Association. *Diagnostic and statistical manual of mental disorders*. 3rd ed. rev. Washington, DC: APA, 1987.

11.   Craine, L.S., Henson, C.H., ColliverjA., and MacLean, D.G. Prevalence of a history of sexual abuse among female psychiatric patients in a state hospital system. *Hospital and Community Psychiatry* (1988) 39:300-304; Lindberg, F.H., and Distad, Lj. Posttraumatic stress disorders in women who experienced childhood incest. *Child Abuse &Neglect* (1985) 9:329-34.

12.   Conte, J.R., and SchuermanjR. Factors associated with an increased impact of child sexual abuse. *Child Abuse & Neglect* (1987) 11,2:201-11; Wolfe, VV, Gentile, C., and Wolfe, D.A. The impact of sexual abuse on children: A PTSD formulation. *Behavior Therapy* (1989) 20:215-28.

13.   Famularo, R., Kinscherff, R., and Fenton, T. Psychiatric diagnoses of maltreated children: Preliminary findings. *Journal of the American Academy of Child and Adolescent Psychiatry* (1992) 31:863-67.

14.   McLeer, S.V, Deblinger, E.B., Esther, B., et al. Sexually abused children at high risk for posttraumatic stress disorder. *Journal of the American Academy of Child and Adolescent Psychiatry* (1992) 31:875-79.

15.   Runtz, M. The influence of coping strategies and social support on recovery from physical and sexual maltreatment during childhood. Doctoral dissertation. University of Manitoba, Canada, 1991. *Dissertation Abstracts International* (1992) 53:573B; Saunders, B.E., Villeponteaux, L.A., Lipovskyj A., et al. Child sexual assault as a risk factor for mental disorders among women: A community survey. *Journal of Interpersonal Violence* (1992) 7:189-204.

16.   Courtois, C.A. *Healing the incest wound: Adult survivors in therapy*. New York: W.W. Norton, 1988; Gelmas, Dj. The persisting negative effects of incest. *Psychiatry* (1983) 46:312-32.

17.   Barahal, R., Waterman, J., and Martm, H. The social-cognitive development of abused children. *Journal of Consulting and Clinical Psychology* (1981) 49:508-16; Oates, R.Y_, Forest, D., and Peacock, A. Self-esteem of abused children. *Child Abuse & Neglect* (1985) 9:159-63; also, see note no. 12, Conte and Schuerman.

18.   Farber, E.D., andjoseph,J.A. The maltreated adolescent: Patterns of physical abuse. *Child Abuse &Neglect* (1985) 9:201-6; Gold, E.R. Long-term effects of sexual victimization in childhood: An attributional approach. *Journal of Consulting and Clinical Psychology* (1986) 54:471-75.

19.   Finkelhor, D., and Browne, A. The traumatic impact of child sexual abuse: A conceptualization. *Americanjournal of Orthoppychiatry* (1985) 55:530-41.

20.   Jehu, D. *Beyond sexual abuse: Therapy with women who were childhood victims*. Chichester, England: Wiley, 1988; Wozencraft, T., Wagner, W., and Pellegrin, A. Depression and suicidal ideation in sexually abused children. *Child Abuse &Neglect* (1991) 15:505-11.

21.   See note no. 18, Gold.

22.   See note no. 20, Jehu; also see note no. 15, Runtz.

23.   For a discussion of the emotional distress reported by survivors of sexual abuse, see note no. 9, Briere; also, see note no. 16, Courtois.

24.   See note no. 2, Browne and Finkelhor, p. 152.

25. Lipovskyj.A., Saunders, B.E., and Murphy, S.M. Depression, anxiety, and behavior problems among victims of father-child sexual assault and nonabused siblings. *Journal of Interpersonal Violence* (1989) 4:452-68; also, see note no. 7, Conte and Berliner.

26. Briere j, and Runtz, M. Post-sexual abuse trauma: Data and implications for clinical practice. *Journal of Interpersonal Violence* (1987) 2:367-79; Peters, S.D. Child sexual abuse and later psychological problems. In *The lasting effects of child sexual abuse.* G.E. Wyatt and Gj. Powell, eds. Newbury Park, CA: Sage, 1988.

27. Lanktree, C.B., Brierej, and Zaidi, L.Y Incidence and impacts of sexual abuse in a child outpatient sample: The role of direct inquiry. *Child Abuse & Neglect* (1991) 15:447-53.

28. Stein, J.A., Golding, J.M., Siegel, J.M., et al. Long-term psychological sequelae of child sexual abuse: The Los Angeles epidemiological catchment area study. In *The lasting effects of child sexual abuse.* G.E. Wyatt and Gj. Powell, eds. Newbury Park, CA: Sage, 1988.

29. Elliott, D.M., and Briere j Sexual abuse trauma among professional women: Validating the Trauma Symptom Checklist-40 (TSC-40). *Child Abuse &Neglect* (1992) 16:391-98; also, see note no. 25. Lipovsky, Saunders, and Murphy.

30. Kolko, Dj., MoserjT, and Weldy, S.R. Behavioral/emotional indications of sexual abuse in child psychiatric inpatients: A controlled comparison with physical abuse. *Child Abuse &Neglect* (1988) 12:529-42.

31. Chu, J.A., and Dill, D.L. Dissociative symptoms in relation to childhood physical and sexual abuse. *American Journal of Psychiatry* (1990) 147:887-92; Swett, C., Surreyj, and Cohen, C. Sexual and physical abuse histories and psychiatric symptoms among male psychiatric outpatients. *American Journal of Psychiatry* (1990) 147:632-36; Elliott, D.M. The impact of child versus adult trauma: Gender and age differences. Paper presented at the 1993 meeting of the International Society for Traumatic Stress Studies. San Antonio, TX, October 1993.

32. See note no. 15, Saunders, Villeponteaux, Lipovsky, et al.

33. Berliner, L., and Wheeler, J.R. Treating the effects of sexual abuse on children. *Journal of Interpersonal Violence* (1987) 2:415-34.

34. Meiselman, F-C. *Incest: A psychological study of causes and effects with treatment recommendations.* San Francisco: jossey~Bass, 1978.

35. Maltz, W., and Holman, B. *Incest and sexuality: A guide to understanding and healing.* Lexington, MA: Lexington Books, 1987.

36. Beitchman,J.H., Zucker, Kj., HoodjE., et al. A review of the short-term effects of child sexual abuse. *Child Abuse &Neglect* (1991) 15:537-56; Friedrich, W.N. Sexual behavior in sexually abused children. In *Treating victims of child sexual abuse.* J. Briere, ed. San Francisco: jossey-Bass, 1991; see note no. 15, Saunders, Villeponteaux, Lipovsky, et al.

37. Cunningham, J., Pearce, T., and Pearce, P. Childhood sexual abuse and medical complaints in adult women. *Journal of Interpersonal Violence* (1988) 3:131-44; Morrison, J. Childhood sexual histories of women with somatization disorder. *American Journal of Psychiatry* (1989) 146:239-41; Springs, RE., and Friedrich, W.N. Health risk behaviors and medical sequelae of childhood sexual abuse. *Mayo Clinic Proceedings* (1992) 67:527-32; Walker, E., Karon, W., Harrop-Griffiths,J., et al. Relationship of chronic pelvic pain to psychiatric diagnosis and childhood sexual abuse. *American Journal of Psychiatry* (1988) 145:75-80.

38. Brierej Invited editorial: Medical symptoms, health risk, and child sexual abuse. *Mayo Clinic Proceedings* (1992) 67:6034.

39. Friedrich, W.N., Beilke, R.L., and Urquiza, Aj. Behavior problems in young sexually abused boys: A comparison study. *Journal of Interpersonal Violence* (March 1988) 3:21-28; Lanktree, C.B., and Brierej Effectiveness of therapy for sexual abuse trauma in children: Changes in Trauma Symptom Checklist for Children (TSC-C) scores. Paper presented at the annual meeting of the International Society for Traumatic Stress Studies. Los Angeles, CA, October 1992; Everson, M.D., Hunter, W.M., Runyon, D., and Edelson, G.A. Maternal support following disclosure of incest. *Annual Progress in Child Psychiatry and Child Development* (1990) 9:292-306.

40. Carmen, Ej., Rieker, RE, and Mills, T Victims of violence and psychiatric illness. *American Journal of Psychiatry* (1984) 141:378-83; Stukas-Davis, C. The influence of childhood sexual abuse and male sex role socialization on adult sexual functioning. Unpublished doctoral dissertation. California School of Professional Psychology, Los Angeles, CA, 1990.

41. Einbender, Aj., and Friedrich, W.N. Psychological functioning and behavior of sexually abused girls. *Journal of Consulting and Clinical Psychology* (1989) 57:155-57; Runtz, M., and Briere, J. Adolescent "acting out" and childhood history of sexual abuse. *Journal of Interpersonal Violence* (1986) 1:326-34.

42. Egeland, B. A longitudinal study of high-risk families: Issues and findings. Paper presented at the Research Forum on Issues in the Longitudinal Study of Child Maltreatment. Toronto, October 1989.

43. See note no. 26, Briere and Runtz; also, see note no. 25, Lipovsky, Saunders, and Murphy.

44. Langevin, R., Handy, L., Hook, H., et al. Are incestuous fathers pedophilic and aggressive? In *Erotic preference, gender identity, and aggression.* R. Langevin, ed. Hillsdale, NJ: Lawrence Erlbaum Associates, 1985; Rokous, E, Carter, D., and Prentkly, R. Sexual and physical abuse in the developmental histories of child molesters. Paper presented at the National Symposium on Child Abuse. Anaheim, CA, April 1988; Smiljanich, K, and Briere j Sexual abuse history and trauma symptoms in a university sample. Unpublished paper presented at a conference of the American Psychological Association. Toronto, Canada, August 1993; also, see note no. 40, Stukas-Davis.

45. Hopper, J., and Lisak, D. The relationship between abuse history and perpetration. Paper presented at the 1993 International Society for Traumatic Stress Studies. San Antonio, TX, October 1993.

Immediate and Long-Term Impacts of Child Sexual Abuse

46. Alexander, P.C. Application of attachment theory to the study of sexual abuse. *Journal of Consulting and Clinical Psychology* (1992) 60:185-95; BowlbyJ. *Separation: Anxiety and anger.* Vol. 2 of *Attachment and loss.* London: Hogarth, 1973.

47. Cole, P.M., and Putnam, EW. Effect of incest on self and social functioning: A developmental psychopathology perspective. *Journal of Consulting and Clinical Psychology* (1992) 60:174-84; Elliott, D.M. Impaired object relations in professional women molested as children. *Psychotherapy* (1994) 31:79-86; also see note no. 16, Courtois.

48. See note no. 47, Elliott.

49. Brierc, J., and Conte, J. Self-reported amnesia for abuse in adults molested as children. *Journal of Traumatic Stress* (1993) 6:21-31; also, see note no. 15, Runtz.

50. Putnam, EW. Dissociative phenomena. In *Dissociative disorders: A clinical review.* D. Spiegel, ed. Lutherville, MD: Sidran, 1993, pp. 1-16; Steinberg, M. The spectrum of depersonalization: Assessment and treatment. In *Dissociative disorders: A clinical review.* D. Spiegel, ed. Luthervillc, MD: Sidran, 1993, pp. 79-103.

51. Also, see note no. 39, Lanktree and Briere.

52. Briere,J., and Runtz, M. Differential adult symptomatology associated with three types of child abuse histories. *Child Abuse & Neglect* (1990) 14:357-64; also, see note no. 11, Lindberg and Distad.

53. van der Kolk, B.A., and Kadish, W. Amnesia, dissociation, and the return of the repressed. In *Psychological trauma.* B.A. van der Kolk, ed. Washington, DC: American Psychiatric Press, 1987, pp. 173-90.

54. Lowenstein, RJ. Psychogenic amnesia and psychogenic fugue: A comprehensive review. In *Childhood antecedents of multiple personality*. P. Kluft, ed. Washington, DC: American Psychiatric Press, 1993, pp. 65-98.

55. Herman, J.L., and Schatzow, E. Recovery and verification of memories of childhood sexual trauma. *Psychoanalytic Psychology* (1987) 4:490-94.

56. See note no. 49, Briere and Conte.

57. Loftus, E.F., Polonsky, S., and Fullilove, M.T. Memories of childhood sexual abuse: Remembering and repressing. *Psychology of Women Quarterly* (1994) 18:67-87.

58. Williams, L. Recall of childhood trauma: A prospective study of women's memories of child sexual abuse. *Journal of Consulting and Clinical Psychology*. In press.

59. For further information on what is often called the "repressed memory debate," see: Briere, J. Studying delayed memories of childhood sexual abuse. *APSAC Advisor* (1992) 5:17-18; Herman, J.L. Adult memories of childhood trauma: Current controversies. Paper presented at the annual meeting of the American Psychiatric Association. San Francisco, GA, May 1993; Loftus, E.E. The reality of repressed memories. *American Psychologist* (1993) 48:518-37.

60. Hibbard, S. Personality and object relational pathology in young adult children of alcoho*lics*. *Psychotherapy* (1989) 26:504-9; Singer, M.I., Petchers, M.K, and Hussey, D. The relationship between sexual abuse and substance abuse among psychiatrically hospitalized adolescents. *Child Abuse & Neglect* (1989) 13:319-25.

61. Dembo, R., Williams, L., LaVoie, L., et al. Physical abuse, sexual victimization, and illicit drug use: Replication of a structural analysis among a new sample of high-risk youths. *Violence and Victims* (1989) 4:121-38; Sullivan, EJ. Association between chemical dependency and sexual problems in nurses. *Journal of Interpersonal Violence* (1988) 3:326-30.

62. See note no. 26, Briere and Runtz.

63. Schneidman, E., Farberow, N., and Litman, R. *Psychology of suicide*. New York: Science House, 1970.

64. Briere, J., and Runtz, M. Suicidal thoughts and behaviours in former sexual abuse victims. Special issue on family violence. *Canadian Journal of Behavioural Science* (1986) 18:413-23.

65. For a discussion of postsexual abuse trauma, see note no. 26, Briere and Runtz.

66. Briere,J., and Zaidi, L.Y. Sexual abuse histories and sequelae in female psychiatric emergency room patients. *American Journal of Psychiatry* (1989) 146:1602-6.

67. Herman, J.L. *Father-daughter incest*. Cambridge: Harvard University Press, 1981.

68. Wyatt, G.E., Newcomb, M., Reederle, M., and Notgrass, C. *Sexual abuse and consensual sex: Women's developmental patterns and outcomes*. Newbury Park, CA: Sage, 1993.

69. Goldfarb, L.A. Sexual abuse antecedents to anorexia nervosa, bulimia, and compulsive overeating: Three case reports. *International Journal of Eating Disorders* (1987) 6:675-80; Root, M.P., and Fallon, P. Treating the victimized bulimic: The functions of binge-purge behavior. *Journal of Interpersonal Violence (1989) 4:90-100*.

70. Piran, N., Lerner, R, Garfinkel, P.E., et al. Personality disorders in anorexic patients. *Intentional Journal of Eating Disorders (1988) 7:589-99;* Steiger, H., and Zanko, M. Sexual traumata among eating-disordered, psychiatric, and normal female groups: Comparison of prevalences and defense styles. *Journal of Interpersonal Violence* (March *1990) 5:74-86.*

71. Pope, H.G., and Hudson,J.I. Is childhood sexual abuse a risk factor for bulimia nervosa? *American Journal of Psychiatry (1992) 149:455-63.*

72. See note no. *69*, Root and Fallon, p. *90*.

73. Walsh, BW., and Rosen, P. *Self-mutilation: Theory, research, and treatment*. New York: Guilford Press, *1988, p. 9.*

74. See note no. *73,* Walsh and Rosen.

75. See note no. 11, Lindberg and Distad.

76. See, for example, Gardner, A.R., and Gardner, AJ. Self-mutilation, obsessionality and narcissism. *International Journal of Psychiatry (1975) 127:127-32;* Grunebaum, H.U., and Kierman, G.L. Wrist slashing. *American Journal of Psychiatry (1967) 124:527-34.*

77. For a discussion of such difficulties in social functioning, see note no. *23,* Friedrich.

78. See note no. *47,* Elliott; also, see note no. *2,* Finkelhor.

79. Friedrich, W.N., Urquiza, A., and Beilke, R.L. Behavior problems in sexually abused young children. *Journal of Pedantic Psychology (1986) 11:47-57.*

80. Mannarino, A.P., Cohen, J.A., Smith, J.A., and Moore-Motily, S. Six- and twelve-month follow-up of sexually abused girls. *Journal of Interpersonal Violence (1991) 6:494-511.*

81. Friedrich, W.N., Grambsch, P., Damon, L., et al. The child sexual behavior inventory: Normative and clinical findings. *Journal of Consulting and Clinical Psychology (1992) 4:303-11;* Gale, J., Thompson, RJ., Moran, T., and Sack, W.H. Sexual abuse in young children: Its clinical presentation and characteristic patterns. *Child Abuse & Neglect (1988) 12:163-70.*

82. Gil, E., and Johnson, T.C. *Sexualized children: Assessment and treatment of sexualized children and children who molest.* Rockville, MD: Launch, *1993;* also, see note no. *81,* Friedrich, Grambsch, Damon, et al.

83. See note no. *82,* Gil and Johnson.

84. See note no. *52,* Briere and Runtz.

85. Russell, D.E.H. *The secret trauma: Incest in the lives of girls and women.* New York: Basic Books, *1986;* Finkelhor, D., HoLaling, G., Lewis, I.A., and Smith, C. Sexual abuse and its relationship to later sexual satisfaction, marital status, religion, and attitudes. *Journal of Interpersonal Violence (1989) 4:279-399.*

86. See note no. *12,* Conte and Schuerman.

87. Runtz, M. The psychosocial adjustment of women who were sexually and physically abused during childhood and early adulthood: A focus on revictimization. Unpublished master's thesis. University of Manitoba, Canada, *1987;* also, see note no. *85,* Russell.

88. See note no. *16,* Courtois; also, see note no. *67,* Herman.

89. Bagley, C., and Young, L. juvenile prostitution and child sexual abuse: A controlled study. *Canadian Journal of Community Mental Health (1987) 6:5-26;* Earls, C.M., and David, H. Early family and sexual experiences of male and female prostitutes. *Canada's Mental Health (1990) 38:7-11;* Simons, R.L., and Whitbeck, L.B. Sexual abuse as a precursor to prostitution and victimization among adolescent and adult homeless women. *Journal of Family Issues (1991) 12:361-79.*

90. Butler, S. *Conspiracy of silence: The trauma of incest.* San Francisco: Volcano, *1979.*

91. Briere, J., and Runtz, M. Childhood sexual abuse: Long-term sequelae and implications for psychological assessment. *Journal of Interpersonal Violence (1993) 8:312-30.*

92. See note no. *12,* Conte and Schuerman; see note no. *29,* Elliott and Briere; also, see note no. *85,* Russell.

93. Elliott, D.M., and Briere, J. Child maltreatment, later revictimization, and adult symptomatology: A causal analysis. Paper presented at the *1993* American Psychological Association Annual Meeting. Toronto, August *1993;* also, see note no. *87,* Runtz.

94. See note no. *47,* Elliott; also, see note no. *39,* Friedrich, Beilke, and Urquiza; also, see note no. *12,* Conte and Schuerman.

95. Berliner, L. Effects of sexual abuse on children. *Violence Update* (1991) 1:1,8, 10-11; Elliott, D,M. Disclosing sexual abuse: Predictors and consequences. Paper presented at the 1993 meeting of the International Society for Traumatic Stress Studies. San Antonio, TX, October 1993.

96. See note no. 12, Conte and Schuerman; also, see note no. 47, Elliott.

97. See note no. 46, Alexander; also, see note no. 47, Cole and Putnam.

Prevalence and Severity of Lifetime Physical and Sexual Victimization Among Incarcerated Women*

Angela Browne, Ph.D.

Brenda Miller, Ph.D.

and
Eugene Maguin, Ph.D.

Introduction

Beginning in the 1960s in the United States, a new area of interpersonal victimization-that of aggression by intimates-began receiving increased attention from researchers, mental and medical health treatment providers, and legal policy-makers. Attention to violence by family members initially focused on the physical abuse of children (Gil, 1970; Kemp, Silverman, Steele, Droegemueller, & Silver, 1962). Public awareness of physical aggression between intimates expanded in the 1970s and 1980s to include new findings on violence between marital partners, particularly violence against wives (Dobash & Dobash, 1979, 1984; Dutton, 1988; Frieze, 1980; Martin, 1976; Pagelow, 1981, 1984; Walker 1979). With the publication of Straus, Gelles, and Steinmetz's (1980) nationally representative incidence study on family violence in 1980, an area of inquiry was born that has remained a focus of extensive research, intervention, and legal policy efforts up to the present (Tjaden & Thoennes, 1996). Research on violence by intimates spans the disciplines of sociology, criminal justice, law, medicine, psychology, psychiatry, and social work, and has stimulated rapid and dramatic changes in legislation, social policy, and public awareness.

As a result of scientific inquiry, we now have an extensive body of knowledge on the incidence and prevalence of physical and sexual aggression by intimates and on potential short- and long-term effects for survivors (see Gelles & Conte, 1990 for a review). However, virtually all empirical research during this period has been based on general population studies or on mental health, medical, court, or shelter samples (Browne & Bassuk, 1997). Except for a few studies, literature on the prevalence of interpersonal violence fails to include individuals who are out of the community serving long-term sentences in correctional settings. This article begins to address this gap by presenting findings from a comprehensive study of victimization histories among incarcerated women in a maximum-security setting. Empirical information on this population is critical, given the sharp increases in the rates of incarceration in the United States over the past 15 years and the economic and human price this increased use of imprisonment exacts.

Changing Patterns of Incarceration in the United States

Although long considered too small a population to warrant extensive consideration, women now constitute the most rapidly growing segment of the prison population and the segment about which we know the least. The United States has the highest rate of incarceration in the industrialized world, even higher than that of former police states such as South Africa and the former Soviet Union (U.S.

*As Previously Published In: International Journal of Law and Psychiatry, Vol. 22, Nos. 3-4. pp. 301-322,1999 Reprinted with permission of Elsevier Science Ltd.

Expands its Lead in the Rate of Imprisonment, 1992). Since 1985, the nation's prison and jail populations have nearly doubled on a per capita basis, to over 1.6 million today. Nearly 30% of this population is imprisoned in three states-California, Texas, and New York (Gilliard & Beck, 1996). During 1995 alone, the number of individuals in prison grew by over 72,000, an increase of 6.8%. On December 31, 1995, 1 in every 167 U.S. residents was incarcerated (Gilliard & Beck, 1996).

The most dramatic increase over the past decade has been in the incarceration of women, which has nearly quadrupled (Beck & Gilliard, 1995). A large part of this rapid growth has been due to the increased use of prison for drug, rather than violence-related, offenses. For example, in 1986, 1 in every 8 incarcerated women was serving time for drug-related offenses; by 1991, that number had risen to 1 in 3 (Snell & Morton, 1994). Even when one considers only those individuals incarcerated in maximum security facilities (a population more likely to be serving time for crimes of violence), less than 60% of currently incarcerated women are incarcerated for violent felonies. In New York State-the state with the third largest prison population in the United States 60% of all women under custody on April 18,1998 were serving time for drug related offenses. About one quarter (26%) were incarcerated for violent felonies committed either by themselves or by a companion. Only a small minority (9%) was incarcerated for property or other offenses.

Long-Term Effects of Violence by Intimates and Reasons for the Incarceration of Women

Parallels between the literature on *long-term effects of violence by intimates* and the *predominant reasons for women's incarceration* (noted above) make a further understanding of imprisoned women's prior trauma histories particularly important. For example, empirical studies have shown a strong association between histories of family violence and development of later alcohol and drug problems in survivors, irrespective of whether samples are drawn from clinical or community populations. (e.g., Downs, Miller, Testa, & Panek, 1992; Polusny & Follete, 1995; Rohsenow, Corbett, & Devine, 1988; Singer, Petchers, & Hussey, 1989; Toray, Coughlin, Vuchinich, & Patricelli, 1991). Women victims of child sexual molestation or severe physical child abuse by parental figures are at significantly higher risk for substance abuse and addiction as teenagers and adults than women who have not had these experiences (Brown & Anderson, 1991; Miller, Downs, & Testa, 1993; Straus & Kantor, 1994; Windle et al., 1995). These findings hold even when risk factors such as the presence of alcoholic parents or sociodemographic variables are controlled. However, most research on connections between drugs and violent victimization has focused on violence related to the business of buying and selling drugs and on the drug subculture; little attention has been given to drug use as a possible *secondary* effect of earlier experiences with aggression or threat.

Girls from physically or sexually abusive homes also are more at risk of separation from their families of origin before adulthood due to out-of-home placements or running away, and then become at increased risk of involvement in drug- or prostitution-related activities. Further, in a prospective cohort study of long-term consequences of severe physical or sexual abuse or neglect in childhood (based on 908 substantiated cases in the Midwest), Widom and Ames (1994) found that children who had experienced severe child abuse or neglect were at significantly higher risk for arrest as juveniles and adults compared to a matched control group. Although the absolute percentage was low, girls who had been sexually abused (compared to girls with *other* types of victimization and to controls) were at increased risk of adult arrests for prostitution.

Finally, one of the most consistently found aftereffects of sexual molestation during childhood is a vulnerability in some survivors to later involvement with violent intimates (e.g., Beitchman et al., 1992; Browne & Finkelhor, 1986). Drug use also increases the likelihood of relationships with intimates who are violent-both to the women and to others-and who are involved in a variety of other criminal activities. Increased exposure to violent intimates increases the risk of defensive acts by women in protection of themselves or a child (e.g., Browne, 1987), as well as the likelihood that women will be present or will otherwise have "certain knowledge" when a crime is committed by an intimate and will therefore be charged with and convicted of involvement with that crime. Thus, some of the long-term effects of victimization by family members may play important roles in the events for which women today are imprisoned.

Prevalence of Lifetime Physical and Sexual Victimization Among Incarcerated Women

Questions about lifetime histories of physical and sexual victimization are just starting to be included in studies of incarcerated women. In most cases, these questions are inserted into studies on other subjects; measurement is abbreviated, question sets lack validity and reliability, and methodologies used predict that resulting prevalence levels may be low. (For example, Finkelhor, 1994 noted that, across studies, prevalence estimates of abuse seem most affected by the number of questions used to measure victimization experiences, with multiple questions yielding the highest endorsements.) The six studies in the literature using U.S. samples are reviewed below.

Findings from National Samples

Only two national studies included victimization questions in surveys with incarcerated women. In 1991, the Bureau of Justice Statistics (BJS) conducted its first nationally representative survey of women in prison, interviewing approximately 1 in every 11 women in state correctional facilities (Snell & Morton, 1994). This survey included three screening questions on lifetime experienced of victimization: (a) *"Have you ever been physically or sexually abused?"*; (b) (If yes to sexual abuse) *"In this incident did someone use force to rape you or attempt to rape you?"*; and (c) (If yes to either) *"Did you know any of the persons who abused you?"* If respondents endorsed any items, they were asked about the number of occurrences, their age, and the perpetrator(s), age(s) at the time, and the relationship category of the perpetrator(s). Of the 38,798 women participants, 43% reported some type of assault prior to that incarceration; 33.5% reported lifetime physical abuse and 33.9% reported lifetime sexual abuse. About half of those reporting abuse had been assaulted by an intimate. More than three quarters of those reporting abuse had been sexually abused or assaulted. Over half (56%) of those who were sexually abused had experienced a completed rape (Snell & Morton, 1994).

Although the BJS sample was large and representative, the methodology used may have suppressed rates. Questions on victimization occurred near the end of the interview in a section on involvement with gangs, and only one question was used to screen for abuse histories. If respondents gave a negative response or refused to answer that questions, no further questions were asked. The BJS methodology also required respondents to *label* actions they experienced as "abuse" in order to endorse the screening item-a technique less likely to reveal experiences with physical or sexual assault by intimates than behavioral indices describing actions without labeling them as inappropriate. A revised BJS survey is currently being conducted in which questions have been reworded to include behavioral descriptors and the question set has been expanded.

The other national survey was conducted by the American Correctional Association (1990) in 1987, using similar methodology. In this sample of 1,720 women, 43% of adult respondents were white non-Hispanic, 36% were African American, and 10% were Hispanic. Respondents were asked whether they had ever been *"the victim of physical abuse (e.g., being beaten, kicked, or tied up)"* and if they had ever been *"the victim of sexual abuse."* If they said yes to either question, they were asked how many times incidents happened, their age at the time of the first incident, the relationship of the perpetrator, whether they disclosed the abuse to anyone, and-if they reported the incident-what happened. Based on these questions, 53% of adult respondents reported ever being physically abused-with 82% of these reporting 3 or more incidents; and 36% reported sexual abuse-with 55% reporting multiple incidents. Over one third (36%) reported physical abuse occurring before age 20, and 30% reported sexual abuse prior to that age, mostly between the ages of 5 and 14. Sexual abuse was most often perpetrated by male family members. One fourth of all respondents reported physical abused by husbands or boyfriends.

Findings from Local Samples

Only four other studies appear in the literature as being conducted in the United States and including victimization questions or obtaining information on sexual trauma. Bloom, Chesney, and Owen (1994) conducted a study of a randomly selected sample of 297 women housed in California's three women's prisons and the California Rehabilitation Center (a coed facility at that time). Women in the sample averaged 32 years of age; over one third (35 %) were African American, 36% were white non-Hispanic, and 17% were Hispanic. Respondents were asked whether they had ever been *"physically abused/ harmed/hit"* as a child, whether they had been *"physically abused/battered"* as an adult; if they had ever been *"sexually abused"* as a child or as an adult, and if they had ever been *"sexually assaulted (using violence)"* as a child or in adulthood. For any positive endorsements, participants were asked how often this occurred and the relationship category of the perpetrator(s). Using these questions, Bloom et al. (1994) found that 29% of California's incarcerated women reported violence by parental caretakers and 31% reported child sexual abuse. Over half (60%) reported being physically assaulted in adulthood, primarily by male partners, and 23% reported adult sexual assault.

Similar findings were obtained by Sargent, Marcus-Mendoza, and Chong (1993) and Fletcher, Rolison, and Moon (1993), in their study of 267 women at a mixed-security level prison in Oklahoma. Women in this sample also had an average age of 32; 48% were White non-Hispanic, 37% were African American, and 9% were Native American. Participants were asked four questions about victimization: if they were *"physically abused"* before age 18 or, after age 18, were *"physically abused by a mate, husband, boyfriend, lover, friend, acquaintance, or partner"*; and if they were *"raped, sexually abused, or molested"* before age 18 or, after age 18, were *"raped (forced to commit sexual acts against your will)."* Questions did not distinguish between assaults by intimates and nonintimates. Based on these questions, over one third (37.5%) reported being physically abused as children and 69% reported being physically abused as adults. Over half (55%) reported experiencing sexual assault; 40% of the sample reported sexual assault in childhood and 38% reported sexual assault as adults. Sargent et al. (1993) noted that, in other analyses, respondents who reported physical or sexual abuse also were more likely to report problems with alcohol or other drugs.

Lake (1993) did post-hoc analyses on reported experiences of abuse by intimates and assault, sexual assault, and robbery by nonintimates among 83 women incarcerated in Washington state in 1986. The average age of these women was 29; over half were White non-Hispanic (63 %), 20.5 % were African American, and 8% were Hispanic. Since the study had been designed primarily to assess criminal behavior, assessments of physical and sexual victimization were quite abbreviated. Physical abuse in childhood was assessed by asking about kinds of *"punishment"* used by parental figures before the respondent's age 12. Respondents were classified as *"abused"* only if a parental figure had punched or kicked her; both design factors could sharply limit resulting prevalence levels. Sexual assault by relatives was described to respondents as someone "using *force or threats"* to make her engage in sex. Other types of sexual abuse were excluded-a potentially large omission. (Since children are socially and legally prohibited from leaving their homes, child victims are often forced to remain in an environment where inappropriate and illegal activities are perpetrated against them, regardless of whether overt threat or force is used.) Given endorsements, questions were asked about the relationship of the respondent to perpetrators, but the study did not include a way to determine whether sexual abuse occurred in childhood. Physical assaults by partners were assessed by asking if the respondent had ever been hit by a spouse or live-in partner (dating violence was not assessed). Physical and sexual assaults by strangers were measured in the same manner as those by intimates.

Using these measures, 29% of respondents reported physical abuse in childhood; 18% reported sexual abuse by relatives-a prevalence somewhat *lower* than that among women in general community-based samples (Finkelhor, 1994). However, 70% reported violence by an intimate partner and nearly half of those reported sustaining injuries severe enough to need medical treatment. Over one-third (37%) reported physical assaults by strangers, and 30% reported sexual assaults; nearly three-quarters reported being physically or sexually assaulted by strangers or robbed. In total, over 85% of the sample reported at least one type of victimization experience. In examining potential correlations between experiences of abuse in childhood and later assaults by partners or nonintimates, Lake reports no evidence of associations between childhood abuse and later victimization. However, this may be an artifact of the small sample size, measurement problems for childhood variables, and the resulting low endorsement - - especially for childhood sexual abuse. Lake also finds family sexual assault uncorrelated with later arrest data, possibly also due to these methodological factors (see also Bonta, Pang, & Wallace-Capretta, 1995 for similar Canadian findings and similar conclusions based on unusually low endorsements of childhood abuse). Finally, Singer, Bussey, Song, and Lunghofer (1995) interviewed 201 women randomly selected from all new admissions to the Cleveland House of Corrections from May to September 1992. (Actively violent or psychotic women were excluded.) Women were an average age of 30; most were African American (73%) or White non-Hispanic (21%). In this municipal jail sample, half of the women were incarcerated for prostitution; 13% were incarcerated for drug offenses or drug-related loitering. Although this study did not specifically ask about intimate violence, 68% of respondents reported being forced into sexual activity as adults, and nearly half (48%) reported being sexually victimized as children.

In sum, the six studies published over the past 10 years suggest a substantial prevalence of physical or sexual assault among incarcerated women. However, these assessments used only three to six direct questions, often requiring that *respondents* decide whether actions by intimates and others qualified as abuse, molestation, battery, or rape. Studies vary widely in their ability to distinguish (a) childhood from adult experiences, (b) perpetration by intimates versus nonintimates, and (c) cumulative experiences of victimization over the lifespan. The research reported here was conducted to lay a foundation of prevalence and severity data-based on comprehensive measures with established validity for evaluating physical and sexual assault-upon which to build future inquiries on the links between later behaviors and lifetime exposure to violence. The purpose of these analyses is not to link victimization experiences to particular types of criminal behaviors, but rather to identify the prevalence of these experiences in a population of incarcerated women. In addition to the importance of establishing parallel knowledge to prevalence and severity findings on other populations, more comprehensive data on the level of prior victimization in incarcerated populations is essential to inform intervention and prevention efforts and criminal justice policy.

Method

Analyses presented here are based on data from a National Institute of Health-funded supplement to a larger National Institute on Drug Abuse (NIDA) prospective study. The NIDA study investigated the impact of family violence on women's drug use based on a sample of 600 women from four groups: shelters for partner violence, drug treatment centers, and community samples matched to these groups for geographical residence and age. Although the NIDA study was comprehensive, only women living in the community were included. This study added a sample of women *(n = 150)* from the societally cost-intensive and rapidly growing women's prison population, representing women who spend extended time out of the community in correctional settings.

The focus of the analyses is the aggregate experiences of incarcerated women in terms of prior victimization histories. The reported prevalence and severity of six types of violence will be discussed: (a) severe physical violence by parental figures, (b) child sexual molestation-both familial and nonfamilial, (c) severe physical aggression and (d) rape by intimate partners in adulthood, and (e) physical and (f) sexual violence by strangers or acquaintances. Data includes detailed information on reported experiences with physical and sexual victimization and threats throughout the lifespan among women serving long-term (over 6 year) prison sentences, as well as reports on resultant injuries and other outcomes. Data do not include reports on victimization while incarcerated.

Setting

These data are drawn from cross-sectional interviews with 150 women entering the general population of Bedford Hills Maximum Security Correctional Facility (BHCF) in Bedford Hills, New York. BHCF, with a population of 760 to 840, is New York State's only maximum security prison for women, as well as the Reception Center for all women sentenced to prison in New York State. A maximum-security facility was chosen for this research because of the assumed presence of a saturated population for inquiry into issues of drug abuse and violent victimization. The relatively longer sentences served by most maximum-security inmates also offered the potential of later follow-up studies with this population.

Respondents

All women entering the general corrections population of BHCF (thus excluding women in reception who were transferred to nonmaximum. security settings) for 26 consecutive months on new charges who met study criteria and had less than 1 year total time away from the community were invited to participate. A list of eligible participants was prepared monthly for the project by the Department of Correctional Services, Division of Program Planning, Research and Evaluation Unit. Because the first few weeks of incarceration can be a chaotic and potentially frightening time, women were invited to participate after they had been in the general corrections population at BHCF for at least 2 months and had had time to become familiar with prison routines and become involved in ongoing program and work activities.

The following categories were excluded from the eligible respondent pool: (a) women with severe mental illness, as determined by the Office of Mental Health Satellite Unit (OMH) at BHCF, (b) women considered a mental health risk at the time of their eligibility due to active suicidal ideation or recent incidents of self-harm (as determined by OMH), (c) women serving disciplinary time in the Segregated Housing Unit (SHU) at the time of their eligibility, and (d) women who were medically hospitalized at the time of their eligibility. For the last three categories, women were given a later opportunity to participate if they returned to the general population and were not considered at special risk. Due to human subject concerns, no women entering BHCF at ages younger than age 18 were accepted into the study.

Of the 304 women entering the general population on new charges with less than 1 year away from the community who were 18 years of age and older during the interviewing frame, 74 (24%) were excluded from the eligible subject pool for mental health *(n = 56)* or medical *(n = 5)* reasons or because they were in SHU (n = 13). Of the 230 women eligible for the project, 68% completed the interview, 9% refused to participate, 11% failed to appear for the call out (scheduled appointment), and 12% were absent from the facility during interview weeks due to being at court or in other facilities.

Demographic Characteristics of Sample

Respondents ranged in age from 18 to 59 years, with a mean and median age of 32 years. Ethnically, the largest group of women were African American (49%); 25% were Hispanic and 12% were White non-Hispanic. Most Hispanics in the sample were from Puerto Rico or other Caribbean countries. The majority of women reported they had never married (53%). However, 23% reported being married or in a common-law relationship at the time of the interview, while 17% were either divorced or separated. The majority of women (78%) had one or more children. Over four fifths (82%) were born in the United States. This sample is similar to recent national data on all women in state prisons in median age (31 years nationally), percent Black (45% nationally), and number who had children (78%; Snell & Morton, 1994). However, the BHCF sample has a higher proportion of Hispanics (25% vs. 14%) and married women (23% vs. 17%), and a lower proportion of White non-Hispanics (12% vs. 36%). Women at BHCF were much less likely to be divorced or separated (17% vs. 32%; Snell & Morton, 1994).

Protocol

Interviews were conducted on prison grounds 1 week each month over a 1-year period. All eligible women were sent a memo at the beginning of each interviewing week explaining the study, reassuring them that all new residents were being invited to participate and they were not being singled out in any way, and informing them that they would be called out to meet a project interviewer who would describe the study to them in more detail. Potential participants were briefed on the study individually by going through the detailed consent form with an interviewer in a private interviewing space. If they agreed to participate, they were interviewed at that time. In most cases the interview protocol took 2.5 to 3.5 hours to complete; the majority of interviews were completed in one sitting. At the conclusion of the interview, respondents were given a resource list in Spanish and English detailing mental health and family violence resources available within the prison setting and how to access those resources.

Interview questions were derived from the NIDA study. Some special considerations for prison data collection, such as time constraints on interviews, limited replication. All questions related to time periods prior to the current incarceration. Interviewers were selected for prior experience with research interviewing on sensitive topics in special settings. All interviewers were women. Interviews were conducted in either English or Spanish, depending on the preference of the interviewee. All interviews were conducted in private with just the participant and the interviewer present.

Measures

Physical Violence. The physical aggression scale of the Conflict Tactics Scales (CTS; Straus, 1979, 1990a, 1990b) was used to obtain data on physically violent actions by childhood caretakers and by intimate partners in adulthood. Developed in the United States in 1971, the CTS has been used in two national samples of more than 8,000 respondents and employed in hundreds of studies in Western countries over the past 27 years. Alpha coefficients of reliability range from .79 to .62. Numerous indicators of concurrent validity, construct validity, and independence from social desirability effects have been demonstrated in research by Straus and others (e.g., see Straus, 1990a, pp. 40-44 and Straus, 1990b, pp. 63-70 for a review). Items give behavioral descriptions of physically aggressive acts with a yes/no or a frequency response for each item. The aggression scale is further divided into "minor" and "severe" violence indexes. The "minor" violence items are threw something at the other; pushed, grabbed, or shoved; slapped or spanked. Severe violence items are: kicked, bit, or punched; hit or tried to hit with an object; beat up; choked (or for parent-to-child violence, burned or scalded); threatened with a knife or gun; and used a knife or gun. Only results from the "severe" violence index are reported here. Although Straus and colleagues (Straus, 1990b; Straus & Gelles, 1990) used the CTS to assess adults' behaviors toward their children, many empirical studies have since used the index as a retrospective measure of abuse in childhood (e.g., Tjaden & Thoennes, 1996).

Severe Physical Violence by Childhood and Adolescent Caretakers. Following Straus and colleagues (Straus, 1990b; Straus & Gelles, 1990), severe physical violence by childhood caretakers was defined as the occurrence of at least one of the following before age 18: being kicked, bit, or hit with a fist; hit with an object; beaten up; burned or scalded; or threatened or assaulted with a knife or gun. In addition, we incorporated the non-CTS item, "having one's life threatened in some other manner." This allowed us to elicit information about violent behaviors not captured by specific CTS items. The prevalence of severe caretaker violence in the family of origin was computed for the women's primary mother figure, primary father figure, and for other childhood caretakers combined. The primary parental figures were those with whom the women had resided the longest (until age 18 or leaving home, whichever came first) or for the longest duration prior to age 13. Other childhood or adolescent caretakers were the mothers or fathers with whom women had resided for the second-longest period of time up until their age 18 or they left home. Although this category may contain people that were not routinely (or at all) involved in caretaking, we use the term *caretakers* for brevity's sake when referring to these three categories in the aggregate.

Child Sexual Molestation. Child sexual molestation was defined as both contact and noncontact sexual experiences occurring before age 18 and involving a person at least 5 years older than the woman at the time of the incident, a relative irrespective of any age difference, or any individual who had forced the respondent to engage in sexual activities. Detailed items described experiences of sexual molestation in three categories: inappropriate exposure, sexual contact (touching), and any form of penetration. Specific sexual experiences included invitations to do something sexual; sexually oriented touching (e.g., breast, abdomen, thighs); oral sex; digital penetration ("other person inserted a finger or object into your vagina or anus"); and intercourse ("other person inserted his penis into your vagina or anus"). Interviewers read the list of items and asked if each item had ever occurred. A measure of total sexual abuse prevalence was constructed from these items. For each endorsement, respondents were asked their age at the time of occurrence, the perpetrator's age if known, and the perpetrator's relationship to them.

This method of using multiple questions of a specific nature rather than a single, more general question, has been shown to produce more reports of sexual abuse (Briere, 1992; Finkelhor, 1994; Peters, Wyatt, & Finkelhor, 1986 Russell, 1986). Interview questions were drawn from previous works by Finkelhor (1979) and Sgroi (1982). Over the past 12 years, the indices of sexual abuse used in this study have been used with over 1400 women across community and treatment settings to help respondents identify sexual abuse experiences (Miller et al., 1993). The data for these variables were taken from a series of questions that elicited information on the first five persons involved in reported incidents of sexual abuse. Community agency involvement was measured by a question that assessed whether the police, juvenile courts, social service agencies, regular (adult) court, or any other official agency was involved with the family as a result of sexual molestation incidents.

Severe Physical Violence by Intimate Adult Partners. Severe physical violence by intimate partners was defined similarly to violence by childhood caretakers, except that-following Straus (1990a)-being "choked, strangled, or smothered" appeared in the adult violence scale. Our definition of severe violence by an adult partner differs in two ways from that of Straus and Gelles (1990). First, as with parental violence, we incorporated the non-CTS item "having one's life threatened in some other manner," enabling us to elicit information about violent behaviors not captured by specific CTS items. In addition, respondents were asked if they had been "threatened with an automobile." Respondents were asked about all *"intimate partners" (by this we mean a male or female you had a romantic or sexual relationship with for 1 month or more)"* since age 14, starting with their *"very first date or lover."* A separate item measured whether women had been harassed, threatened, or assaulted by any ex-partners after an intimate relationship had ended.

Threats of Harm by Intimate Partners. Threats of harm to self or others by the women's assailants were measured by items that were asked of all women about threats by an intimate partner, irrespective of whether they reported severe partner violence. These threats included (a) to kill themselves, (b) to kill the respondent, or (c) to kill the respondent's relatives or friends.

Medical Outcomes of Partner Violence. The prevalence of injuries sustained by women as a result of severe violence was measured by a series of questions adapted from Walker (1984), increasing in severity from "no visible injury but painful" to "permanent injury to eyes, head, joints, back, or limbs" (Browne, 1987; Walker, 1984). This set of items was asked if severe violence was reported by any intimate adult partner. The total injury prevalence was constructed of all injury items except the "no visible injury but painful" item. Thus, a positive response to the total injury prevalence indicates that the attack resulted in at least minor bruises, cuts, burns, or blackened eyes. Respondents were also asked if they needed or received medical treatment as a result of partner violence.

Other Outcomes of Partner Violence. Other outcome measures of partner violence included whether the woman had moved away from an intimate partner to escape his/her violence, whether the woman or others had ever called the police related to a partner's violence, whether the woman had ever obtained a restraining order, and whether charges had ever been filed related to partner violence.

Lifetime Physical and Sexual Victimization by Strangers. Victimization by persons *other* than parental caretakers or intimate partners was assessed by five items that asked whether women had ever: (a) had something taken from them by force (e.g., been held up or mugged); (b) been beaten up or attacked with a dangerous object such as a rock or bottle; (c) been knifed, shot at, or attacked with another weapon; (d) been threatened with assault (excluding telephone threats) or threatened with a knife, gun, or some other weapon; or (e) been raped. Those reporting experiences in any of these categories were asked how many times this had occurred between their ages of 10 and 17, since they turned 18, and in the 6 months prior to this incarceration, and the number and relationship of perpetrators involved.

Results

Severe Physical Violence by Childhood and Adolescent Caretakers

Overall, results show that a substantial majority of the sample of women in the general corrections population reported having experienced sexual molestation or severe violence prior to the current incarceration. Over two thirds (70%) reported experiencing severe physical violence from a childhood or adolescent caretaker or parent. Just over half (51%) reported that their primary female caretaker had inflicted physical violence, and over one quarter (29%) reported that their primary male caretaker had severely physically attacked them. Seventeen percent reported that other caretakers had inflicted severe physical violence (Table 1).

TABLE 1 Severe Physical Violence by Childhood and Adolescent Caretakers

Any caretaker/other adult in household	70%
Primary female caretaker	51%
Primarily male caretaker	29%
Other caretakers	17%

N = 150.

Child Sexual Molestation

Over half of all respondents (59%) reported some form of sexual abuse during childhood or adolescence. Nearly half (49%) of all respondents reported experiencing exposure; 51% reported sexual touching, and 41% reported experiencing vaginal, oral, or anal penetration. Of those women reporting sexual molestation, 27% reported biological or adoptive fathers or stepfathers as the perpetrators (surprisingly, fathers were just as likely as stepfathers to be the reported perpetrators); nearly half (42%) of the sample reported sexual victimization by other male relatives (excluding foster parents). Just over half of those who reported molestation (56%) gave nonrelatives (including foster parents) as the perpetrators. Finally, a small minority (2%) of the sample reported that they had been victimized by a female relative. Over half (51%) of those reporting childhood or adolescent sexual abuse reported that their first molestation occurred between the ages of 0 and 9. For nearly half of those reporting childhood sexual abuse (42%), the duration of the abuse was estimated to exceed 1 year. Over one quarter estimated the duration as more than 3 years. Among women reporting childhood sexual abuse, only one quarter (24%) reported that their experiences of molestation had come to the attention of outside authorities. When an outside agency was reported as involved, the police or a social service agency were most often mentioned (21% and 10%, respectively). Interestingly, few women reported that either juvenile or adult courts became involved (6% and 9%, respectively) (see Table 2).

TABLE 2 Child Sexual Molestation

Type of molestation	
Any	59
Exposure	49
Sexual touching	51
Vaginal, oral or anal penetration	41
Of those reporting molestation (any type)	**(n = 89)**
Relationship of perpetrator(s)	
Father or stepfather	27
Other male relatives	42
Female relatives	2
Nonrelatives (includes foster parents)	56
Age at first molestation experience	
0 through 9 years	51
10 through 14 years	42
15 through 17 years	8
Duration of molestation experience	
Only once or <1 month	23
1 month to 1 year	36
More than 1 year to 3 years or less	15
More than 3 years to 5 years or less	15
More than 5 years	12
Intervention by outside agency	
Any	24
Police involvement	21
Adult court involvement	9
Juvenile court involvement	6
Social service agency involvement	10

*N= 150.

Severe Physical Violence by Intimate Adult Partners

Experiences of severe physical violence by intimate partners in adulthood were reported by three-quarters (75%) of all respondents. Sixty percent reported being kicked, bitten, or hit with a fist; over half (57%) reported being beaten up; 50% reported being hit with an object able to do damage. Even when only the most *severe* sounding items are considered, 40% of all respondents reported being choked, strangled, or smothered; 36% reported being threatened with a knife or gun; and one quarter reported being cut with a knife or shot at by an intimate partner. In addition, over one third (35%) reported that they had experienced marital rape or been forced to participate in other sexual activity (Table 3).

Threats of Harm by Intimate Partners. Verbal threats of severe harm were also commonly reported: Over half of all respondents (53%) reported that a partner had threatened to kill them; over one third (36%) reported that a partner had threatened to kill himself. Homicide threats were reported as extending to the women's friends and relatives in 16% of the cases.

TABLE 3 Severe Physical Violence by Intimate Adult Partners

Physical violence by an intimate partner	%
Any	75
Kick, bit, or hit with a fist	60
Hit with an object able to do damage	50
Beat up	57
Burned or scalded	7
Choked, strangled, or smothered	40
Threatened with a knife or a gun	36
Actually used a knife or a gun	24
Threatened life with an automobile	7
Threatened life in some other manner	21
Forced sex by an intimate partner	35
Threats of harm by intimate partners	
Any	56
Threatened to kill respondent	53
Threatened to kill self	36
Threatened to kill respondent's relatives or friends	16
Medical outcomes of partner violence	
Physically injured by a partner	62
Most prevalent injuries	
Minor bruises	56
Severe bruises	38
Concussion	21
Broken bones	17
Needed medical treatment	46
Other outcomes of partner violence	
Assaulted, threatened, or harassed postseparation	50
Obtained restraining order	37
Charges were filed	28

*N= 150.

Medical Outcomes of Partner Violence. Nearly two thirds of all respondents (62%) reported that they had been injured by an intimate partner during adulthood. Although minor bruises were the most common form of injury mentioned (with 56% reporting this injury), over one fifth of all respondents (21%) reported suffering a concussion and 17% reported broken bones as a result of a partner's violence. Nearly half (46%) reported that they needed medical treatment for injuries inflicted by their partner.

Other Outcomes of Partner Violence. Over one third (37%) of the total sample reported obtaining an order of protection related to partner violence, and over one quarter (28%) reported that charges had been filed. Half of all respondents who had ever *ended* a relationship with an intimate partner reported that they had been physically assaulted, threatened, or harassed after separation.

Physical and Sexual Violence by Nonintimates

The final dimension of lifetime violent victimization assessed was criminal victimization by "nonintimates": persons other than parental figures or intimate partners. Three quarters (77%) of all respondents reported that they had been the target of some form of victimization by others, which ranged from threats of assaults involving weapons to physical and sexual attacks. The most common forms of criminal victimization mentioned were muggings (reported by 49% of the sample) and threats of assaults involving weapons (also reported by 49% of the sample). Only slightly less common were violent assaults, reported by 38% of respondents. Again, more than one quarter (28%)

of all respondents reported being knifed or shot at. Violent sexual attacks were reported by one third of the sample. When all forms of violence are considered together, only 6% of respondents did *not* report experiencing at least one physical or sexual attack during their lifetime (Table 4).

TABLE 4 Physical and Sexual Violence by Nonintimates"

Physical or sexual violence	%
Any	77
Held-up/mugged	49
Threatened to beat up/threatened with a weapon	49
Beaten up/physically attacked	38
Knifed or shot at	28
Other physical assault	2
Raped/attacked sexually	33

* = 150.

Relationship of Childhood Victimization to Adult Victimization

Finally we examined whether women who reported different types of victimization prior to age 18 were also more likely to report physical or sexual attack in adulthood. Overall, 80% of women reporting that they experienced *severe physical violence by* parental caretakers in childhood or adolescence also reported later experiencing *severe physical violence* by an intimate partner. (In contrast, 62% of women who did not report experiencing severe assault by parental caretakers reported severe physical violence by a partner.) Similarly, women who reported being *sexually molested* before age 18 were much more likely to report *sexual assaults by nonintimates* during adulthood than women who reported no sexual intrusions during childhood (40% vs. 23%) (Table 5).

TABLE 5 Relationship of Childhood Victimization to Adult Victimization

	Childhood victimization			
	Severe violence by caretakers		Child sexual molestation	
Adult victimization	Yes (%)	No (%)	Yes (%)	No (%)
Severe partner violence (75%)	80.0*	62.2*	80.9	65.6
Sexual assaults -				
nonintimates (33%)	35.0	28.9	40.2*	23.0*
Physical assaults -				
nonintimates (72%)	75.0	64.4	76.1	65.6

*Chi-square test, p<.05.

Discussion

These findings suggest that violence across the lifespan for women incarcerated in the general population of a maximum-security prison is pervasive and severe. Lifetime prevalence rates of severe violence by intimates reported in this study far exceed those for all acts of physical abuse reported by women in the general female population-as identified in a recent national random sample of 8,000 U.S. women-of 40% for physical abuse by parental caretakers and 22% for violence by adult partners (Tjaden & Thoennes, 1996; Tjaden, personal communication, 1996). Similarly, the 59% lifetime prevalence rate of child sexual molestation stands in stark contrast to the 20 to 27% prevalence rates obtained in community-based samples (Finkelhor, 1994).

For these incarcerated women, experiences of physical and sexual assault began early. According to these reports, by age 11, over two thirds (66%) of those experiencing child sexual abuse had already been molested; 71% of those assaulted by caretakers had already experienced severe violence by a parental figure. Reports of childhood victimization strongly predict reported revictimization later in life. Women who reported severe physical violence by parental figures were 29% more likely to report that they later became involved with an intimate adult partner who was physically violent; women who reported childhood sexual molestation were 75% more likely to endorse violent sexual assault items than women who did not report childhood molestation.

In thinking about implications of early experiences of violence, we have primarily emphasized the parallels between long-term effects of experiences with violence and predominant reasons for women's incarceration. It is also true that there is an association between involvement in drug abuse and/or illegal activities and an increased risk of physical and sexual victimization. Since 82% of the sample reported experiencing severe parental violence and/or childhood sexual abuse before reaching adulthood, it is unlikely that victimization precipitated simply by drug use or criminal activity increased the cumulative lifetime prevalence figure significantly. However, the high rates of reported victimization by adult partners and nonintimates undoubtedly was driven, in part, by respondents' involvement in illegal drug use and other illegal activities.

This study offers several strengths. Interviews were conducted with women entering the general population of the prison facility rather than with participants in special programs or mental health interventions, thus enhancing the generalizability of findings to incarcerated women in other facilities. The study was designed to distinguish (a) childhood from adult experiences, (b) perpetration by intimates versus nonintimates, and (c) cumulative experiences of victimization over the lifespan. Measures of key domains were detailed and comprehensive, with proven validity and long histories of use in other empirical studies. All key measures were based on behavioral indices; respondents were never asked to label intimates as abusive in order to endorse a question or to respond to questions based on their personal definition of battery, abuse, or molestation. In line with Finkelhor's (1994) earlier observations, the higher prevalence rates identified in this study compared to earlier inquiries among incarcerated women underscore the importance of research utilizing comprehensive and validated measures of victimization.

The study also has several limitations. Lifetime prevalence rates of the types of violence under investigation may be underreported. For purposes of comparability and due to our concerns about strains on mental health resources within BHCF, severely and chronically mentally ill women and women considered to be mental health risks were excluded from the study. Although research with mentally ill inpatient populations and women who self-mutilate or seriously consider suicide suggest a high prevalence rate of past physical and sexual victimization, we believe a study specifically focused on the severely mentally distressed would be most appropriate for assessing their trauma histories. Women who refused to participate in this study also may have lowered prevalence findings, due to the exclusion of their histories. A memo that accompanied each notice of call-out described the study as including questions about relationships with family and intimate partners. In informally stating their reasons for refusal at the time of call-out, many of those refusing referred to this sentence and said that they had "had things happen to them that they wanted to forget." Self-report techniques also risk, underreporting of sensitive or painful information by participants due to shame or actual repression of traumatic childhood experiences (e.g., Widom & Ames, 1994). In this study, respondents sometimes asked to skip questions on sexual molestation or abuse by parents or said that responding to those questions would be disloyal to their families.

Although record data of private events such as violence by intimates severely underreport their actual occurrence in a population, self-report techniques risk both under- and overreporting. Thus, lifetime prevalence levels of violence in this study also may be overreported. For example, some participants may have felt that manufacturing stories of early abuse experiences would help justify their later incarceration. The structure of the interview and the interviewing process was designed to minimize this possibility; respondents were not asked about reasons for their current incarceration or precursors to it and knew that interviewers were blind to their criminal history and the charges for which they were serving time. Still it may have occurred. If overreporting did occur with some participants, it would not be enough to eliminate the phenomenon. For example, even if prevalence levels were overreported by 20%, this would reduce the intensity and severity, but results would still represent a phenomenon of significant magnitude and implications for policies related to incarcerated female populations.

Implications for Research

Despite these caveats, this study-along with a few others-suggests that there is a sufficiently high prevalence of severe physical and sexual assault across the lifespan among incarcerated women to warrant further inquiries on how trauma histories relate to later imprisonment. Research directions suggested by this and other studies (e.g., Widom & Ames, 1994) include investigations of: (a) mechanisms by which victimization by intimates *contribute* to women's later involvement in the criminal justice system; (b) what types of background characteristics, resiliency and support factors, and/or trauma profiles *differentiate* women with trauma histories who become involved with the criminal justice system from women with trauma histories who do not; (c) the *impact* of victimization histories on women's prison adjustment and needs for mental health and other interventions while incarcerated; and (d) what *types* of early interventions or interventions during incarceration might offset negative effects of trauma and promote a positive readjustment to the community upon release. The pervasiveness of reported abuse experiences in this study did not suggest that victimization histories *per se* would be correlated with particular types of crimes. However, future studies that wanted to be specifically predictive could possibly look at *profiles* of abuse histories among women that might be related to specific types of criminal offenses.

Implications for Interventions and Programs

Levels of severe physical assault and sexual molestation in early childhood identified in this study are particularly troubling in their potential for long-lasting psychological and behavioral outcomes (e.g., Beitchman et al., 1991, 1992; Bryer, Nelson, Miller, & Kroll, 1987; Finkelhor, 1995; Herman, 1992). Time spent in an incarcerated setting provides an opportunity for targeted interventions that could markedly improve the potential for adjustment within the incarcerated setting and successful reintegration when women return to the community (e.g., Morash, Haarr, & Rucker, 1995).

For example, a study completed by the New York State Department of Correctional Services (DOCS) Division of Program Planning, Research and Evaluation (Canestrini, 1994) found evidence of specific short-term effects on recidivism for women who had participated in an on-site program for survivors of family violence. The program was comprehensive, with educational activities, support groups, and individual counseling. In addition, small groups addressed issues of survivors of child abuse, child sexual abuse/incest, and partner violence, as well as those of women who killed adult partners and women with child-related crimes. The DOCS study followed up all women (220) who had participated in the Family Violence Program at BHCF between 1988 and April 1994 and were subsequently released. Control variables for the study included type of crime, second felony offender status, ethnicity, and age at release.

After a 21-month follow-up, women with 6 to 12 months in the program had less than *half* the recidivism rate (10% vs. 24%) as women released during the same period who did not participate in the program, even when type of crime, second felony offender status, ethnicity, and age at release were controlled. Women with less than 6 months in the program had the second highest rate of return: 19%. Although the researchers did not speculate on factors affecting this outcome, this -study illustrates the potential impact on recidivism of focused interventions that deal directly with histories of traumatic victimization. Beyond the humanitarian issues of providing support and intervention to individuals in our society who are suffering, addressing some of the long-term effects of violent victimization is particularly important in incarcerated populations. If left unaddressed, posttrauma effects-potentially part of the pathway leading *to* incarceration-would be expected to markedly worsen the prognosis for a successful return to life outside correctional facilities upon release.

Implications for Policy

The number of imprisoned women in the United States has nearly quadrupled over the past 15 years. An increased understanding of the precursors to imprisonment for women is now timely and critical. Incarceration as a "solution of choice" for drug-related offenses is a radically costly alternative, both for individual taxpayers and on a state and federal level. Costs for holding one individual in jail or prison in New York City are now estimated at $58,000 per year (Singer et at., 1995). Estimates for the cost of building one prison cell range from $52,000 to $94,000 for a maximum security facility, in 1990 dollars *(America Behind Bars,* 1992; cf. Byrne, Lurigio, & Petersilia, 1992). Yet the current level of growth in the U.S. prison population would require building a 1,000-bed prison every 6 days (Beck & Gilliard, 1995; Langan, 1991). Alternative responses to substance abuse and other effects of earlier trauma would be far more cost effective than the total expenses of arrest, prosecution, incarceration, and parole.

The authors would like to acknowledge the contributions of the following persons in the conduct of this research: Bedford Hills Correctional Facility Administration and staff; Department of Corrections Division of Program Planning Research and Evaluation Unit staff; Project Manager Pam Varker; Project Interviewers

Margaret Feerick, Susan Piercey, Judy Rodriguez, Angela Taylor, and Alessandra Testa, and the 150 women who shared with us the experiences of their lives.

This work was supported by grants from the National Institute on Drug Abuse Grant No. R01DA06795-04, -Impact of Family Violence on Women's Drug Use," *Brenda A. Miller, PI, Bill Downs and Angela Browne,* CO-Pls; and a Women's Health Supplement Award from the National Institutes of Health, *Brenda A. Miller* and *Angela Browne, Co-Pls.*

Address correspondence and reprint requests to Angela Browne, Harvard Injury Control Research Center, Harvard School of Public Health, 677 Huntington Avenue, 4th Floor, Boston, MA 02115, USA.

References

American Correctional Association. (1990). *The female offender. What does the future hold?* Washington, DC: St. Mary's Press.

America Behind Bars. (1992). New York: Edna McConnell Clark Foundation.

Beck, A. J., & Gilliard, D. K. (1995). *Prisoners in 1994.* Washington, DC: United States Department of Justice.

Beitchman, J. H., Zucker, K. J., Hood, J. E., DaCosta, J. E., Akman, D., & Cassavia, E. (1991). A review of the short-term effects of child sexual abuse. *Child Abuse and Neglect, 15,* 537-556.

Beitchman, J. H., Zucker, K. J., Hood, J. E. DaCosta, G. A., Akman, D., & Cassavia, E. (1992). A review of the long-term effects of child sexual abuse. *Child Abuse and Neglect,* 16, 101-118.

Bloom, B., Chesney, L. M., & Owen, B. (1994). *Women in California prisons: Hidden victims of the war on drugs.* San Francisco, CA: Center on Juvenile and Criminal Justice.

Bonta, J., Pang, B., & Wallace- Capretta, S. (1995). Predictors of recidivism among incarcerated female offenders. *The Prison Journal,* 75,277-294.

Briere, J. (1992). Methodological issues in the study of sexual abuse effects. *Journal of Consulting and Clinical Psychology,* 60,196-203.

Brown, G. R., & Anderson, B. (1991). Psychiatric morbidity in adult inpatients with childhood histories of sexual and physical abuse. *American Journal of Psychiatry,* 148, 55-61.

Browne, A. (1987). *When battered women kill.* New York: The Free Press.

Browne, A., & Bassuk, S. S. (1997). Intimate violence in the lives of homeless and poor housed women: Prevalence and patterns in an ethnically diverse sample. *American Journal of Orthopsychiatry,* 6, 261-278.

Browne, A., & Finkelhor, D. (1986). Impact of child sexual abuse: A review of the research. *Psychological Bulletin,* 99, 66-77.

Bryer, J. B., Nelson, B. A., Miller, J. B., & Kroll, P. A. (1987). Childhood sexual and physical abuse as factors in adult psychiatric illness. *American Journal of Psychiatry,* 144, 1426-1430.

Byrne, J., Lurigio, A., & Petersilia, J. (1992). *Smart sentencing. The emergence of intermediate sanctions.* Newbury Park, CA: Sage.

Canestrini, K. (1994). Follow-tip *study of the Bedford Hills Family Violence Program.* Albany, NY: State of New York Department of Correctional Services, Division of Program Planning, Research and Evaluation.

Dobash, R. E., & Dobash, R. (1979). *Violence against wives.* New York: The Free Press.
Dobash, R. E., & Dobash, R. (1984). The nature and antecedents of violent events. *British Journal of Criminology,* 24, 269-298.

Downs, W. R., Miller, B. A., Testa, M., & Panek, D. (1992). Long-term effects of parent-to-child violence for women. *Journal of Interpersonal Violence, 7,* 365-382.

Dutton, D. G. (1988). *The domestic assault of women: Psychological and criminal justice perspectives.* Boston, MA: Allyn and Bacon.

Finkelhor, D. (1979). *Sexually victimized children.* New York: Free Press.

Finkelhor, D. (1994). The International epidemiology of child sexual abuse. *Child Abuse and Neglect, 18,* 409-417.

Finkelhor, D. (1995). The victimization of children: A developmental perspective. *American Psychologist,* 49, 173-183.

Pletcher, B. R., Rolison, G. L., & Moon, D. G. (1993).The woman prisoner. In B. R. Fletcher, L. D. Shaver, & D. G. Moon (Eds.), *Women prisoners: A forgotten population (pp.* 15-26). Westport, CT: Praeger.

Frieze, 1. (1980). *Causes and consequences of marital rape.* Paper presented at the Annual Meeting of the American Psychological Association, Montreal, Canada.

Gelles, R. J., & Conte, J. R. (1990). Domestic violence and sexual abuse of children: A review of research in the eighties. *Journal of Marriage and the Family,* 52, 1045-1058.

Gil, D. G. (1970). *Violence against children.* Cambridge, MA: Harvard University Press.

Gilliard, D. K., & Beck, A. J. (1996). *Prison and jail inmates, 1995.* Washington, DC: United States Department of Justice.

Herman, J. L (1992). *Trauma and recovery.* New York: Harper Collins.

Kemp, C. H., Silverman, F. N., Steele, B. F., Droegemuellcr, W., & Silver, H. K. (1962). The battered-child syndrome. *Journal of the American Medical Association,* 181, 105-112.

Lake, E. S. (1993). An exploration of the violent victim experiences of female offenders. *Violence and Victims,* 8, 41-51.

Langan. P. A. (1991). America's soaring prison population. *Science,* 251, 1568-1573.

Martin, D. (1976). *Battered wives.* San Francisco, CA: Glide.

Miller, B. A., Downs, W. R., & Testa, M. (1993). Interrelationships between victimization experiences and women's alcohol use. *Journal of Studies on Alcohol,* (Suppl. 11), 109-117.

Morash, M., Haarr, R. N., & Rucker, L. (1995). A Comparison of programming for women and men in U.S. prisons in the 1980s. *Crime and Delinquency,* 40, 197-221.

Pagelow, M. D. (1981). *Women -battering: Victims and their experiences.* Beverly Hills, CA: Sage.

Pagelow, M. D. (1984). *Family violence.* New York: Praeger.

Peters, S. D., Wyatt, G. E., & Finkelhor, D. (1986). Prevalence. In D. Finkelhor (Ed.), *A sourcebook on child sexual abuse* (pp. 15-59). Beverly Hills, CA: Sage Publications.

Polusny, M. A., & Follete, V. M. (1995). Long-term correlates of child sexual abuse: Theory and review of the empirical literature. *Applied Preventive Psychology,* 4,143-166.

Rohsenow, D. J., Corbett, R., & Devine, D. (1988). Molested as children: A hidden contribution to substance abuse? *Journal of Substance Abuse Treatment,* 5,13-18.

Russell, D. E. H. (1986). *The secret trauma: Incest in the lives of girls and women.* New York: Basic Books.

Sargent, E., Marcus-Mendoza, S., & Chong, H. Y. (1993). Abuse and the woman prisoner. In B. R. Fletcher, L. D. Shaver, & D. G. Moon (Eds.), *Women prisoners: A forgotten population* (pp. 54-64). Westport, CM Praeger.

Sgroi, S. M. (1982). *Handbook of clinical intervention in child sexual abuse.* Lexington, MA: D.C. Heath

Singer, M. I., Bussey, J., Song, L. Y., & Lunghofer, L. (1995). The psychosocial issues of women serving time in jail. *Social Work,* 40,103-113.

Singer, M. I., Petchers, M. K., & Hussey, D. (1989). The relationship between sexual abuse among psychiatrically hospitalized adolescents. *Child Abuse and Neglect,* 13,319-325.

Snell, T. L., & Morton, D. C. (1994). *Women in prison: Survey of state prison inmates,* 1991. Washington, DC: U.S. Department of Justice.

Straus, M. A. (1979). Measuring intrafamily conflict and violence: The Conflict Tactics (CT) Scales. *Journal of Marriage and the Family,* 41, 75-88.

Straus, M. A. (1990a). Measuring intrafamily conflict and violence: The Conflict Tactics (CT) Scales. In M. A. Straus & R. J. Gelles (Eds.), *Physical violence in American families: Risk factors and adaptations to violence in 8,145 families (pp.* 29-45). New Brunswick, NJ: Transaction.

Straus, M. A. (1990b). The Conflict Tactics Scales and its critics: An evaluation of new data on validity and reliability. In M. A. Straus & R. J. Gelles (Eds.), *Physical violence in american families: Risk factors and adaptations to violence in 8,145 families (pp.* 49-79). New Brunswick, NJ: Transaction.

Straus, M. A., & Gelles, R. J. (Eds.). (1990). *Physical violence in American families. risk factors and adaptations to violence in 8,145 families.* New Brunswick, NJ: Transaction.

Straus, M. A., Gelles, R. J., & Steinmetz, S. (1980). *Behind closed doors: Violence in the American family.* Garden City, NY: Anchor Press.

Straus, M. A., & Kantor, G. K. (1994). Corporal punishment of adolescents by parents: A risk factor in the epidemiology of depression, suicide, alcohol abuse, child abuse, and wife beating. *Adolescence,* 29,543-561.

Tjaden, P., & Thoennes, N. (1996). *Violence against women: Preliminary findings from the violence against women in America survey.* Denver, CO: Center for Policy Research.

Toray, T., Coughlin, C., Vuchinich, S., & Patricelli, P. (1991). Gender differences associated with adolescent substance abuse: Comparisons and implications for treatment. *Family Relations, 40,338-344.*

U.S. expands its lead in the rate of imprisonment. (1992). *New York Times, February 11, p. C18.*

Walker, L. E. (1979). *The battered woman.* New York: Harper and Row.

Walker, L. E. (1984). *The battered woman syndrome.* New York: Springer.

Widom, C., & Ames, M. A. (1994). Criminal consequences of childhood sexual victimization. *Child Abuse and Neglect,* 18,303-318.

Windle, M., Windle, R. C., Scheidt, D. M., & Miller, G. B. (1995). Physical and sexual abuse and associated mental disorders among alcoholic inpatients. *American Journal of Psychiatry,* 152,1322-1328.

The Effects of Early Sexual Abuse on Later Sexual Victimization Among Female Homeless and Runaway Adolescents*

Kimberly A. Tyler

Dan R. Hoyt and Les B. Whitbeck

Introduction

Negative developmental outcomes have been reported for adolescents with a history of sexual abuse. Depression, poor self-esteem, substance abuse, inappropriate sexual behavior, suicidal ideation, running away, and prostitution, are just some of the effects that have been noted (Beitchman, Zucker, Hood, da Costa, & Akman, 1991; Browne & Finkelhor, 1986; Silbert & Pines, 1981). Runaways, in particular, tend to suffer from much higher rates of childhood sexual abuse compared to other adolescents (cf. Bayatpour, Wells, & Holford, 1992; Janus, McCormack, Burgess, & Harman, 1987). Furthermore, females are more likely to be sexually abused compared to males (Finkelhor, 1993; Finkelhor & Dziuba-Leatherman, 1994).

Runaways who have experienced early family abuse are at risk for re-victimization on the streets (Whitbeck, Hoyt, & Ackley, 1997a). Research demonstrates that the abuse indirectly influences street victimization by increasing a young woman's ties to deviant peers that may facilitate experimentation with various sorts of deviant behaviors (Simons & Whitbeck, 1991; Whitbeck & Simons, 1990, 1993). Furthermore, the social context of street life also may increase the probability of sexual victimization among female homeless and runaway adolescents.

Rates of Early Childhood Sexual Abuse

Although there are no reliable statistics on how many cases of childhood sexual abuse occur each year, it is estimated that one in four girls and one in ten boys will suffer from victimization (Finkelhor, 1993). The risk for sexual abuse rises in pre-adolescence and girls are at higher risk compared to boys. Statistics on childhood sexual abuse only exist for those cases that are reported to child protection agencies or law enforcement offices. According to Finkelhor (1994), the actual number of cases being reported to child abuse authorities are 2.4 cases per 1,000.

Although only 15% of child sexual abuse cases have been substantiated (Finkelhor, 1994), the actual number of cases are expected to be much higher since sexual abuse is underreported by both male and female children (Becker, 1988). Retrospective reports of rates of childhood sexual abuse range anywhere from 20% (Fleming, Mullen, & Bammer, 1997) to a high of 60% (Peters, 1988). Studies done on adolescents and youths report a range of percentages similar to those found in adult retrospective reports. Bayatpour and associates (1992) reported that almost 12% of teens they surveyed had been sexually abused, whereas Kellogg and Hoffman (1997) found much higher rates of sexual victimization among females (54%) compared to males (15%). Although the estimated rates vary across studies, the clear pattern is for high rates of abuse whether using retrospective reports or youth samples.

*A version of this paper was presented at the Midwest Sociological Society Meetings in Kansas City, April 1998.

Studies find even higher rates of abuse among homeless and runaway adolescents. Some research revealed that more than 50% of adolescents studied reported being sexually abused (Janus et al., 1987; Silbert & Pines, 1981). Moreover, gender differences revealed that females experienced much high rates of sexual abuse (73%) compared to their male counterparts (38%) (McCormack, Janus, & Burgess, 1986).

The Effects of Early Sexual Abuse

The negative developmental outcomes that adolescents experience as a result of early childhood sexual abuse have been divided into both short-and long-term consequences. Short-term effects of childhood sexual abuse included depression, low self-esteem, and suicidal behavior/ideation. Other commonly reported behavior among sexually abused adolescents included running away, substance abuse, and promiscuity (Beitchman et al., 1991). In addition to those short-term effects listed above, fear, anger, hostility, and inappropriate sexual behavior also have been noted as other possible short-term consequences (Browne & Finkelhor, 1986). Long-term effects of childhood sexual abuse included promiscuity, depression, difficulty trusting others, self-destructive behavior, and re-victimization (Beitchman et al., 1992; Browne & Finkelhor, 1986).

Risk Amplification Model

The present study views the transition of adolescents from home to the street from a risk amplification model (Whitbeck, Hoyt, & Yoder, 1999). Based on life course developmental theory (Elder, 1997) and social interaction theory (Patterson, 1982), this model holds that runaway adolescents often leave dysfunctional and disorganized homes where street experiences amplify negative developmental effects originating in the family and these developmental problems set the stage for later victimization.

Patterson has argued that coercive families provide "basic training" for antisocial behaviors (Patterson, Dishion, & Bank, 1984) which is the result of continuous failure on the part of the parents to use effective discipline techniques in controlling coercive exchanges between family members. Through this training, the child learns to control other family members through coercion and these interaction styles are generalized into other contexts. These coercive and abusive behaviors become coping styles that are carried with the adolescent into peer interactions which results in rejection by normal peer groups (Patterson et al., 1984; Patterson, DeBaryshe, & Ramsey, 1989). As adolescents leave their dysfunctional/abusive families, interaction patterns learned at home are carried into early independence. The "basic training" for antisocial behavior in the family now becomes "advanced training" on the streets. The combination of antisocial behavior and rejection by conventional peers leads adolescents to form ties with deviant peer groups which are important for explaining adolescents subsequent involvement in risky, deviant behaviors (Whitbeck et al., 1999).

Once adolescents are on the street, the social environment in which they interact becomes significant. The effects of risks and abuse that were experienced in the home become amplified on the street (Whitbeck et al., 1999). Victimization theories, which define the social context in which crime occurs, are useful for explaining how the social environment in which runaway adolescents interact on a day to day basis puts them at risk for victimization. Living on the streets exposes runaways to both criminals and potential offenders. Exposure to crime, and the fact that runaways are easily preyed upon because of their age, increases their risk for victimization. Specifically, lifestyle-exposure theory (Hindelang, Gottfredson, & Garofalo, 1978) and routine activity theory (Cohen & Felson, 1979) argue that the lifestyles and daily routines of people's everyday lives are related to differential exposure to dangerous places and people which creates the potential for crime opportunities, therefore, increased victimization.

In summary, early life exposure to dysfunctional homes places these youth on trajectories for early independence. Subsequently, the lifestyles and daily routines that many of these runaways engage in on a regular basis in order to survive, puts them in a particular social environment where they are exposed to dangerous people and places. Existing in such an environment and lacking conventional ties, these young people are at increased risk of being sexually victimized.

Sexually Abused Adolescents on the Streets

A fully recursive model was hypothesized to investigate the cumulative effects of caretaker sexual abuse (Figure 1). It was expected that early sexual abuse would be negatively associated with the age at which the adolescent first left home (Arrow A). Childhood sexual abuse typically occurs between eight and twelve years of age (Finkelhor, 1984), therefore, children who have been abused sexually are likely to run at earlier ages. Early sexual abuse was predicted to increase the total time the adolescent spent in unsupervised settings (Arrow B). A history of family abuse has been found to be associated with the amount of time that adolescents spend out on their own (Janus et al., 1987; Whitbeck et al., 1999). Further, an abusive family background was predicted to increase the likelihood of associating with friends who sold sex (Arrow C). Research demonstrates that children from abusive backgrounds drift into associations with deviant peers (Patterson, 1982; Whitbeck et al., 1997a). Direct effects also were hypothesized for early sexual abuse on number of different sexual partners, trading sex, and alcohol/drug use (Arrows D). Numerous studies have linked abuse by parents or caretakers to numerous sexual partners (Bagley & Young, 1987), trading sex (Silbert & Pines, 1981; Weisberg, 1985; Widom & Kuhns, 1996), and substance use (Dembo et al., 1989). Finally, early sexual abuse was hypothesized to directly influence sexual victimization (Arrow E). Adolescents from abusive backgrounds often experience emotional problems such as depression and poor self-esteem (Beitchman et al., 1991; Morrow & Sorell, 1989) which may make them more vulnerable targets on the streets.

It was expected that adolescents who ran for the first time at an early age would have spent more time in unsupervised living arrangements (Arrow F) and to have associated with friends who sold sex (Arrow G). Spending time on the street has been found to be associated with deviant peers and engaging in criminal street networks (Hagan & McCarthy, 1997). Further, it was expected that age on own would be associated with number of different sexual partners, trading sex, and substance use (Arrows H). Young people who are on the streets from an early age are likely to have greater exposure to risky behaviors as well as crime and criminals. Finally, being on the street at an early age increases exposure and risk. Following this, it was expected that age on own would be associated with sexual victimization (Arrow I).

Because it increases the amount of time at risk for participation in risky behaviors, a positive association was predicted between total time on own and number of different sexual partners, trading sex, and substance use (Arrows J). Being on the street also exposes these young people to dangerous people and places, therefore, it was expected that time on own would positively predict sexual victimization (Arrow K). Associating with deviant peers who sell sex was expected to positively predict number of different sexual partners, trading sex, and substance use (Arrows L). Further, associating with friends who sell sex is likely to increase the adolescents' chances of interacting with sexually violent customers. As such, a positive association was expected between friends selling sex and sexual victimization (Arrow M).

Finally, based on other studies of victimization among runaway and homeless adolescents (McCarthy & Hagan, 1992; Whitbeck & Simons, 1990, 1993; Whitbeck et al., 1997a) high risk behaviors (numerous sexual partners, trading sex, substance use) were expected to increase the risk for sexual victimization while on the street (Arrows N).

157

Figure 1. **Hypothesized model for female sexual victimization.**

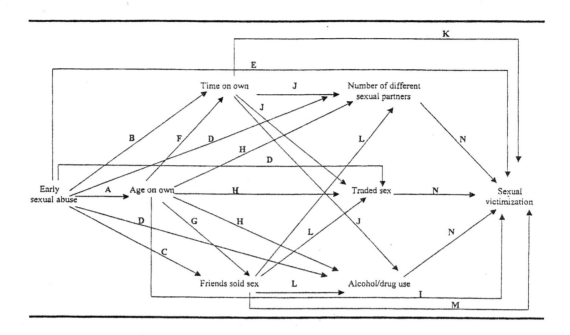

Method

Participants

The sample is from the Midwest Homeless and Runaway Adolescent Project (MHRAP), a four-state study of runaway adolescents from Missouri, Iowa, Nebraska, and Kansas. Of the total 602 adolescents that were interviewed, only the females (N = 361) were used for these analyses. Young people were interviewed directly on the streets, in shelters, and in drop-in centers by outreach workers who were trained youth workers with considerable experience interviewing and interacting with this group of young people. They were very familiar with local street cultures and were already known and trusted by many of the runaways. Respondents were recruited as part of the participating agencies' regular intake and outreach programs. Agencies were selected for participation in the study based on their having an existing street outreach program in addition to shelter and/or transitional living facilities. All but one of the study agencies had a street outreach van. This agency had an inner city drop-in center that catered to street youth. There were a total of six agencies: two in St. Louis, one each in Kansas City, Wichita, Lincoln, and Des Moines.

Upon initial contact, the interviewers read the consent statement to the youth and explained the study procedures. Respondents were informed that they could refuse participation, refuse single questions, or stop participating in the interview at any time. They also were informed that reports of abuse by adults must be reported by law and that steps would be taken for their protection in the event of disclosure of plans to harm themselves. Adolescents signed the consent form prior to starting the interview. The adolescents were not living under parental supervision at the time of the interview and were considered emancipated. Referral and support services were offered to youths on the street and provided to youths in shelters by the agencies as part of their outreach programs. Agreeing to be interviewed was not a precondition for any of the services the agencies provided. Interviews lasted about 1-½ hours. A snack was provided during a break in the interview process and the adolescent received $15 for participation.

Response rates ranged from a low of 71% to a high of 100%. The average response rate across all agencies was 93%. Although response rates were high, there were few street intercepts that may have resulted in a bias selection process since the harder-core adolescents who do not use shelters may have been omitted.

Of the 361 females who were interviewed, the majority were White (64%) or African-American (22%). Four percent were Hispanic and the remaining 10% were either Asian, American Indian, bi-racial, or multi-racial. These young women ranged in age from 12 to 22 years with a mean of 16 years. Many of these runaways have been on their own for the first time at a very young age. The median age at first time on own was 14 years. In addition, these young women had spent between 1 day and 7.1 years on the street with a median of 13 days. Thirty-two percent of the young women were sexually abused while still living at home and 21% of all females were sexually victimized while on the street. Approximately 11% have experienced both early sexual abuse and street sexual victimization.

Measures

Early sexual abuse consisted of two items that asked respondents how often a parent or guardian had ever made a verbal request for sexual activity or had ever forced them to engage in sexual activity while living at home. The two items were summed and dichotomized such that 0 = it had never happened and 1 = it had happened at least once. This item was adapted from Whitbeck and Simons (1990). The bivariate correlation between these two items was .80.

- *Age on own* was a single item that asked the adolescent how old she was when leaving home and being on her own for the first time.
- *Time on own* was measured by the total amount of time the respondent had been either on the street or in unsupervised living arrangements (e.g., living with friends, having an apartment) since living away from home.
- *Friends sold sex* was measured using four items that asked young women if any of their close friends had ever sold sexual favors for money or drugs and/or food or shelter and if they knew anyone who had traded sex for food or shelter and/or money or drugs since being on the street. Response categories were 0 (*no*) and 1 (*yes*). Cronbach's alpha for friends selling sex was .83 for females.
- *Number of different sexual partners* was a single item that asked participants to indicate the total number of different people they had sex with in the past twelve months.
- *Trading sex* was assessed using two items where the respondents were asked if they had ever traded sex for food or shelter and if they had ever traded sex for money or drugs since being on the street. The two items were summed and then dichotomized such that those who had never traded sex were coded as 0 and those who had traded sex were coded as 1. The bivariate correlation between these two items was .56.
- *Alcohol/drug use* was measured using 11 items in which adolescents were asked about frequency of use of beer, hard liquor, marijuana, cocaine, amphetamines and other hard drugs during the past twelve months. Each item was dichotomized so that response categories were 0 (*no*) and 1 (*yes*) and then each of the 11 dichotomized items were summed into a single scale.

Response categories ranged from 0 (*never*) to 11 (*many times*). Cronbach's alpha for this measure was .81 for females.

- *Sexual victimization* while on the street consisted of two items in which the young women were asked if they had ever been forced to do something sexual and if they had been sexually assaulted or raped (adapted from Whitbeck & Simons, 1990). Due to skewness, response categories were summed and then dichotomized into 0 (*no*) and 1 (*at least once*). The bivariate correlation between these two variables was .80.

Procedure

A path model that focused on risk factors associated with sexual victimization while on the streets among female homeless and runaway adolescents was estimated using generalized least squares (Joreskog & Sorbom, 1993). Thus, each of the standardized path coefficients β for arrows leading to a specific dependent variable were estimated simultaneously with all other variables predicted to influence the measure in question. This is a fully saturated model that fits the data perfectly; therefore, fit indices are not reported. Independent variables included early sexual abuse at home, age on own, time on own, friends selling sex, number of different sexual partners, trading sex, and alcohol/drug use. Due to listwise deletion, the sample was reduced to 333 cases for these analyses.

Results

Table 1 shows the correlation matrix for the variables included in the present analyses. Early sexual abuse was significantly associated with age on own ($r = -.21$) and time on own ($r = .12$) suggesting that victims of sexual abuse were more likely to have run away from home at earlier ages and to have spent more time on the streets or in unsupervised living arrangements. Young women with a history of sexual abuse engaged in survival sex ($r = .11$), had friends who traded sex ($r = .14$), and reported being sexually victimized while on the street ($r = .21$). Those who left home at a young age spent more time on their own ($r = -.19$), traded sex ($r = -.14$), had friends who sold sex ($r = -.13$), and reported being sexually victimized ($r = -.12$). The more time spent on the street or in unsupervised living arrangements, the more likely adolescents had engaged in survival sex ($r = .14$), affiliated with friends who sold sex ($r = .17$), used large amounts of alcohol/drugs ($r = .16$), and reported being sexually victimized ($r = .18$). Those who associated with deviant peers who had sold sex reported multiple sex partners ($r = .19$), selling sex ($r = .31$), high rates of substance use ($r = .22$), and being a victim of sexual assault ($r = .35$). Engaging in sexual intercourse with multiple partners was associated with survival sex ($r = .37$), high rates of substance use ($r = .30$), and being sexually victimized ($r = .19$). Female adolescents who engaged in survival sex reported higher rates of alcohol/drug use ($r = .28$) and sexual assault ($r = .29$). Finally, substance use was significantly associated with sexual victimization on the street ($r = .25$).

The results of the path model for sexual victimization among female homeless and runaway adolescents is shown in Figure 2 (only significant paths shown). The model revealed that early sexual abuse was positively associated with time on own indicating that young women from sexually abusive family backgrounds were likely to have spent a greater portion of their time on the streets or in unsupervised living arrangements ($\beta = .13$) compared to their non-abused counterparts. Early sexual abuse negatively affected age on own ($\beta = -.17$) suggesting that adolescents with a history of sexual abuse were more likely to have run at earlier ages as a result of the abuse. A history of sexual abuse also was positively associated with friends selling sex ($\beta = .34$) and trading sex ($\beta = .08$) indicating that young women who were previously sexually abused were more likely to have affiliated with friends who sold sex as well as having engaged in trading sex for food, shelter, money, and/or drugs. Early sexual abuse also had a direct positive effect on sexual victimization ($\beta = .29$) indicating that young women from abusive family backgrounds were more likely to have reported being sexually victimized on the street.

Table 1   Correlation Matrix for Female Sexual Victimization (N = 333)

		1	2	3	4	5	6	7	8
1.	Early sexual abuse	--							
2.	Age on own	-.21**	--						
3.	Time on own	.12*	-.19**	--					
4.	Friends sold sex	.14**	-.13*	.17**	--				
5.	Different sex partners	.04	-.06	.10	.19**	--			
6.	Traded sex	.11*	-.14*	.14*	.31**	.37**	--		
7.	Alcohol/drug use	.10	-.10	.16**	.22**	.30**	.28**	--	
8.	Sexual victimization	.21**	-.12*	.18**	.35**	.19**	.29**	.25**	--
M		.310	13.58	3.90	1.10	2.53	.066	3.02	.200
SD		.463	2.46	1.82	1.43	4.59	.248	2.38	.401

*$p < .05$. **$p < .01$.

Figure 2

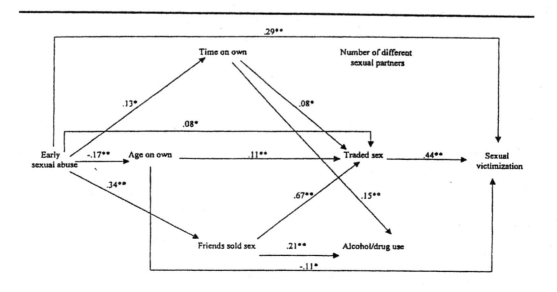

Figure 2:   Path Model for Female Sexual Victimization
NOTE: Only significant paths shown. $R^2 = .39$.
* $p < .05$. **$p < .01$.

Age on own positively predicted trading sex ($\beta = .11$) suggesting that older adolescents were more likely to have traded sex for food, shelter, money, and/or drugs compared to their younger counterparts. Further, age on own negatively affected sexual victimization ($\beta = -.11$) indicating that the earlier that adolescents find themselves on the street, the greater the likelihood of being sexually victimized. Spending more time out on their own increased the likelihood of these adolescents trading sex ($\beta = .08$). In addition, young women who spent more time out on their own reported higher rates of alcohol/drug use ($\beta = .15$).

Friends selling sex was strongly associated with adolescents trading sex ($\beta = .67$) and alcohol/drug use ($\beta = .21$). Finally, trading sex was positively associated with sexual victimization ($\beta = .44$) suggesting that young women who had traded sex for food, shelter, money, and/or drugs were more likely to have been sexually victimized compared to those who had not engaged in such behaviors. The model for female sexual victimization explained 39% of the variance (see Table 2 for all the standardized regression coefficients).

Table 2 Standardized Regression Coefficients for Female Sexual Victimization (N = 333)

Variable	Age on own	Time on own	Friends sold sex	Different sex partners	Traded sex	Alcohol/ drug use	Sexual victimization
Early sexual abuse	-.17**	.13*	.34**	.10	.08*	-.01	.29**
Age on own		-.05	.02	.06	.11**	-.01	-.11*
Time on own				.09	.08*	.15**	.06
Friends sold sex				.06	.67**	.21**	-.04
Different sex partners							-.02
Traded sex							.44**
Alcohol/drug use							.07
R^2	.03	.02	.12	.03	.53	.08	.39

*$p < .05$. **$p < .01$.

The decomposition of the effects of independent variables on the dependent variables (Joreskog & Sorbom, 1993) is presented in Table 3. The results indicated that although sexual abuse had a direct effect on sexual victimization, it also had indirect effects. That is, sexual abuse indirectly affected sexual victimization via age on own, time on own, friends selling sex, and trading sex. The effects of time on own and friends selling sex on sexual victimization were all indirect through trading sex. Young women who had friends who sold sex were more likely to have engaged in survival sex that resulted in their being sexually victimized.

Consistent with previous research (Whitbeck et al., 1997a; Whitbeck et al., 1999; Whitbeck & Simons, 1990), our results indicated that those with a history of sexual abuse were likely to be re-victimized on the street. The effects of early sexual abuse were found to have both direct and indirect effects on street sexual victimization. In terms of direct effects, given the fact that many adolescents who experience sexual abuse within the home are likely to suffer psychological and emotional problems (Beitchman et al., 1991), it is possible that they bring these problems to the street, thereby making them vulnerable targets, easily preyed upon by potential offenders. As such, the effects of early sexual abuse in combination with the social context of street life are likely to put these young women at increased risk for sexual victimization on the street. The indirect effects are consistent with risk amplification (Whitbeck et al., 1997a) in that adolescents are likely to leave home at an early age due to sexual abuse and to associate with deviant peers upon entering the street environment. Consistent with this perspective and victimization theories (Cohen & Felson, 1979; Hindelang et al., 1978), spending time on the street and engaging in high-risk behaviors puts these young people in threatening situations.

Table 3 Decomposition of Effects for Female Sexual Victimization (N = 333)

	Age on own	Time on own	Friends sold sex	Different sex partners	Traded sex	Alcohol/ drug use	Sexual victimization
Early sexual abuse							
Direct	-.17**	.13*	.34**	.10	.08*	-.01	.29**
Indirect	.00	.01	.00	.02	.22**	.09**	.15**
Total	-.17**	.14*	.34**	.13*	.30**	.09	.44**
Age on own							
Direct		-.05	.02	.06	.11**	-.01	-.11*
Indirect		.00	.00	.00	.01	.00	.05
Total		-.05	.02	.05	.12*	-.01	-.07
Time on own							
Direct				.09	.08*	.15**	.06
Indirect				.00	.00	.00	.04*
Total				.09	.08*	.15**	.10*
Friends sold sex							
Direct				.06	.67**	.21**	-.04
Indirect				.00	.00	.00	.31**
Total				.06	.67**	.21**	.27**
Different sex partners							
Direct							-.02
Indirect							.00
Total							-.02
Traded sex							.44**
Direct							.00
Indirect							.44**
Total							
Alcohol/drug use							.07
							.00
Direct							.07
Indirect							
Total							

*p < .05. **p < .01.

Close proximity to potential offenders exposes these youth to crime and criminals where the risk for victimization is greater. In particular, the combination of early emotional and psychological problems and the high-risk environment in which these adolescents interact on a daily basis results in an increased risk for sexual victimization.

Although substance use and number of different sexual partners were significantly associated with sexual victimization at the bivariate level, these associations are not significant when simultaneously controlling for the effects of all the other variables. Both substance use and number of different sexual partners are highly correlated with trading sex which accounts for much of the variation in sexual victimization.

Some limitations should be noted in the present study. The use of cross-sectional data does not allow us to test causal interpretations and limits the strength of our argument regarding the amplification of effects. However, the intervening variables, which represent street experiences, have significant effects for young women's risk for sexual victimization and are consistent with the hypothesized relationships. Another limit is the use of adolescent self-reports. Because the information was provided by the adolescent only, it is difficult to determine the extent of potential bias. However, research comparing runaway youth and parent reports has found that these youth do not appear to be over-reporting abuse in the home (Whitbeck, Hoyt, & Ackley, 1997b). Another limitation is the retrospective nature of some of the measures. For example, time on own required adolescents to think back to all the times they had been on the street or in unsupervised living arrangements. It is likely that some young people may have not been able to recall every instance they were on the street or the actual duration of that stay. Finally, the term sexual activity was not defined for the adolescents in the questions dealing with early sexual abuse; therefore, the definition was left up to the interpretation of each respondent.

Notwithstanding these concerns, the results have practical implications for those who work with homeless and runaway adolescents. Foremost is the fact that many of these young women have experienced early sexual abuse in the home at the hands of a parent or guardian. Policies that require runaways to return home only put these youth at further risk for future victimization. A second policy implication deals with life on the streets for these adolescents. Associating with deviant peers and participating in deviant behaviors increase risk for victimization. The pattern of exploitation and victimization within the family and on the streets has serious and cumulative developmental consequences. Early interception and intervention for runaways to break this cycle is needed through increased funding for safe-houses, drop-in centers, and especially for street-based outreach workers. In terms of future research, it may be helpful to determine who is sexually victimizing these young women on the street. Research demonstrates that associating with deviant peer groups increases the adolescents' chances of engaging in deviant, risky subsistence strategies (Hagan & McCarthy, 1997; Whitbeck et al., 1999) and such behaviors increase risk for victimization (Lauritsen, Sampson, & Laub, 1991). Determining whether deviant peers, strangers, or both, are sexually victimizing these young women may be important information for street-based outreach workers when determining what course of action should be taken when dealing with victims of sexual victimization.

In summary, young women who leave dysfunctional and disorganized families to escape the abuse often find themselves faced with similar problems once they enter the street environment. Plagued by financial problems, such as lack of food and shelter, these young adolescents become vulnerable to the dangers of survival in an often hostile and exploitative street environment. Existing in such an environment increases these young women's chances of being re-victimized time and time again.

Requests for reprints should be addressed to Kimberly A. Tyler, University of Central Florida, Department of Sociology & Anthropology, Orlando, FL 32816-1360.
Phone Number: (407) 823-2227. Fax: (407) 823-3026.

This article is based on research supported by a grant from the National Institute of Mental Health (MH50140). Les B. Whitbeck, Principal Investigator.

References

Bagley, C., & Young, L. (1987). Juvenile prostitution and child sexual abuse: A controlled study. *Canadian Journal of Community Mental Health, 6,* 5-26.

Bayatpour, M., Wells, R. D., & Holford, S. (1992). Physical and sexual abuse as predictors of substance use and suicide among pregnant teenagers. *Journal of Adolescent Health, 13,* 128-132.

Becker, J. V. (1988). The effects of child sexual abuse on adolescent sexual offenders. In G. E. Wyatt & G. J. Powell (Eds.), *Lasting effects of child sexual abuse* (pp. 193-207). Newbury Park, CA: Sage Publications, Inc.

Beitchman, J. H., Zucker, K. J., Hood, J. E., da Costa, G. A., & Akman, D. (1991). A review of the short-term effects of child sexual abuse. *Child Abuse & Neglect, 15,* 537-556.

Beitchman, J. H., Zucker, K. J., Hood, J. E., da Costa, G. A., Akman, D., & Cassavia, E. (1992). A review of the long-term effects of child sexual abuse. *Child Abuse & Neglect, 16,* 101-118.

Browne, A., & Finkelhor, D. (1986). Impact of child sexual abuse: A review of the research. *Psychological Bulletin, 99,* 66-77.

Cohen, L. E., & Felson, M. (1979). Social change and crime rate trends: A routine activity approach. *American Sociological Review, 44,* 588-608.

Dembo, R., Williams, L., LaVoie, L., Berry, E., Getreu, A., Wish, E. D., Schmeidler, J., & Washburn, M. (1989). Physical abuse, sexual victimization, and illicit drug use: Replication of a structural analysis among a new sample of high-risk youths. *Violence and Victims, 4,* 121-138.

Elder, G. (1997). Life course and human development. In R. Lerner (Ed.), *Handbook of child psychology, volume 1: Theoretical models of human development* (pp. 939-991). New York, NY: Wiley.

Finkelhor, D. (1984). *Child sexual abuse: New theory and research.* New York, NY: Free Press.

Finkelhor, D. (1993). Epidemiological factors in the clinical identification of child sexual abuse. *Child Abuse & Neglect, 17,* 67-70.

Finkelhor, D. (1994). Current information on the scope and nature of child sexual abuse. *The Future of Children, 4,* 31-53.

Finkelhor, D., & Dziuba-Leatherman, J. (1994). Children as victims of violence: A national survey. *Pediatrics, 94,* 413-420.

Fleming, J., Mullen, P., & Bammer, G. (1997). A study of potential risk factors for sexualabuse in childhood. *Child Abuse & Neglect, 21,* 49-58.

Hagan, J., & McCarthy B. (1997). *Mean streets: Youth crime and homelessness.* New York, NY:Cambridge University Press.

Hindelang, M. J., Gottfredson, M. R., & Garofalo, J. (1978). *Victims of personal crime: An empirical foundation for a theory of personal victimization.* Cambridge, MA: Ballinger.

Janus, M., McCormack, A., Burgess, A. W., & Hartman, C. (1987). *Adolescent runaways: Causes and consequences.* Lexington, MA: Lexington Books.

Joreskog, K., & Sorbom, D. (1993). *LISREL 8: User's reference guide.* Chicago, IL: Scientific Software.

Kellogg, N. D., & Hoffman, T. J. (1997). Child sexual revictimization by multiple perpetrators. *Child Abuse & Neglect, 21,* 953-964.

Lauritsen, J. L., Sampson, R. J., & Laub, J. H. (1991). The link between offending and victimization among adolescents. *Criminology, 29,* 265-291.

McCarthy, B., & Hagan, J. (1992). Surviving on the street: The experiences of homeless youth. *Journal of Adolescent Research, 7,* 412-430.

McCormack, A., Janus, M., & Burgess, A. W. (1986). Runaway youths and sexual victimization: Gender differences in an adolescent runaway population. *Child Abuse & Neglect, 10,* 387-395.

Morrow, K. B., & Sorell, G. T. (1989). Factors affecting self-esteem, depression, and negative behaviors in sexually abused female adolescents. *Journal of Marriage and the Family, 51,* 677-686.

Patterson, G. R. (1982). *Coercive family processes.* Eugene, OR: Castilia.

Patterson, G. R., DeBaryshe, B. D., & Ramsey, E. (1989). A developmental perspective on antisocial behavior. *American Psychologist, 44,* 329-335.

Patterson, G. R., Dishion, T. J., & Bank, L. (1984). Family interaction: A process model of deviancy training. *Aggressive Behavior, 10,* 253-267.

Peters, S. D. (1988). Child sexual abuse and later psychological problems. In G. E. Wyatt & G. J. Powell (Eds.), *Lasting effects of child sexual abuse* (pp. 101-117). Newbury Park, CA: Sage Publications, Inc.

Silbert, M. H., & Pines, A. M. (1981). Sexual child abuse as an antecedent to prostitution. *Child Abuse & Neglect, 5,* 407-411.

Simons, R. L., & Whitbeck, L. B. (1991). Sexual abuse as a precursor to prostitution and victimization among adolescent and adult homeless women. *Journal of Family Issues, 12,* 361-379.

Weisberg, D. K. (1985). *Children of the night: A study of adolescent prostitution.* Lexington, MA: Lexington Books.

Whitbeck, L. B., Hoyt, D. R., & Ackley, K.A. (1997a). Abusive family backgrounds and later victimization among runaway and homeless adolescents. *Journal of Research on Adolescence, 7,* 375-392.

Whitbeck, L. B., Hoyt, D. R., & Ackley, K. A. (1997b). Families of homeless and runaway adolescents: A comparison of parent/caretaker and adolescent perspectives on parenting, family violence, and adolescent conduct. *Child Abuse & Neglect, 21,* 517-528.

Whitbeck, L. B., Hoyt, D. R., & Yoder, K. A. (1999). A risk-amplification model of victimization and depressive symptoms among runaway and homeless adolescents. *American Journal of Community Psychology, 27,* 273-296.

Whitbeck, L. B., & Simons, R. L. (1990). Life on the streets: The victimization of runaway and homeless adolescents. *Youth & Society, 22,* 108-125.

Whitbeck, L. B., & Simons, R. L. (1993). A comparison of adaptive strategies and patterns of victimization among homeless adolescents and adults. *Violence and Victims, 8,* 135-152.

Widom, C. S., & Kuhns, J. B. (1996). Childhood victimization and subsequent risk for promiscuity, prostitution, and teenage pregnancy: A prospective study. *American Journal of Public Health, 86,* 1607-1612.

Early Family Life and Victimization in the Lives of Women*

Claire Burke Draucker, RN, Ph.D.

Introduction

Violence against women, including physical and sexual abuse by intimate others, is a major public health problem and an important topic for nursing research (Campbell, Harris, & Lee, 1995; Sampselle et al., 1992). Based on data from a national probability sample, Strauss and Gelles (1990) estimate that each year 2 million women in the United States are severely assaulted by a male partner. In a national prevalence study conducted by the National Victims Center (1992), 14% of the women surveyed reported having been forcibly raped in their lifetime. For many women, victimization begins in childhood. Data from the National Incidence Study - 2, sponsored by the National Center on Child Abuse and Neglect (USDHHS, 1988), indicates that the incidence of childhood physical abuse is 5.7 cases per 1000 children; emotional abuse is 3.4 cases per 1000 children; and sexual abuse is 2.5 cases per 1000 children. A third national incidence study of childhood abuse and maltreatment is currently underway (Kolko, 1996).

Victimization, both in childhood and adulthood, is an etiological factor in a variety of mental health problems, including depression, substance abuse, eating disorders, and self-destructive behavior (Koss, 1990). Most victims of violence experience a period of distress following a violent incident, which, if unresolved, can develop into a symptom pattern that includes anxiety responses, constriction of affect, altered self-efficacy, and sexual dysfunction (Koss, 1990). Experiences of violence often result in acute physical health problems, such as injury stemming from the violent episode, and long-term health consequences, such as stress-related chronic illnesses (Koss & Heslet, 1992).

For women, childhood maltreatment, especially sexual abuse, has been shown to be associated with increased risk for interpersonal victimization later in life. Researchers have reported relationships between childhood sexual abuse and later experiences of sexual and physical abuse (Elliot & Briere, 1993; McCord, 1985; Russell, 1986), battering (Briere, 1984), nonconsensual sexual experiences (Fromuth, 1986), and marital rape (Shields & Hanneke, 1988). Path modeling has been used to examine the complex relationships between childhood abuse and later negative outcomes, including further victimization. Elliot and Briere (1993), for example, used this approach to explicate the relationships among child abuse, quality of family environment, adult trauma, and several measures of current functioning in a sample of 2,953 professional women. The researchers highlight three noteworthy findings based on their model. First, family environment was related to parental substance abuse, childhood physical abuse, and sexual molestation. Second, childhood sexual and physical abuse were related to adult sexual assault, whereas a negative family environment and childhood physical abuse were related to adult physical assault. Finally, several indices of current functioning (e.g., lower life dissatisfaction, psychological distress, disruptions in interpersonal relationships) were differentially associated with various combinations of the predictor variables. Wyatt, Newcomb, and Riederle (1993) used structural equation modeling to examine the relationships

*Early Family Life and Victimization in the Lives of Women Claire Burke Draucker, RN, Ph.D. As previously Published in : Research In Nursing & Health, 1997, 20, 399 – 412 Copyright © 1997 John Wiley & Sons Inc. Reprinted by permission of Jossey-Bass, Inc. a subsidiary of John Wiley & Sons, Inc.
Running head: EARLY FAMILY LIFE

Key words: childhood abuse, family health, victimization, cognitive processes, social support among family context (i.e., parent education, sexual socialization, quality of family life) and child, adolescent, and adult consensual and abusive sexual experiences in a stratified probability sample of 248 women in Los Angeles County. The final path model indicated multiple relationships among the variables. One pertinent finding was that women who were severely sexually abused and women who reported less closeness in their family of origin were more likely to be victimized throughout their lives.

Little is known about the nature of the relationship between childhood abuse and victimization in adulthood and few investigators have examined variables that might mediate this relationship. For example, the use of coping processes to resolve early trauma or the quality of current interpersonal relationships have not been examined as factors that might attenuate a lifespan pattern of abuse.

The purpose of this study was to test a causal model designed to identify relationships among early family life experiences, including the overall emotional health of the family of origin and incidents of child abuse and maltreatment; the use of cognitive coping mechanisms to resolve earlier negative experiences and the availability of social support; and experiences of interpersonal victimization in a sample of adult women (see Figure 1). If childhood experiences that predispose women to interpersonal victimization later in life are identified and if it can be determined what coping mechanisms and sources of support mitigate the negative effects of these experiences, the relationship between childhood and adult abuse can be better understood. The model may assist nurses and other health professionals in identifying women at risk for on-going victimization and in planning therapeutic interventions that facilitate the resolution of early life experiences associated with abuse throughout the lifespan.

Figure 1. Proposed casual model.

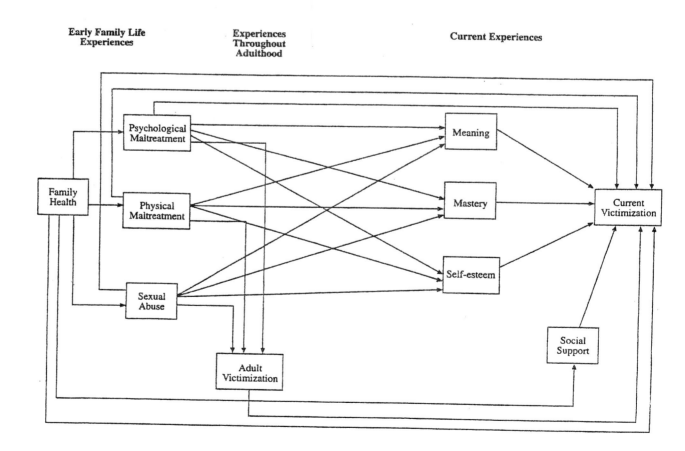

According to Hovestadt, Anderson, Piercy, Cochran, and Fine (1985), autonomy and intimacy are two essential components of healthy family life. Autonomy is developed when all family members are encouraged to express their thoughts and feelings, accept personal responsibility, display respect for each other, and deal openly with separation and loss. Intimacy is developed when families create a warm atmosphere in the home, encourage the expression of a wide range of feelings, deal with conflicts without undue stress, and promote sensitivity toward others and trust in the goodness of human nature. Family health is considered a basic and enduring aspect of family life that begins developing when a family is formed. Therefore, family health is considered an exogenous variable that influences all other variables in the model, including three childhood abuse variables: the extent of psychological maltreatment experienced in the family of origin, the extent of physical maltreatment experienced in the family of origin, and the extent of sexual abuse experienced in, or outside, the family of origin.

It was hypothesized that poor family health and childhood abuse are related to current victimization, defined as the extent of interpersonal victimization recently or presently being experienced, but that these relationships are mediated by several factors. Mediating variables in the model include adult victimization, defined as the degree of victimization experienced throughout adulthood; the level of accomplishment of three cognitive coping tasks used to deal with earlier negative experiences; and the degree of perceived social support. The cognitive coping tasks were drawn from the theory of cognitive adaptation (Taylor, 1983). Taylor proposes that successfully searching for meaning in negative experiences, reestablishing a sense of mastery following negative experiences, and regaining self-esteem lost through negative experiences facilitate adaptation to stressful life events. Social support was included in the model based on the mediational theory of social support (Quittner, Gluechauf, & Jackson, 1990), which suggests social support can mitigate the stressful impact of negative life events.

Method

Sample

Women (N = 622) from several communities in Northeast Ohio participated in the study. Participants ranged in age from 18 to 84, with an average age of 41 (SD = 12.82), and had varied racial, occupational, and financial backgrounds. However, the sample was largely Caucasian (n = 556, 89%). The modal woman was a professional (n = 272, 44%) with an income over $40,000 ($n$ = 216, 42%).

Measures

Family health: the self-perceived levels of emotional health in one's family of origin during childhood, was measured by the Family-of-Origin Scale (FOS, Hovestadt et al., 1985). The FOS consists of 40 items measured on a 5-point scale reflecting the constructs of family autonomy and intimacy. Scores range from 40 to 200, with higher scores indicating a greater degree of perceived family health. A 2-week test-retest reliability of .97, a Cronbach's alpha of .75, and a standardized item alpha of .97 are reported (Hovestadt et al., 1985). The Cronbach's alpha coefficient obtained for the present sample was .98. Evidence of content and contruct validity has been reported (Hovestadt et al., 1985).

Psychological maltreatment: the frequency of childhood experiences of parental behaviors that are primarily verbal but result in psychological pain or distress, was measured by the Psychological Maltreatment Scale (Briere & Runtz, 1988). The respondents were asked to indicate on a 7-point scale ranging from 0 (never) to 6 (more than 20 times a year) the frequency that they experienced seven types of parental psychological maltreatment (yell at you, insult you, criticize you, try to make you feel guilty, ridicule or humiliate you, embarrass you in front of others, make you feel like a bad person) in an average year prior to age 16. Scores range from 0 to 42, with higher scores indicating more psychological maltreatment. An internal consistency of .87 is reported (Briere & Runtz, 1988). The Cronbach's alpha coefficient obtained for the present sample was .93. The authors provide evidence of construct validity based on significant correlations with several measures of long-term symptoms often associated with trauma (e.g., interpersonal sensitivity, dissociation, depression) in a sample of college students (Briere & Runtz, 1988).

Physical maltreatment: the frequency of childhood experiences of parental behaviors typically associated with physical pain and/or fear of physical injury, was measured by the Physical Maltreatment Scale (Briere & Runtz, 1988). The respondents were asked to indicate on a 7-point scale ranging from 0 (never) to 6 (more than 20 times a year) the frequency that they experienced five types of parental physical maltreatment (slap you, hit you really hard, beat you, punch you, kick you) in a year at the worst point prior to age 16. Scores range from 0 to 30, with higher scores indicating more physical maltreatment. An internal consistency of .75 is reported. The Cronbach's alpha obtained for the present sample was .86. As with the psychological maltreatment scale, evidence of construct validity was based on significant correlations with several measures of long-term symptoms often associated with trauma (e.g., interpersonal sensitivity, dissociation, depression) in a sample of college students (Briere & Runtz, 1988).

Childhood sexual abuse: sexual experiences with a person at least five years older, whether or not the experiences involved physical contact, was measured by the Severity of Childhood Sexual Abuse Scale, designed for the purpose of this study. The items were based on prior research (Browne & Finkelhor, 1986) in which characteristics of childhood sexual abuse experiences most frequently associated with negative effects was identified. The first item measured on a 5-point scale ranging from 0 (no abuse) to 4 (abuse with violence) the greatest degree of penetration and physical violence involved in the sexual abuse incidents. The second item measured on a 7-point scale ranging from 0 (no abuse) to 6 (abuse by a parent) the greatest degree of closeness in relationship between the victim and offender(s). The third item measured on a 5-point scale ranging from 0 (no abuse) to 4 (too many to count) the total number of sexual abuse incidents experienced. Scores range from 0 to 14 with higher scores indicating more severe sexual abuse. The Cronbach's alpha coefficient obtained for the present sample was .92. Because the scale was developed for the purpose of this study, validity data has not been accrued.

Adult victimization: the extent of victimization experienced throughout adulthood, including the frequency of experiences of rape/sexual assault and battering and emotional abuse in intimate relationships, was measured by the Adult Victimization Scale, designed for the purpose of this study. The respondents were asked if, as adults, they have experienced rape/sexual assault (0 = no; 1 = yes, one assault; 2 = yes, more than one assault), battering in an intimate relationship (0 = no; 1 = yes, in one relationship; 2 = yes, in more than one relationship), and emotional abuse in an intimate relationship (0 = no; 1 = yes, one relationship; and 2 = yes, more than one relationship). Scores range from 0 to 6 with higher scores indicating a greater degree of victimization throughout adulthood. The Cronbach's alpha coefficient obtained for the present sample was .70. Because the scale was developed for the purpose of this study, construct validity data are not yet available.

Meaning: the degree of accomplishment of the cognitive coping task of finding meaning in negative experiences, was measured by the revised meaning subscale of the Cognitive Adaptation Scale (Draucker, 1989). The original subscale was designed to measure the extent to which survivors of incest had found meaning in their incest experiences. For the purpose of this study, the scale was revised for use with all women, not just survivors of incest. The scale consists of 5 items asking respondents to indicate on a 5-point scale the extent to which they agree with statements reflecting a successful search for meaning in negative childhood experiences. The statements, based on Taylor's (1983) description of the meaning coping task, reflect the processes of having "made peace" with difficult or negative experiences, believing that some good or benefit had come out of the negative experiences, and ceasing to experience distress related to understanding "why" negative events occurred. Scores range from 5 to 25, with higher scores indicating a greater degree of the accomplishment of the meaning task. For the original meaning subscale, a test-retest coefficient of .75 and an alpha coefficient of .50 are reported (Draucker, 1995). The Cronbach's alpha coefficient obtained for the revised scale in the present sample was .71. Evidence of the construct validity of the original subscale is based on moderate correlations with several measures of well being, including the Beck Depression Inventory (Beck, 1978), r = -. 55, p < .001; the Coopersmith Self-esteem Inventory (Coopersmith, 1981), r = .55, p < .001; and the Social Adjustment Scale - Self-Report (Weissman & Bothwell, 1976), r = -.51, p < .001 (Draucker, 1988).

Mastery, the degree of accomplishment of the cognitive coping task of regaining a sense of mastery following negative experiences, was measured by the mastery subscale of the Cognitive Adaptation Scale (Draucker, 1989; 1995). This subscale consists of three items asking respondents to indicate on a 5-point scale the degree to which they believe they have the ability to handle situations to achieve the results they desire, to set limits on the behaviors of others, and to prevent themselves from being abused or exploited in their personal relationships. Scores range from 3 to 15, with higher scores indicating a greater degree of the accomplishment of the mastery task. For the mastery subscale, a test-retest coefficient of .71 and an alpha coefficient of .76 are reported (Draucker, 1989; 1995). The Cronbach's alpha coefficient obtained for the present sample was .74. Evidence of the construct validity of the subscale is based on moderate correlations with several measures of well being, including the Beck Depression Inventory (Beck, 1978), r = -. 46, p < .001; the Coopersmith Self-esteem Inventory (Coopersmith, 1981), r = .44, p < .001; and the Social Adjustment Scale - Self-Report (Weissman & Bothwell, 1976), r = -. 35, p < .001 (Draucker, 1988).

Self-esteem, the degree of accomplishment of the self-enhancement coping task, was measured by the Coopersmith Self-Esteem Inventory (Coopersmith, 1981). This instrument contains 25 favorable or unfavorable self-statements. Respondents are asked to indicate if the statements are like me or unlike me and receive 4 points for each positive self-esteem item endorsed. Scores range from 0 to 100 with higher scores indicating greater self-esteem. Kuder-Richardson 20s ranging from .74 to .92 and test-retest reliability coefficients of .80 to .82 are reported (Coopersmith, 1981). The Cronbach's alpha coefficient obtained for the present sample was .89. Coopersmith provides evidence of the construct and predictive validity of the SEI.

Social support, the perception of the degree of social support in one's life, was measured by Part 2 of the Personal Resource Questionnaire (PRQ85, Weinert, 1987). The PRQ85, Part 2, contains 25 items measured on a 7-point Likert scale reflecting the following dimensions of social support: provision for attachment/intimacy, social integration, opportunity for nurturant behaviors, reassurance of worth as an individual and in role accomplishments, and availability of informational, emotional, and material help (Weiss, 1974). Scores range from 25 to 175 with higher scores reflecting greater perceived social support. An internal consistency reliability coefficient of .89 is reported (Wienert, 1987). The Cronbach's alpha coefficient obtained for the present sample was .93. Evidence of the content, face, construct, and predictive validity of the instrument has been reported (Brandt & Weinert, 1981; Weinert, 1987; Weinert & Tilden, 1990).

Current victimization, the extent of victimization experienced within the past year, was measured by the Current Abuse Scale (Draucker, 1995). The scale consists of six items asking respondents to indicate on a 4-point scale the frequency and degree of severity of the emotional, physical, and sexual abuse they experience in their current relationships. For the purpose of this study, the items were reworded to inquire about abuse experienced within the past year. The items include definitions and examples of each type of abuse. Scores range from 0 to 18, with higher scores indicating a greater degree of victimization. A test-retest reliability of .79 and an alpha coefficient of .84 are reported. The Cronbach's alpha coefficient obtained for the present sample was .83. Evidence of construct validity includes moderate correlations with the social introversion (r = .23, p < . 01) and guilt (r = .24, p < .01) subscales of Berndt=s (1990) Multiscale Depression Inventory (Draucker, 1989) .

Procedures

Announcements of the study were placed in newspapers of major metropolitan areas in Northeast Ohio (e.g., Akron, Cleveland, Youngstown) as well as in smaller community-based newspapers. In addition, posters containing the study announcements were displayed in rural, urban, and suburban public centers at which women are likely to gather (e.g., YMCAs, Community Centers). The announcements indicated that the study was about A early family life and adult experiences in the lives of women and included a brief description of the study, criteria for participation (women over the age of 18 who could complete a survey in English), and an invitation to call a toll-free line for further information or to request a survey packet. The survey packets consisted of an information letter describing details of the study, including risks and benefits; the questionnaire; a pre-stamped return envelope to return the questionnaire anonymously; and a postcard for participants to return separately with their name and address if they wished to have the study results sent to them.

A total of 833 survey packets were distributed. Seven hundred and fifty-two women (752) called a toll-free line and requested survey packets and another 71 packets were given directly by the investigator or research assistants to individuals who expressed an interest in the study. Six hundred and twenty-three (623) surveys were returned (75% of those distributed) and all but one were sufficiently complete to be included in data analysis.

Results

The childhood abuse histories of the sample are outlined in Table 1. Childhood psychological and physical maltreatment were measured as continuous variables; however, the frequencies and percentages of responses to certain items from each of these scales are displayed in Table 1 to reflect the portion of the sample who experienced behaviors that would typically be considered abusive. Approximately 28% of the participants experienced emotionally abusive behaviors over 20 times in an average year. Twenty-one percent of the participants were beaten and a smaller group were punched (13%) or kicked (9%) at least once at the worst point in their childhood.

Fifty-three percent (n=326) of the sample indicated that they had experienced sexual abuse before the age of 16. The type of sexual abuse incidents, the relationship of the offender(s) to the participant, the number of incidents, and the age at which the first incident occurred are outlined in Table 1.

Table 1 Childhood Abuse Histories of the Sample

Characteristic	Response	f	%[c]
Child Psychological Maltreatment	Ridicule/Humiliate[a]		
	Between 1 and 20 times	240	39%
	Over 20 times	150	24%
	Make you feel like a bad person		
	Between 1 and 20 times	241	39%
	Over 20 times	175	28%
Child Physical Maltreatment	Beaten[b]		
	Between 1 and 20 times	129	21%
	Over 20 times	37	6%
	Punched		
	Between 1 and 20 times	61	10%
	Over 20 times	19	3%
	Kicked		
	Between 1 and 20 times	50	8%
	Over 20 times	9	1%
Child Sexual Abuse	Type of incidents		
	Sexual/no physical contact	199	32%
	Physical contact/no intercourse	274	44%
	Intercourse	106	17%
	With violence	51	8%
	Relationship of offender		
	Stranger	79	13%
	Acquaintance	128	21%
	Family friend/authority figure	106	17%
	Extended family member	123	20%
	Sibling	54	9%
	Parent/step-parent/foster parent	83	13%
	Number of incidents		
	One	70	11%
	Several (2-10)	170	27%
	Many (over 10)	40	6%
	Too many to count	46	7%
	Age at first incident		
	Infant	6	1%
	Toddler (1 to 3 years)	16	3%
	Preschooler (4 to 6 years)	68	11%
	School-aged (7 to 12 years)	155	25%
	Adolescent (13 years or over)	93	15%

Note: [a]Frequencies represent an average year prior to age 16. [b]Frequencies represent the worst year prior to age 16. [c] % = percent of total sample.

The adult abuse histories of the sample are displayed in Table 2. As indicated, 29% of the sample had experienced one or more sexual assaults, 35% had experienced battering in one or more intimate relationships, and approximately 62% had experienced emotional abuse in one or more intimate relationships. Within the past year, almost 50% had experienced at least occasional emotional abuse and a small portion of the sample had experienced at least occasional physical (4%) and/or sexual abuse (11%).

Table 2 Adult Abuse Histories of the Sample

Characteristic	Response	f	%
Adult Victimization (anytime in adulthood)	Rape/sexual assault		
	No	440	71%
	Yes, one assault	99	16%
	Yes, more than one assault	80	13%
	Battering in an intimate relationship		
	No	403	65%
	Yes, one relationship	153	25%
	Yes, more than one relationship	63	10%
	Emotional abuse in an intimate relationship		
	No	232	37%
	Yes, one relationship	251	40%
	Yes, more than one relationship	135	22%
Current Victimization (within the past year)	Emotional Abuse		
	Frequency		
	Never	145	23%
	Seldom	177	29%
	Occasional	170	27%
	Frequent	123	20%
Current Victimization (within the past year)	Degree of Severity		
	None	154	25%
	Slight	236	38%
	Moderate	151	24%
	Severe	75	12%
	Physical Abuse		
	Frequency		
	Never	527	85%
	Seldom	63	10%
	Occasional	18	3%
	Frequent	8	1%
	Degree of Severity		
	None	529	85%
	Slight	59	10%
	Moderate	20	3%
	Severe	8	1%
	Sexual Abuse		
	Frequency		
	Never	439	71%
	Seldom	106	17%
	Occasional	50	8%
	Frequent	21	3%
Current Victimization (within the past year	Degree of Severity		
	None	454	73%
	Slight	118	19%
	Moderate	28	5%
	Severe	15	2%

Analysis of the Causal Model

The descriptive statistics for the scales measuring the 10 major variables in the causal model are presented in Table 3. Several of the measures (psychological and physical maltreatment, adult victimization, and current victimization) have large standard deviations indicating heterogeneity of the sample. The zero-order correlations between the major variables are presented in Table 4. All correlations were statistically significant.

Table 3 Descriptive Statistics for the Ten Major Scales

Scale	Range	M	SD
		Statistic	
Family Health	40-198	111.00	37.19
Psychological Maltreatment	0-42	23.90	13.56
Physical Maltreatment	0-30	5.30	6.77
Sexual Abuse	0-13	3.12	3.34
Adult Victimization	0-6	1.71	1.70
Meaning	5-25	19.20	3.43
Mastery	3-15	11.37	2.57
Self-Esteem	4-100	66.59	24.36
Social Support	40-175	136.22	24.11
Current Victimization	0-18	3.87	3.47

Path modeling was used to compare the theoretical structures of the model with empirical data to determine fit. The LISREL VII program (Joreskeg & Sorbom, 1989) was used for simultaneous estimation of the proposed paths. However, as only one empirical indicator of each variable was used, assessment of a measurement model was not conducted.

As it is common practice to report several indices of fit (Bollen & Long, 1993), the GFI (goodness of fit index) and AGFI (adjusted goodness of fit index), both scaled to indicate adequate fit if they are over .90 (Joreskog & Sorbom, 1986), were calculated in addition to the $\div^2$ estimator. The stability index, an indication that the data fit the model as precisely as the constraints allow, and the coefficient of determination (R^2), the amount of variance in all the variables accounted for by the model, also were determined.

The following statistics were obtained for the original model: $\div^2(19, N = 622) = 978.42$, $p < .01$; GFI = .721; AGFI = .194. The goodness of fit indices were well below the criterion of .9, confirming the lack of fit shown by the $\div^2$. The coefficient of determination was .651 and the stability index was .232. Approximately 27% of the variance of the outcome variable, current victimization, were accounted for by the model.

As the original model did not fit the data well, the model was revised. The path coefficients and modification indices were studied. The modification indices in a LISREL analysis (Joreskeg & Sorbom, 1989) indicate which non-estimated paths, if included, would maximally improve the fit of the model. Paths with non-significant coefficients were deleted and new paths, identified by the highest modification indices, were added if such additions were theoretically and logically justifiable. For example, path additions representing relationships among variables that were likely to have occurred concurrently and that were conceptually linked (e.g., the three types of childhood

175

maltreatment) were allowed. This process has been referred to as a theory trimming (Youngblut, 1994).

Table 4 Zero-order Correlations between Ten Major Variables

Varia-bles	Family Health (FH)	Psycho-logical Maltreat-ment (PsM)	Physical Maltreat-ment (PhM)	Sexual Abuse (SA)	Adult Victimi-zation (AV)	Mean-ing (Me)	Mastery (Ma)	Self-esteem (SE)	Social Support (SS)	Current Victimi-zation (CV)
FH	1.00	-.74**	-.47**	-.32**	-.34**	.25**	.22**	.35**	.40**	-.24**
PsM		1.00	.58**	.32**	.32**	-.15**	-.15**	-.34**	-.30**	.27**
PhM			1.00	.39**	.30**	-.17**	-.17**	-.29**	-.28**	.29**
SA				1.00	.35**	-.10*	-.19**	-.23**	-.18**	.27**
AV					1.00	-.20**	-.20**	-.28**	-.32**	.45**
Me						1.00	.46**	.48**	.46**	-.27**
Ma							1.00	.55**	.53**	-.39**
SE								1.00	.61**	-.41**
SS									1.00	-.39**
CV										1.00

*p — .05. **p — .05

This process proceeded in steps, as indicated in Table 5, until no meaningful improvement in the model was detected. The decision to retain the sixth model was made based on a good residual pattern, low $\div^2$ value, small difference between the GFI and the AGFI, and low modification indices. Also, the sixth model exhibited a greater degree of parsimony than did the fifth model. Thus 9 paths were added to the original model and 16 were deleted. All of the path coefficients were statistically significant and the goodness of fit index was almost at a maximum.

Table 5 Statistics Used to Determine Final Model

Revision Number	Path Added	Path Removed	Statistic			
			X^2	Stability	GFI	AGFI
Original Model	-	-	978	23	.72	.19
1	SE 6 SS SE 6 Ma Ma 6 SS	PsM 6 AV PsM 6 Ma SA 6 Me SA 6 CV Me 6 CV	455	.58	.87	.68
2	SE 6 Me PsM 6 PhM	PsM 6 CV PhM 6 Ma SA 6 Ma	184	.84	.95	.87
3	PhM 6 SA	PsM 6 Me PhM 6 Me	128	.83	.96	.91
4	Me 6 Ma	FH 6 PhM FH 6 CV	97	.73	.97	.93
5	AV 6 SE FH 6 SE	SS 6 CV	68	.75	.98	.95
6 (Final Model)		PsM 6 SE PhM 6 SE SA 6 SE	79	.75	.98	.95

Note: FH = Family Health PsM = Psychological Maltreatment PhM = Physical Maltreatment SA = Sexual Abuse AV = Adult Victimization Me = Meaning Ma = Mastery SE = Self Esteem SS = Social Support CV = Current Victimization

For the final revised model, the following statistics were obtained: $\div^2$ (26, $\underline{N}$ = 622) = 78.98, $\underline{p}$ < .01; GFI = .975; and the AGFI = .948. Although the $\div^2$ statistic was still significant, possibly due to the large sample size (Boyd, Frey, & Aaronson, 1988), the other indices suggested adequate fit. The total coefficient of determination was .605 and the stability index was .745. The model accounted for about 60% of the total variance and the data fits the model as precisely as constraints allow. Approximately 33% of the variance of the outcome variable, current victimization, was accounted for by the revised model.

The indirect and total effects of the variables in the revised model are shown in Table 6. The revised model, with the standardized path coefficients and the squared multiple correlation coefficients, is depicted in Figure 2. The structures of the original and the final model were compared. The original model essentially posited relationships between variables representing experiences occurring at different points throughout the lifespan. Early family life variables were hypothesized to predict current victimization, and intervening factors were hypothesized to mediate these relationships. Unlike the original model, the revised model reflected the intercorrelation of variables that supposedly occurred contemporaneously. For example, the revised model accounts for the intercorrelations among the three childhood abuse variables, among the cognitive coping variables, and among the cognitive coping variables and social support. These intercorrelations become important in understanding the complexity of the relationship between early family life experiences and current victimization. Because the revised model is a better fit with the data, the path coefficients in the revised model will be addressed. The revised model, however, is only a numerical indication of how the variables might relate to each other and should be validated with another group of subjects.

A complex network of significant pathways reflected multiple, mediated intercorrelations among the variables. The effects discussed below are displayed in Figure 2 (direct effects) and Table 6 (indirect effects). Paths mediated by one or more of the victimization variables are considered abuse pathways whereas paths not mediated by one of these variables are considered nonabuse pathways.

The early family life variables were related to one another by several paths. Poor family health indirectly predicted sexual abuse via psychological and physical maltreatment. This path is considered an abuse pathway as it was mediated by physical and/or psychological maltreatment. However, family health also directly predicted sexual abuse; in other words, poor family health was related to sexual abuse even when the effects of other forms of maltreatment were controlled. This path is therefore considered a nonabuse pathway as it was not mediated by either maltreatment variable.

Table 6 Indirect and Total Effects Among the Variables in the Final Model

	Predictor Variables									
Effect Variables	FH	PsM	PhM	SA	AV	Me	Ma	SE	SS	CV
PsM	0	0	0	0	0	0	0	0	0	0
	-.75*	0	0	0	0	0	0	0	0	0
PhM	-.43*	0	0	0	0	0	0	0	0	0
	.43*	.57	0	0	0	0	0	.02	0	0
SA	-.14*	.18*	0	0	0	0	0	0	0	0
	31*	.18*	.32*	0	0	0	0	0	0	0
AV	.12*	.11*	.07*	.00	0	0	0	0	0	0
	-.34*	.11*	.19*	.22*	0	0	0	0	0	0
Me	.20*	.01*	-.02*	.02*	.09*	0	0	0	0	0
	.20*	-.01*	-.02*	-.02	-.09*	0	0	.52*	0	0
Ma	.22*	.01*	-.02*	.02*	-.10*	0	0	.12*	0	0
	.22	-.01*	-.02*	-.02*	-.10*	.23*	0	.58*	0	0
SE	.06*	.02*	-.03*	.04*	0	0	0	0	0	0
	.38*	-.02*	-.03*	-.04*	-.18*	0	0	0	0	0
SS	.22*	-.01*	-.02*	.02*	-.10*	.06*	0	.14*	0	0
	.39*	-.01*	-.02*	-.02*	-.10*	.06*	.25*	.58*	0	0
CV	-.27*	.11*	.07*	.09*	.05*	-.05*	0	-.13*	0	0
	-.27*	.11*	.18*	.09*	.39*	-.05*	-.22*	-.28*	0	0

Note: Indirect effects are on top, total effects are on the bottom * = p_ <.01. FH = Family Health PsM = Psychological Maltreatment PhM = Physical Maltreatment SA = Sexual Abuse AV = Adult Victimization Me = Meaning Ma = Mastery SE = Self Esteem SS = Social Support CV = Current Victimization

Figure 2. Standardized path coefficients and squared multiple correlation coefficients for the final model.

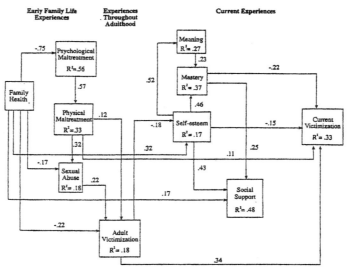

The relationships between the early family life variables and adult victimization showed similar abuse and nonabuse patterns. Poor family health indirectly predicted adult victimization by several abuse pathways; one path involved all three types of abuse, one bypassed sexual abuse, and another bypassed physical and psychological maltreatment. However, there was also a nonabuse pathway that connected family health directly to adult victimization without mediation by any of the three childhood abuse variables.

Several major pathways connected the early family life variables and current victimization. Many of these paths were mediated by adult victimization, for example, family health to adult victimization (either directly or indirectly via the childhood abuse variables) to current victimization. However, a few of the pathways between the early family life variables and current victimization were not mediated by adult victimization (e.g., family health to psychological maltreatment to physical maltreatment to current victimization) and one pathway was not mediated by adult victimization or by any child abuse variable (family health to the cognitive variables to current victimization).

Several pathways leading from the early family life variables and/or adult victimization to current victimization were mediated by the three cognitive variables. Self-esteem served as a "hub" variable of the cognitive triad, as the early family life variables predicted self-esteem directly (e.g., family health to self-esteem) and indirectly (via adult victimization) and self-esteem then predicted current victimization directly or indirectly (via the other cognitive variables).

Social support was not related to current victimization. However, several pathways linked the early family life variables to social support either directly (e.g., family health to social support) or indirectly via the adult victimization and/or cognitive variables. Many of the same paths that led to current victimization also led to social support.

Discussion

The results are consistent with other causal models (Elliot & Briere, 1993; Wyatt et al., 1993) that point to a complex relationship between childhood and adult victimization, strongly influenced by the general emotional health of the family of origin. The multiple intercorrelations among the early family life variables support an ecological perspective of childhood maltreatment (Briere & Runtz, 1988); that is, childhood abuse typically occurs in an environment of problematic family dynamics often involving several types of maltreatment.

The mechanisms by which early family experiences are associated with later victimization are represented by multiple pathways. The types of paths (abuse and nonabuse) that connect childhood experiences and current victimization may be explained by different dynamics. The abuse pathways, indicating multiple abuse experiences over time, may reflect a lifespan pattern of abuse. Wyatt et al. (1993), noting a strong positive association between intra- and extra-family sexual abuse and later victimization, stated, "Sexually abused girls may learn that they are powerless and helpless with regard to unwanted and inappropriate sexual invasion and that there is no safety either in or outside of the home" (p. 124-125). Similarly, Koss (1990) hypothesized that abused girls may come to believe that violence is "part of being female" (p. 376).

The nonabuse pathways, however, indicate that problematic family dynamics predict victimization even beyond the effects accounted for by prior abuse experiences. Koss (1990) has suggested that decreased self-esteem, confusion regarding personal boundaries, and limited skills of self-protection render repeatedly abused individuals susceptible to further victimization. These characteristics also could stem from a negative family environment that may not involve overt abuse. Farmer (1989) identified eight problematic family interaction patterns including denial, inconsistency and unpredictability, lack of empathy, lack of clear boundaries, role reversal, a closed family system, incongruent communication, and too much or too little conflict. Any of these dynamics might lead to disruption in the development of the child's ability to form healthy interpersonal relationships. Subsequent abusive relationships might be one result of such disruption.

The similarity of the paths leading to current victimization and to social support also suggests that factors associated with victimization may be predictive of other aspects of interpersonal functioning as well. Events that predispose some women to further victimization may cause other women to avoid relationships altogether, thereby protecting themselves from further abuse, but leaving them feeling socially isolated and devoid of support

This model differs from the previous models discussed (Elliot & Briere, 1993; Wyatt et al., 1993) by inclusion of the cognitive variables, which further explained the relationships between early and current abuse. All the pathways that include the cognitive variables suggest that the manner in which the self and negative events are cognitively appraised can influence the degree of victimization currently being experienced. A positive self-concept, a sense of mastery, and having found meaning in negative experiences can mitigate the impact of prior negative events.

The findings suggest possible clinical implications. Clearly, the general family environment, as well as experiences of maltreatment, have an impact on future interpersonal relationships. Therefore, the overall quality of family life, including elements such as autonomy and intimacy, should be included in all assessments of children. Similarly, when working with women who are seeking to end a cycle of violence in their lives, childhood abuse, negative family interactions, and the cumulative effects of on-going abuse throughout the lifespan all should be considered. Some authorities (Berliner, 1993; Mullen, 1993) have cautioned clinicians not to focus on any one childhood trauma, such as childhood sexual abuse, as the sole etiology of current distress. Mullen (1993) stated, for example, "The time has come to stop being dazzled by CSA (child sexual abuse) and its sequelae and, while giving it its full and proper weight, view it within the context of those other social, family, and interpersonal factors that contribute to the development of disorder" (p. 431). The findings of this study support such advice.

The findings also point to the potential promise of therapeutic interventions aimed at facilitating the accomplishments of the cognitive tasks. Cognitive approaches have been used to facilitate increased self-esteem (Briere, 1992) and mastery (Walker, 1994) in women who have experienced interpersonal violence in their lives. Therapy aimed at finding meaning in childhood abuse experiences (Clarke, 1993) also has been shown to be effective.

The major limitation of the study was the retrospective, correlational, and cross-sectional nature of the design that prohibits empirical validation of causality suggested by the arrows in the model. Whereas retrospective designs can "illuminate associations between perceived event and symptom, only prospective designs can reliably examine the relationship between historical event and symptom" (Nash, Hulsey, Harralson, & Lambert, p. 282). In this study, many factors could have influenced the participant's recall and evaluation of events that occurred throughout their lives, especially in their childhoods. For example, current functioning and quality of life, therapy experiences, and intervening life events all could affect how participants now perceive their early family life experiences. The accomplishment of the cognitive tasks, some of which by definition are appraisals of early negative events, could affect how these events are remembered and described. Further, many of the relationships between the variables are likely to be bi-directional, whereas the model implies unidirectionality. For example, an incident of childhood sexual abuse may influence family health (as well as be influenced by it) by causing the family to become more secretive and less trusting than it might have otherwise been. Similarly, problems with self-esteem and sense of mastery could lead to experiences of victimization but could be influenced by such experiences as well.

The essentially middle class and ethnically homogeneous sample limits the generalizability of the findings. Also, the self-selection of the sample and the large sample size could possibly have inflated the correlations among the variables. All participants volunteered for the study in response to an announcement about "early family life and adult experiences in the lives of women." Respondents may have been individuals who perceived an important connection between their childhood experiences and their experiences in adulthood and therefore responded to the ad. This also may account for the large portion of the sample (63%) who reported childhood sexual abuse.

The psychometric properties of some of the instruments also contributed to the study's limitations. The internal reliability of the measures of adult victimization, meaning, and mastery were marginally adequate. While measurement of the extent of adult victimization experienced throughout the lifespan likely could be accomplished by a more detailed scale (such as the Current Abuse Scale), the quantitative measurement of cognitive processes remains a challenge. These processes best may be explored by a qualitative approach. Also, for several measures designed by the investigator (e.g., severity of child sexual abuse, adult victimization), validity has not been established. Ultimately, multi-scale assessment of the constructs of interest should be used so that a structural equation model with latent variables could be tested, thereby avoiding the assumption of perfect reliability of the scales, as was the case in this path analysis.

Although the revised model contained nine predictor variables and was designed to fit optimally with the data collected from the current sample, the model accounted for only 33% of the variance in the outcome variable, current victimization. The remaining 67% of the variance remains unexplained. To further explicate the relationships in the model, the type and nature of abuse experiences in adulthood may need to be differentiated. For example, the variables in the model may predict abuse by an intimate other, but not assault by a stranger. Also, as the Briere and Elliot (1993) model suggests, different types of childhood abuse (sexual versus physical) differentially predict to some degree the types of abuse experienced in adulthood.

The model focuses on victimizing experiences of women throughout their lives and on their appraisals of those experiences, but does not address external forces that contribute to violence against women and that may account for the unexplained variance. For example, socioeconomic status was not included in the model. While a model focusing on women's experience with, and responses to, victimization across the lifespan can be helpful to clinicians working with individuals seeking to end a "cycle of violence" in their lives and to researchers attempting to explicate the psychodynamic factors that contribute to the victimization of women, such models may imply that women's experiences and cognitive processes are the major factors in explaining abuse while ignoring potential external factors. Several authors (Campbell et al., 1995; Fine, 1993) have suggested that such research has the potential of casting blame on the victims of violence. Fine (1993) states, "To focus on the individual, although it may be practically useful given our access to women but not their domestic contexts, contributes to a discourse that finally blames individual survivors, for the source of social inequity is sought inside their bodies and minds" (p. 280). Therefore, relevant social, political, or economic factors should be identified and included along with family and psychological variables in comprehensive models explaining the victimization of adult women.

This study was supported by an Academic Research Enhancement Award from NINR - R15 - NR03330-01.

References

Brandt, P. A. & Weinert, C. (1981). The PRQ - A social support measure. *Nursing Research 30*, 277-280.

Beck, A. T. (1978). *Beck Depression Inventory*. Philadelphia: Center for Cognitive Therapy.

Berliner, L. (1993). Sexual abuse effects or not? *Journal of Interpersonal Violence 8*, 428-429.

Berndt, D. J. (1986). *Multiscore Depression Inventory*. Los Angeles: Western Psychological Services.

Bollen, K. A., & Long, J. S. (1993). *Testing structural equation models*. Newbury Park: Sage.

Boyd, C. J., Frey, M.A., & Aaronson, L. S. (1988). Structural equation modeling and nursing research: Part I. *Nursing Research 37*, 249-251.

Briere, J. (1984, April). *The effects of childhood sexual abuse on later psychological functioning: Defining a "post-sexual abuse syndrome."* Paper presented at the Third National Conference on Sexual Victimization of Children, Washington, D.C.

Briere, J. (1992). *Child abuse trauma: Theory and treatment of lasting effects*. Newbury Park, CA: Sage.

Briere, J., & Runtz, M. (1988). Multivariate correlates of childhood psychological and physical maltreatment among university women. *Child Abuse and Neglect, 12,* 331-341.

Browne, A., & Finkelhor, D. (1986). Impact of child sexual abuse: A review of the research. *Psychological Bulletin, 99,* 66-77.

Campbell, J. C., Harris, M. J., & Lee, R. K. (1995). Violence research: An overview. *Scholarly Inquiry for Nursing Practice: An International Journal 9*, 105-126.

Clarke, K. M. (1993). Creation of meaning in incest survivors. *Journal of Cognitive Psychotherapy 7*, 195-203.

Coopersmith, S. (1981). *Self-esteem inventories.* Palo Alto, CA: Consulting Psychologist Press.

Draucker, C. B. (1988). The cognitive adaptation of female incest survivors. *Dissertation Abstracts International, 49 (12B)*, 5515.

Draucker, C. B. (1989). Cognitive adaptation of female incest survivors. *Journal of Consulting and Clinical Psychology, 57,* 668-670.

Draucker, C. B. (1995). A coping model: Adult survivors of childhood sexual abuse. *Journal of Interpersonal Violence, 10,* 159-175.

Elliot, D. M., & Briere, J. (1993, August). *Childhood maltreatment, later revictimization, and adult symptomatology: A causal analysis.* Paper presented at the 101st Annual Meeting of The American Psychological Association, Toronto, Canada.

Farmer, S. (1989). *Adult children of abusive parents*. Chicago: Contemporary Books.

Fine, M. (1993). The politics of research and activism: Violence against women. In P. B. Bart & E. G. Moran (Eds.)., *Violence against women: The bloody footprints.* (pp. 278-287). Newbury Park, CA: Sage.

Finkelhor, D., Hotaling, G., Lewis, I. A., & Smith, C. (1990). Sexual abuse in a national survey of adult men and women: Prevalence, characteristics, and risk factors. *Child Abuse and Neglect, 14,* 19-28.

Fromuth, M. E. (1986). The relationship of childhood sexual abuse with later psychological and sexual adjustment in a sample of college women. *Child Abuse and Neglect, 10,* 5-15.

Hovestadt, A. J., Anderson, W. T., Piercy, F. P., Cochran, S. W., & Fine, M. (1985). A family-of-origin scale. *Journal of Marital and Family Therapy, 11*(3), 287-297.

Joreskog, K., & Sorbom, D. (1989). *LISREL VI Analysis of linear structural relationships by maximum likelihood, instrument variables, and least square methods.* Mooresville, IN: Scientific Software.

Kolko, J. D. (1996). Child physical abuse. In J. Briere, L. Berliner, J. A. Bulkley, C. Jenny, & Reid, T. (Eds.), *The APSAC handbook on child maltreatment* (pp. 21-50). Thousand Oaks, CA.:Sage.

Koss, M. P. (1990). The women's mental health research agenda: Violence against women. *American Psychologist, 45,* 374-380.

Koss, M. P., & Heslet, L. (1992). Somatic consequences of violence against women. *Archives of Family Medicine, 1,* 53-59.

McCord, J. (1985). Long-term adjustment in female survivors of incest: An exploratory study. Doctoral dissertation, California School of Professional Psychology, 1985. *Dissertation Abstracts International, 46,* 650-651B.

Mullen, P. E. (1993). Child sexual abuse and adult mental health. *Journal of Interpersonal Violence 8,* 429-431.

Nash, M. R., Hulsey, T. L., Sexton, M. C., Harralson, T. L., & Lambert, W. (1993). Long-term sequelae of childhood sexual abuse: Perceived family environment, psychopathology, and dissociation. *Journal of Consulting and Clinical Psychology, 61,* 276-283.

National Victims Center (1992). *Rape in America: A report to the nation.* Arlington, VA: Author.

Quittner, A. L., Glueckouf, R. L., & Jackson, D. N. (1990). Chronic parenting stress: Moderating versus mediating effects of social support. *Journal of Personality and Social Psychology, 59,* 1266-1278.

Russell, D. E. H. (1986). *The secret trauma: Incest in the lives of girls and women.* New York: Basic Books.

Sampselle, C. M., Bernhard, L., Kerr, R. B., Opie, N., Perley, M. J., & Pitzer, M. (1992). Violence against women: The scope and significance of the problems. In C. M. Sampselle (Ed.), *Violence against women* (pp. 3-14). New York: Hemisphere.

Shields, N. M., & Hanneke, C. R. (1988). Multiple sexual victimization: The case of incest and marital rape. In G.T. Hotaling, D. Finkelhor, J.T. Kirkpatrick, & M. A. Straus (Eds.), *Family abuse and its consequences* (pp. 255-269). Newbury Park: Sage.

Straus, M. A., & Gelles, R. J. (1990). *Physical violence in American families: Risk factors and adaptation to violence in 8,145 families.* New Brunswick, NJ: Transaction.

Taylor, S. E. (1983). Adjustment to threatening events: A theory of cognitive adaptation. *American Psychologist, 38,* 1161-1173.

U. S. Department of Health and Human Services. (1988). *Study findings: Study of the national incidence and prevalence of child abuse and neglect* (Contract No. 105-85-1702). Washington, D.C. U. S. Department of Health and Human Services.

Walker, E. A. (1994). *Abused women and survivor therapy.* Washington, D. C.: The American Psychological Association.

Weinert, C. (1987). A social support measure: PRQ 85. *Nursing Research, 36,* 273-277.

Weinert, C. & Tilden, V. P. (1990). Measures of social support: Assessment of validity. *Nursing Research 39,* 212-216.

Weiss, R. (1974). The provisions of social relationships. In Z. Rubin (Ed.), *Doing unto others* (pp. 17-26). Englewood Cliffs, NJ: Prentice-Hall.

Weissman, M. M., & Bothwell, S. (1976). Assessment of social adjustment by patient self-report. *Archives of General Psychiatry, 33,* 1111-1115

Wyatt, G. E., Newcomb, M. D., & Riederle, M. H. (1993). *Sexual abuse and consensual sex.* Newbury Park, CA: Sage.

Youngblut, J. M. (1994). A consumer's guide to causal modeling: Part II. *Journal of Pediatric Nursing 9*, 409-413.

Why Is It So Difficult For The Epidemic Of Child Abuse To Be Taken Seriously?
David L. Chadwick Endowed Lecture*

Delivered by:
Frank W. Putnam, MD

Introduction

The title of my lecture is a question that has bothered me for many years. In the last year, it has become a burning question as I watch from a position at the federal level and see the incredible contraction of resources that go into the area of child abuse and neglect and into the larger area of domestic violence.

What we are seeing is a real dissolution of leadership, programmatic leadership, at the federal level. Some of it has to do with the legal and political transitions that have occurred - to which Judge Elias referred in the preceding presentation (Elias, 1998). Some of this loss of programmatic leadership, however, has to do with changes in scientific thinking and scientific paradigms. I will say more about this in a few minutes. .

This morning, I am going to give a three-part talk (they seem to be popular among speakers). First, I am going to address the problem of making and communicating the public policy case for the importance and the enormous costs of child abuse. I realize here that I am preaching to the choir in many ways. But I want to make a case that has not been argued often. This is a case in terms of monetary costs as a warrant of the impact of child abuse and neglect upon our society. The magnitude and nature of these costs are only beginning to be appreciated. Many of the factors contributing to these costs have not been included in prior analyses.

The second part of my talk is a question. It is also a continuation in many ways of what we have just heard from Judge Elias. "Why - given these absolutely enormous costs - why is child abuse and neglect not taken seriously, particularly by the federal government? Why are we not allocating resources that are commensurate with the impact of child abuse and neglect on our society?"

The third part of my talk is a set of suggestions about what we can do - as a field, as individuals, and as organizations - to convey the immensity of these costs to others not in the field, and to stimulate the allocation of resources for prevention, treatment, and research that are truly commensurate with the costs of child abuse and neglect.

Let me begin with a few disclaimers. First I want to say that the opinions that I am going express today are my own. They do not represent the National Institute of Mental Health, the United States Public Health Service or the Department of Health and Human Services, which are hierarchy of organizations that I work for. I hereby assume all responsibility for these opinions.

During the course of this talk I am going to make some comparisons with other public health problems: cancer, AIDS, and heart disease. These comparisons are intended to provide understandable benchmarks against which we can measure the impact of child abuse, the magnitude

*As Presented at The San Diego Conference on Responding to the Maltreatment of Children January 30, 1998
Audio Transcription by: Kirk Laughead (1998)
Edited by: Diane Martin and Kirk Laughead (1998)
Final version edited and referenced by Frank Putnam, January, 1999

185

of child abuse, and the monetary cost of child abuse. In no way do I wish to suggest that cancer, AIDS, or heart disease are not serious public health problems or that they are not deserving of the resources that are provided for services and treatment. Rather, I wish to demonstrate that the impact of child abuse and neglect on our society is equivalent to these other major public health problems. Yet we are receiving only a fraction of the resources that are allocated to the prevention, treatment, and research of cancer, AIDS and heart disease.

When I speak of costs today I am going to be speaking of monetary costs. These are costs that are tangible for our society. As I have indicated, individual costs are really incalculable. In many respects, they cannot be measured. Those of you who work with victims of child abuse and neglect understand what I mean.

Finally, with respect to my sources of data: I have searched for the best sources of data that I can find to make comparisons among these conditions. I will try to remember to cite these sources as I go along. Many of these comparisons are somewhat rough. They are often based on data sets that are from about 1992-1996. These are the most current public domain data sets that I can locate. Indeed, one of my principal recommendations is going to be that we get a much more rigorous accounting of the cost of child abuse and neglect. This should be undertaken by appropriate professionals with experience in tabulating both the direct and indirect costs of public health problems in general.

Determining the scope of child abuse and neglect and the societal costs.

Two statistics are generally used to measure the scope of a public health problem. These are incidence and prevalence. Incidence is defined as the number of new cases detected in a defined period of time, which is then divided, by the number of individuals who are eligible to become new cases. Typically this is expressed as a number such as the number of new cases per 1,000 individuals who are susceptible per year. Prevalence is the number of existing cases at any point in time, divided by the total population from which that sample was drawn. Typically it is expressed as a percentage.

If you examine the statistics on the incidence and prevalence of child abuse and neglect you encounter an enormous range in the figures. Typically they differ by several fold but it is not difficult to find studies that differ by as much as twenty fold in terms of the incidence and prevalence. These substantial differences, in part, fuel the controversy that rages around child abuse statistics.

One consistent finding that emerges looking across all of these data sets is that general population surveys usually report incidence and prevalence figures that are three to four times higher than officially based or officially counted cases. Several reasons that have been advanced for these large differences.

Probably the first and foremost is that many cases of child abuse and neglect are never reported to authorities or officials and therefore are not counted in the official tabulations. General population surveys are probably much closer to the truth in terms of incidence and prevalence figures. But there are other differences, such as differences in definition. What one investigator counts as a case another discounts. Definitional differences make comparisons difficult but there are ways to adjust.

There are also differences in how samples are selected and differences in response rates. We find in general that when response rates are low you often get very abnormal prevalence figures. Various critiques address this problem and I am not going to dwell on it (e.g., Gorey & Leslie, 1997). For our purposes today, the best statistics that I can identify are the set of incidence figures that were generated by National Incidence studies funded by the National Center on Child Abuse and Neglect (NCCAN) (Sedlak& Broadhurst, 1996).

I chose to use incidence figures because the 1993 report by the National Academy of Sciences, Understanding Child Abuse and Neglect, recommended incidence figures as the single best measure of the scope of the problem (National Academy of Science, 1993). The National Incidence studies employ a probability sample, which gathers data on reported and unreported cases. This is accomplished through an informant network that includes investigatory agencies and professionals such as physicians and educators.

The third National Incidence study, the most recent study, dates to 1993 and used 5,600 informants in 42 counties of the United States (Sedlak & Broadhurst, 1996). It found that the incidence rate for all forms of child abuse and neglect was forty children per thousand children per year. That yielded approximately 1.6 million new cases of child abuse and neglect per year. This agrees reasonably well with a number of other estimates. For example, in officially counted cases taken recently, there are about two and a half to three million reported cases of which about half are substantiated by Child Protective Services (CPS) agencies.

Now in comparison, for cancer there is a very sophisticated epidemiological network called SEER, which stands for Surveillance, Epidemiology, and End Results. SEER uses a sample that is approximately ten percent of the U.S. population. The comparable SEER incidence statistic (1994), for all forms of cancer across all age groups, is 3.9 individuals per thousand per year. In other words, the incidence rate for child abuse and neglect is approximately ten times higher than the incidence rate for all forms of cancer. The SEER cancer incidence statistics translate into about 1.3 to 1.4 million new cases of cancer per year (1994 data). So even though children make up a minority of the U.S. population, we have at least as many new cases of child abuse and neglect in this country every year as we have new cases of cancer in the entire U.S. population.

Over the last decade or so, the incidence of cancer has been relatively stable. Although certain forms of cancer have increased while other forms have decreased; the overall incidence has remained about the same. At any given time, in this country there are about 8 million Americans living with some form of cancer.

Over the approximately same time period, the National Incidence studies indicate that we have had significant increases in the number of abused and neglected children. For example, the National Incidence Study Number Two (1986) found a 66% increase in child abuse and neglect over the NIS One Study (1980). In particular, physical abuse increased 58% and sexual abuse increased 300%. The Third National Incidence Study (1993), found a 200% increase in overall child abuse and neglect over the NIS Study Number Two, with a 400% increase in the number of children seriously injured (Sedlak & Broadhurst, 1996).

Thus, we find an incidence rate for child abuse and neglect that is about ten times as high as the incidence rate for all forms of cancer. This yields an approximately equal number of new cases per year for these two major public health problems. Comparison of incidence across three methodologically similar studies spanning thirteen years suggests that the incidence of child abuse and neglect is increasing dramatically; whereas the incidence of cancer is stable or declining slightly over the same period. This is one reasonable index of the magnitude of the problem.

Just how much money is child abuse and neglect costing our society?

We increasingly realize that there are a lot of different costs that must be entered into calculations of the fiscal impact of child abuse and neglect. Much of this realization is the result of clinical research over the last decade. We have known for a long time about many of the direct costs, particularly the costs of legal investigations and proceedings, in-home services, out-of-home placements, and the costs of direct treatment of the children and their families. What we are just beginning to appreciate, - and it is not widely appreciated yet - is the enormity of the indirect costs of child abuse and neglect.

I will begin with the psychiatric costs. This is one area where we now have literally hundreds of studies showing the psychiatric consequences of child abuse and neglect. One of the most consistent findings that has emerged over and over in study after study is the linkage between histories of having child maltreatment and developing depression (e.g., Levitan, Parikh, Lesage, Hegadoren, Adams, Kennedy, & Goering, 1998). In fact, if you look at a sample of individuals that have been abused and a group of people who have not been abused, you find rates of depression that are two or three times higher in the abused subjects. This is especially true for women. In fact recent analyses suggest that the discrepancy in rates of depression between males and females may be largely explainable by the much higher incidence of abuse, particularly sexual abuse, in females (Breslau, Davis, Patricia, Peterson, & Schultz, 1997; Nolen-Hoeksema, 1995).

We also find that the risk for suicide and suicide attempts is remarkably increased in individuals with histories of child abuse and neglect compared to those who have not been abused. This is true with both depressed and non-depressed samples. The increased risk is about two to three fold higher but has been reported to be much as six to twelve times higher in people with histories of maltreatment compared to people without such a history (e.g., Felitti, Anda, Nordenberg, Williamson, Spitz, Edwards, Koss, & Marks, 1998).

Another disorder that has been now widely associated with histories of maltreatment is Borderline Personality Disorder (BPD) (Guzder, Paris, Zelkowitz, & Marchessault, 1996; Silk, Lee, Hill, & Lohr, 1995). This is an extremely common psychiatric diagnosis and one that is notoriously difficult to treat. It is now well recognized that a large percentage of individuals who qualify for this diagnosis have histories of severe maltreatment, particularly sexual abuse. BPD represents yet another indirect consequence.

Regarding Posttraumatic Stress Disorder (PTSD), recent epidemiological studies suggest that as many as 8% of the American population qualify for PTSD (Breslau, Davis, Andreski, & Peterson, 1991). PTSD is also proving to be a very difficult disorder to treat. A large percentage of the individuals who qualify for PTSD in the epidemiological studies have histories of child abuse. We find that experiences of child abuse have direct effects and indirect effects on developing PTSD. That is, a certain percentage of individuals report their child abuse experiences as the traumatic experiences that are associated with their post traumatic symptoms. We are also discovering a discovery made first in Vietnam veterans (Bremner, Southwick, Johnson, Yehuda, & Charney, 1993) - that a history of having been abused in childhood is a strong risk factor for developing PTSD as a result of some other trauma that happens in adulthood especially, rape or combat. In the Persian Gulf War, a history of childhood abuse, proved to be the largest predisposing factor for developing PTSD in combat (Engel, Engel, Campbell, & McFall, 1993; Wolfe, Sharkansky, Read, Dawson, Martin, & Ouimette, 1998).

Another connection that is really just beginning to reach a larger level of awareness is the strong relationship between child abuse and substance abuse. Again this is best established for women. We have now well over a score of studies, including some very large population sample studies, with upwards of four to eight thousand individuals involved (Felitti et al., 1998; Wilsnack & Wilsnack, 1993). We find that a history of having been abused in childhood is the single largest risk factor for developing a substance abuse disorder in women. This is true for both alcohol and drugs.

What is also just beginning to be appreciated now - although not very widely - is the strength of the relationships between major medical illness, the propensity to utilize medical services, and a history of childhood maltreatment. This has been shown by a number of studies to be particularly true for gastrointestinal disorders, functional bowel disease, pelvic and GYN disorders. Not well appreciated yet, is the fact that a history of childhood maltreatment seems to be a major risk factor for a number of health risk behaviors such as smoking, alcohol use, and poor diet (Felitti, Anda, Nordenberg, Williamson, Spitz, Edwards, Koss, & Marks, 1998).

Recently about three or four studies made the discovery that a history of childhood abuse, usually physical and sexual abuse, in combination, seems to be an extraordinarily important risk factor for high-risk sexual behaviors that have two major consequences. The first is early pregnancy in teenagers. (Becker-Lausen & Rickel, 1995). The second is that the risk for AIDS - and other sexually transmitted diseases - is dramatically increased in child abuse victims. Indeed a recent large scale study by Cunningham, Stiffman, Dore, and Earls indicates that a history of a combination of physical and sexual abuse is the largest risk factor for high risk behaviors related to the transmission of AIDS in adolescents (Cunningham, Stiffman, Dore, & Earls, 1994).

So, in summary, research is finding important connections between child abuse and a number of major health problems in this country such as AIDS, substance abuse, and health risk behaviors. We do not fully understand how child abuse operates as a major risk factor for these costly outcomes, but the strength of these relationships indicates that a substantial percentage of the attributable risk for these outcomes can be ascribed to experiences of child abuse and neglect.

In the area of education, we find that a disproportionate number of abused and neglected children are represented in special education placements. In particular, disorders like Attention Deficit Hyperactivity Disorder are vastly over-represented in maltreated children compared to general population samples. About thirty percent of maltreatment children have cognitive impairments. About fifty percent have significant trouble in school including misconduct and truancy and about twenty-five percent require special educational services (Hyman & McDowell, 1977; van der Kolk, Crozier, & Hopper, 1998).

Usually figured into the indirect costs of other disorders such as cancer, AIDS or heart disease are costs of lost personal productivity. We do not really have the good figures on these losses from child abuse and neglect, but they should be counted as they are for other disorders. For example, in her seminal study of 930 women residents of San Francisco, Russell (1986) found that incest victims were twice as likely as non-victims to be unemployed at the time of the interview (Russell, 1986). Other studies indicate that sex abuse victims have more job turnover and more negative work experiences (Fairbanks, Ebert, & Zarkin, 1999). When aggregated across the millions of child abuse victims, such effects probably add several billions of dollars to the total costs of child abuse and neglect.

Finally, we should look at the criminal and legal system costs that are indirectly associated with child abuse and neglect (Miller, Cohen, & Wiersema, 1996). We know that a history of child abuse and neglect is a risk factor for both perpetration of violent crime, particularly sexual assault, and a risk factor for re-victimization. A variety of studies, at least twelve studies by my count, show that women who have a history of having been sexually abused in childhood have a two- to three-fold higher risk for rape as adults (e.g., Messman & Long, 1996).

Rape is the single most potent traumatic stressor in terms of the development of PostTraumatic Stress Disorder. Large-scale epidemiological studies find PTSD following a rape in about 50-80% of victims (e.g., Breslau, Davis, Andreski, & Peterson, 1991; Resnick, Kilpatrick, Dansky, Saunders, & Best, 1993). That is in marked contrast to most other traumas such as combat or auto accidents where the PTSD rates typically range between five and ten percent of exposed individuals. Thus rape is an extremely potent traumatic stressor that has long term consequences. And, for reasons we do not fully understand, a history of child abuse at least doubles a woman's risk of rape (Messman & Long, 1996).

How do we put a dollar amount on all of these direct and indirect costs?

This has not been done well, yet. I could only locate three studies that have attempted to systematically assess the costs of child abuse and neglect. One was funded by the National Center of Child Abuse and Neglect and conducted in Colorado (Gould & O'Brian, 1995). This study looked at indirect and direct costs. It did not, however, look extensively at medical costs or psychiatric costs. Nonetheless, it concluded that for the state of Colorado, the direct and indirect costs of child abuse and neglect were $402 million a year.

Another study, unpublished at present, funded by the Michigan Children's Trust, looked at essentially the same factors in Michigan (Caldwell, 1992). This study estimated the annual costs of child abuse and neglect at $823 million for the state of Michigan. For purposes of argument, if you average those two studies and multiply them by fifty for the fifty states, you come out with a yearly cost of $30 billion in direct and indirect costs to the United States for child abuse and neglect. Finally, a study by the National Institute of Justice placed the annual national costs of child abuse and neglect at $56 billion (Miller et al., 1996). Each of these studies included a somewhat different set of costs - but all concluded that the annual total costs are enormous.

Now what can we compare this to?

Well, if we look at cancer which is a benchmark that I have been using here, you find that the American Cancer Society estimates that the 1996 yearly costs of cancer to the United States were $104 billion (American Cancer Society, 1998). However, $57 billion of that was accounted for by the costs associated with mortality, that is, the final stages of dying of cancer. It costs a lot to die these days - at least of cancer.

If we look at the cancer costs that are associated with morbidity that is, the direct medical costs and indirect costs in lost productivity we arrive at a figure of about $47 billion. This is reasonably comparable to the estimate that I gave you for child abuse and neglect.

Now, I would emphasize that my figures for the costs of child abuse and neglect are rough. They are, however, sufficiently within the ballpark to show that in terms of numbers of affected individuals and direct and indirect monetary costs, child abuse and neglect is comparable to well accepted major public health problems such as cancer, which are widely regarded as deserving of significant resources.

Given the magnitude of this problem, what has been the response?

This is the second part of my talk. What do we have? Well, we have at the Federal level a weak, disorganized, and uncoordinated response. This is not because those of us who are federal workers are not interested in this problem. In fact, we have our own interagency working group, who meet on a regular basis to inform each other about relevant activities in our respective agencies and try to coordinate initiatives across the federal agencies. But we are all middle level at best. We do not have much influence on policy. The best that we can do is to make recommendations to our respective bosses. There is no truly centralized coordination of effort.

There are programs at the Department of Health and Human Services through the Administration for Children Youth and Families, primarily the National Center for Child Abuse and Neglect and also some programs in what is known as the Children's Bureau. You should be aware that the National Center of Child Abuse and Neglect is being downgraded to the level of an office this year. It will lose much of its programmatic independence. In addition, much of their discretionary budget, which was never large, will be lost for research funding.

Through the Public Health Service we have programs at the National Institute of Mental Health, the National Institute of Child Health and Human Development, the National Institute of Alcohol and Alcohol Abuse, and now recently through the National Institute of Drug Abuse and the Center for Disease Control. The total monies committed by all of these programs is only about ten million dollars exclusively devoted to child abuse and, another $23.7 million for potentially related research. This figure is the result of a recent survey of all of the grants through the Public Health Service and the NIH in the area of child abuse and neglect (Varmus, 1997). This total is not a yearly commitment. This is a total commitment spread across three to five year for grants currently awarded. We also have some programs through the U.S. Department of Education, Department of Justice, and the U.S. Department of Defense.

Another look at the total federal research budget for child abuse and neglect is contained in the National Academy of Science's report, Understanding Child Abuse (National Academy of Science, 1993). In 1992, the total federal research commitment - including treatment programs, demonstration programs, and research grants - was $142 million. Using the (conservative) $30 billion estimate derived above, that translates into an investment of one nickel (5 cents) for every one hundred dollars in societal costs.

In contrast, we have a large, well-funded, federal research and medical establishment dedicated to fighting cancer. The annual budget at the National Cancer Institute is over $2.3 billion. And it has been near this level for many years. Annual Federal cancer research expenditures are roughly two dollars for every one hundred dollars of the estimated annual costs. In addition to Federal agencies such as the National Cancer Institute, we have large private organizations, for example, the American Cancer Society, and a variety of foundations contributing to these efforts.

In summary, there is a multi-billion-dollar research base reliably renewed on an annual basis for cancer treatment and prevention. Nothing remotely similar to this exists for child abuse and neglect. For cancer, there is an annual research investment that is approximately 2% of national annual costs (using the full $104 Billion estimate from the American Cancer Society above). This is a forty-fold discrepancy in research investment for the same dollar costs to society.

Another telling statistic that I encountered in my search was a report by the National Academy of Sciences, a 1993 study entitled Understanding Violence (Reiss & Roth, 1993). This report included a comparison of the Federal research dollars spent on deaths associated with violence and deaths attributed to cancer, AIDS, and heart disease. Our government is spending $31 per death attributable to any form of violence. In contrast we are spending $794 per death attributed to cancer, $441 for a life lost to heart disease, and $697 for a life lost to AIDS. This is a 14- to 25-fold discrepancy in research money per life lost. Again, using a common metric, we find an enormous disparity between what we are willing to spend for violence and other equivalent public health problems.

Why has there been so little response to this enormous problem?

Why are lives lost to violence less worthy than lives lost to cancer or AIDS? Why do we have such an enormous discrepancy between the kinds of resources we will devote to those disorders and conditions, which are serious public health problems, and to all forms of violence?

I think that this is because child abuse and neglect and family violence are not viewed as a genuine problem at the Federal level by those who run the agencies that develop and administer public health programs. The conflicting and contradictory statistics that I described make it easy for many people to dismiss child abuse and neglect as a problem. In fact, critics delight in pointing to the high rates of unsubstantiated cases, typically running about 50% in the CPS System. They suggest that the majority of reports are "false" and therefore that child abuse and neglect are over-dramatized as problems.

Judge Elias gave a wonderful discussion of how the media tends to prey on these inconsistencies. Thus I will devote little additional time to the role of the media. But, I think that it is difficult to make a strong case for child abuse and neglect until we have good and widely credible incidence and prevalence statistics. In particular, the contradictory media details are confusing to the public and the policy makers. We find that many of the media discussions become largely focused on individual cases. The media lacks a larger perspective on scope and costs of child abuse and neglect to this country.

Irrespective of the merits of any individual case, the media is largely focused on the theme of victims and villains. For a while the victims of child abuse were also viewed as the 'victims' in the media. Recently they have been transformed into the "villains". The alleged perpetrators are now recast as the "victims" in many news stories. At best, this has neutralized the impact on the public of stories about child abuse and neglect. As Judge Elias rightly concluded we have a very strong backlash in the media. Part of the reason is that the media are not paying attention to the enormous societal costs of child abuse and neglect. If you read or see discussions of cancer, AIDS, or heart disease in the media, they talk about the numbers of cases, the costs, what is being done, and what resources are devoted to fixing the problem. We do not see this information included in media discussions of child abuse and neglect.

Another problem is the enormous complexity of representing to others the scope of child abuse and neglect and the larger issue of domestic violence. It is even difficult for many of us to comprehend. We have so many different disciplines involved. Pediatrics, medicine, nursing, psychiatry, psychology, social work, law enforcement, family systems, substance abuse, the education system and many other disciplines. We do not know each other very well. We do not understand each other's roles very well. We do not speak the same professional languages. None of us is truly qualified to represent the field as a whole. All of us can only communicate some part of it.

When I am interviewed by the media and try to make a case for the magnitude of the societal impact of child abuse and neglect, I see the reporter's eyes glaze over. They only seem to want to know about that one memorable case that personifies or illustrates child abuse. They do not want to talk about the larger problems. We need to find ways to represent information on the scope and costs that are more palatable.

As I alluded to at the beginning of my talk, increasingly at the Federal scientific leadership level, child abuse and neglect are not viewed as a solvable scientific problems. Conflicting data, the disagreements about definitions, the messy methodology that is inherent in working with disturbed families, and the chronic level of low funding make this a very unattractive area. Budding young investigators looking for an area to launch a career, scientific administrators looking for fields ripe for breakthroughs, and institute directors seeking to change the course of science, can not be bothered with child abuse and neglect. There is no obvious pay off for those self-interests.

The hot new scientific paradigm is molecular biology. Medical and psychiatric molecular biology is focused on a genetic model of disease if you saw the State of the Union Address (1998), you heard President Clinton describe scientific progress as measured by the increasing rapidity with which we can sequence genes. In fact, he specifically mentioned going from nine years for one gene to only nine days for another. This is where the current generation of scientific administers are placing their bets - not to mention the enormous capital investments pouring in from the private sector.

Is there a child abuse gene? While you might think that is a bad joke, this is a question that I am asked in all seriousness by scientific administrators. How do I know that there is not a child abuse gene? Why aren't we looking for a child abuse gene in our work? After all, child abuse is transmitted across generations, isn't it? None of the data that we have indicates that there is a significant genetic component to child abuse. This is a complex social behavior that can be transmitted across generations. We can change this behavior with psychosocial, legal and structural interventions - not genetic ones.

Increasingly we have a situation where the fashionable scientific tools of molecular genetics and molecular neuroscience are dictating what are considered fundable scientific problems. You have probably heard the old saying that if your only tool is a hammer, then every problem becomes a nail. What we have here is a 20th or 21st century twist on that. If your most elegant tool, your most status-bestowing tool, is a: gene sequencer. Then every problem becomes molecular genetic. Thus, by this standard, child abuse and neglect is not a problem that is worthy of scientific interest to the current scientific administration.

A generation ago physicists and rocket engineers dominated the decision making of American science, and we had great engineering projects such as the space race. Now these influential positions are held by molecular biologists and molecular geneticists, and our grandest scientific agendas involve sequencing the entire human genome, and thus theoretically finding genetic treatments for all diseases.

I will remind you that at this point in time we have sequenced less than 3% of the human genome, which is estimated to be roughly a hundred thousand genes (Koonin, 1998). No one really knows how big our genome, is. We have not even finished a single chromosome. One of the problems that is emerging is that even if you have a 99.99% accuracy rate in your sequence of the human genome. Even making only one error in every ten thousand base pairs sequenced, you will still have an enormous cumulative error when you start looking at millions and millions and millions of bases. This is a problem that has not been widely acknowledged (Rowen, Mahairas, & Hood, 1997). When the human genome is finished, supposedly around the year 2005, we will know the entire nucleotide sequences of three or four anonymous individuals. We will not know what most of those genes do individually, much less how they interact with each other and the environment in developing children.

Another problem that has not been widely acknowledged in the scientific rush to embrace molecular genetic technology is the fact that there have been over two thousand trials of various gene therapies and not a single trial has worked to date (Verma & Somia, 1997). Not a single trial of gene therapy had worked to date. But you don't hear about that! We are told that medical progress hinges on allocating ever more funds for molecular biology.

For many years, there has been a NIMH peer grant review committee that reviews and approves funding for research on violence, abuse and neglect. That committee will go out of existence in June of 1998. Future grants submitted for research on violence, abuse and neglect will go to the NIH in general rather than to a NIMH committee composed of scientists familiar with research on abuse and trauma.

As far as we can tell at this time, this new review committee is going to be dominated by molecular neurobiologists and geneticists. Abuse research studies will be competing with molecular genetic studies and judged largely by molecular neurobiologists and geneticists. Given the very messy research problems, with which we must deal, we are not going to be able to compete with those glamorous technologies. We simply do not and can not have the elegance and rigor of the molecular sciences. In the eyes of those who are now - and increasingly in future will be making the decisions of who and what gets funded, child abuse and neglect is viewed as unscientific and not deserving of support for "purely scientific reasons." This is going to be a very serious problem in the next few years. It threatens to stifle the field unless we can mobilize a larger awareness that child abuse and neglect is a public health problem of the first magnitude.

There is a fourth reason why I think that child abuse and neglect is not taken as seriously as it should be by the general public and scientific leadership. David Chadwick has called this the "invisible force" in the public debate (Chadwick, 1994). We heard about it from Judge Elias as "backlash" or the "dark force." I have always thought of it as the dark force myself. There is, in fact, a group of people (probably a substantial number of people if you think about the prevalence rates we have for just sexual abuse alone: 15% to 20% of women and 8% to 10% of men) who have a great deal to lose if sexual abuse and child abuse in general is revealed or prevented.

Although largely invisible, this group is influential. Especially in the media where they have been active behind the scenes in shaping knee-jerk stereotypes of intrusive child protective service workers, hysterical therapists, and manipulated patients. Many of us have encountered interference with our work. Sometimes this is ignorance or honest disagreement, but sometimes it can only be ascribed to malevolent attempts to suppress or discredit the dissemination of information on the scope and consequences of child abuse and neglect. Every apparent contradiction, every disagreement in interpretation of data, every ostensible discrepancy, every legally unsubstantiated case, every weakness in research methodology is seized upon by these individuals and used to obscure the larger picture and to discredit the child protection movement. This invisible force is very influential, is very powerful, and is very skillful in its use of the media and the legal system to covertly advance its agenda.

So what can we do? What is it that we can do, as a field, as individuals, as organizations?

We have to take a cooperative, collaborative, inter-disciplinary, multidisciplinary approach to the epidemic of child abuse and neglect. Because no single organization or profession is going to be very effective in this climate. We must work together and share knowledge. We must make what we know accessible to others, both professionals and the general public. We must understand that no discipline, no profession, no organization owns or controls the child abuse agenda. That progress can only be made as a multidisciplinary collaboration among individuals at the local level and organizations at the national and international level.

We desperately need better statistics. Statistics that are credible, defensible, and that can give us as good prevalence and incidence rates as we can achieve. This requires large, methodologically rigorous, population based, epidemiological studies of child abuse and neglect (Gorey & Leslie, 1997). Nothing else will suffice. This is going to be difficult. Researchers who have attempted such studies understand that there are many difficult ethical issues and many difficult methodological questions. In truth, traditional epidemiologists have avoided these studies because of their inherent difficulties.

I saw this acted out at the National Institute of Mental Health when they were planning a set of studies that were going to determine the incidence and prevalence of mental disorders in children and adolescents for the United States. Surprisingly, we do not have any comprehensive population based studies of serious mental problems in children and adolescents. To correct this, the NIMH proposed a multi-site study. At the last moment this study was canceled for reasons that I won't go into here. However, there were some preliminary studies that were conducted to test methodology. With one exception, you could not get investigators in these preliminary studies to ask about child abuse. They just would not do it. They were afraid of their obligations under the mandated reporting laws. They were not willing to stand up to these difficult questions. We are going to have to find a way to do this.

We need a good accounting of the societal costs of child abuse and neglect and violence in general. We also need to increasingly link all of these forms of violence - child abuse, domestic violence, and rape - with each other. Because they are interconnected in many perpetuating ways. Viewing them as separate and independent weakens our public position and misses important opportunities to deal with them in a concerted fashion. By looking at this larger picture we can coordinate prevention, intervention and research efforts to reduce family violence across its many manifestations.

We can tap the experience accrued in other health care economic analyses to come up with reasonable and defensible cost accounting. This is an extremely important point. David Chadwick has made this point in the past (Chadwick, 1988). If we don't understand the costs, if we can't account for the costs, how can we calculate cost-benefit analyses? How are we going to be able to show that interventions and prevention programs are effective? To make a compelling case, we have to understand what the dollars spent on those programs save us' in terms of direct and indirect costs.

Cost-benefit estimates have been done for both of the studies that I referred to: the Colorado study and the Michigan study. They were remarkably the same in that $1 spent on prevention would probably save about $20 in direct and indirect costs. If reasonably accurate, these savings would be considered extremely cost effective. In cancer prevention, they are pleased if one dollar spent on prevention/intervention saves about three dollars in other costs. So potentially, we have some very strong, very powerful arguments that spending money for prevention and early intervention could save far more in direct and indirect costs.

We need ways to represent and to integrate the information that we already have about the scope, costs, causes, and interventions in the area of child abuse and neglect and family violence. This is something that does not fit easily into a book. Even if it does fit into a book, it is not very accessible and or easy to follow. Besides, you can not get many members of the media (or scientific administrators) to read books. Nor can you get them to read scientific articles.

We need to make our information accessible in other ways. Fortunately, we now have computer technologies for representation of complexly interconnected information. Tools such as hyper-media and search engines. I won't spend a lot of time on this. Perhaps it sounds a bit geeky or nerdy to some. But actually it is an extraordinarily powerful way to represent the kinds of information we have. Interconnected information, which is multi-disciplinary. Information which can be linked in direct and indirect ways. Connections that vary along probability relationships and level of certainty. These kinds of linkages can be represented in a more honest way than they are in a linear representation, such as in a textbook.

So, if we were to develop a computerized representation of our collective knowledge; it would permit in-depth access to information tailored to the user's needs. This body of information could be easily updated, refined, abridged, and disseminated. So that it grows in scope, accuracy, and availability over time. It would become an indispensable tool. Not just for students, but for all of us who are in one discipline and need to know what is known in other disciplines. As well as for the media, for policy makers, and for concerned others who may use it to discover things we professionals missed. Such collected and interconnected bodies of knowledge are increasingly appearing on the World Wide Web and as CDROM databases. Although not a trivial undertaking, this can be done without enormous costs, especially as various collections of relevant information and data have already been compiled, indexed and loosely interconnected.

We need a more centralized federal leadership for research and funding in the area of violence. I would call for the creation of a National Institute of Violence and Traumatology, or in deference to David Finkelhor, an Institute of Violence and Victimology. A center where we could coordinate the programmatic development of research and interventional treatment programs. Where we would have a centralized review process which is truly informed about the state of the field and can make judgments about the quality of science in this area. This would be true and fair peer review.

And finally, with respect to this "invisible force," I think that we have to do a number of things. One is to conduct our practice with the most consistency, the highest standards, and in ways that minimize controversy. We need to refine and disseminate our standards and methodologies, and to develop better-validated techniques for objective documentation of abuse and neglect.

We also need to clearly establish and to get on the table in a public fashion - for both the legal system and the media - the understanding that there are no perfect interviews, there are no perfect protective service, psychological or medical evaluations. No matter how experienced or skillful the interviewer or how technically sophisticated the methodology or documentation there will always be things that can be questioned and attacked. Every case is unique. Every case is complex. Every case is embedded within a much larger psychosocial context that can never be fully investigated or revealed.

We have to be clear with ourselves and with others about what constitutes competent professional work. We can establish what is sufficient documentation beyond which technical flaws or differences in interpretation do not matter. We need to sort out the criticisms and separate those that are legitimate from those that are malicious. The legitimate criticisms should be looked at and learned from. As for the malicious criticisms, there is little to do but to endure them. We should, of course, rebut them for the record. But we will not change many minds on the other side. We must prove them wrong in the larger arenas of science and public interest.

In terms of a national agenda, we need to clearly and forcefully communicate information about the scope, the costs, and the causes of child abuse and neglect and family violence. We have a very strong case. If you look at it with respect to the benchmarks that I have provided for cancer, we have a public health problem that certainly ranks in the top five public health problems in this country. We need to make this case. We need to make the linkages of child abuse with substance abuse, AIDS, medical costs, psychiatric costs, lost productivity and other indirect costs.

As for that "dark force", we need to let the light of truth - scientific, clinical, and forensic truth - reveal them for what they are. The truth will out. There will be justice. And there can be peace.

Thank you very much.

References

American Cancer Society (1998). Cancer facts and figures. American Cancer Society Web Site, World Wide Web.

Becker-Lausen, E., & Rickel, A. (1995). Integration of teen pregnancy and child abuse research: Identifying mediator variables for pregnancy outcome. *Journal of Primary Prevention, 16,* 39-53.

Bremner, D. J., Southwick, S. M., Johnson, D. R., Yehuda, R., & Charney, D. S. (1993). Childhood physical abuse and combat-related posttraumatic stress disorder in Vietnam veterans. *American Journal of Psychiatry,* 150, 235-239.

Breslau, N., Davis, G., Patricia, A., Peterson, E., & Schultz, L. (1997). Sex Differences. in Posttraumatic Stress Disorder. *Archives of General Psychiatry, 54,* 1044-1048.

Breslau, N., Davis, G. C., Andreski, P., & Peterson, E. (1991). Traumatic events and posttraumatic stress disorder in an urban population of young adults. *Archives of General Psychiatry, 48,* 216-222.

Caldwell, R. (1992). *The costs of child abuse vs. child abuse prevention,* Michigan Children's Trust Fund, Lansing: distributed by Robert Caldwell, Dept of Psychology, Michigan State University, East Lansing, MI 48824-1117.

Chadwick, D. (1988). Community organization of services needed to deal with child abuse. In D. Bross & R. Krugman (Eds.), *The new child protection team handbook.* (pp. 398-408). New York, NY: Garland Publishing.

Chadwick, D. (1994). A response to 'The impact of 'moral panic' on professional behavior in cases of child sexual abuse'. *Journal of Child Sexual Abuse, 3,* 127-131.

Cunningham, R., Stiffman, A., Dore, P., & Earls, F. (1994). The association of physical and sexual abuse with HIV risk behaviors in adolescence and young adulthood: Implications for public health. *Child Abuse & Neglect,* 233-245.

Elias, H. (1998). ? In *San Diego Conference on Responding to Child Maltreatment,* - Town and Country Resort Hotel, San Diego, CA:

Engel, C., Engel, A., Campbell, S., & McFall, M. (1993). Posttraumatic stress disorder symptoms and precombat sexual and physical abuse in Desert Storm veterans. *Journal of Nervous & Mental Disease, 181,* 683-688.

Fairbanks, J., Ebert, L., & Zarkin, G. (1999). Socioeconomic consequences of traumatic stress. In P. Saigh & J. Bremner (Eds.), *Posttraumatic stress disorder: A comprehensive text* (pp. 180-198). Boston, MA: Allyn and Bacon.

Felitti, V., Anda, R., Nordenberg, D., Williamson, D., Spitz, A., Edwards, V., Koss, M., & Marks, J. (1998). Relationship of childhood abuse and household dysfunction ' to many of the leading causes of death in adults: The adverse childhood experiences (ACE) study. *American Journal of Preventative Medicine, 14,* 245-258.

Gorey, K.,.& Leslie, D. (1997). The prevalence of child sexual abuse: Integrative review adjustment for potential response and measurement biases. *Child Muse and Neglect, 21,* 391-398.

Gould, M., & O'Brian, T. (1995). *Child maltreatment in Colorado: The value of prevention and the cost of failure to prevent* (No. 3G994140). Colorado Children's Trust Fund -distributed by the Clearinghouse on Child Abuse and Neglect Information, P.O. Box 1182, Washington, DC 20013.

Guzder, J., Pads, J., Zelkowitz, P., & Marchessault, K. (1996). Risk Factors for Borderline Pathology in Children. *Journal of the American Academy of Child and Adolescent Psychiatry* 35, 26-33.

Hyman, I., & McDowell, E. (1977). The social costs of maltreatment of children in the schools: Mental health considerations. In *Conference on the social costs of maltreatment of children,* Rutgers, NJ:

Koonin, S. (1998). An independent perspective on the Human Genome Project. *Science,* 279, 36-37.

Levitan, R., Parikh, S., Lesage, A., Hegadoren, K., Adams, M., Kennedy, S -', & Goering, P. (1998). Major depression in 'individuals with a history of childhood physical or sexual abuse: Relationship to neurovegetative features, mania and gender. *American Journal of Psychiatry, 155*, 1746-1752.

Messman, T., & Long, P. (1996). Child sexual abuse and its relationship to revictimization in adult women: A review. *Clinical Psychology Reviews, 1 6*_397-420.

Miller, T., Cohen, R., & Wiersema, B. (1996). *Victim costs and consequences: A new look_*, National Institute of Justice (DOJ), Washington, DC.

National Academy of Science (1993). *Understanding child abuse and neglect_* Washington, DC: National Academy Press.

Nolen-Hoeksema, S. (1995). Epidemiology and theories of gender differences in unipolar depression. In M. Seeman (Eds.), *Gender and psychopathology_* (pp. 63-87). Washington, DC: American Psychiatric Press.

Reiss, A., & Roth, J. (Ed.). (1993). *Understanding and preventing violence_* Washington, DC: National Academy Press.

Resnick, H., Kilpatrick, D. G., Dansky, B. S., Saunders, B. G., & Best, C. L. (1993). Prevalence of civilian trauma and posttraumatic stress disorder in a representative national sample of women. *Journal of Consulting and Clinical Psychology 51*, 984-991.

Rowen, L., Mahairas, G., & Hood, L. (1997). Sequencing the human genome. *Science, 278*, 605-607.

Russell, D. (1986). *The secret trauma: Incest in the lives of girls and women_* New York: Basic Books.

Sedlak, A., & Broadhurst, D. (1996). *Executive summary of the Third National Incidence Study of Child Abuse and Neglect_* National Center on Child Abuse and Neglect (DHHS).

Silk, K., Lee, S., Hill, E., & Lohr, N. (1995). Borderline Personality Disorder Symptoms and Severity of Sexual Abuse. *American Journal of Psychiatry 152_* 1059-1064.

van der Kolk, B., Crozier, J., & Hopper, J. (1998). *Child abuse in American: prevalence, costs, consequences and intervention* Nathan Cummings Foundation, Mill Valley, CA.

Varmus, H. (1997). *NIH research on child abuse and neglect Current status and future pla*ns National Institutes of Health, Bethesda, MD.

Verma, I., & Somia, N. (1997). Gene therapy - promises, problems and prospects. *Nature 389,_* 239-242.

Wilsnack, S., & Wilsnack, R. (1993). Epidemiological research on women's drinking: Recent progress and directions for the 1990s. In E. Gomberg, E. Lisansky, & T. Nirenberg (Eds.), *Women and substance abuse* (pp. 62-99). Norwood, NJ: Ablex Publishing Corp.

Wolfe, J., Sharkansky, E., Read, J., Dawson, R., Martin, J., & Ouimette, P. (1998). Sexual harassment and assault as predictors of PTSD symptomatology among U.S. female Persian Gulf War military personnel. *Journal of Interpersonal Violence, 13*, 40-57.

Cost and Benefit Simulation Analysis of Catastrophic Maltreatment

Sachiko Nobuyasu

Introduction

The impact of a comprehensive treatment on a child's life: an economic analysis

It is more sensible that the millions now being spent would be far better and more humanely spent in those initiatives that are to lessen the long term costs associated with the care of these young victims (Baladerian, 1993)

It is a great concern to see the human costs caused by child abuse. In 1991, the National Center on Child Abuse and Neglect indicates that 141,700 children have suffered serious injury as a result of child abuse and neglect (NCCAN, 1991). Estimates, in particular, concerning disabilities caused by abuse are provided by Nora J. Baladerian (1991) who claims that at least 18,000 children per year are permanently disabled by abuse and neglect, suffer mental retardation or sensory and motor impairments, and often require lifelong services which can cost an average of approximately $20,000 throughout the life of each child. Her study suggests that at least ten times as many children survive severe abuse as die from it, and that a staggering 9.5 to 28 percent of all disabled persons in the United States may have been made so by child abuse and neglect (Baladerian, 1991). Although the mentioned data raises serious concern about child abuse, apparently, there are no parameters that can detect exactly which children live and which die. Furthermore, there are no rigorous scientific findings on such disabilities (NRC, 1993).

The proposed analysis is organized in the following way:
1. *To illustrate* the general statistics of child abuse in New York State;
2. *To compute* the overall costs associated with child abuse in New York State;
3. *To set* a number of basic assumptions for a comprehensive Catastrophic Maltreatment (CM) treatment;
4. *To estimate* the average cost for a comprehensive CM treatment;
5. *To define* the assumptions for a "good' CM treatment;
6. *To provide* a simulated Cost-Benefit (C&B) analysis of the CM treatment.

1. General Child Abuse Statistics in New York State

Lately, the phenomenon of child abuse (which indicates all types of abuse regardless of its severity) has increased and even in the international figures United States shows the highest rates of abuse (although this may be due to more transparency towards the issue; ABCAN, 1995). Only in 1995, 128,896 cases of suspected abuse or maltreatment were reported in New York State involving approximately 211,445 children (all reports were investigated). As of April 3, 1993, local districts had made a determination on 84 percent of reported cases (88,229). Of these determined cases, 24,525 or 28% were "indicated". Most of these indicated cases (99%) was verified by the State Central Register (SCR). Since most findings of abuse and maltreatment at the local level are confirmed upon SCR review, it is likely that the actual number of indicated cases in New York State may be slightly higher than the 24,228 cases which had been verified by the SCR at the time these data were prepared (Department of Social Services, Bureau of Services Information Systems, personal communication, 1994a).

Adapted from the author's Appendix of *Cost and Benefit Simulation Analysis of Catastrophic Maltreatment*, a Master's Thesis from Cornell University, 1997.

In New York State in 1992 there were 10,295 allegations of sexual abuse made in reported cases of abuse and maltreatment. The proportion of allegations of sexual abuse to the total number of allegations of abuse and maltreatment remained relatively stable between 1980 and 1992 at three to five percent (Department of Social Services, Bureau of Services Information Systems, personal communication, 1994a).

In 1997, there were 7 child fatalities in New York State (New York State Department of Social Services, personal communication, 1997). However, data show that there has been a decrease in the number of child fatalities in the last three years: according to the NYS DSS, in 1992, 165 children died from alleged abuse or maltreatment. Forty-nine of these allegations were confirmed, 33 were determined to be unfounded, and determinations were still pending for 83 of the deaths (Department of Social Services, Bureau of Services Information Systems, personal communication, 1994).

2. Computing Child Abuse Overall Costs in New York State

It is difficult to measure the exact overall costs involved in child maltreatment because of the several factors involved which are intangible at times (e.g.; the intensity of the child's attachment to his parents or the discomfort of a procedure) and because information is often biased by some methodological flaws. Below, I will provide a general description of the major costs associated with child abuse such as medical care, foster care, special education, psychological services, and juvenile justice costs. However, these figures are not comprehensive since some cost data are not obtainable. Since the given estimates of child abuse reports are based on a general definition of abuse, conservative values will be considered in the computation of each cost category. The previous and the following data have been obtained, as a personal communication, from the Department of Social Services, the Department of Correctional Services, and the Office of Mental Health in Albany, New York State.

Category A: Medical Treatment of Injuries Due to Abuse

Not all abused children require hospitalization. Nationwide, about 3.2 percent of abused children require medical treatment for serious physical injuries (McCurdy and Daro, 1993). Applying this percentage to New York State's abused children which is 59,207, it yields an estimated 1,895 children requiring hospitalization. Since data concerning medical treatment and hospitalization at the New York State's Department of Social Services was not available, the figures provided by Blue Cross/Blue Shield of Michigan (Caldwell, 1992) were considered: in 1991 the average stay in hospital for NY children with injuries was 4.5 days and the average cost per child was $5,498. There are no estimates that indicate the extent of child abuse not requiring hospitalization except for the medical treatment. Therefore, the total medical costs for abused children in NYS are ***$10,418.710 annually**.*

*COMPUTATION:
$5,498*# of CM children = $5,498*1.895 = $10.4 million

Category B: Special Education Costs

Children who have been exposed to abuse do encounter more difficulties than those who have not been abused throughout their lives. Several of these difficulties were identified by the National Clinical Evaluation Study:
- Approximately 30% of abused children have some type of language or cognitive impairment;
- Over 50% of abused children have socio-emotional problems;
- Approximately 14% of abused children exhibit self-mutilative or other self-destructive behavior;
- Over 50% of abused children have difficulty in school (also, poor attendance and misconduct);

- Over 22% of abused children have a learning disorder;
- School-based special education services cost about $655 per child annually (Daro, 1988, p.154).

Based on these figures, at least 25% of all abused children which is 14.801(from the number of indicated cases) will need some special educational services for a minimum of 1 year during their school time. Therefore, the costs for NY due to special education services provided to maltreated children are **_9.7 million dollars annually*_**.

*COMPUTATION:
$655*# of CM children = $655*14.801 = $9.7 million

Category C: Protective Services Costs

As previously said, according to the New York State Department of Social Services,(personal communication) in 1995, the division conducted the investigation on 128,896 reports of suspected child abuse and maltreatment involving 211,445 children. Generally, the total budget at the Protective Services Division of NYS DSS is equal to approximately $7 million dollars and about 82.5% is for staff costs which leads to an amount of **_$5.7 million dollars annually_** (NYS DSS, 1997). Due to unavailability of data, the costs do not include other expenditures related to child abuse services.

COMPUTATION:
$5.7 million/ #of CM children = $5.7 million/ 211.445 = $26,600 (CPS staff costs/child)

Category D: Foster Care Costs (See note)

In New York State the total number of children in out-of-home placements/foster care as of 12/31/96 is 52,419. The average cost of this service is $457 per child per month. However, not all abused children are placed in foster care. Daro (1988) cites a figure from the American Association for Protecting Children that only 18% of abused children are actually removed, even temporarily, from their homes. Applying such percentage to the number of indicated abused children in NYS, a number of 9.435 children would be placed in foster care each year. Although there is not an average length of stay in foster care for children who have been abused in New York since this varies from case to case, the estimated average stay in foster care for these children suggested by Daro (1988) of 7.68 months was used for this analysis. Therefore, New York spends *approximately **3.31 million dollars annually*** *on foster care placement of children* who have been exposed to abuse.

COMPUTATION:
$457*7.68*# of CM children = $457*7.68*9.435 = $3.31 million

Note: Apparently, the child's stay in foster care is intended to be temporary; the parents retain the right to resume custody at a later day. However, the existing foster care is not a temporary one, even after termination of the rights. There is a 50% chance that a child will stay in a foster care for almost 2-3 years. Only in a few cases where the parental rights are terminated, then, the child is placed for adoption.

Category E: Juvenile Justice System:

Literature (Alfaro, 1981; Bolton, et al., 1977) illustrating the relationship between child abuse and later criminal activity is available. Studies that have been conducted in this field have reported that almost 80% of all incarcerated youth offenders were victims of child abuse. It is not meant to imply that all abused children get involved with the juvenile justice system, which is, in fact, represented only by a minority. In 1983, McCord studied the long-term consequences of child abuse and neglect and found that approximately 20% (a percentage that was later defined reasonable from

Lewis, et al. in 1989) of abused children were convicted of serious juvenile crime such as theft, burglary or assault. Since the systems of police, courts are also involved in this process, it is difficult to commensurate the exact costs, however, the available data shows that in New York the average cost of an inmate (adult or youth) in a corrective facility per year is estimated approximately $27,639. The average length (including adults and youths) of incarceration is about 32 months (however, it will use a more conservative period of 15 months which represents the average stay of a youth inmate in Michigan's juvenile corrections system; Caldwell, 1992). Since not all children involved in the juvenile justice system get incarcerated, a conservative number (1/3 of all convicted youth) of 3943 is considered. The state of New York's expenditures associated with children from abusive households who become involved in *juvenile delinquent behavior is approximately 109 million dollars annually* (without the costs involving the police and the courts).

COMPUTATION:
$27,639/12months = $2,303
$2,303*15months = $34,548 (average cost per child in correctional facility)
$27,639*3943 = $109 million

Category F: Adult Criminality

In 1987, Loeber showed the high correlation between child abuse and adult criminality, indicating the presence of a high probability that an abused child will later get involved with the criminal justice system. It appears that on average approximately 25.3% of juvenile offenders are later incarcerated as adults. If 20% of children from abusive homes are involved in juvenile delinquency and 25.3% of these later become inmates in the adult criminal justice system, 998 (which is 20%*3943) children will become involved in the adult criminal justice system. If the average cost due to incarceration is 27,639 per inmate per year (excluding the other expenses, see above) and the average stay per adult is 32 months, then the *costs associated with adult criminality in New York are 27.6 million dollars annually*.

Category G: Psychological Problems

The psychological effects of child abuse can have a negative and long lasting impact on the life of these children and, as many studies show, they can be manifested in a variety of ways accordingly to the subjectivity of the individual. Several researchers have conducted studies showing a relationship between child abuse and developmental impairments. To mention some of them: Appelbaum noticed the presence of developmental retardation in infants as a concomitant of physical child abuse (1977); other impairments in children have been found due to emotional abuse (Dean, 1979; Green 1978a) as well as the development of psychological and emotional limitations as consequences of different patterns of maltreatment (Egeland, 1983). In her forty-year follow-up of abused boys, McCord (1983, p.269) found that, "Among the 97 neglected or abused children, 44 had become criminal, alcoholic, mentally ill, or had died before reaching age 35". Children from abusive households have also been found to have poorer psychosocial adjustment than non-maltreated children (Lamphear, 1986). Finally, a study conducted by Scott (1992) found that children sexually abused were almost four times as likely to develop psychiatric disorders, once adults.

Since there is no data that show how many abused children will need psychological treatment, very conservative figures were used. It is assumed that 1% of abused children will need inpatient psychiatric hospitalization in their lifetime; then, 5% of abused children will be treated through outpatient therapy. The average attendance of outpatient treatment is assumed to be 20 sessions, (which represents the common limit of insurance coverage for mental health treatment). With respect to average duration of inpatient treatment, data from Michigan's Department of Mental Health (Caldwell, 1992) are used whose figure is 110 days of stay (however, for children is a longer length) in any public mental health hospital. Although data from Michigan (Caldwell, 1992) show that inpatient psychological treatment per child costs about $330 a day, a more conservative number of $200 is used; for outpatient psychological therapy, a cost of $75 an hour for 20 sessions ($1500). In sum, assuming these values to be sufficiently realistic, the *total cost for psychological care for maltreated children in New York State is about 17.5 million dollars annually**.

COMPUTATION:
a) Psychiatric Inpatient Annual Cost/Child: $200/day*110 days = $22,000
b) Psychiatric Inpatient Annual Total Cost: $22,000*1%(59.207) = $13,024.000
c) Psychiatric Outpatient Annual Cost/Child: $75/hr*20 sess = $1500
d) Psychiatric Outpatient Annual Total Cost: $1500*5%(59.027) = $4,440.000
 e) Total Psychiatric Care Cost/Child: $22,000 + $1,500 = $23,500

3. CM Comprehensive Treatment: Basic Assumptions
In order to estimate the cost of a comprehensive CM treatment, certain basic assumptions have to be made. The assumptions are:

a.)   There is *no change of money value* throughout the treatment's length;
b.)   The average length of the treatment is *6 years* (however, it may differ for the subjective circumstances and responsiveness of each child);
c.)   The treatment is provided for *all CM children*;
d.)   Children are *aged through high school* (including infants would change several assumptions since their needs vary from those of children aged 5 or more);
e.)   The rate of population growth is *constant* (thus, no impact on the available resources);
f.)   The number of children being abused stays the *same for 6 years*;
g.)   Politics is a *neutral* factor;
h.)   At present, the welfare reform is *not* implemented;
i.)   The costs represent *only* state level costs (not county level ones);
j.)   The analysis will be conducted on a standard comprehensive treatment for children aged *above 5 years* (infants are not included);
k.)   The costs are *only* related to the special treatment and not the additional administrative costs associated to the fast track system (i.e., extra training, paper work);
l.)   The catastrophic maltreatment has been *qualitatively tested*;
m.)   A *sample of* 592 CM children is considered:

Since the data indicates that severely abused children represents only a small percentage, in order to represent victims of CM, a conservative value of 1% was extrapolated from 59,207 which is the number of children involved in indicated cases in New York State.

4. The Cost for a CM Comprehensive Treatment: A Tentative Estimate (See note 1)
Virtually, the estimated costs of CM treatment are focused on long-term psychological services; in fact, as a key element to help the child to overcome the trauma of CM, the emphasis is given to the psychological treatment. Therefore, the treatment is conceived as follows:

a) *Psychotherapy Treatment* to the child (1 month is subtracted in the 1st year counted as hospitalization period):
First 2 years, 2 times per week (48 weeks per year), thus
→ Total of 184 Sessions (44 Sess + 48 Sess) @ $70.00 = $12,880
Additional 2 years, 1 time per week (48 weeks per year), thus
→ Total of 96 Sessions (48 Sess * 2) @ $70.00 = $6,720

Additional 2 years, 1 time per month (12 times per year), thus
→ Total of 24 Sessions (12 Sess * 2) @ $70.00 = $1,680

b) *Psychiatric Consultation* with caregivers (ex., teachers) being provided along with the treatment above:
First year, 1 hour per week → Total of 48 hours @ $70.00 = $3,360
Second year, 1 hour every 2 weeks → Total of 24 hours @ $70.00 = $1,680
Additional 4 years, 1 hour per month → Total of 12 hours @ $70.00 = $840

c) *Additional Expenses in Educational Support* (e.g., Special Educational Program or a tutor) (See note 2):
Length of 4 years, 4 hours per week (35 weeks per year, excluding summer time), thus
→ Total of 560 hours (140 weeks * 4) @ $25.00 = $14,000

d) *Additional Support Program during non-school hours* (See note 3):
Length of 4 years, 2 hours per day/5 days per week (for academic year), thus
→ Total of 1400 hours (35 weeks*5 days*2 hours*4 years) @ $10.00 = $14,000
Length of 2 years, 8 hours per day/5 days per week (for summer), thus
→ Total of 480 hours (12 weeks*5 days*8 hours*2 years) @ $10.00 = $9,600
Thus, the **Total Cost of CM Comprehensive Treatment per child** =
= $21,280+$5,880+$9,600+$14,000 = **$50,760**

Note1: The following treatment estimates are based on an informed clinical judgment.
Note2: There are subsidies provided for specialized foster care and adoption that could replace the support educational program (item c) and thus drop its cost from the overall expenses of the comprehensive treatment. For example, in NYS for special children there are subsidies up to $879/month and for exceptional children up to $1,332/month, in need of 24 hours care (New York State Department of Social Services, personal communication 1996). Of course, such provisions may vary accordingly to the age of the child and the length of stay in the program. It is worth adding that there are costs associated with foster care regardless of whether the child is catastrophically maltreated (therefore, those costs will not be counted in the analysis).
Note3: This program will be provided after school hours during academic year and all day during summer.

Additional Information:
    Costs for parental services to the abusive parents are not included since the premise is that, upon a finding of a CM child, the focus of the treatment will be on the child. Furthermore, the immediate treatment of injuries due to abuse is assumed to be a fixed cost since it would be provided in any case of maltreatment. The treatment is costly, however, those expenses will be distributed among the different cost categories already mentioned in the previous paragraphs.

5. What Do We Mean by Successful Treatment?
    Considering the many subjective factors associated with quantifying all the costs for the CM treatment (i.e., one child may be more responsive than another to the treatment) as well as the ones involved in measuring the expected benefits such as the happiness of a child, it is difficult to give an exact measure of what could be called a successful CM treatment. Therefore, in order to simplify the computation, a set of tentative criteria are given. Such criteria, describing a minimum satisfactory outcome from the treatment, will be identified with the following characteristics:
1) *The treated individual is out of jail*, and 2) *the treated individual is being employed*.
6. Simulation of CM Treatment Cost-Benefit Analysis

The technique of simulated cost-benefit analysis that I will use is intended to compare the costs caused by child abuse to the required costs (all of which are identified specifically so that they cannot be spent on other things), for providing a comprehensive CM intensive treatment. Despite the possible existing methodological flaws (Dubowitz, 1990), the following is a tentative analysis to show the cost-effectiveness of CM treatment in terms of total net savings, according to different percentages of responsive children to CM treatment. Such a simulation will illustrate not only the savings both socially and financially derived from the received benefits inherent to the treatment provided but also the earnings the state government can gain by providing such a treatment.

The percentages used in the simulation's three scenarios were established with the understanding that many issues are involved in the distribution of maltreated children in society; for example, the unique circumstances surrounding a particular child.

Three alternative scenarios will be analyzed:

Status Quo Condition: No comprehensive treatment is provided. It is assumed that 45% of these children are on chronic welfare assistance; 45% of them will get involved as a youth or an adult in the criminal justice system, and the remaining 10% is the only population able to recover (without the treatment) and contribute with taxes to the society;

1. The *minimum* rate of successful treatment is achieved (20% of all recipients);
2. The *satisfactory* rate of successful treatment is achieved (40% of recipients);
3. The *hoped* rate of successful treatment is achieved (60% of all recipients);
4. The rate at which the treatment breaks even (BEP).

Note: The optimum rate of successful treatment would be ideally 80% but it won't be discussed in this paper.

Benefit from the Treatment is composed by:
1) *Lifetime income of recovered CM children* ($25,999*33yrs = $857,967)
    The lifetime income should be seen as a generator of social benefit to the whole society across the time. The revenues that government receive from the taxable income is just an expression of the social benefits that come from the income. The difference is that taxes go directly to the government (taxes were not computed because they are included in the benefits from the lifetime income).

2.) *Social Costs saved with the treatment* (computed below). Such costs are composed by all cost categories just mentioned. However, child protective service staff's cost (CPS) is assumed to be equal for all children. The percentages in each cost category are based on child abuse figures, although they are a little adjusted (higher values) to the CM's special nature of abuse.

The *cost categories, relative percentages and number of children* (computed by the total number of indicated abused children which is 592) are:
1. Juvenile Delinquency (JD): 20%*592 = 118.4 children
2. Adult Criminality (AC): 20%*25.3%*592 = 30 children
3. Foster Care (FC): 18%*592 = 106.56 children
4. Psychiatric Care (PC): 25%*592 = 148 children
5. Medical Care (MC): 40%*592 = 177.6 children
6. Special Education Cost (SEC): 2%*592 = 11.44 children

Total of : 118.4 + 30 + 106.56 + 148 + 177.6 + 11.44 = 592 children
Annual Cost per child of each category:

JD: $27,639
AC: $27,639
FC: $457*7.68months = $3,509
PC: $22,000+$1,500 = $23,500
MC: $5,498
SEC: $655
CPS's Staff Cost: $26.95

Therefore, the *Total Annual Saved Cost for All 592 children* is equal to:
JD children*JD annual cost = $27,630*118.4 = $3,271,392
AC children*AC annual cost = $27,639*30 = $829,170
FC children*FC annual cost = $3,509*106.56 = $373,919
PC children*PC annual cost = $23,500*148 = $3,478,000
MC children*MC annual cost = $5,498*177.6 = $976,444
SEC children*SEC annual cost = $655*11.44 = $7,493
CPS total cost = 592*$26.95 = $15,954

As a result, by adding all of above components, the total saved cost by the CM treatment is equal to:
$3,271,392+$829,170+$373,919+$3,478,000+$976,444+7,493+$15954 = **$8,952,372**

Assumptions for the Simulation of CM Treatment:
Assumption 1: The recovery percentage represents the number of CM children who are believed to be completely healed from the trauma.
Assumption 2: The percentage of recovered CM children will determine the same percentage in terms of costs saved by the treatment. There is a direct cause-effect relationship between children who recover and costs saved by the treatment.
Assumption 3: The number of CM children will remain the same for the length of the comprehensive treatment.
Assumption 4: The distribution of costs will stay constant for those years.

Scenario BEP, where about **6%** of CM children are recovered:

Cost saved w/treatment = $8,952,372*6% = $537,142
Lifetime Income Recovered = $857,967*6%*592 = $30,474,987
Total Benefit from Treatment = $30,474,987 + $537,142 = **$31,012,129**
Total Cost Treatment = **$30,049,920**
Net Benefit = $31,012,129 - $30,049,920 = **$962,209**

The Break-Even-Point (BEP) can be obtained with solely a percentage of about 6%. Such a result indicates that the treatment offsets the immediate costs with a fairly low number of recovered CM children.

A) Scenario 1, where **20%** of CM children are recovered:

Cost saved w/treatment = $8,952,372*20% = $1,790,474
Lifetime Income Recovered = $857,967*592*20% = $101,583,292
Total Benefit from Treatment = $101,583,292 + $1,790,474 = **$103,373,766**
Total Cost Treatment (6 years) = $50,760*592children = **$30,049,920**
Net Benefit = $103,373,766 - $30,049,920 = **$73,323,846**

B) Scenario 2, where **40%** of CM children are recovered:

Cost saved w/treatment = $8,952,372*40% = $3,580,948
Lifetime Income Recovered = $857,967*592*40% = $203,166,585
Total Benefit from Treatment = $203,166,585 + $3,580,948 = **$206,747,533**
Total Cost Treatment = $30,049,920
Net Benefit = $206,747,533 - $30,049,920 = **$176,697,613**

C) Scenario 3, where **60%** of CM children are recovered:

Cost saved w/treatment = $8,952,372*60% = $5,371,423
Lifetime Income Recovered = $857,967*60%*592 = $304,749,878
Total Benefit from treatment = $304,749,878 + $5,371,423 = **$310,121,301**
Total Cost Treatment = $30,049,920
Net Benefit = $310,121301 – $30,049920 = **$280,071,381**

The above three scenarios (See graph below) are illustrative examples of the cost-effectiveness of this treatment. In fact, as the number of recovered CM children increases, the social benefits become greater as well. The intensive nature of CM treatment appears to make the service quite successful. Yet, the analysis above was a simulation, thus, whether the treatment is truly effective or not remains an empirical question. Furthermore, as I said previously, there are several factors that have a significant impact on the effectiveness of such treatment according to the subjective response of the child under therapy. There are findings that show the relevance of psychological treatments. The study conducted by Culp, Heide, and Richardson (1987) demonstrated that remediation of developmental delays in maltreated children under the age of six years can be accomplished through an intensive day treatment program. The program was based on a cognitive developmental model whose focus was to provide an environment to facilitate these children to build self-esteem, and to recognize and deal with their own feelings. The results were developmental gains for the treated children in the areas of fine motor, cognitive, gross motor, social/emotional, and language.

Since we are in a capitalistic society, some may raise the question whether the net marginal long term social savings specifically deriving from catastrophic maltreatment would be greater than the benefits generated by the use of the same dollars into the system. However, the core issue here is not about "marginal benefits", rather it is about what a morally responsible society should do to help children who have been exposed to such horrible abuses. Furthermore, if the question of whether responsible parents should pay for irresponsible parents, then the answer is that a morally responsible society should break down the common distinction that is made between my children and your children, for all children are our children and as such these children should be able to rely on all of us. The bottom line is that deterring child abuse through a collective response from the entire community is not only morally right but it is also the most realistic way to deal with this social problem. Families, in fact, do not exist like entities in alienation; families are embedded in their societies and can learn to build responsible parenting only when supported by their society.

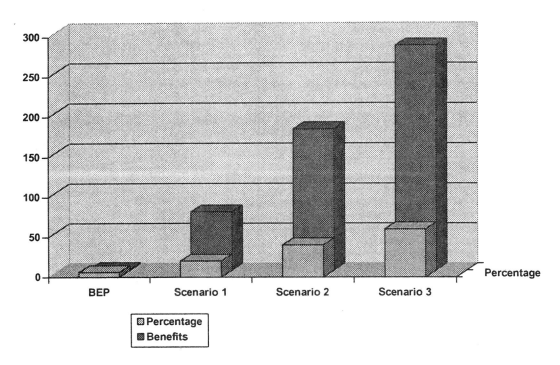

**Simulation Analysis of CM Treatment
(in millions)**

Concluding Thoughts: Issues to be Addressed in the Cost-Benefit Analysis

Reducing the present and future pain to children caused by abusive parents is considered a worthy public policy objective. The CM treatment appears to be a satisfactory one, although preventive efforts would likely offset, at an earlier stage, even more social costs generated by child abuse (Daro, 1988). To give one example, there are findings that demonstrate that intentionally injured children use more hospital resources resulting in higher injury-related health care costs that could be significantly reduced by efforts directed at preventing intentional injuries (Wright and Litaker, 1996).

Indeed, if not only direct but also all indirect expenditures (i.e., the cost in medical time as well as in financial terms [$63,000 annually] of initial investigations, Summers and Molyneux, 1992) are considered, dealing with child abuse is a costly task. By all means, costs should not be the sole determinant of policy, but in the face of scarcity as we are, costs are an appropriate contributor to the decision-making process for to fight child abuse significant public funds will be needed.

Cost-benefit analysis is the principal analytical framework used to evaluate public expenditures or, in other words, if the total benefits of a public action out weight its total costs. However, in social service planning this analysis has certain limits. To give one example, the quantification of benefits and costs is problematic for programs designed to improve the quality of life or to prolong it (like CM proposal). Apparently, the need to somewhat measure the worth of a human life has made policy-makers equate it with the individual's contribution to the Gross National Product or with his or her potential earnings, a standard that, however, according to Scheffler and Paringer (1980) works against who are in an economical disadvantaged position. Given this standard, one would place less value on the outcome of a program designed to assist a college students than pregnant teen-agers on welfare assistance simply because one group can be expected to have greater lifetime earnings than the other.

It should also be mentioned that emotional support or other non-market human interactions pose an insurmountable measurement task for any researcher seeking to quantify a person's absolute contribution and thus worth to the society. For instance, the "willingness to pay" criterion to determine a person's worth still would not reduce bias, since one's willingness to pay is largely determined by one's income, the degree to which society assigns a monetary value to the service, and the availability of other sources of the desired good. A bias for those who do not have a support network (Daro, 1988).

Finally, the cost and benefit method requires that future costs and benefits be discounted or be ascribed a current value generally below what they would be worth if they were accrued in the present (Armstrong, 1983). In fact, the basic rationale for this system is that everyone would prefer to have something now more than in the future, or that present gains are more valuable than the anticipation of future gains (Daro, 1988). Virtually, discounting allows to reduce a stream of costs and benefits to a single amount that can be compared across different programs. Although this system of evaluation is a logical one from an economic perspective, on the other hand, it can be misleading when it is time to compare programs that produce benefits sooner over those that produce the same overall benefits but do so over a longer period of time since systematically it would favor the former ones. As Scheffler and Paringer (1980) said, all things being equal in terms of the total earnings preserved, programs targeted to individuals who are currently in their prime working years will be identified as producing greater total present benefits than programs serving young children.

References

Advisory Board on Child Abuse and Neglect (U.S. ABCAN); *A Nation's Shame: Fatal Child Abuse and Neglect in the United States;* U.S. Department of Health and Human Services; Fifth Report; April, 1995.

Alfaro, J. (1981). Report on the Relationship Between Child Abuse and Neglect and Later Socially Deviant Behavior. In R.J. Runner & Y.E. Walker (Eds.), *Exploring the Relationship Between Child Abuse and Delinquency,* Montclair, NJ: Allanheald, Osmun.

Appelbaum, A (1977). Developmental Retardation in Infants as a Concomitant of Physical Child Abuse. *Journal of Abnormal Child Psychology, 5,* 417-423.

Armstrong, A. K. (1983). Economic Analysis of a Child Abuse and Neglect Treatment Program. *Child Welfare,* Vol.LXII, No1, Jan.-Feb.

Baladerian, N. J (1991). *Abuse Causes Disabilities: Disability and the Family.* Culver City, CA: Spectrum Institute.

Baladerian, N. J. (1993). *Written Testimony: Hearing on Child Maltreatment-Related Fatalities.* Pittsburgh, Pennsylvania: Sponsored by the U.S. Advisory Board on Child Abuse and Neglect.

Bolton, F.G., Reich, J. W., & Gutierres, S. E. (1977). Delinquency Patterns in Maltreated Children and Siblings. *Victimology; 2*; 349-357.

Caldwell, R. A. (1992). *The Costs of Child Abuse vs. Child Abuse Prevention: Michigan's Experience.* Lansing, MI: Michigan's Children's Trust Fund.

Culp E. R., Heide J., & Richardson, M. T. (1987). Maltreated Children's Developmental Scores: Treatment versus Non-Treatment. *Child Abuse & Neglect, Vol.11,* 29-34.

Daro D. (1988). *Confronting Child Abuse: Research for Effective Program Design.* New York: The Free Press.

Dean, D. (1979). Emotional Abuse of Children. *Children Today, 8;* 8-20, 37.

Dubowitz, H. (1990). Costs and Effectiveness of Interventions in Child Maltreatment. *Child Abuse and Neglect; Vol.14,* 177-186.

Egeland, B., Sraufe, A., & Erickson, M. (1983). The Development of Consequences of Different Patterns of Maltreatment. *Child Abuse and Neglect.* 7:4, 459-469.

Green, A. H. (1978). Self-Destructive Behavior in Battered Children; *American Journal of Psychiatry*; *135*; 414-42.

Lamphear, V. S. (1986). The Psychosocial Adjustment of Maltreated Children: Methodological Limitations and Guidelines for Future Research. *Child Abuse and Neglect*; *Vol. 10,* 63-69.

Lewis, D. O., Mallouh, C., & Webb, V. (1989). Child Abuse, Delinquency, and Violent Criminality. In, D. Cicchetti & V. Carlson (Eds.), *Child Maltreatment: Theory and Research on the Causes and Consequences of Child Abuse and Neglect* (pp. 707-721). New York: Cambridge University Press.

Loeber, R., & Stouthamer-Loeber, M. (1987). Prediction. In H. C. Quay (Ed.), *Handbook of Juvenile Delinquency* (pp. 325-382). New York: Wiley.

McCord, J. (1983). A Forty Year Perspective on Effects of Child Abuse and Neglect. *Child Abuse and Neglect,* Vol. 7, 265-270.

McCurdy K., & Daro D. (1993). *Current Trends in Child Abuse Reporting and Fatalities: The Results of the 1992 Annual Fifty State Survey*; Chicago: National Committee for Prevention of Child Abuse, 13-16.

National Center on Child Abuse and Neglect (NCCAN) (1991). *National Incidence and Prevalence of Child Abuse and Neglect: The 1988 Revised Report* (NIS-2) [Westat]; Washington, D.C.; Department of Health and Human Services.

National Research Council (NRC) (1993). *Understanding Child Abuse and Neglect.* Washington, D.C.: National Academy of Sciences.

Scott, K. D. (1992). Childhood Sexual Abuse: Impact on a Community's Mental Health Status; *Child Abuse and Neglect*, Vol. 16, 285-295.

Scheffler, R., & Paringer, L. (1980). A Review of the Economic Evidence on Prevention; *Medical Care*, 18, 473-484.

Summers, C. L., & Molyneux, E. M. (1992). *Suspected Child Abuse: Cost in Medical Time and Finance.* Accident and Emergency Department; Royal Liverpool Children's Hospital; Liverpool, 15.

Convening A National Call to Action: Working Toward the Elimination of Child Maltreatment

The Economics*

Mark Courtney, Ph.D.

Introduction

By way of introduction, I ask the question: Why should we care about the economics of child maltreatment? After all, isn't the suffering of one child, let alone the legions of children that we know are abused and neglected each year, enough to warrant serious attention? Shouldn't the ranking of child maltreatment on the social problem agenda be more a function of the calculus of human well being rather than the calculus of the bottom line? Perhaps, but like it or not, economics has played, and will continue to play, a significant role in debates over how society should respond to the problem of child maltreatment.

The economics of child maltreatment manifests itself in a number of ways. Defenders of services for abused children or for families where abuse has taken place point at estimates of the long-term costs of child maltreatment, such as delinquency and mental illness, to justify funding for their interventions. Prevention advocates use data on the costs of intervention programs to argue for the need for more prevention, based on the assumption that preventing maltreatment will lower the costs of intervention. Critics of social policies such as welfare reform point at the high cost of protecting children to argue for caution in making radical changes to social institutions that support families, and policy makers want to know which practices and policies protect the greatest number of children for the lowest price. There is simply no escaping the fact that the economics of child maltreatment influences how we view the problem.

But what do we really mean when we talk about the "economics" of child maltreatment? Are we referring to the costs in pain and suffering to those who are subjected to maltreatment? Or are we interested in the costs of lost earnings and socially deviant behavior of those impaired by maltreatment? What about the costs of administering the variety of "services" provided in order to prevent or respond to child maltreatment (e.g., various forms of public assistance, family resource centers, home visitation programs, juvenile and family courts, child protective services, health and mental health care provided to ameliorate the consequences of child maltreatment, or out-of-home care for maltreated children)? Of course, only some of these costs can be estimated, and even then with only a modicum of accuracy.

Arguably, all of the costs that I have described and more should be included in any accounting of the economics of child maltreatment. But even if we could come up with a total dollar figure, some important issues would be missed in doing so. First, many of the costs associated with child maltreatment are, to a large extent, a reflection of the construction of child maltreatment as a social problem and society's corresponding response to its perception of this problem. In other words, if we as a society chose not to respond in some of the ways that we currently do, we would "save money" so to speak, at least in terms of child welfare services expenditures. Conversely, the costs of child protection could be much greater than they currently are, all else being equal, if communities chose to set a much higher standard of what is acceptable parenting. For example, widening the net in terms of what level of harm to children warrants state intervention in families increases the demand for, and hence the cost of, child protective services. Similarly, the reason taxpayers currently bear the cost of out-of-home care of maltreated children is because we chose, relatively recently in our history, to

*As presented at the San Diego Conference on Responding to Child Maltreatment January 26, 1999

remove children from their homes when the courts determine that this is necessary for their safety. This is not to say that reducing state efforts to prevent or respond to child maltreatment would not have other costs to children and society, only that such costs would largely show up "outside" of the budgets of the child welfare system. Put bluntly; if we simply decided that we no longer cared as a society if children were maltreated, the costs of programs devoted specifically to addressing child maltreatment would be zero.

Second, adding up the costs of child maltreatment does not explicitly acknowledge the fact that most of these costs are the result of our failure to prevent child maltreatment in the first place, and that such estimates only make sense in the context of knowledge about the expense of preventing or ameliorating the effects of maltreatment. It is one thing to know that a social problem has costs, but such knowledge is most useful when one knows how such costs could be reduced, and how expensive cost-reduction efforts might be. In other words, knowledge of the costs associated with child maltreatment would not, in and of itself, constitute a cost-benefit analysis of efforts to reduce maltreatment.

The "bottom-line" then, in terms of the economics of child maltreatment, cannot be determined without an understanding of:

1. How child maltreatment is currently socially constructed and what responses to abuse society will sanction.
2. How the costs of preventing child maltreatment and of reducing its consequences.

Unfortunately, the first criterion is a moving target, as evidenced by the rapid changes in child protection law and practice over the past 30 years. Also unfortunate is our relatively rudimentary knowledge of the cost-effectiveness of child maltreatment prevention and intervention efforts.

Before examining what we know, and do not know, about the economics of child maltreatment, I would like to add another wrinkle to the discussion. Specifically, that the costs of preventing and responding to child maltreatment cannot be understood without thoughtful reference to the fact that the lower economic tiers of our population suffer most from maltreatment. The most recent National Incidence Study of Child Abuse and Neglect (Sedlak & Broadhurst, 1996) found that children from families with incomes below $15,000 per year, or roughly the poverty level for a family of four, were 22 times more likely to experience observable harm from child maltreatment than children from families with annual incomes above $30,000. Moreover, as I will point out in more detail in a moment, the lion's share of government funding for child protection programs is directed at children from low-income families (U.S. House of Representatives, Committee on Ways and Means, 1998). Whatever one's understanding of the powerful relationship between poverty and child maltreatment, and to be sure there is disagreement about why this observed relationship exists, there can be no denying that it does exist. I hope to show that this has profound implications for attempts to understand the economics of child maltreatment in an era of welfare reform.

I would like to make three observations today. First, we know relatively little about the economic consequences of child maltreatment for a number of reasons, but the unquantified costs are undoubtedly quite large. Second, child welfare services programs-one area where we have at least reasonable estimates-are very costly. Three, the powerful role that public assistance programs have played in the lives of most maltreating families ensures that the way in which state and local government and private human services programs respond to "welfare reform" will play a large role in the future costs of child maltreatment. These observations lead me to make some recommendations for our National Call to Action.

The Total Costs of Child Maltreatment

Truth be told, no meaningful estimates are available regarding the overall costs of child maltreatment. This dearth of information has many causes. Perhaps most importantly, the "human costs" of child maltreatment are difficult to quantify in monetary terms. For example, how does one put a price on the pain and suffering experienced by a person who has lost the ability to form intimate relationships as a consequence of abuse or neglect. I could easily present a long list of such examples to illustrate my point, but suffice it to say that no serious effort has been made to quantify the human costs of child maltreatment.

But what about costs that ought to be more easy to capture, such as those associated with the responses of various social institutions to the problem of child maltreatment? The institutions that help prevent and cope with the problem are myriad: public assistance and family support programs, schools, health and mental health care systems, police and the courts, juvenile and adult corrections, and, of course, the child welfare services system. Unfortunately, even these costs are very difficult to clearly identify. Putting aside for the moment the costs of the child welfare system itself, the most significant problem in identifying the fiscal impact of child maltreatment on the institutions I have just listed is the well-known difficulty of establishing causal relationships between child maltreatment and various undesired outcomes for those who are maltreated. Did child maltreatment per se cause the event or behavior that led to a particular cost to an institution? An ecological perspective on child abuse and neglect calls for an appreciation of the interrelatedness of child maltreatment and a host of other serious problems including poverty, racial discrimination, domestic violence, parental mental illness and substance abuse, and so on. Parsing out the costs of one of these problems from those of another is challenging to say the least and as a result it has not been done.

Complicating matters more is the fact that the social institutions most affected by child maltreatment have done very little to account for the costs of maltreatment. For example, there are no meaningful national estimates of the considerable court expenses associated with processing the jurisdictional, dispositional, and permanency planning hearings required to supervise the care of the half-million maltreated children currently in out-of-home placement and the quarter-million or so who entered care last year, let alone the hundreds of thousands of children who end up in court but are not removed from the care of their families. Similarly, although researchers have found that health care expenses of children admitted to hospitals as a consequence of abuse are much higher than for children admitted for other reasons (Wright & Litaker, 1996; Irazuta et al., 1997), no comprehensive and reliable data exist at the state or national level on the costs of providing health care in response to child abuse or neglect.

In short, no historical or current estimates of the overall costs of child maltreatment exist that would stand any level of serious scrutiny, due both to a lack of interest historically, and to the problems that I have just described. About all that can be said about the costs of child maltreatment 100 years ago is that nearly all of them were born directly by the children and families involved or indirectly by everyone through the loss of full participation in society by those who had been maltreated. Not much of a formal child protection system existed then, reflecting the low priority child maltreatment had on the social agenda at that time, and what did exist was most certainly not very costly.

Although more current estimates of various costs of child maltreatment must be taken with more than a grain of salt, they do give some idea of the potential magnitude of expenditures. For example, the American Humane Association (1994) (sic) has estimated that the costs of providing a broad range of services to maltreated children and their families was approximately $11.4 billion in 1993. They based this figure on their own estimates of the costs of foster care, investigating child abuse and neglect, and providing in-home services to families reported for maltreatment, and on estimates of the National Committee to Prevent Child Abuse (1994) of the child maltreatment-related costs of hospitalization of children with serious physical injuries, in-patient mental health services, care of seriously endangered juveniles in specialized service facilities, and counseling of abuse victims and their families. Even this rather sobering estimate does not include a number of important costs such as the value of lost productivity and earnings loss, special education services required by maltreated children, drug and alcohol treatment, juvenile court proceedings, and potential dependency on public assistance programs. In the 1980s, Deborah Daro (1988) (sic) conservatively estimated that the cost in lost earnings of the relatively small group of maltreated children with serious injuries-about 24,000 in 1985-was $658 million to $1.3 billion per year.

Dr. Jack Westman (1994) estimated the costs of "incompetent parenting" in making his argument for licensing parents in the interest of preventing child abuse and neglect. To be sure, the definition of incompetent parenting used in his calculations goes beyond what would normally be defined as abuse and neglect. For example, he assumes that chronic welfare dependency is a consequence of incompetent parenting. Though some of the architects of welfare reform might see things this way, I would assert that this assumption as well as some of the others Westman makes is open to serious criticism. Still, his numbers give pause. Dr. Westman estimates that the total annual cost of incompetent parenting in the U.S. is $38.6 billion per year, $17.8 billion in costs of criminal recidivism, $12.4 billion in expenses associated with welfare dependency, and $8.4 billion in child abuse and neglect services.

The Cost Of Government-Funded Child Protection

Although no reliable data on the overall costs of child maltreatment exist, relatively accurate recent estimates of the costs of operating the child welfare services system are available, as are trend data on federal expenditures for child welfare programs. Such data are useful in gauging the political commitment to responding to child maltreatment, the cost of that commitment, and the relative emphasis placed on prevention services as opposed to intervention. Before examining trends in federal funding and estimates of current government expenditures, a brief look at the history of federal funding for child protection is in order.

The federal government's role in providing child welfare services dates to the enactment of the Social Security Act in 1935, whereby the Children's Bureau was given funding under the Title IV-B Child Welfare Services program to provide, through the states, an array of services to children and their families. Title IV-13 funding, however, was not substantial and states, localities, and private philanthropy largely funded child welfare programs until 1961. In that year federal assistance to help states make maintenance payments for children placed out of their homes by a child welfare agency was first provided under the old Aid to Dependent Children (ADC) program (Title IV-A of the Social Security Act), later renamed Aid to Families with Dependent Children (AFDC). These payments were made to foster parents, and later to group care providers, to reimburse them for the costs of providing out-of-home care. The federal role grew out of the recognition that some states were denying ADC payments to children whose homes were deemed "unfit." The 1961 regulations required that either states continue ADC payments and improve conditions in the home or provide out-of-home care for the child. Thus, from the beginning, the federal foster care program was essentially a poverty program, a fact often missing from discussions of child protection.

The "rediscovery" of child abuse and neglect during the 1960s and early '70s led in 1974 to federal legislation requiring that child abuse be reported by professionals who interact with children, the Child Abuse Prevention and Treatment Act (CAPTA, Public Law 93-247). Although CAPTA provides important policy direction for the states, and no doubt contributed to the rapid increase in reports of child maltreatment to child protection authorities during the 1980s and early 1990s, it has never been a major source of funding for child protection. In recent years funding for programs authorized under the law has ranged between 60 and 80 million dollars (Collins, 1997).

By the late 1970s the perception that many children were being placed inappropriately in foster care or were spending inordinate amounts of time in the system contributed to demands for reform of the existing child welfare services system. That gave rise to The Adoption Assistance and Child Welfare Act of 1980 (Public Law 96-272). In essence, the focus on "permanency planning" in Public

Law 96-272 calls for prompt and decisive action to maintain children in their own homes or place them, as quickly as possible, in permanent homes with other families (preferably guardianship or adoption). Public Law 96-272 retained the entitlement status of federal foster care funding but separated foster care from AFDC by creating a new Title IV-E foster care program. It also created an entitlement program of payments to families who adopted foster children with "special needs." In fiscal year 1996, the federal government spent $3.67 billion on foster care and adoption assistance (U.S. House of Representatives, Committee on Ways and Means, 1998).

The goal of preventing out-of-home placement of maltreated children is also manifested in the movement for "'family preservation" services. Family preservation programs aim to help families safely care for their own children. Although states can use federal funds from Title IVB and the Title XX Social Services Block Grant for family preservation and child maltreatment prevention services, the perception that such funding was inadequate, given competing demands, contributed to the creation in 1993 of Part 2 of the Title IV-B program, the federal Family Preservation and Support Program, which sets aside funds to be used by the states for family preservation and support planning and services (U.S. House of Representatives, Committee on Ways and Means, 1998). "Family preservation" services are intended for children and families, including extended and adoptive families, that are at risk of having children placed in out-of home care due to abuse or neglect or are in the process of having children returned home from care. "Family support services" are intended to help families that are not yet in crisis and to prevent child maltreatment from occurring. The program was renamed Promoting Safe and Stable Families in 1997 via the Adoption and Safe Families Act. Its funds can now be used for family reunification and adoption preservation in addition to family preservation and support. Federal funding for Part I of Title IV-B, the Child Welfare Services program, was $277 million in 1996, whereas $225 million was appropriated for Part 2, Promoting Safe and Stable Families.

In addition to IV-B, IV-E and CAPTA monies, states are also able to fund child protection programs using federal dollars provided under the Title XX Social Services Block Grant and, until 1997 when it was collapsed into the welfare reform block grant, from Title IV-A Emergency Assistance (EA). Title XX was created in 1975 and is currently a capped entitlement to the states. It provides states with wide discretion in determining the services to be provided and the groups that may be eligible for services. Due to minimal reporting requirements there are no trend data available on how states actually chose to allocate Title XX funds among various social services, but fiscal year 1996 funding for Title XX was $2.3 8 billion (U.S. House of Representatives, Committee on Ways and Means, 1998).

The Emergency Assistance program, which was authorized under Title IV-A primarily to help states cope with national disasters, evolved in many states into a child welfare program helping to handle emergencies associated with child maltreatment, domestic violence, and family crises such as homelessness. EA was an uncapped entitlement program with federal expenditures of $1.6 billion in 1996 (U.S. House of Representatives, Committee on Ways and Means, 1998).

Trends in federal funding for child protection show the discrepancy in spending between out-of home care expenditures on the one hand and all other services for maltreated children and their families on the other. Federal expenditures for foster care and adoption maintenance payments and administration leapt from $610 million to $3.67 billion between 1986 and 1996, an increase of over 500 percent (U.S. House of Representatives, Committee on Ways and Means, 1998). Caseload trends do not account for all of this growth, however, since the rate of growth over this period in the number of children either in foster care or receiving adoption subsidies was less than half the rate of growth in expenditures.

Although foster care spending has grown faster than the foster care caseload, funding for child protective services investigations and services to families and children has not kept pace with demand. Between 1986 and 1996 Title IV-B Child Welfare Services spending increased only about 40 percent from $198 million to $277 million, less than the growth in child maltreatment reports over this period

(Wang & Daro, 1997; U.S. House of Representatives, Committee on Ways and Means, 1998). Similarly, although a large but unknown portion of funds provided by the Title XX social services block grant are spent by the states on child protective services, these funds have declined in both nominal and real terms since 1986. Even the addition of Title IV-13 Promoting Safe and Stable Families funding to the equation does not do much to seriously address the mismatch between funding for "front end" services (i.e., child maltreatment prevention efforts and in-home services to children and families) and "deep end" services (i.e., out-of-home care): The $3.67 billion spent by the federal government during 1996 on Title IV-E foster care and adoption assistance was over seven times as much as total Title IV-B services spending. Moreover, even if states chose to use all of the Social Services Block Grant for child protection-a very unlikely scenario-federal foster care and adoption spending would still outstrip federal spending on services for maltreated children and their families.

Whereas figures on federal child welfare services and foster care spending give a sense of trends in the cost to government of child protection, clearly this is only part of the picture. State and local governments also fund child protection and current reporting practices make it impossible to routinely account for how much federal Title XX and Medicaid dollars are used to fund child protection.

Fortunately, as part of its study of the ongoing transfer of responsibility for social programs from the federal government to the states through its New Federalism Project, The Urban Institute has undertaken a comprehensive analysis of government funding of child welfare services. Based on a detailed survey of state officials responsible for administering programs that might engage in child protection activities, The Urban Institute has estimated that federal, state, and local governments spent a total of $14.4 billion on child welfare services in 1996 (Geen, 1998). This estimate is undoubtedly low given that it excludes certain types of expenditures that 20 states were not able to account for. Approximately 44 percent of the total was federal spending, 44 percent state, and 13 percent local. Of the total, 56 percent was spent on out-of-home care for abused and neglected children, 7 percent on adoption, and 43 percent on other services. The range in spending across states reflects the wide diversity in the level of state response to child maltreatment: Estimated per-child expenditures in 1996 on child welfare programs ranged from under $200 in Mississippi to over $500 in the District of Columbia. Expenditures per poor child-a more realistic measure of demand-ranged from less than $200 in Mississippi to over $3,700 in New Hampshire.

Comparing the Urban Institute's estimate of federal spending on child welfare services to other federal expenditures on children provides a sobering perspective on the economics of child maltreatment. In 1996, the federal government spent more on child welfare programs than on a number of other crucial family support programs for children and families including the School Lunch and Breakfast program, Title 1, Supplemental Security Income (SSI) for children, the Women Infants and Children (WIC) nutrition program, Head Start, and child care (Office of Management and Budget, 1997; U.S. House of Representatives, Committee on Ways and Means, 1998). In fact, child protection costs the federal government more than Head Start and childcare combined.

The Economic Safety Net and the Costs of Child Maltreatment

Thus, the economic costs of child maltreatment are considerable, even by the relatively conservative measure of funding for government programs devoted to responding to child abuse and neglect. But before suggesting some actions that might be taken to both better understand the economics of child maltreatment and to use that understanding to reduce the incidence of harm to children, I would like to return to my earlier observation about the powerful relationship between familial poverty and child maltreatment. Nearly all of the significant sources of government funding for child protection that I have just discussed are targeted toward low-income children and families. Hence, the lion's share of the currently measurable costs of child maltreatment are associated with children from low-income families. Indeed, this has become increasingly the case over the years. For example, in 1986 about 40 percent of children in foster care came from AFDC-eligible families whereas by 1996 that percentage had risen to over 53 percent (U.S. House of Representatives, Committee on Ways and Means, 1998). Even these numbers are undoubtedly low given the historical propensity of many states to do a poor job of establishing Title IV-E eligibility for children in state care. For example, recently the director of Los Angeles County's child welfare program observed that over 90 percent of children in out-of-home care in Los Angeles were Title IV-E eligible and by definition poor (Digre, 1998).

Since low-income families clearly account for most governmental expenditures related to child maltreatment, it behooves those of us interested in the costs of child maltreatment to pay close attention to significant changes in public programs that support low-income families. In the current context, the most important of these changes is welfare reform. For the first time in U.S. history our nation finds itself with a national commitment, albeit arguably inadequate, to protecting children from child abuse and neglect, but with no commitment of financial assistance to low-income families in times of need. Indeed, the renewed emphasis in the Adoption and Safe Families Act on child safety comes just in the wake of the radical revamping of the safety net for poor families. This profound change will take time for families as well as administrators of both public assistance and child protection programs to comprehend.

Much of welfare reform's impact on the child welfare system will depend on how states and localities prioritize the competing demands of moving parents into the work force, preserving families, and protecting children. Will the conflicting demands of the new work-based programs and the child welfare system be reconciled, and if so, how? On the one hand, states that adopt an unforgiving emphasis on the use of financial sanctions to enforce work and that provide minimal support for poor families may have to increasingly use coercive state intervention to protect children. If parents are denied assistance because no jobs are available, or because they could not or did not comply with program requirements, their children will be placed in harm's way. Even if child welfare agencies or private charities had the resources to provide basic necessities to all these families, such intervention would be inconsistent with the welfare reform interest in punishing parents for their failure to work.

Current child protection policy only justifies state intervention in confirmed cases of child maltreatment, not simply because a parent does not work. Nevertheless, states choosing a "tough" approach to welfare reform will find it difficult to ignore the plight of children in families that are denied economic support, and may seek to expand state intervention to protect children: Simply defining poverty-related neglect as off-limits to child protective services intervention is unlikely to save child welfare administrators from the need to intervene in desperate cases (Rycraft, 1990). In such states, child welfare agencies are likely to protect children from harm in sanctioned families by placing them in out-of-home care, increasing child protection costs in the process.

On the other hand, states that reform their welfare systems to include family support and guarantee both work and child care for those who strive to improve themselves may reduce the need for child welfare services, and improve the effectiveness of the supports they do provide. Such states can offer a range of supportive services such as job training, parenting education and support groups, and substance abuse treatment to improve the prospects that parents will succeed in making the transition to work. States can also impose financial sanctions incrementally, rather than abruptly terminating benefits, to lessen the likelihood that children will be placed in desperate situations. Most important, states can identify families that require child welfare intervention before children have been seriously harmed. In such a "gentle" approach to welfare reform, work-based public assistance programs can function as part of a comprehensive web of supports for families and children, and thereby complement the functioning of the child welfare system (Knitzer & Bernard, 1997).

Whatever the approach to welfare reform, however, state policy makers and child welfare administrators will face critical questions in the new era. Will the child protective services system wait until it is confronted with concrete evidence of child maltreatment before providing services to families who have been denied benefits under the new work-based programs? Alternatively, will parental refusal or inability to participate in the new programs, in and of itself, become grounds for coercive intervention by child welfare authorities? Can a way be found to reconcile the demands for work, family preservation and child protection? Answers to these questions are central to what welfare reform will mean to the most desperate of America's children and what it will cost to ensure their safety. More fundamentally, these questions remind us of how much the economics of child maltreatment at any given point in time reflect the nature of the social contract between society as a whole and its least fortunate families.

Summary

No reliable estimates exist of the overall costs to society of child maltreatment that will withstand serious examination. Arguably, some of the most important human costs of maltreatment are unquantifiable. Moreover, in many cases it is difficult if not impossible to separate the economics of child abuse and neglect from the economics of a host of other problems facing families. Still, even conservative estimates of government spending on behalf of abused and neglected children and their families illustrate that child maltreatment costs society a great deal, with much of that expense going for deep-end intervention rather than family support and prevention. Government expenditures directed at this social problem have grown rapidly since the rediscovery of child abuse in the 1960s and now exceed spending for a number of essential supports for children and families. Moreover, the new era of continuing commitment to child protection in the context of a revised social contract with the nation's poor raises serious questions about the economics of child maltreatment in the future.

Recommendations

My recommendations for the National Call to Action are intended to address two separate but related aspects of improving our understanding of the economics of child maltreatment. First, the recommendations are intended to increase our knowledge of the costs of maltreatment and the costs of interventions intended to either prevent or minimize the consequences of maltreatment. Second, they address the broader issue of how attributes of the system of supports provided to families affect the incidence and costs of child maltreatment. I will describe the kinds of research and analysis that will be necessary to achieve these goals and then present some short- and long-term strategies for ensuring that the work takes place.

What kind of research and evaluation will help to improve knowledge about the costs of child maltreatment and the costs and benefits of prevention and intervention? Several approaches come to mind. Advances in the use of administrative data to track both the pathways of maltreated children through various service systems and the cost of such services could increase our knowledge base fairly rapidly. Optimally this requires linking administrative data on children and families across systems (e.g., data on vital statistics, Medicaid utilization, child abuse and neglect reports, court intervention, out-of-home care, and public assistance utilization). Some headway has been made in this regard and interesting insights obtained in the process, but much more needs to be done. This work usually requires close collaboration between researchers and the administrators of public programs. More researchers will also need to be trained in the use of appropriate methods for analyzing such data.

More traditional longitudinal cost-effectiveness and cost-benefit studies are also needed. Too many ideas about how to reduce the incidence and consequences of child maltreatment have quickly become seen as panaceas before any serious analysis of their cost and effectiveness has been done. In general, cost-effectiveness studies examine how much a particular benefit might cost given a specified intervention. Typically, either competing interventions that cost approximately the same amount are compared in terms of their effectiveness, or the costs of competing interventions that achieve identical results are compared. Some cost-effectiveness studies of child maltreatment prevention and intervention programs have been done, but scholars agree that the gaps in this body of research are enormous. Cost-benefit analyses go beyond cost effectiveness studies in attempting to actually capture all of the costs of a particular intervention and all of its benefits. This kind of analysis requires that both costs and benefits be specified in monetary terms, a task that can be quite difficult under the best of circumstances, let alone when the costs are as difficult to identify as they are in the case of child maltreatment. Not surprisingly, although advocates often make back-of-the-napkin estimates of the "savings" that they believe result from programs that they support, very little reasonably rigorous cost-benefit analysis of child maltreatment prevention and intervention has been done, the recent work by Lynn Karoly and her colleagues at the RAND Corporation on early childhood intervention being a notable exception (Karoly et al., 1998).

In general, the types of research that I have just described are forms of services research, as opposed to basic research on child maltreatment. I am not arguing against more basic research on child abuse and neglect by social, behavioral, and life scientists, but such research in and of itself simply will not go far enough in improving our understanding of the economics of child maltreatment. There is a desperate need for more applied research and evaluation in this area.

In addition to conducting basic research on the costs of child abuse and neglect and the effectiveness of particular prevention and intervention programs, now is the time to begin to assess the relative impact of various constellations of welfare reform and community-based family supports on the costs of child maltreatment. The common wisdom among cutting-edge scholars and practitioners struggling with how to prevent child maltreatment is that efforts must be comprehensive (i.e., addressing the complete range of family strengths and challenges), flexible, in many cases intensive, and long-term. There is also a growing recognition that the comprehensiveness and often community-wide nature of the most promising approaches to supporting children and families require new methods of evaluation. The systems-reform and community saturation initiatives currently gaining momentum are simply not amenable to traditional experimental evaluation designs, a fact reflected in the work of evaluation researchers such as Heather Weiss at the Harvard Family Research Project.

Ironically, welfare reform offers a unique opportunity to better understand how various ways of going about supporting families affects the incidence and cost of child maltreatment. It does so by throwing into question the basic economic safety net for children and families and allowing states and localities wide latitude in whether and how they choose to reconstitute the safety net. As a result, our nation is likely to see the gradual evolution of a wide variety of approaches to providing health care, social services, work-based public assistance, childcare, and education, particularly to low-income families. Some communities will choose to integrate these services so as to support parents to both parent effectively and participate successfully in the labor market. If the current wisdom in the field of child maltreatment prevention and intervention is correct, these communities will experience much lower rates of child maltreatment and other social pathologies, and their attendant costs, than communities with less supportive strategies for reform.

But we will only learn more about the impact of this grand social experiment on the economics of child abuse and neglect if we set out to do so immediately. Currently states are running large surpluses under the Temporary Assistance to Needy Families block grant, but this will not last forever. Any significant economic downturn could rapidly eliminate the flexibility states now have to experiment with work-based public assistance. Few studies currently in the field even attempt to do justice to the impact of welfare reform on the economics of child maltreatment. For example, whereas the Urban Institute's New Federalism Project will provide much information about state-level variation in welfare reform strategies, it will miss much of the most interesting variation in service integration and redesign at the local level. What is needed are studies of how the thousand flowers that bloom in response to the new federalism affect the conditions of families, particularly low-income families, and how differing strategies affect the incidence of child maltreatment and the costs of responding to maltreatment within these communities. This will require the refinement of existing research methods and probably the development of new ones as well (Piliavin & Courtney, 1997).

All of the activities I have described above require significant funding and many of them require either the development of new research methodologies or at least training of more scholars capable of conducting the necessary work. My recommendations for specific action are intended to help meet these needs. *First, in the next budget cycle and thereafter the federal government should appropriate at least one percent of what is spent on child protection programs by the federal government to research and evaluation focused specifically on the costs of child maltreatment and the cost-effectiveness of prevention and intervention programs directed at child maltreatment.* This would amount to approximately $65 million per year based on the Urban Institute's estimate of $6.5 billion spent by the federal government in 1996. Since by far most of the federal funds spent on child protection are administered by the Administration on Children, Youth and Families within the Department of Health and Human Services, these research and evaluation dollars should be administered by ACYF and most appropriately by the Children's Bureau since it is responsible for child protection programs. It is nothing less than a disgrace that our nation has engaged for decades in what has become a multi-billion dollar experiment on maltreated children and their families while paying virtually no attention to the costs and outcomes of this experiment. To further put this into perspective, consider the fact that the Children's Bureau operates over $4 billion in child welfare programs including Title IV-B and Title IV-E but has never in recent memory had more than about two-tenths of one percent of its budget ($7 million) to spend on research and evaluation. For the past three years its research and evaluation budget has been zero.

Second, following the recent recommendation of the Institute for the Advancement of Social Work Research, the U.S. Department of Health and Human Services should develop a new National Institute on Strong Families and Communities parallel in structure to a NIH institute. Such an institute would recognize the inextricably linked set of challenges facing vulnerable children, the appropriateness of family- and community-based responses, and the need for applied research on the cost-effectiveness of prevention and interventions efforts. In the words of the Institute for the Advancement of Social Work Research White Paper on the topic: "an interdisciplinary institute ... would promote service- and community-focused research, generating knowledge and technical innovations that would drive policies and programs to strengthen families and communities. These policies and programs would result in future savings that result from fewer families becoming involved in cycles of family violence and child abuse, adolescent pregnancy, school drop-out, alcohol and drug abuse, and crime and violence. In contrast to the current disjuncture between solution-focused research and outcome/cost analysis, NISFC supported studies would address issues of effectiveness and cost. Technology transfer issues would be considered even in early-stage developmental studies, through systematic contacts with service providers, family and community representatives" (Institute for the Advancement of Social Work Research, 1998, pp. 13-14). Development of such a resource will of course take time, but the sooner it is done the better.

Both of these recommendations would help address the need for additional funding for research on the economics of child maltreatment. Whereas the first recommendation recognizes the dearth of services research on child maltreatment prevention and intervention, the latter emphasizes the need to factor into the economics of child maltreatment the relationship between child abuse and neglect and other issues. Following these recommendations would also help to develop the expertise and support the group of scholars necessary to improve our grasp of the economics of child maltreatment.

Third, where this is not already taking place, child advocates and administrators of programs for maltreated children should immediately seek to form alliances with the entire spectrum of child and family service providers in order to ensure that state and local TANF programs become part of an integrated system of supports for vulnerable families and children. Without a concerted attempt to create working models of how communities can help parents both to work and parent we will have missed a golden opportunity to explore the larger economics of child maltreatment: We will have failed to learn how the quality, or lack thereof, of society's social contract with families conditions the level of harm experienced by children within their families.

Obviously such efforts will not be successful everywhere. In particular, many managers of TANF programs may be too focused on the new bottom line of caseload reduction as an end in itself to see the wisdom of working creatively with the broad array of support systems for families and children. Nevertheless, the TANF block grant offers an unparalleled opportunity to manifest the vision of many prevention advocates. TANF funds are relatively plentiful right now and may be used for a wide variety of supports for families. Moreover, in the wake of rapid reduction in public assistance caseloads, the residual TANF population in many states is made up largely of parents facing a host of challenges that threaten both their ability to move successfully into the labor force and to safely parent their children. Reminding TANF administrators of these facts can help to convince them that they should coordinate efforts-and perhaps even share some of their arguably temporary wealth-with other health and human service systems that promote healthy family functioning.

Many organizations and interest groups have an interest in supporting such an effort. Most notable are the organizations representing institutions and professions that consume much of the spending on child protection in the U.S.. Their members know firsthand about the costs in both human and monetary terms of child maltreatment. Moreover, they owe it to taxpayers and children at risk of maltreatment to make sure that the programs and services they provide are cost effective. Such organizations include the National Association of Public Child Welfare Administrators and its parent the American Public Human Services Association, the Child Welfare League of America, the National Association of Social Workers, the American Psychological Association, the American Public Health Association, the American Medical Association, the American Psychiatric Association, the American Academy of Pediatrics, and the American Professional Society on Abuse of Children. Child advocacy and prevention advocates such as the National Committee for the Prevention of Child Abuse, the Children's Defense Fund, the National Children's Alliance, and the American Humane Association should also support this. If funds are to be shifted from the deep end to the front end of efforts to protect children, then evaluation research must be conducted not only on the costs and benefits of prevention and early intervention, but also on how to make the deep end (i.e., foster and group care) work cost effectively. Failing to do so will only run the risk that out-of-home care will continue to break the child welfare bank.

The time is ripe for a major investment in understanding the economics of child abuse and neglect. This investment would pay off both in terms of a better understanding of how much child maltreatment really costs society, and therefore how much more important it should be taken by policy makers, and in greater knowledge about the costs of effectively preventing and responding to maltreatment. Such an investment should be a major part of convening A National Call To Action: Toward The Elimination of Child Maltreatment.

References

Institute for the Advancement of Social Work Research (1998). *Strengthening America's families and communities: Applying R&D in re-inventing human services systems*. Unpublished paper, dated July 1998. Washington, D.C.: Author.

Irazuzta, J. E., McJunkin, J. E., Danadian, K., Arnold, F., & Zhang, J. (1997). Outcome and cost of child abuse. *Child Abuse and Neglect, 21*, 751-7.

Karoly, L. A., Greenwood, P. W., Everingham, S. S., Hoube, J., Kilburn, M. R., Rydell, C. P., Sanders, M., & Chiesa, J. (1998). *Investing in our children: What we know and don't know about the costs and benefits of early childhood interventions*. Santa Monica, CA: The RAND Corporation.

Knitzer, J. & Bernard, S. (1997). *The New Welfare Law and Vulnerable Families: Implications for Child Welfare/Child Protection Systems*. New York: National Center for Children in Poverty.

National Committee to Prevent Child Abuse (1994). *Building healthy families America system: A summary of costs and benefits.* Unpublished monograph. Chicago, IL: Author

Office of Management and Budget, Executive Office of the President of the United States (1997). *Budget of the United States Government, Fiscal Year 1998.* Washington, D.C.: U.S. Government Printing Office.

Piliavin, 1. & Courtney, M. E. (1997). Interstate comparison of welfare reform programs. *Focus, 18*(3): 29-32.

Rycraft, J. R. (1990). Redefining abuse and neglect: A narrower focus could affect children at risk. *Public Welfare, 48*, 1, 14-21.

Sedlak, A. J. & Broadhurst, D. D. (1996). *The Third National Incidence Study of Child Abuse and Neglect (NIS-3).* Washington, D.C.: U.S. Department of Health and Human Services.

U.S. House of Representatives, Committee on Ways and Means (1998*). 1998 Green Book: Background Material and Data on Programs Within the Jurisdiction of the Committee on Ways and Means*, Washington, D.C.: U.S. Government Printing Office.

Wang C.T. & Daro, D. (1997). *Current Trends in Child Abuse Reporting and Fatalities: Results of the 1996 Annual 50-State Survey. Chicago: National Committee to Prevent Child Abuse.*

Westman, J. C. (1994). *Licensing parents: Can we prevent child abuse and neglect?* New York: Insight Books.

Wright, M. S. & Litaker, D. (1996). Childhood victims of violence. Hospital utilization by children with intentional injuries. *Archives of pediatrics and adolescent medicine, 150*, 415-20.

Child Abuse in America:
Prevalence, Costs, Consequences and Intervention*

Bessel A. van der Kolk, M.D.
Joe Crozier, M.P.M.
James Hopper, Ph.D.

Section 1: Summary of Extent and Demographics of Child Maltreatment

Total Incidences of Reported and Substantiated Abuse

In 1997, Child Protective Services nationwide received information that an estimated 3,195,000 children were allegedly being abused and/or neglected (Wang & Daro, 1997). The number of child abuse/neglect cases being reported to CPS has risen steadily since 1988. The total percentage increase over the ten years from 1988 to 1997 is 41%. Despite the marked increase in cases being reported to CPS for investigation, the number of substantiated cases of child abuse and neglect have remained virtually unchanged since 1993. In 1993 the number of substantiated cases involved 1,009,000 children compared with 1,054,000 in 1997. From 1993 to 1997, the number of substantiated cases has involved 15 out of every 1,000 children each year, or 33% of all alleged incidences. (Wang & Daro, 1997). Figure 1 plots the change both reported and substantiated cases of maltreatment. In *Current Trends in Child Abuse Reporting and Fatalities: The Results of the 1997 Annual Fifty State Survey,* Wang and Daro underscore the difficulties involved in accurately estimating these numbers. They mention the wide variation in data collection methods for the 50 states.

FIGURE 1: Incidence of child maltreatment

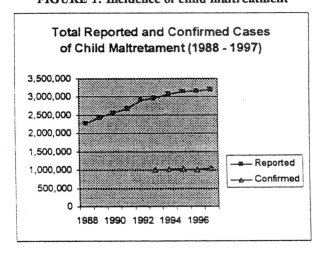

Total Reported and Confirmed Cases of Child Maltretament (1988 - 1997)

*Adapted from The Executive Summary, Child Abuse in America. Sponsored by the Nathan Cummings Foundation; Sections of the report were reprinted with permission of Bessel A. van der Kolk, M.D. For full report or for further information, visit the Trauma Center website at: www.traumacenter.org

223

Child Fatalities

Wang and Daro estimated that 1185 children died in 1996 due to child abuse and neglect. This represents a 34% increase over the estimate of 798 in 1985.

The Types of Abuse

In reported cases of child abuse, the breakdown by types of abuse in substantiated cases is shown in Figure 2. Neglect is most common, at 52%. Physical abuse came in second, at 26%. Sexual abuse cases were the third most common, representing 7% of all cases. Emotional abuse cases represented 4% of all instances, and 11% of cases fell into a miscellaneous "other" category. Types of cases that fall into the substantial "other" category include multiple types of maltreatment, medical and educational neglect, substance and/or alcohol abuse or dependency, lack of supervision, threat of harm, "bizarre" discipline and imminent risk (Wang & Daro, 1997).

FIGURE 2: Types of abuse

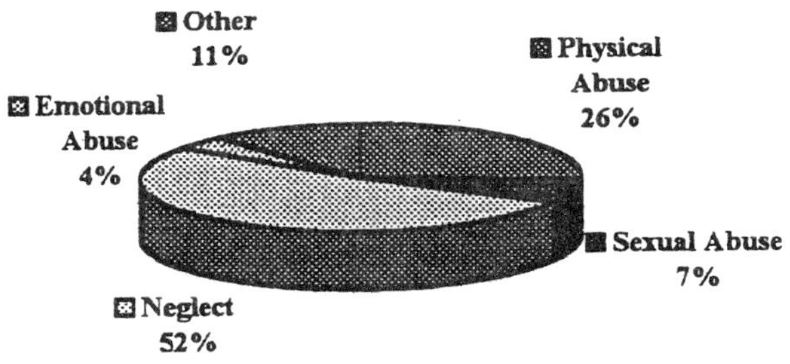

Primary Presenting Problems

Families involved in child maltreatment cases often have a number of compounding problems that increase the likelihood of maltreatment. The most prevalent of these problems is alcohol or substance abuse or dependence: 88% of surveyed states reported substance/alcohol abuse as one of the top two primary presenting problems. The second most common problem was poverty or economical strains. This was reported by 5 1% of the states surveyed. The third most common problem was parental capacity or skills, which was cited by 39% of the responding states. These problems often arise because of parental mental illness, poor understanding on the part of the parents of normal child development, or young maternal age (Wang & Daro, 1997).

Relationship of the Victim to the Perpetrator in Substantiated Cases of Abuse

The overwhelming majority of perpetrators of violence against children are the parents of the children themselves, constituting 81 % of the total population of child abuse/neglect perpetrators. Other relatives of the child made up 10.6 % of the total perpetrator population. Therefore, only 8.4% of perpetrators are not related to the child they abuse/neglect in any way. The relationships of victims to perpetrators are summarized in Figure 3 (CWLA, 1997).

FIGURE 3: Relationship of victims to perpetrators

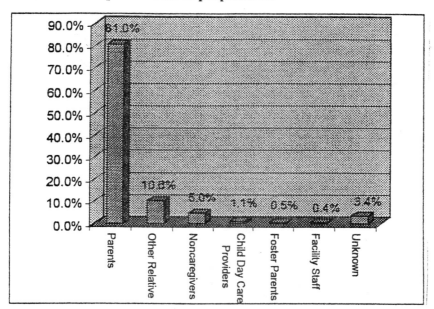

Gender of Perpetrators of Child Abuse and Neglect

Among maltreated children, 65% were victimized by a female and 54% by a male. The type of abuse was related to the gender of the perpetrator. Children were twice as likely to be neglected by females than males, 87% versus 43%, respectively. This is consistent with the fact that women still represent the vast majority of primary caregivers. Males were more likely to physically abuse children than females (67% versus 40%, respectively). Sexual abuse was the category most strongly linked with males: 89% of sexually abused children were abused by males and 12% by females (Abbreviated NIS-3).

The Relationship Between Gender and Child Maltreatment

Females were slightly over-represented among maltreated children in comparison with their distribution in the population: of all maltreated children, 53% are females, while females constitute only 49% of all US children (CWLA, 1997). These findings are summarized in Figure 4.

According to NIS-3, girls were sexually abused three times more often than boys while boys had 24% greater risk of serious injury from abuse and were 18% more likely to be emotionally neglected. From NIS-2 to NIS-3 boys' rate of physical neglect and emotional abuse rose faster than girls' rate. Also, from NIS-2 to NIS-3, boys' rate of fatal injury increased while the rate for girls decreased.

FIGURE 4

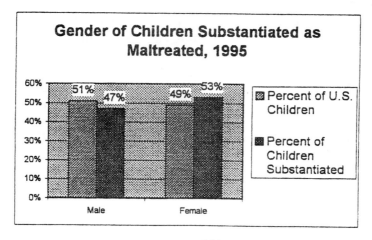

Distribution of Child Abuse and Neglect by Child's Age

The age distribution of substantiated abuse cases closely matches the age distribution for children in the U. S. The one age group that is under-represented in substantiated abuse cases is children 13 and older. They make up 21% of maltreated children and 27% of the total child population. One explanation is that children over 13 are more able to defend themselves against abuse or to run away from their abusers (CWLA, 1997). The age distribution of maltreated children is presented in Figure 5.

FIGURE 5

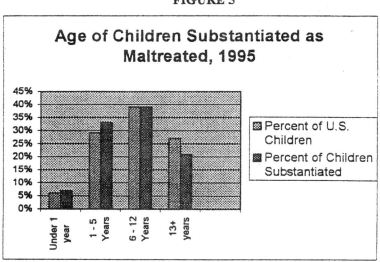

The Race/Ethnicity of Children Substantiated as Maltreated

Most races or ethnic groups were under-represented in child maltreatment cases compared to their share of the population as a whole. Caucasian children make up 66% of the population, while only 57% of the maltreatment cases Latino children represent 14% of the total child population, and 12% of the maltreatment cases. Native American children comprise 4% of the child population, and 2% of the maltreated child population. Asian Pacific Islander children make up 1% of both the population and the maltreatment cases. However, African American children, while representing only 15% of the population, made up 28% of all the substantiated child abuse cases. The researchers caution against drawing any conclusions from this data, saying it "may not reflect an accurate picture" due to "a strong need to understand factors related to substantiation, and in particular, to the interaction in decision making of race/ethnicity, family and environmental strengths, and risks, both among community reporters and mandated service providers, and in the service delivery system as a whole. (CWLA, 1997). This data is represented in Figure 6.

FIGURE 6

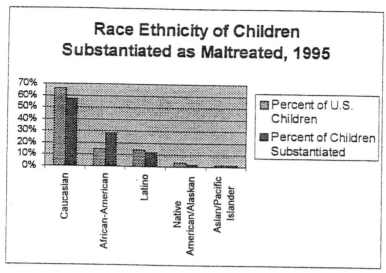

The Relationship Between Family Structure and Maltreatment

Coming from a single-parent household was a grave risk factor for child maltreatment. Compared with their counterparts living with both parents, children in single-parent families had:

1. 77% greater risk of being harmed by physical abuse (using the stringent Harm Standard) and a 63% greater risk of experiencing any countable physical abuse (using the Endangerment Standard);
2. 87% greater risk of being harmed by physical neglect and a 165% greater risk of experiencing any countable physical neglect
3. 74% greater risk of being harmed by emotional neglect and a 64% greater risk of experiencing any countable emotional neglect
4. 220% (or more than three times) greater risk of being educationally neglected;
5. approximately 80% greater risk of suffering serious injury or harm from abuse or neglect
6. approximately 90% greater risk of receiving moderate injury or harm as a result of child maltreatment
7. 120% (or more than two times) greater risk of being endangered by some type of child abuse or neglect.

Furthermore, within single-parent homes, if the single parent was a father rather than a mother, the children were approximately one and two-thirds times more likely to be physically abused. Obvious explanations for why single parenting is such an aggravating factor in child maltreatment include the added stresses of being a single parent, and inadequate social, emotional and financial support (NIS-3).

Family size was also an important consideration. The relationship was non-linear. Children from large families (with 4 or more children) were at greatest risk for educational and physical neglect. Children from medium-sized families (2-3 children) were at the lowest risk for maltreatment. Children from large families were 3 times more likely than there peers from medium sized families to be educationally neglected, and more than 2 times more likely to be physically neglected.

According to a DHHS study done in 1993, between 40 and 50% of child maltreatment incidences occur in families with income below the poverty level (less than 15% of all families have income in this range). Another 40 to 50% of maltreatment incidences occur in the approximately 35% of American families whose income is less than national median, but above the poverty level. Thus, approximately 90% of all child maltreatment incidences occur in families whose income is below the national median while less than 10% of maltreatment incidences occur in families whose income is greater than the national median. Compared to children in families whose income is above the national median, children in families below the median but above the poverty level are five to seven times more likely to be abused, children in families below the poverty level are 13 to 17 times more likely to be abused. (pg. 110) Maltreated children are four times more likely to be supported by public assistance (Wolfe, 1994, p. 227). According to the NIS-3, these findings cannot be plausibly explained away by the "higher visibility of lower-income families " to CPS.

Compared to children from families, for whom yearly income was above $30,000, children from families with an income below $15,000 a year were:

1. 22-25 times more likely to be maltreated (difference depends on whether using the more stringent Harm Standard, or the looser Endangerment Standard)
2. 14 times more likely to suffer harm from some variety of abuse
3. 44 times more likely to be neglected
4. 12-16 times more likely to be physically abused
5. 18 times more likely to be sexually abused
6. 13-18 times more likely to be emotionally abused
7. 40-48 times more likely to suffer physical neglect
8. 27-29 times more likely to suffer emotional neglect
9. 56 times more likely to be educationally neglected
10. 60 times more likely to die from maltreatment under the definition used by Harm Standard
11. 22 times more likely to die from maltreatment under definition used by Endangerment Standard
12. 22 times more likely to suffer serious injury from maltreatment
13. 18-20 times more likely to be moderately injured from maltreatment
14. 39-57 times more likely to be classified as having incurred an injury from maltreatment
15. 31 times more likely to be considered in imminent danger, although not yet injured, from maltreatment

Consequences of Child Maltreatment

Introduction

The devastating consequences of child maltreatment are manifested in numerous facets of a child's life from decreased performance at school to diminished physical and mental health to increased deviant behavior. This section highlights these consequences and presents evidence from the child maltreatment literature.

Psychobiology of Maltreatment

- Brain matures in use-dependent manner (Perry et al., 1995)
- Maltreatment of children may impair the normal development of the brain and have lasting effects on cognition, behavior, affects and social interaction.
- The organizing sensitive brain of an infants or young children is more malleable to experience than a mature brain (Perry et al., 1995)

- The neurotransmitter systems, neuroendocrine systems, and immune systems mediate the physiological mechanisms for coping with stress and trauma. Maltreatment may result in dysfunction in these systems:
    - Neurotransmitter systems involved: Catecholamine, Serotonin, Benzodiazepine Receptor System, Endogenous Opiate System
    - Neuroendocrine systems involved: HPA axis, HPT axis, HPGH (growth hormone) axis, BPGN (gonadal) axis
    - Immune system: during intense stress the HPA axis and SNS suppress immune response. (DeBellis & Putnam, 1994)
- Children have two broad modes of responses to extreme stress: hyperarousal and dissociation. Adult-like hyperarousal (fight or flight) may not be an adaptive stress response for children beyond notifying caretakers.
    - In the hyperarousal continuum, children respond to a threat with increased SNS activation (increases in heart rate, blood pressure, respiration, release of stored sugar, an increase in muscle tone, hypervigilance, and tuning out non-critical information). The immune system, HPA (along with release of ACTH and cortisol) and other stress response systems in the brain are also activated. The locus coeruleus is essential in mediating the stress response. The ventral tegmental nucleus also has a role in regulating the sympathetic nuclei in the pons/medulla (Perry et al., 1995). Perry and colleagues conclude that hyperarousal leads to sensitization whereby weaker stimuli and generalized stimuli can also provoke the hyperarousal response. Over time trauma may result in motor hyperactivity, anxiety, behavioral impulsivity, sleep problems, tachycardia, hypertension, and a variety of neuroendocrine abnormalities (Perry et al., 1995).
    - In the dissociation continuum (the freeze/surrender response): Children use a variety of dissociative techniques: "going to a 'different place', assuming persona of heroes or animals, a sense of 'watching a movie that I was in' or 'just floating' - ciassic depersonalization, and derealization responses." Psychobiology of dissociation includes increased CNS activation, increases in epinephrine and related stress hormones (as with hyperarousal); the difference lies in the increased parasympathetic activation as evidenced by dramatic increases in vagal tone, decreasing blood pressure and heart rate-sometimes resulting in fainting despite the increases in circulating epinephrine. The endogenous opioid systems may also be involved in mediating the dissociative responses as well as other brainstem, midbrain, and limbic region neurotransmitters (van der Kolk, 1989, 1994).
- Findings of increased urinary catecholamines and abnormal cortisol in sexually abused girls are consistent with reports from men with combat-related PTSD (DeBellis & Putnam, 1994).
- Abnormalities in HPA Axis, HPT Axis, testosterone, androstedione in sexually abused girls (DeBellis & Putnam, 1994).
- Early sexual maturation.
- Biological abnormalities may drive hyperactivity, anxiety, behavioral impulsivity, sleep problems, tachycardia, hypertension, and a variety of neuroendocrine abnormalities seen in abused children

Effects on Learning/Occupational Functioning

- Maltreated children have more behavioral problems and perform significantly worse in school (Daro, 1988).
    ⇒30% of abused children have some type of language or cognitive impairment
    ⇒Over 50% have trouble in school (including poor attendance and misconduct)

⇒Over 22% have a learning disorder

⇒Approximately 25% require special education services at some point (Caldwell, 1992; Gianconia et al., 1995)

- Significant differences in various aspects of academic performance are found between maltreated and nonmalterated groups of children:

Table 1.

Criterion	Abused (N=19) LSM[a]	Neglected (N=40) LSM	Nonmaltreated (N=60)	P
Overall	2.75**	2.78**	3.21	.0041
Language	44.82*	42.73*	63.02	.0082
Math	39.50**	43.28*	63.05	.0022
Reading	.	195.26*	218.02	.0256
Working (below average)	2.28**	2.30*	3.11	.0033
Learning (below average)	2.30**	2.63	3.23	.0024
Problem behavior (teacher)	46.56**	28.80	21.19	.0046
Problem behavior (parent)	57.81**	34.29	26.37	.0002

* Significant difference from nonmalterated group at .05 level; ** Significant difference from nonmaltreated group at .0 1 level; [a]Least squares means adjusted for SES and time; *Missing data from high SES cell From: Kurtz, Gaudin, Wodarski & Howing, 1993

Neglected boys have lower IQ's than physically abused and nonmaltreated groups of boys; physically abused and neglected girls have lower IQ's than nonmaltreated girls (Rogeness, et al., 1986 cited in Malinosky-Rummel & Hansen, 1993). A survey found that incest victims were twice as likely as nonvictims to be unemployed. Additionally, women who reported experiencing serious trauma were more likely to have "negative socioeconomic outcomes" (Russell, 1986). Maltreated children show higher rates of disability after their maltreatment (Sullivan & Knutson, 1998)

Table 2.

Disability	Prior to Maltreatment (N=581)	Following Maltreatment (N=844)
Behavior Disorders	16.9	52.6
None	41.7	18.9
Speech/Language	11.4	7.3
Mental Retardation	5.5	4.3
Hearing Impairment	10.7	3.3
Learning Disability	4.2	5.7
Other Disability	4.9	3.5
Health Impairments	3.2	1.6
Attention Deficit Disorder (w/o Conduct Disorder)	1.5	2.8

X^2 [13, N=1425]= 197.9; p <.0001; From Sullivan & Knutson, 1998

Cycle of Violence

- 20% of parents who were abused as children go on to abuse their own children (Straus et al., 1980)
- 75% of perpetrators of child sexual abuse reported their own childhood sexual abuse experience (based on a survey of 24 sex offenders in Romano & De Luca, 1997).
- Physical abuse and neglect are associated with the highest rates of arrest for violent offenses:

TABLE 3.

Abuse Group	N	Arrest for Any Violent Offense
Physical Abuse Only	76	21%
Neglect Only	609	20%
Physical Abuse and Neglect	70	16%
Controls	667	14%
Sexual Abuse and Other Abuse	28	11%
Sexual Abuse Only	125	9%

From: Widom & Maxfield, 1996

- Widom and Maxfield used a logistic regression analysis to examine variables that predict eventual arrest for a violent crime. Table 4 depicts the results of that regression:

TABLE 4.

	B	Standard Error	Odds Ratio
Male	1.86[1]	.19	6.40
Black	1.41'	.16	4.09
Physical Abuse	.65'	.33	1.91
Neglect	43[2]	.17	1.55
Sexual Abuse	24[4]	.38	
Age in 1994	.07[2]	.02	1.07

[1]$p{:}{<}.001$; [2]$p{<}.01$; [3]$p{<}.05$; [4]Not Significant

Criminal Behavior

- Abused and neglected children have a higher likelihood of arrests for delinquency, adult criminality, and violent criminal behavior than matched controls" (Widom & Maxfield, 1996). In a prospective study using a matched control group (N=1575), Widom and Maxfield found that maltreated children were 1.8 times more likely to be arrested as a juvenile, 1.5 times more likely to be arrested as an adult, and 1.35 times more likely to be arrested for a violent crime. Table 5 depicts these results:

TABLE 5.

Arrests (%)	Abuse/Neglect Group	Control Group	Odds Ratio
Juvenile	27.4%	17. 2[1]	1.80
Male	35%	23%[1]	1.80
Female	20%	11%[1]	1.94
Adult	41.6%	32..5%[1]	1.47
Male	55%	49%[3]	
Female	28%	16%[1]	2.09
Any Violent Crime	18.1%	13..9%[3]	1.35
Male	28%	24%[4]	
Female	8%	4%[2]	2.38

[1]$p{\le},001$; [2]$p{\le}0\,1.$, [3]Significant with $P{\le}.05$ with one-tailed test; [4]Not significant

- Child maltreatment has proportionally greater impact on the criminal behavior of females as shown above in Table 5.
- The majority of juvenile offenders are arrested again as adults although adult arrest rates for juvenile offenders differ slightly between maltreated and nonmaltreated groups-71% for the maltreated group versus 66% for the nonmaltreated group (Widom & Maxfield, 1996).
- Maltreated children have more involvement with the juvenile justice system (Lewis et al., 1989).
- Other research has found that 20% of maltreated children are convicted for a serious juvenile crime (McCord 1983, cited in Caldwell, 1992; Lewis et al., 1989).

Substance Abuse

- Traumatized children are more likely to be substance abusers than their nonmaltreated peers. In a community sample of 384 18-year olds, 25% of children with PTSD were substance abusers, compared to 14.9% of children who were traumatized only (no PTSD), and 3.7% of children who did not experience significant trauma (Gianconia et al.,1995).
- 15.1 % of abused children, 21.0% of neglected children, and 5.7% of control group were found to have substance abuse disorders (N=7,103; abused=63; neglect=84; both=4; controls=6,952). Based on Wave 11 (new cases of abuse and neglect) of NIMH's Epidemiological Catchment Area Study (Chaffin, Kelleher, & Hollenberg, 1996).
- Abused children are at elevated risk for alcohol dependence and alcohol abuse as depicted in Table 6. These results are based on a sample of adolescents (132 with alcohol dependence; 52 with alcohol abuse; 73 controls from the community)

TABLE 6

	Alcohol Dependence vs. Control		Alcohol Abuse vs. Control	
	Odds Ratio	95% CI	Odds Ratio	95% CI
Physical Abuse	5.8*	1.7- 19.7	11.7**	3.2- 45.5
Sexual Abuse and Rape	21.3 *	2.8-160.1	17.6*	2.2-141.2
Violent Victimization	5.2*	1.5- 18.2	4.2*	1.3- 21.8

N=257
*P<.01;**P<.00I From: Clark, Lesnick, & Hegedus, 1997

Psychiatric Sequelae

1. Multiple behavioral and emotional expressions of trauma

- "Multiply abused infants and toddlers often experience developmental delays across a broad spectrum, including cognitive, language, motor, and socialization skills" (Culp, Heide, & Richardson, 1987)
- In a sample of sexually abused children (Kendall-Tackett, Williams, & Finkelhor, 1993):
  ⇒ 68% exhibited anxiety symptoms
  ⇒ 41 % depressive symptoms
  ⇒ 31% regressive behaviors
  ⇒ 36% inappropriate sexual behaviors
- Self-mutilation (van der Kolk et al., 1991) symptoms have been found to correlate with child physical and/or sexual abuse.
- *Substance abuse and depression have been found to correlate with parents who maltreat their children* (Swanson et al., cited in Chaffin, Kelleher, & Hollenberg, 1996). The odds ratio for the likelihood of maltreatment by severely depressed mothers compared to non-depressed mothers is 3.95 for abuse and 1.87 for neglect (Zuravin, 1988 cited in Chaffin, Kelleher, & Hollenberg, 1996). Out of 206 cases involving serious child abuse and neglect at Boston Juvenile Court, 43% cases

Court, 43% cases involved at least one parent with a documented problem with drugs or alcohol (Chaffin, Kelleher, & Hollenberg, 1996).
- Traumatized children develop a variety of psychiatric diagnoses
  - Table 7 contains a breakout of psychopathology in a sample of physically and sexually abused children. The results are presented for victims of sexual abuse only, physical abuse only, and combined.

TABLE 7

| | | **ABUSE GROUPS** | | | | | | |
| | | Sexual (N=127) | | Physical (N=43) | | Both (N=34) | | Control* |
Diagnoses	**Total** %	**Boys** %	**Girls** %	**Boys** %	**Girls** %	**Boys** %	**Girls** %	%
ADHD	29	40	22	36	10	67	26	3-5
Oppositional Defiant Disorder	36	46	22	56	20	64	47	7
Conduct Disorder	21	44	11	21	10	67	21	4
Major Depression	13	12	11	12	20	8	32	5
Bipolar Disorders	9	4	9	9	20	0	21	1
Dysthymia	19	16	13	24	20	17	42	
Separation Anxiety Overanxious	59	44	58	48	100	59	79	9
Phobic	36	44	36	24	30	25	58	10
Obsessive-Compulsive	14	0	14	18	20	8	27	0.5
Avoidant	10	12	7	18	30	8	0	
PTSD	34	20	35	18	50	58	53	>6%

*Based on various studies. See Appendix B for a full citation. Source: Ackerman et al., 1998. Subjects included 62% outpatients, 25% inpatients, and 13% were referrals from local agencies.

- McCord conducted a 40-year follow up of 97 abused or neglected boys. In this group 44 (45%) had become criminal, alcoholic, mentally ill, or had died before reaching age 35 (McCord, 1983).

2. PTSD (Core symptoms of intrusions, avoidance, and hyperarousal)
- The DSM model of PTSD is not directly applicable to maltreated children-the DSM does not include an alternate set of developmentally relevant symptoms for children and adolescents. PTSD in maltreated children may be better understood as a dimensional category rather than all-or-none (Putnam, 1998).
- Trauma researchers have recently proposed that a diagnosis of complex PTSD be added as a new diagnostic category. This diagnosis would include a number of alterations that often accompany exposure to long term interpersonal victimization such as difficulties with self-concept, affect regulation, and interpersonal functioning (van der Kolk et al., 1994).
- In a sample of 90 abused children and adolescents (Wolfe et al., 1994 cited in Putnam, 1998):
  ⇒ 80% met DSM-based re-experiencing criteria
  ⇒ 64.4% met avoidant criteria
  ⇒ 66.7% met the hyperarousal criteria
  ⇒ 48.9% met the PTSD criteria
  - The PTSD group contained more females and older children and was more likely to have been abused for a year or longer
- Studies of survivors of sexual abuse find PTSD rates ranging from 20.7% to 90% (cited in Pelcovitz and Kaplan)

- PTSD is three times more likely when the victim is under 11 compared to over age 11 (Davidson & Smith cited in Pelcovitz & Kaplan, 1996).
- Abuse related variables (severity, duration, coercion, relationship to abuser) accounted for 26.9% of PTSD variance after controlling for IQ, age, gender, receptive language ability, and the nature of the abuse. Guilt and blame account for 10. 1% of the variance (Wolfe et al., 1994 cited in Putnam, 1998).
- "Depression, aggression, hypersexuality, suicide, self-mutilation (and risk taking), dissociation, problems with affect regulation, somatization, impulsivity, hyperactivity and attentional problems, low self-esteem, and other disturbances of self-image are among the more common symptoms reported in maltreated children" (Putnam, 1998)
- **"Most attempts at treatment for maltreated children are more focused on nonPTSD symptoms such as aggression and hypersexuality than on PTSD symptoms. Children 'and adolescents have yet to reap any significant benefits from the treatment studies of adults with PTSD "(Putnam, 1998).**
- A survey from an ongoing longitudinal study of 384 18-year old subjects (from mostly white, working or lower middle income level families) indicated that 43% experienced some form of trauma, and 6.3% of the total (or 14.5% of those experiencing trauma) were diagnosed with PTSD based on DSM criteria. Various trauma categories resulted in the same general pattern of symptoms except for rape victims of rape were 8 times more likely to have avoidance or numbing symptoms, 12 times more likely to report symptoms lasting more than one month, and seven times more likely to meet all DSM III-R criteria for PTSD. On average, rape victims experienced twice as many total lifetime symptoms as adolescents with all other traumas combined. In general, females were six times more likely than males to develop PTSD after experiencing trauma (Gianconia et al., 1995).
  - Based on the community sample discussed above, Table 8 depicts the prevalence of psychiatric disorders among three groups of adolescents: Diagnosed with PTSD, Trauma Only (no PTSD diagnosis), and No Trauma (Gianconia et al., 1995).

TABLE 8

Psychiatric Disorder	Lifetime % of Group	Current (1 YR) % of Group
Major Depression		
PTSD	41.7	29.2
Trauma Only	9.2	7.1
No Trauma	5.9	4.6
Phobia		
PTSD	29.2	29.2
Trauma Only	12.1	10.6
No Trauma	8.7	7.8
Alcohol Dependence		
PTSD	45.8	37.5
Trauma Only	31.4	27.9
No Trauma	16.6	15.7
Drug Dependence		
PTSD	25.0	20.8
Trauma Only	14.9	12.8
No Trauma	3.7	1.8
Two or More Disorders		
PTSD	45.8	41.7
Trauma Only	23.4	21.3
No Trauma	12.3	9.6
Three or More Disorders		
PTSD	33.3	20.8
Trauma Only	7.1	3.5
No Trauma	2.3	0.9

- Based on the community sample discussed above, Table 9 depicts the risks for various problem behaviors for three groups of adolescents: Diagnosed with PTSD, Trauma Only (no PTSD diagnosis), and No Trauma (Gianconia et al., 1995).

TABLE 9

RISK AREA	% of GROUP
Clinical Range on Internalizing Problems∧	
PTSD	16.8
Trauma Only	DNA
No Trauma	4.6
Clinical Range on Externalizing Problems∧	
PTSD	33.3
Trauma Only	13.5
No Trauma	4.1
Attempted Suicide	
PTSD	16.7
Trauma Only	5.7
No Trauma	1.8
Rated Health as "Fair of Poor"	
PTSD	37.5
Trauma Only	21.3
No Trauma	10.0
>= 3 Sick Days/Month in Past Year	
PTSD	25.0
Trauma Only	12.2
No Trauma	5.1
Suspended/Expelled in Past Year*	
PTSD	25.0
Trauma Only	37.6
No Trauma	26.9

*Not Statistically Significant∧ Based on Youth Self Report (YSR)

Health

- 30% of abused children have chronic health problems (Daro, 1988).
- 3.2% of abused children require hospitalization for serious injuries secondary to child abuse (Daro, 1988).
- In a survey of patients at a pediatric intensive care unit, 1.4% of admissions were due to child abuse. 17% of deaths were due to child abuse. Child abuse patients had the highest "Severity of Illness" scores (Irazuzta, 1997).
- Persons reporting having experienced 4 or more categories of child maltreatment and/or household dysfunction (out of 7) are more likely to engage in health-risk behaviors **and have poorer adult** health outcomes than those reporting fewer of these experiences (Felitti et al., 1998):
  ⇒ 4 - 12 times greater risk for alcoholism, depression, drug abuse, and suicide attempt
  ⇒ 2 - 4 times greater risk for smoking, poor self-rated health,≥50 sex partners, and sexually transmitted disease
  ⇒ 1:4 - 1.6 times greater risk for physical inactivity and obesity
  ⇒ *1. 6 - 2.9 times greater risk for the following diseases: ischemic heart disease, cancer, chronic lung disease, skeletal fractures, hepatitis, stroke, diabetes, and liver disease.*
- Women with sexual abuse histories are more prevalent than those without abuse histories among women suffering from chronic pelvic pain (Harrop-Griffiths et al., 1988), gastrointestinal problems (Drossman et al., 1990; Leserman et al., 1998), and from neurological complaints including headaches and backaches (Berkowitz, 1998).

- Health service utilization was 2 1/2 times greater in college women who reported childhood sexual abuse compared to control group-N=51 (Berkowitz, 1998).
- Women with severe abuse history had worse physical health, greater pain, greater number of non-GI somatic symptoms, number of days disabled by illness, number of physician visits and greater functional distress (Leserman, et al., 1998)

Monetized Cost to Society of Child Maltreatment

Estimates of the annual monetized impact of child abuse range from $8.5 *billion* to $56 *billion* (American Humane Association, 1994 and National Institute of Justice – Miller et al., 1996, respectively).

National Institute of Justice (NIJ) Study in 1996 (Miller et al., 1996)

1. The NIJ report was published in February 1996 and is the result of a two-year multidisciplinary effort to estimate the costs and consequences of personal crime in America. The authors considered both the direct costs (medical, lost earnings, public programs for victims, etc.) and indirect costs (pain, suffering, diminished quality of life) of crime.
2. The total annual direct costs of all crime were estimated to be $105 billion. When indirect costs were included this number increased to $450 billion. Of this total, $426 billion were associated with violent crime.
3. Violence against children accounts for 20% of the direct costs and 35% of the combined direct and indirect costs of crime. Child abuse particularly accounts for $56 billion or 12.4% of the total. The following is a breakout of the $56 billion in losses due to child abuse:

TABLE 10.

Rape	$9 billion
Other Sexual Abuse	$14 billion
Physical Abuse	$24 billion
Emotional Abuse	$9 billion

4. The following are the estimated costs of child abuse per victimization (NIJ, Miller et al., 1996):

TABLE 11

	Mental Health Only	Medical Care/Ambulance	Total
Child Abuse	*$2,500*	*$430*	*$60,000*
Sexual Abuse (Including Rape)	$5,800	$490	$99,000
Physical Abuse	$2,700	$790	$67,000
Emotional Abuse	$2,700	$0	$27,000

5. A survey of 168 mental health professionals indicates that 25 - 50% (or more) of child abuse victims receive mental health care. An estimated 49% of recent victims of sexual abuse and 42% of recent victims of physical abuse receive mental health care (Miller et al., 1996).
6. Despite the fact that mental health costs are the "largest component of tangible losses for most forms of child abuse and rape," the cost of mental health care is one of the least studied areas of the costs of crime while are costs are the (Miller et al., 1996).

American Humane Association (AHA), 1994 & National Committee for the Prevention of Child Abuse (NCPCA), 1998

1. NCPCA study (1998) reports that for victims of abuse the cost per family for layperson counseling is $2,860. They assumed that I in 5 abuse victims receives counseling and that the estimated annual cost for these services is $814,756,800 (based on 1,424,400 confirmed cases from the 1988 NIS).
2. AHA estimates and FY97 appropriations:

TABLE 12

Foster Care	$3,500,000,000	(Estimate)
Specialized Service Facilities	$945,356,200	(Estimate)
In-patient Mental Health Facilities	$2,848,800,000	(Estimate)
Family Preservation Services	$240,000,000	(Appropriation)

3. The annual cost of child maltreatment is $8.5 billion (beyond what is spent on investigations and providing in-home child protective services). According to ARA this figure does not include: long-term impairment, lost productivity and loss of future earnings, special education services, drug and alcohol treatment, cost of juvenile court proceedings, potential welfare dependency, family reunification services (NCPCA, 1994 cited in AHA, 1994).
4. If only the most serious abuse victims received services (about 3% of total) it would still cost more than $662 million-based on service costs ranging from $2,860 to $28,000 (Daro, 1988, cited in Wolfe, 1994).

Medicaid Patients in Massachusetts: The cost impact of trauma

TABLE 13: NUMBER OF CASES UNDER EACH DIAGNOSIS

PTSD	DEPRESSION	PANIC	BIPOLAR	DID
22802	*22897*	*13281*	*1463*	*1228*
PTSD + Depression	2986			
PTSD + Panic	1277			
PTSD + Bipolar	217			
PTSD/DID	669			
Total PTSD	27,950 = 7% of total Medicaid population in MA			

- Table 14 shows that PTSD and DID (which usually involves severe trauma) are the most common diagnoses in the Medicaid population. PTSD diagnosis accounts for 10 times as many patient days as depression. DID-while only accounting for just over 1200 cases causes the single largest expense per diagnosis. Based on these figures the estimated annual cost for traumatized Medicaid patients in Massachusetts is $47 million.

TABLE 14: MENTAL HEALTHCARE UTILIZATION PER DIAGNOSIS

	IP Days	IP Admits	24 Hr.	Crisis	ARTP	Day Rx
PTSD	*8536*	*622*	*38*	*962*	*9360*	*15873*
DID	*7598*	*926*	*45*	*219*	*59*	*2601*
Bipolar	*869*	*72*	*34*	*153*	*100*	*2398*
Depression	*836*	*89*	*10*	*552*	*3561*	*7009*
Panic	*5036*	*644*	*55*	*181*	*89*	*1989*

Resources devoted to Child Abuse vs. Cancer

- Annual incidence of cancer and child abuse are approximately equal
- Colorado NCCAN Study: annual cost $ 402 Million
- Michigan Children's Trust: $ 823 Million
- Estimated US annual child abuse cost yearly: $ 56 Billion
  (direct costs + lost productivity and quality of life)
- Annual cost of cancer in US: $ 47 Billion
  (direct medical cost + lost productivity)
- Annual budget National Cancer Research Institute: $ 2.3 Billion
- Annual budget of programs related to child abuse $ 14.2 Million
  by National Institutes of Mental Health, National
  Institute for Child Health and Human development,
  National Institute for Drug Abuse, Center for Disease Control in 1992.

Outcomes for Treated versus Non-Treated Victims of Child Maltreatment

Outcome studies with victims of child maltreatment can be grouped into two main types: one type focuses on mental health outcomes while the other type focuses on social outcomes such as criminality and cost. A few studies and programs bridge the gap between the two types: "wraparound" services (such as Wisconsin's Integrated Service Providers) and multisystemic therapy (as formulated Scott Henggeler's work). Positive outcomes-to varying extents-have been found in much of the literature.

Compared to untreated children, those receiving appropriate mental health treatment are likely to show a decrease in mental health problems such as depression, anxiety, fear, and acting out. Appropriate treatment appears to involve a combination of addressing the child's particular symptoms in combination with parent education or therapy. Due to the lack of long term follow up in much of the treatment outcome literature, it is unclear whether the treated group fares better than the untreated group over time. For an overview of research regarding the prevalence of psychopathology in children, see Appendix A at the end of this article.

A Rand Corporation review of the outcome literature indicates that some forms of intervention can effectively reduce eventual criminality, improve performance in school, increase the likelihood of employment and enhance cognitive development. Rand reviewed reports from programs such as The Syracuse University Research Development Program which involved providing pre- and post-natal care to families from the third trimester on as well as daycare for the first five years after birth. A 10-year follow-up showed that program participation was correlated with a number of positive outcomes such as higher positive self-regard among the children and more prosocial parental attitudes. Notably, 22% of children in the control group had been referred to probation while only 4% of the children in the experimental group were referred (Lally, Mangione, & Honig, 1992). In addition, a New York program that involved home visitation for the first two years after birth resulted in reduced reports of child abuse and neglect from 19% for the no services group to 4% for the treatment group.

In addition, the NCPCA cites a study by Victoria Seitz in which low-income parents received home visits, health care, and day care services, following the birth of their first child. A follow-up survey was conducted ten years after then end of the program. The survey results showed that compared to the control group, parents who participated in the program reported higher educational levels, greater financial independence, and their children performed better performance in school (NCPCA, 1994).

In general, the studies focused on social outcomes have found that positive outcomes for at-risk youths were correlated with the following types of interventions: home visitation/daycare, parent training, graduation incentives, and delinquent supervision. A comparison of program costs versus cost savings due to reduced criminality reveals that all four of these programs are likely to pay for themselves in the long run.

Research related to programs that bridge the gap between social outcome- and mental health- foci have also reported positive outcomes. In one study using multisystemic therapy with delinquent youth, the recidivism rate in the treated group was 22% compared to 72% for the group that only receiving counseling. Additionally, Wisonsin's Integrated Service Providers (ISPs) have found in their work with severely emotionally disturbed children that ISPs lead to reduced residential placement, reduced hospitalization, reduced criminal behavior, and reduced cost.

Some of the studies focused on social outcomes pertain to a larger target population than maltreated children. These programs often include children considered "at-risk" for negative outcomes due to family income level, neighborhoods, family structure, etc.

In conclusion, children in "at-risk" situations who do not receive adequate services are more likely to suffer from mental health problems, have trouble in school, abuse drugs, become pregnant, and have contact with the juvenile and adult justice systems. The child maltreatment literature indicates that treating child victims and providing appropriate services decreases the child's suffering as well as decreases the negative outcomes for our society as a whole.

References

Ackerman, P.T., Newton, J.E.O., McPherson, W.B., Jones, J.G., & Dykman, R.A. (1998) Prevalence of post traumatic stress disorder and other psychiatric diagnoses in three groups of abused children (sexual, physical, and both). *Child Abuse and Neglect.* 22 (8):759-774.

American Humane Association. (1994). Twenty years after CAPTA: A portrait of the child protective services system.

Anderson, J.C., Williams, S., McGee, R., & Silva, P.A. (1987). DSM-III disorders in preadolescent children: Prevalence in a large sample from the general population. *Archives of General Psychiatry.* 44:69-76.

Benjamin, R.S., Costello, E.J., & Warren, M. (1990). Anxiety disorders in a pediatric sample. *Journal of Anxiety Disorders.* 4:293-316.

Berkowitz, C.D. (1998). Medical consequences of child sexual abuse. *Child Abuse & Neglect.* 22(6):541-550.

Birmaher, B., Ryan, N.D., Williamson, D.E., Brent, D.A., Kaufman, J., Dahl, R.E., Perel, J., & Nelson, B. (1996). Childhood and adolescent depression: A review of the past 10 years. *Journal of the American Academy of Child and Adolescent Psychiatry.* 3 5:1427-143 7.

Caldwell, R.A. (1992). The costs of child abuse vs. child abuse prevention: Michigan's experience. Michigan Children's Trust Fund.

Cantwell, D.P. (1996). Attention deficit disorder: A review of the past 10 years. *Journal of the American Academy of Child and Adolescent Psychiatry.* 3 5:978-988.

Chaffin, M., Kelleher, K., & Hollenberg, J. (1996). Onset of physical abuse and neglect: Psychiatric, substance abuse, and social risk factors from prospective community data. *Child Abuse &Neglect.* 20(3):191-203.

Children's Welfare League of America. (1997). *Child Abuse and Neglect: A Look at the Fifty States (199 7).*

Clark, D.B., Lesnick, L., & Hegedus, A.M. (1997). Traumas and other adverse life events in adolescents with alcohol abuse and dependence. *Journal of the American Academy of Child Adolescent Psychiatry.* 36(12):1744-1751.

Culp E. R., Heide J., & Richardson, M. T. (1987). Maltreated Children's Developmetal Scores: Treatment versus Non-Treatment. *Child Abuse and Neglect, Vol.11.* 29-34.

Daro, D. (1998). Public Opinion and Behaviors Regarding Child Abuse Prevention 1998 Survey. Center on Child Abuse and Prevention Research, National Committee to Prevent Child Abuse.

De Bellis, M.D., & Putnam, F.W. 1994. The psychobiology of childhood maltreatment. *Child and Adolescent Psychiatric Clinics of North America.* 3(4):663-678.

Drossman, D. A., Leserman, J., Nachman, G., L,i Z. M., Gluck, H., Toomey, T. C., & Mitchell, C. M. (1990). Sexual and physical abuse in women with functional or organic gastrointestinal disorders. *Annals of Internal Medicine,113*(11), 828-833.

Flament, M.F., Whitaker, A. Rapoport, JL. et al. (1998). Obsessive compulsive disorder in adolescence: an epidemiological study. *Journal of the American Academy of Child and Adolescent Psychiatry.* 27:764-771.

Gianconia, R.M., Reiherz, H.Z., Silverman, A.B., Pakiz, B., Frost, A.K., & Cohen, E. (1995). Traumas and posttraumatic stress disorder in a community population of older adolescents. *Journal of American Academy of Child and Adolescent Psychiatry.* 34:13 691380.

Harrop-Griffiths, J., Katon, W., Walker, E., Holm, L., Russo, J., & Hickok, L. (1988). The association between chronic pelvic pain, psychiatric diagnoses, and childhood sexual abuse. *Obstetrics & Gynecolology*, 71, 589-594.

Irazuzta, J.E., McJunkin, J.E., Danadian, K., Arnold, F., & Zhang, J. 1997. Outcome and cost of child abuse. *Child Abuse& Neglect.* 21(8):751-757.

Kendall-Tackett, K.A, Williams, L.M., & Finkelhor, D. (1993). Impact of sexual abuse on children: A review and synthesis of recent empirical studies. *Psychological Bulletin, 113,* 164-180.

Kurtz, P.D., Gaudin, J.M. Jr., Wodarski, J.S., & Howing, P.T. (1993). Maltreatment and the school-aged child: School performance consequences. *Child Abuse &Neglect.* 17(5):581-589.

Lally, R., Mangione, & Honig (1992). More pride, less delinquency: Findings from ten-year follow up study of the Syracuse University Family Development Research Program. In *The zero to three child care anthology, 1984-1992* (pp. 95-103). Los Angeles, CA: Rand Corporation.

Leserman, J., Li, Z., Drossman, D. A., & Hu, Y. J. (1998). Selected symptoms associated with sexual and physical abuse history among female patients with gastrointestinal disorders: the impact on subsequent health care visits. *Psychological Medicine,* 28, 417-425.

Lewinsohn, P.M., Klein, D.N., & Seeley, JR. (1995). Bipolar disorders in a community sample of older adolescents: Prevalence, phenomenolgy, comorbidity, and course.

Lewis, D. O., Mallouh, C., & Webb, V. (1989). Child Abuse, Delinquency, and Violent Criminality; in, D. Cicchetti and V. Carlson (Eds.) *Child Maltreatment: Theory and Research on the Causes and Consequences of Child Abuse and Neglect* (pp. 707-721). New York: Cambridge University Press; 1989.

Malinosky-Rummell, R., & Hansen, D.J. (1993). Long-term consequences of childhood physical abuse. *Psychological Bulletin.* 114(l):68-79.

McCord, J. (1983). A Forty Year Perspective on Effects of Child Abuse and Neglect. *Child Abuse and Neglect;* Vol. 7, 265-270.

Miller, T., Cohen, R., & Wiersema, B. (1996). *Victim costs and consequences: A new look,* National Institute of Justice (DOJ), Washington, DC.

National Committee to Prevent Child Abuse. (1998). Child Abuse and Neglect Statistics.

Pelkovitz, D., & Kaplan, S. (1996). Post-traumatic stress disorder in children and adolescents. *Child and Adolescent Psychiatry Clinics of North America.* 3(2):449-469.

Perry, B. D. (1997). Incubated in terror: Neurodevelopmental factors in the "cycle of violence." In J. Osofsky (Ed.), *Children, Youth and Violence: The Search for Solutions* (pp. 124-148). New York: Guilford.

Perry, B.D., Pollard, R.A., Blakley, T.L., Baker, W.L., & Vigilante, D. (1995). Childhood trauma, the neurobiology of adaptation and use-dependent development of the brain: How states become traits. *Infant Mental Health Journal, 16,* 271-291

Putnam, F. (1998). Trauma models of the effects of childhood maltreatment. *Journal of Aggression, Maltreatment and Trauma.* 2(1,3):51-66.

Romano, E., & De Luca, R.V. (1997). Exploring the relationship between childhood sexual abuse and adult sexual perpetration. *Journal of Family Violence.* 12(l):85-98.

Russell, D. E. (1986). *The secret trauma: Incest in the lives of girls and women.* New York: Basic Books, Inc.

Shaffer, D., Fisher, P., Dulcan, M., Davies, M., Piacentini, J., Schwab-Stone, ME., Lahey, B.B., Bourdon, K., Jensen, P.J., Bird, H.R., Canino, G., & Reiger, D.A. (1996). The NPAH diagnostic interview schedule for children version 2.3 (DISC-2.3): Description, acceptability, prevalence rates, and performance in the MECA study. *Journal of the American Academy of Child and Adolescent Psychiatry.* 3 5:865-877.

Straus, M. A., Gelles, R. J., & Steinmetz, S. K. (1980). *Behind closed doors: Violence in the American Family.* Garden City, NY: Doubleday.

Sullivan, P.M., & Knutson, I. F. (1998). The association between child Maltreatment and disabilities in a hospital-based epidemiological study. *Child Abuse & Neglect.* 22(4):271288.

van der Kolk, B. A. (1989). The compulsion to repeat the trauma: Reenactment, revictimization, and masochism. *Treatment of Victims of Sexual Abuse. 12(2).* 389-411.

van der Kolk, B. A. (1994). The body keeps the score: Memory and the evolving psychobiology of posttraumatic stress. *Harvard Review of Psychiatry, 1,* 253-265.

van der Kolk, B. A., Perry, C., & Herman, J. L. (1991). Childhood origins of self-destructive behavior. *American Journal of Psychiatry, 148,* 1665-1671.

Wang, C.T., & Daro, D.(1997). Current trends in child abuse reporting and fatalities: The results of the 1997 annual fifty state survey. Center on Child Abuse Prevention Research, National Committee to Prevent Child Abuse.

Wolfe, D.A. , The role of intervention and treatment services in the prevention of child abuse and neglect. In *Protecting Childrenf rom Abuse and Neglect.* Eds. Melton, G. and Barry, F. Guilford: New York, 1994.

Appendix A   Prevalence of Psychopathology in Children

DISORDER	PREVALENCE	REFERENCE
PTSD	>6	Giaconia RM, Reiherz HZ, Silverman AB, Pakiz B, Frost AK, Cohen E, (1995), Traumas and posttraumatic stress disorder in a community population of older adolescents. J Am Acad Child Adolesc Psychiatry 34:1369-1380
OCD	0.5%	Flament NW, Whitaker A, Rapoport JL et al. (1988), Obsessive compulsive disorder in adolescence: and epidemiological study J Am Acad Child Adolesc Psychiatry -.764-77127
ADD	3 5%	Cantwell DP, (1996), Attention Deficit Disorder: A review of the Past 10 years. J Am Acad Child Adolesc Psychiat 35:978-988
Anxiety: Separation Anxiety Disorder	3.5 (age 11)	Anderson JC, Williams S, Mc Gee R, Silva PA (1987), DSM-III disorders in preadolescent children: Prevalence in a large sample from the general population Arch Gen Psychiat 44:69-76
	4.1 (ages 7-11)	Benjamin RS, Costello EJ, Warren M (1990), Anxiety disorders in a pediatric sample. J Anx Disord 4:293-316
	2.9 (age 11)	Anderson JC, Williams S, Mc Gee R, Silva PA (1987), DSM-III disorders in preadolescent children: Prevalence in a large sample from the general population. Arch Gen Psychiatry 44:69-76
Anxiety Overanxious Disorder	4.6 (ages 7-11)	Benjamin RS, Costello EJ, Warren M (1990), Anxiety disorders in a pediatric sample. J Anx Disord 4:293-316
	2.4 (age 11)	Anderson JC, Williams S, Mc Gee R, Silva PA (1987), DSM-111 disorders in preadolescent children: Prevalence in a large sample from the general population Arch Gen Psychiat 44:69-76
Anxiety Simple Phobia	9.2 (ages 7-11)	Benjamin RS, Costello EJ, Warren M (1990), Anxiety disorders in a pediatric sample. J Anx Disord 4:293-316
Anxiety: Social Phobia	1 %(age 11)	Anderson JC, Williams S, Mc Gee R, Silva PA (1987), DSM-111 disorders in preadolescent children: Prevalence in a large sample from the general population Arch Gen Psychiat 44:69-76
Depression	0.4 % - 2.5 % (children) 0.4% - 8.3% (adoelscents)	Birmaher B, Ryan ND, Williamson DE, Brent DA, Kaufman J, Dahl RE, Perel J, Nelson B (1996), Childhood and Adolescent Depression: A review of the Past10 years. J Am Acad Child Adolesc Psychiatry 35:1427-1437
Oppositional Defiant Disorder	6.5 % (ages 9-17)	Shaffer D, Fisher P, Dulcan M, Davies M, Piacentini J, Schwab-Stone NE, Lahey BB, Bourdon K, Jensen PJ, Bird M Canino G, Regier DA (1996), The NIMH Diagnostic Interview Schedule for Children Version 2.3 (DISC-2.3): Description, Acceptability, Prevalence Rates, and Performance in the MECA Study. J Am Acad Child Adolesc Psychiat 35:865-877
Conduct Disorder	3.9 % (ages 9-17)	Shaffer D, Fisher P, Dulcan M, Davies M, Piacentini J, Schwab-Stone ME, Lahey BB, Bourdon K, Jensen PJ, Bird HR Canino G, Regier DA(1996), The NIMH Diagnostic Interview Schedule for Children Version 2.3 (DISC-2.3): Description Acceptability, Prevalence Rates, and Performance in the MECA Study. J Am Acad Child Adolesc Psychiat 35:865-877
Any Disruptive Behavior Disorders	11.5 % (ages 9-17)	Shaffer D, Fisher P, Dulcan M, Davies M, Piacentini J, Schwab-Stone ME Lahey BB, Bourdon K, Jensen PJ, Bird M Canino G, Regier DA (1996), The NIMH Diagnostic Interview Schedule for Children Version 2.3 (DISC-2.3): Description Acceptability, Prevalence Rates, and Performance in the MECA Study. I Am Acad Child Adolesc Psychiat 35:865-877
Bipolar Disorders	1 % (ages 14-18)	Lewinsohn PM, Klein DN, Seeley JR (1995), Bipolar Disorders in a Community Sample of Older Adolescents: Prevalence, Phenomenology, Comorbidity, and Course.